WERE ADAM A

We are all familiar with the

Eve in the Garden of Eden and how

is not widely known is that there are many other ancient religious documents which describe this event. And these tell a different and startling story!

For example, according to sources in the *Haggadah*, the wellspring of Jewish oral tradition, the consequences of their eating the forbidden fruit is described this way:

> The first result was that Adam and Eve became naked. Before, their bodies had been overlaid with a *horny skin* and enveloped with the *cloud of glory.* No sooner had they violated the command given them then the *cloud of glory* and the *horny skin* dropped from them, and they stood there in their nakedness and ashamed (emphasis ours).

In another early source, a Christian Gnostic tract that dates to the First Century AD, the same episode is described as follows:

> Now Eve believed the words of the serpent. She looked at the tree. She took some of its fruit and ate, and she gave to her husband also, and he ate too. Then their mind opened. For when they ate, the light of knowledge shone for them; they knew that they were naked with regard to knowledge. When they saw their makers, they loathed them since they were *beastly forms.* They understood very much.

These are but two of the many references in early religious literature which indicate that the Adam and Eve of the Garden of Eden were physically different from modern man. There are also many myths of ancient Mesopotamia which also reveal that our ancestors may have been reptilian types — the "horny skin" and "cloud of glory" referring to their lustrous reptilian hide.

Since Adam and Eve were created in "the image of god" it is evident that our ancient gods were not human mammals like us but an alien reptilian form. Perhaps this is why the ancient gods did not want to be seen by mankind.

FLYING SERPENTS AND DRAGONS

The Story of Man's Reptilian Past

The Evidence that We are the Children of Ancient Astronauts and Serpent-Gods

New Revised Edition

By

R. A. Boulay

ISBN 1-885395-38-8

PUBLISHED BY:

THE BOOK TREE
c/o Post Office Box 724
Escondido, California 92033

Call for Our Free Catalog 1 (800) 700-TREE

LAYOUT AND DESIGN BY:

Tedd St. Rain

COVER ART BY:

Brad Weinman

TABLE OF CONTENTS

LIST OF ILLUSTRATIONS

LIST OF ILLUSTRATIONS (Continued)

PREFACE TO THE REVISED EDITION

This book is a revised edition of *Flying Serpents and Dragons* which was published by the author in 1990, and incorporates new material which has since become available. In addition, much related matter has been added from *Dragon Power*, the author's second book on the subject.

Although it is not a new notion that our gods and ancestors were probably alien reptile forms, *Flying Serpents and Dragons* was the first (and only) comprehensive in-depth study based on ancient documents, both religious and secular. In this work, no attempt has been made to provide supporting physical evidence, which is beyond the purview of this book.

Without the groundwork laid by three great writers who had a powerful influence on this author, this work would not have been possible. They are Velikovsky, von Daniken, and Sitchin. Immanuel Velikovsky reintroduced the theory of catastrophic evolution in the 1950's for which he was villified by mainstream science. His revised chronology is used in this book and it was an invaluable help in putting all the pieces together. Erich von Daniken introduced a whole generation to the idea that our ancestors may have come from outer space and that their presence was world-wide; an idea which seems to have taken firm hold today. Zecharia Sitchin who, in his series on the Anunnaki called *The Earth Chronicles*, described in detail who these extraterrestrials who colonized the land of Mesopotamia were, and how they created modern man as a slave race.

When *Flying Serpents and Dragons* came out in 1990, the idea of our ancestors being reptiles seemed to be complete fantasy. However, events have transpired since then which have softened the impact of this work and today it is debated world-wide and even suggested that indeed our ancestors may have been reptilian astronauts.

Following established academic convention, Sumerian words are shown in capital letters such as ANUNNA, and Semitic (Akkadian, Babylonian, etc.) words are in italics such as *Anunnaki*, both being names for the serpent gods.

ABOUT THE AUTHOR

Rene Andrew Boulay graduated from George Washington University in 1950 where he did his graduate work in history. He joined the National Security Agency as a cryptologist and intelligence reporter where he worked in various analytical activities. Mr. Boulay also taught at the National Cryptologic School. The study of ancient history has always been his avocation and upon retiring from government service in 1979 has devoted his energies to solving the puzzles and mysteries of history. The culmination of over ten years of research was the publication of *Flying Serpents and Dragons* in 1990.

If you wish to contact the author please write to:

R.A. Boulay
P.O. Box 7701
Clearwater, FL 33758

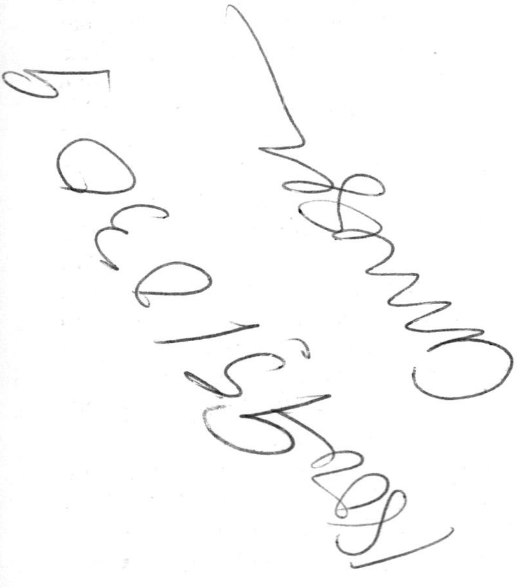

PROLOGUE

Why Were The Ancient Gods So Shy?

In ancient Mesopotamia, the Sumerian gods resided in a temple atop a ziggurat, a stepped pyramid raised above the plain. Here they were sheltered from the general public. In this sanctuary or "cella" they rested and dined in privacy, shielded by drawn curtains from their attending priests. One wonders if their table manners were so atrocious that they had to be hidden even from their retainers. Or was it something more insidious?

In the Old Testament, the overriding need for privacy for the Hebrew God Yahweh (Jehovah) is also emphasized. During the event known as the Exodus, the deity lived in a curtained area inside the sacred enclosure. He was never seen. Specific instructions were given to Moses on how to prepare the food which was left on a grill near the curtained quarters of the deity for him to snack in privacy.

On Mount Sinai, when Moses asked to see the face of his god, he was told sharply that "you cannot see my face, for man may not see me and live." This prohibition against being seen by humans is repeated throughout the scriptures. It was carried to an extreme when it became an injunction of not to make a "graven image" or likeness of the deity. Apparently no one was allowed to guess what he looked like lest they stumble on the truth.

Why the taboo? Could it be possible that its appearance would be so foreign and repulsive that it would upset mankind, and therefore it had to be withheld from man? One would logically assume that if the gods were so superior and grand as indicated in the scriptures, that they would be flattered and pleased to have man see them and copy their magnificence.

Only a privileged few were allowed to even approach the deities. In the Torah it was the Levite priesthood. In Mesopotamia it was the demi-gods: the offspring of the mating of a god and a human. These half-divine creatures formed the aristocracy, and were entrusted by the gods to see to their needs and to form a barrier with mankind. Even these "changelings" as they were called, were somewhat strange in appearance and probably had certain non-human characteristics. The fabled Gilgamesh for example, had something odd in his appearance that made him stand out and be feared by normal men. The Biblical Patriarchs before the Deluge also had unusual physical characteristics as shown by the irrational behavior of Noah when he was seen naked by his sons.

According to the ancient Babylonian tradition, as reported by Berossus, the Babylonian priest writing in Athens in the Third Century BC, Man's ancestry and origin can be traced to one Oannes, the amphibious creature that came out of the Persian Gulf to teach the arts of civilization to man. Berossus called them *Annedoti* which means "the repulsive ones" in Greek. He also refers to them as *musarus* or "an abomination." It is in this way that Babylonian tradition credits the founding of civilization to a creature which they considered to be a "repulsive abomination."

If the tradition had been invented, a more normal attitude would have been to glorify these creatures as splendid gods or heroes. Yet the fact that they chose to describe their ancestors this way argues for the authenticity of the account.

Ancient references to "serpent gods," "flying serpents," and "dragons" are quite common. The reptilian appearance of the gods in the Old Testament was a well-kept secret; occasionally it is perceptible, as for example the obvious worship of the *seraph* or "brazen serpent" during the Exodus which in certain rabbinical sources is equated with Yahweh. The Sumerians were more candid and in their epics, which can be traced as far back as 3000 BC, called their gods U-SHUM-GAL, or "great fiery flying serpent." Sumerian dictionaries avoid trying to explain this perplexing problem by merely translating the word as "dragon" without comment.

The sad fact is that in the West we have created God in our image and not the other way around. In this way we have hidden the true identity of our creators. Many other world civilizations take pride in the fact that they were descended from "dragons" or "flying serpents." The oldest of Chinese books, the mysterious *Yih King*, claims that the first humans were formed by the ancient goddess Nu Kua who was a dragon. Early Chinese emperors boasted of being descendants of this ancient dragon goddess.

In the civilization of India, the oldest and most revered of the Hindu classics, the *Ramayana* and the *Mahabharata* concern the intercourse of early man with their serpent-god ancestors. Central American and African mythology is also replete with stories of how flying serpents and dragon-like beings descended from the heavens and taught man the basics of civilization.

In our search of ancient literature, both secular and religious, we are ovewhelmed with the enormous amount of references to dragon-like beings. If it is a constructor of early man's imagination, how could it have been so universal? These dragons were obviously serpent-gods who could fly about the heavens at will in their craft that had a flaming appearance, probably a rocket exhaust of some kind.

INTRODUCTION

The accepted academic view is that dragons and flying serpents were just fabulous animals, the product of early man's fertile imagination. In view of the fact that their appearance is so universal it is difficult to accept this theory. It is more probable that the dragon symbolism may be the manifestation of something else — the result of traumatic events so deeply rooted in man's subconscious that the knowledge of their true nature has been suppressed. These dragons or flying serpents apparently co-existed with ancient man who portrayed them as gods who could effortlessly move about the skies in their "fiery chariots" or "boats of heaven." They lived in the sky in a "heavenly abode" from where they often descended to interfere in the affairs of man.

The earliest known culture of our Earth is that of Mesopotamia, which can be traced back archaeologically to 3500 BC. Its colonization by these creatures is described in one of the most significant of ancient documents: the so-called Sumerian *King List*. Dated to the Third Millennium BC, the *King List* provides the succession of the kings of Sumer and the lengths of their reign since the beginning of time. It describes the coming of their ancestors and their descent to Earth to establish a number of cities on the alluvial plain of Mesopotamia.

The Sumerian people referred to these gods as Anunna, literally the sons of AN, their chief god and leader. Their later Semitic name was Anunnaki. We will show that the Anunna were an alien race of sapient reptiles. They required a labor force to do the necessary menial work and for this reason a primitive man was created. They accomplished this by combining the characteristics of the native ape-man with their own saurian nature. In this way they produced the "Adam" of the Old Testament. This Adam was half human and half reptile, what can be called a Homo-saurus. It was a failed experiment for the main reason it was a "mule" and could not reproduce itself.

As conditions began to change on Earth and the climate dried out, food was not as plentiful and it was decided to modify the "Adam" and give it reproductive powers. For this reason it was given more mammalian traits. This is the Biblical "Fall of Man" where Adam achieved "knowing" or the ability to reproduce sexually. As a result of this genetic modification, man lost most of his saurian nature — his shiny, luminous skin and scaly hide. He acquired mammalian characteristics — a soft flexible skin, body hair, the need to sweat, and the ability to produce live young. He no longer ran around naked. He now had to wear clothing for comfort and protection. For all purposes he was a Homo sapiens. The modern man or Cro-Magnon Man had arrived on the scene. The experiment was a great success and man multiplied rapidly. The gods considered this a necessary evil and never forgave mankind for straying so far from the reptilian pattern.

During the years before the Deluge, he was sorely tested by the "divine" creators. Some of them descended to Earth to mate with human women. Known in the Old Testament as the "Nefilim" they not only produced mixed offspring but also conducted genetic experiments which went awry at times and produced monstrous forms. This was a trying period for mankind, for in this era he was literally food for the gods. The turmoil on Earth was ended abruptly by the onset of a natural catastrophe, known as the Deluge or Great Flood. The gods retreated to their spaceship and left mankind to perish along with their semi-divine offspring. After the waters subsided they descended once more to establish new cities on the plains of Mesopotamia.

Again mating with humans they produced a race of semi-divine beings to rule their empire on Earth. A race of warrior-gods was established in the land of the Middle East. As descendants of the Nefilim they were know as Rephaim, a barbaric race of giant men which plagued humanity for thousands of years and was not entirely eliminated until the days of Saul and David.

CHAPTER 1

THE DRAGONS OF E

Dragons Everywhere!

Dragons have permeated world consciousness to th found in the mythology and literature of all world civilizations. Som take the form of a flying reptile, often times they are flying serpents breathing fire. Usually they are quite friendly beneficient creatures, but in certain cultures they are considered as the source of evil.

A catalog of all the appearances of dragons in the culture of Europe, China, India, the Middle East, and the Americas would be an enormous task in itself. Suffice it to say that the idea of a fiery, flying serpent is found everywhere. In many places it is a substratum to historical traditions. In England, for example, there are over 70 towns and villages which have dragons in their folklore. In China they are the ancestors of Emperors. Our investigations into the origin of the dragon must, by necessity, be limited to the major significant stories of these cultures.

In order to discover their origins we shall wend our way back through history and follow the trail of the dragon. Our journey in time takes us back through the Medieval Period in Europe, and the early Christian Church. Roman and Greek legends lead us to Asia Minor where many of their stories originated, and from there we proceed to the Semitic civilizations of the Middle East.

We shall find that the Levant, the ancient name for the lands of Palestine, Syria, Lebanon, and Jordan, was an offshoot of the parent civilization of Mesopotamia. As we follow the spoor of the dragon, we travel back to the Assyrian, the Babylonian, the Akkadian, and finally back to the prototype or mother of all civilizations, the Sumerian.

It is here in the myths and stories of Sumer that we first see references to the dragon. These ancient Sumerian myths were the source of the dragon-slayer motif and many of the stories of the Old Testament, such as the Creation of Man, the Fall of Man, and the Fall of Lucifer. It was the manipulation of these legends by the ancient Hebrew priesthood, and later the early Christian Church, which obscured their real and original meaning and provided the serpent with an evil reputation.

Myth versus History

There is an area of activity which man shares with no other creature on Earth. This is the recording of memory and the maintaining of chronicles. In this way, man is able to transfer short-term memory to long-term memory and thus learn from the passage of time beyond the limits of one lifetime. Man is the only living creature to experience history, for it is his ability to record memory, and to transmit memory from generation to generation which creates "history."

Conventional scholarship insists on a rigorous distinction between "history" and "myth." In this paradigm, history consists of documented facts such as names, dates, battles, treaties, revolutions, political and social events, etc. Myth on the other hand, is dismissed as belonging to the realm of fantasy, poetry, and fiction. Yet for people in the past the two were inseparable.

In fact, all myth is derived from historical fact or event. This event is the ch is added to and embroidered by successive generations. It historical fact, that is, their "myth." Written history actually con-xture of these two — fact and myth. The same is true of political, nd social events. Myth must also be given a certain amount of cre-here there is separate historical fact to support it — archaeological evi-wall paintings and reliefs, statues, and other artifacts. We all know that gels" did not have wings, especially those flimsy ones shown in religious intings. These wings are symbolic of the gods and their minions, of their abil-ity to fly about the Earth and to reach a "heavenly abode." Probably the best example of myth overtaking history is the appearance of the "dragon" in the religious literature of the Judeo-Christian tradition.

It is now accepted fact that the Old Testament, especially the *Book of Genesis*, is an abbreviated version of myriads of documents available to the early chroniclers who assembled the scriptures. Many of these ancient documents are available to the serious researcher who can chose from a vast amount of Pseudepigraphal and Apocryphal books which expand on the stories of the Old Testament, a rich Jewish oral tradition that is summarized under the name of *Haggadah*, and numerous religious documents that have survived only in other languages besides Hebrew, such as Latin, Ethiopic, Slavic, and Coptic.

The Legged Snakes of Eden

According to Genesis and other documents, and long before humans ever existed, the serpent lived in the Garden of Eden and did all the necessary work to maintain it. This Biblical serpent was not just a lowly snake; it could converse with Eve, and knew the truth about the Tree of Knowledge. It was of such a stature that it unhesitatingly challenged the deity. Genesis concedes this point when it asserts that "the serpent was the shrewdest of all the world beasts that God had made."

Ancient Jewish legends describe the serpent of Eden as manlike — he looked like a man and talked like a man. The part of the *Haggadah* which deals with the Creation depicts the serpent who inhabited the garden as an upright creature that stood on two feet and who was equal in height to the "camel." He was said to be the lord over all the beasts of Eden. "God spoke to the serpent: 'I created you to be king over all the animals. I created you to be of an upright position." In the *Haggadah* there seems to be little doubt that he was legged and walked like a man. The tempter of Eve was not actually a serpent. It had legs like other animals. Therefore, the many representations of the temptation of Eve which shows it as a snake curled around the Tree of Knowledge are really based on a misunderstanding of the scriptural text.

In the *Book of Genesis*, the serpent was severely punished for his role in the downfall of Adam and Eve. His fate was henceforth to crawl on his belly. In this way, Genesis implies that at one time the serpent was a legged creature and lost his limbs as a result of the eating of the forbidden fruit. Sources in the *Haggadah* are more explicit and plainly state that "his hands and feet were hacked off."

In appearance, the legged serpent must have been a fearsome creature, dominating all the animals as well as man. In fact, Genesis states that when Adam and Eve were expelled from Eden they wore "shirts of skin." But since Adam and Eve were vegetarian during this period and man was not allowed to eat meat until after the Deluge, these "skins" must have been sloughed off by the reptiles. Many ancient documents verity this.

Ancient Jewish legends indicate that the clothes worn by Adam and Eve

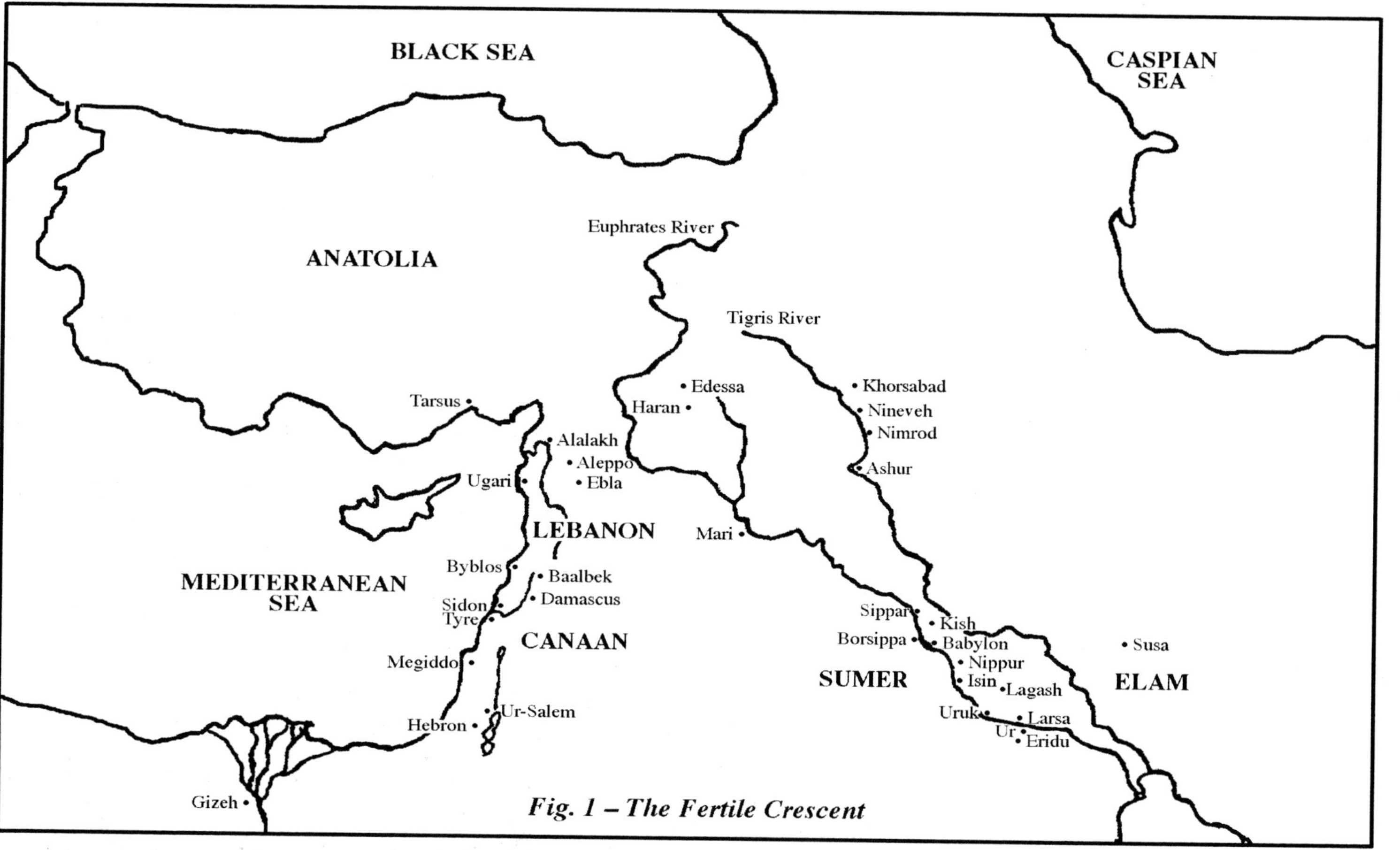

Fig. 1 – The Fertile Crescent

were not only made of reptile skins but that they protected them from predators: "When they wore the coats, Adam and Eve were told, all creatures on Earth would fear them." The serpent skins were symbolic of the ruling race, and not only reminded Adam and Eve of their origin, but also acted as a talisman to safeguard them from wild creatures.

The notion of the serpent as evil is a fairly recent one, for it is one that has evolved during the early Christian era. In actuality, the Biblical serpent is often connected with godly knowledge, healing and immortality. The Hebrew word for the creature who tempted Eve is *nahash* which is usually translated as serpent, but means literally "he who knows all secrets."

It was the *Book of Genesis* that ordained an eternal emnity between reptiles and humans, and the dragon/serpent became the symbol of temptation and evil. In recalling other legends of the dragon's destructiveness, humans were provided with ample excuse to seek out and kill every "dragon" in the land. "Dragons" which had been sacred and objects of veneration in Greek and Roman homes and oracles soon disappeared, and were no longer available for transmitting their wisdom.

The Winged Dragons of Eden

Sometimes the ancient religious sources allow dragon references to slip through. One such document called the *Apocalypse of Abraham* found only in the Slavonic language and dated to the First Century AD, and which is the testimony of the patriarch, clearly depicts the serpent which tempted Eve as a winged dragon:

> And they were standing under a tree in Eden and the fruit of the tree was like the appearance of a bunch of grapes on the vine. And behind the tree was standing something like a dragon in form, but having hands and feet, just like a man's, on his back six wings on the right and six on the left. He was holding the grapes of the tree and feeding them to the two I saw entwined with each other.

The legend of the dragon was quite pervasive in early religious literature. It is seen in another old document called the *Testament of Solomon*, which refers to the building of the temple at Jerusalem by Solomon. Dated to the First Century AD, and found only in Greek, it describes how the dragon interfered with the constructor of the temple.

Described as "a wallowing dragon, having the limbs of a dragon and wings on its back, the face and feet of a man," it's fiery breath burned up all the wood to be used in the building of the temple. It also set the forest of Lebanon on fire. Solomon subdued it and put it to work cutting stone for the temple. The idea of a dragon obstructing the construction of the temple seems bizarre to us today, but two thousand years ago it was not so fanciful and it shows the preoccupation of the religious authorities with the symbol of the dragon.

Many of the angels of the Old Testament were winged, especially the Cherubim (singular Cherub) and the Seraphim (singular Seraph). In fact, the Seraphim are often described in obscure religious sources as dragons. Probably the best known of the dragons of the scriptures is the one found in the *Book of Revelation* where the dragon represents evil and the great Satan, which persecutes Israel and the Christian Church. It is referred to as the "the great red dragon, with seven heads and ten horns and a long tail." According to this book, man would worship the dragon just before the end of the World.

The Seraphim: The Flying Serpent or Dragon of Moses

In the Old Testament explicit references to our serpent-god ancestors have been all but eliminated over the centuries through a long process of selection and editing. When allusions to winged serpents are found they are usually interpreted as merely allegorical. However, there is a strange incident related in the *Book of Numbers* concerning a bronzed or brazen serpent which raises many questions that are not fully addressed by Biblical scholars.

During the second year of the Exodus, and after the tribes had left the comforts of Mount Sinai and were struggling across the wasteland, they had a skirmish with the King of Arad in the Negeb, and the Hebrews prevailed after much difficulty. The incident of the brazen serpent happened at that time:

> The people grew restive on the journey, and the people spoke against the Lord and against Moses, "Why did you make us leave Egypt to die in the Wilderness? There is no bread and water, and we have come to loathe this miserable manna." The Lord sent *Seraph* serpents among the people. They bit the people and many of the Israelites died. The people came to Moses and said, "We sinned by speaking against the Lord and against you. Intercede with the Lord to take away the serpents from us." And Moses interceded for the people. Then the Lord said to Moses, "Make a *Seraph* figure and mount it on a standard. And if anyone who is bitten looks at it, he shall recover." Moses made a brazen serpent and mounted it on a standard and when anyone was bitten by a serpent, he would look at the brazen serpent and recover.

It is difficult to escape the conclusion that the meaning of the incident is obviously idolatry, an activity stringently forbidden in the scriptures. The "seraph" of Moses apparently had healing powers, an attribute which appears time and time again with the flying serpent.

The Hebrew word *Seraph* is an unusual one and appears only a few times in the books of the Old Testament. In the *Book of Isaiah* the *Seraph* is referred to as *me ofef seraph* or literally "flying serpent." It is associated with the Philistines and the Negeb, lands which were traditionally the home of the so-called serpent people, the descendants of the Nefilim after the Deluge. The reference in Isaiah is as follows:

> In the year that King Ahaz died came this oracle: "Rejoice ye not, O Philistia, all of you, that the rod which smote you is broken, for from the serpent's root will come forth an adder, and its fruit will be a flying serpent *(me ofef seraph)*. And the first born of the poor will feed and the needy lie down in safety; but I will kill the root with famine and the remnant he will slay."

This flying serpent appears again in Isaiah 30 when he refers to the land of the Negeb as "a land of trouble and anguish from where came the lioness and the lion, the viper and the *me ofef seraph*."

The brazen serpent of Moses which was made at God's command, was revered in the Temple sanctuary in Jerusalem until the days of King Hezekiah in the Eighth Century BC. According to the *Second Book of Kings*:

> In the third year of the reign of Hezekiah he did the following: He removed the high places, and broke the pillars and cut down the Asherah. And he broke in pieces the bronze serpent *(seraph)* that Moses had made, for until those days the people of Israel had burned incense to it; it was called *Neshushtan*.

The Asherah mentioned here were shrines to the Canaanite goddess Astarte and were representative figures of the goddess mounted on a wooden pole. It apparently stood side by side with the "Nehushtan," which was the brazen flying serpent also mounted on a pole. Nehushtan is a form of the word *nahash*, that is, the serpent of the Garden of Eden and actually means "he who knows all." It is doubtful that this was the original seraph made by Moses about 1450 BC, and that it survived until this time. In either case, it demonstrates that the worship of the serpent-gods as exemplified by a flying serpent, was well established among the Israelites during the period of the Kings and the Judges, and suggests that Yahweh had at one time been identified with the flying serpent. This association is discussed later on.

The term *seraph* has worried Biblical translators and commentators over the years. It is translated as "fiery serpent" in the King James version of the Bible, but the modern tendency is not to translate the word at all but to render the Hebrew as given. Seraph does not fit any convenient classification or translation. It seems more probable that it is a borrowed word from the Canaanites who acquired it from their Mesopotamian heritage.

The seraphim (plural form) were supposedly part of the heavenly host and along with the Cherubim and Opannim, guarded the heavenly throne. The *Hebrew Apocalypse of Enoch*, a pseudepigraphic document written in the Fifth Century AD, describes the heavenly abode where there are four Seraphim or winged angels who guard the throne but do not serve on the divine chariot or *Shekinah*. These Seraphim have six wings. This same six-winged creature is also described in the *Book of Isaiah* (6:1-2) wherein the prophet says:

> In the year that King Uzziah died I saw the Lord sitting upon a throne, high and lifted up; and his train filled the Temple. Above him stood the Seraphim; each had six wings: with two he covered his face, and with two he covered his feet, and with two he flew.

The early Hebrews apparently equated dragons with flying serpents both which came under the name Seraphim, the "angels" who guarded the heavenly throne. This information is also found in Gnostic documents which contain numerous references to the Seraphim or "dragon-shaped angels" who were the guardians of the heavens.

The Origin of the Term Seraphim

The roots of the term Seraphim may well be in Mesopotamia. The flying or fiery serpent atop the pole worshipped for its healing properties symbolically represents Enki, the Sumerian God of healing, who is often represented by the serpent or snake symbol. There is also a curious resemblance of the snake wrapped around the pole, later used by the Greeks as the *caduceus* or symbol of healing. In Sumerian art the serpent is a symbol of immortality as we shall see.

In the famous *Epic of Gilgamesh*, the hero is frustrated in his bid for immortality when the gods, through his grandfather Utnapishtim (the Sumerian Noah) refuse to bestow upon him this gift. Not to let Gilgamesh go home empty-handed, Utnapishtim provides him with information on how to obtain a magical plant which heals and prolongs life. After obtaining the plant, Gilgamesh plans to take it to his home city of Uruk and there to share it with his fellow citizens. On his way home he stops by a pool to bathe, leaving the plant unattended on shore with his clothes. As he is bathing and much to his horror, a snake grabs the magical plant and takes off with it, shedding its skin as it goes, thus symbolizing the act of regeneration. In this epic the serpent is called *seru* and the similarity of the word to "seraph" is striking and suggests a common origin.

The serpent-people, or Nagas of ancient Sanskrit sources who are said to have inhabited the mountains of India and Tibet were called *sarpa.* The theosophist H. P. Blavasky published a comprehensive study of these ancient people in her remarkable work *The Secret Doctrine.* She asserts that the "nagas" or "sarpa" of India are "unquestionably the Jewish Seraphim of the Old Testament as derived from the term *serapi* meaning "serpent."

While these flying serpents or dragons are found in the culture of people throughout the world, they are usually considered to be benevolent creatures and in most cases are the actual ancestors of man. This is why the European view of the dragon as evil is unique. This evil nature of dragons is prevalent in Jewish literature such as the Mishnah, the part of the Talmud which is the Jewish commentary on ethical behavior. In a discussion on which pictures or images are permitted, dragons are proscribed:

> If one finds utensils upon which is the figure of the Sun or Moon or a Dragon, he casts them into the Dead Sea (a symbol of destruction). Pictures of all planets are permissible except that of the Sun and Moon, and that of the Dragon.

The warning against depicting dragons is repeated in other Tractates of the Talmud. While representations of all the other planets are permitted, the Sun, the Moon, and the Dragon are specifically prohibited, This seems strange; it is probably due to the fact that the Sun and Moon are associated with Sumerian gods of Palestine and Lebanon — Shamash being the Sumerian Sun god and the Moon being the symbol of Sin, a major god of the pantheon (The Sinai is named after him). The dragon, of course, represents the entire Sumerian pantheon, all being reptilian gods.

Denizens of the Garden of Eden

Genesis is not very helpful in identifying the inhabitants of the Garden of Eden. Adam was clearly the first and only "human." Then Eve was created from his "rib" or TI to provide him with a mate. Most critics now agree that the creation of Eve from Adam's rib was an early Hebrew distortion with the purpose of establishing male dominance. The Genesis-type of creation lacks any parallel in Mid-Eastern mythology. The Sumerian and Semitic term for "rib" also means "life." The early editors of Genesis either made a whopping error of translation or purposely distorted the real meaning of TI. It seems more logical that the word TI represents the "life force" or "essence of life," the meaning which the earlier Sumerians used when they referred to the creation of man.

Early Christian and Hebrew writings reveal that there were other inhabitants of the Garden of Eden. In the Gnostic view of the creation of Adam, the original occupant of the garden was Sophia who gave the "breath of life" to Adam and then provided her daughter Zoe as a wife to Adam.

In the early rabbinical comments on the Torah, as they are found in the *Midrash*, the original denizen of Eden was Lilith, and Adam was created to be her mate. She rejected Adam mainly because she would not assume a subordinate or recumbent position in sexual intercourse. She left the Garden of Eden and only then was Eve created as a mate.

According to sources as found in the Genesis Rabbah, a *Midrash* account on the *Book of Genesis*, compiled in the Fifth Century in Palestine, Eve was not created from Adam's rib but rather from his tail, which had been part of his body. God cut this off and the stump, now a useless coccyx, is still carried by Adam's descendants. Thus the Adam who occupied the Garden of Eden lost his reptilian tail as a result of the Fall. Perhaps the stump was left as a reminder to man of his reptilian ancestry by a facetious god.

It would thus appear that the early religious sources believed that there were a number of primitives occupying the garden, of which but two have been expunged from the scriptures. Nowhere is there a mention of the creation of offspring, and like in the Sumerian accounts, the denizens of Eden must have been "clones," that is, creatures formed or created individually by the hand of the creator god. What is also clear in the religious accounts other than Genesis, is the dominance of the female image, the "mother of all living" as was often said of Eve. The symbolism of the mother goddess as representing fertility and the mother Earth is completely missing from Genesis and may have been deliberately eliminated.

Homo-saurus, The Primitive Man of Eden

In the epics of Mesopotamia, Man's creation was secondary and even incidental to the creation of the universe and to the colonization of this planet by the alien visitors. Man's creation was conceived and executed not as an end in itself or as a natural development of the civilization of Mesopotamia, but rather as an expedient to satisfy a group of discontented aliens. Man's purpose was to serve the gods; man was meant to be the breadwinner, the laborer, and the caretaker of the gods.

The Sumerian accounts make it clear that the Adam of the Bible was not the Homo sapiens of today. He was what one might call Homo-saurus, a hybrid mammal-saurian creature that was to become our ancestor and the first step in the creation of modern man. In just a few years, man had taken a quantum jump in evolution. He had suddenly evolved from the wild ape-man to a hybrid that would become a new species known as Cro-Magnon Man.

The hybrid that was created probably looked reptilian since he was created in the image of his gods. Genesis is very specific about this, for it states, "then God said 'I will make man in my image, after my likeness." Later, as man intermarried with his species, the reptilian strain deteriorated and he became more mammal-like, and less and less reptilian in appearance. The mammal genes dominated the reptilian ones and man became more "human" and less god-like. It explains Man's "sinful" nature and his "fall from grace." Original sin was Man's deviation from the basic reptilian or godly pattern. Genesis makes the point repeatedly that before the Fall, man was naked while he occupied the Garden of Eden. It was not until he ate of the forbidden fruit that he realized that he was naked and put on clothing. Other ancient religious sources support this condition of man, but they also reveal the reason why he was naked.

According to the *Haggadah*, the bodies of Adam and Eve "had been overlaid with a horny skin," and moreover, of Adam it was said that "it was as bright as daylight and covered his body like a luminous garment." Adam thus had the outward appearance of a reptile, with its scaly and shiny skin. It was for this reason that Adam and Eve did not wear nor did they need clothing for protection or for comfort.

The *Book of Genesis* also makes it clear that Adam did not sweat while he was in the Garden of Eden. That was his punishment for eating the forbidden fruit, for he was told, "by the sweat of your face shall you earn your bread." Adam did not sweat before the Fall for the simple reason that sweating is characteristic of mammals and not reptiles. As long as they remained in the Garden of Eden, Adam and Eve did not propagate. They were "mules" and could not reproduce their own kind. The incident which the Bible refers to as the Fall of Man was his acquiring the ability to procreate by taking on many of the traits of mammals. It is explicit in Eve's punishment that she is to bear the pangs of live birth like a mammal.

These processes and changes which created modern man are reported elsewhere in this work. These changes are probably best illustrated by a tract from a Gnostic document which states, that because of the eating of the forbidden fruit "they saw their makers, they loathed them since they were beastly forms." The appearance of such a statement in the early Christian literature is amazing and makes it abundantly clear why the Gnostics were persecuted by the fathers of the early Church who declared Gnosticism anathema and its followers punishable by death.

CHAPTER 2

THE "INVISIBLE" BIBLE

It is now generally accepted that the *Book of Genesis* is a condensed version of actual events in Man's early history. Moreover, Genesis raises more questions than it answers. In order to understand this book, and explain the omissions and contradictions, scholars of the last 300 years have intensively studied both the sacred texts and the related writings from which Genesis was probably derived. In the words of Saint Jerome, Genesis is said to be "The most difficult and the most obscure of the sacred books; Genesis contains as many secrets as words, and each word conceals several others."

The early chroniclers who compiled Genesis placed little emphasis on events which took place before the Deluge. This section is particularly short and vague, and consists of only seven short chapters. The events of this period are ambiguous and the subject often changes abruptly, indicating that there have been many omissions and changes, presumably committed by succeeding priestly editors and transcribers.

Basically there were two main channels that transmitted information on the events described in Genesis. One is the vast amount of religious literature commenting on these events, and the other is the secular sources which were the fountainhead of these events. If Abraham came from "Ur of the Chaldees" in Mesopotamia around 2000 BC, he presumably brought with him the stories that make up the events described in Genesis, especially those before the Deluge.

When the Old Testament was first written down, about the Seventh or Sixth Century BC, many documents were either not available or were deliberately left out for political reasons. Many non-Hebrew texts such as those found in the Pseudepigrapha were not included, The Pseudepigrapha was actually completely lost from the transmitted heritage and was not recovered until after the Old Testament had become fixed in the form we know today.

What was retained in the Old Testament after centuries of emendation by the priesthood was a highly introspective version of the enormous literature available to them. Manuscripts such as the three books of Enoch, Jubilees, and other documents tell a different story of the Garden of Eden, of the Creation, and of the Fall of Man. These and many other "lost" books of the Bible explain many of the puzzles and inconsistencies of the Old Testament.

The Hebrew Literature

The Torah in its narrowest sense signifies the Pentateuch, otherwise known as the Five Books of Moses, the first part of the Hebrew Bible. In its wider sense, however, it denotes all the ramifications of the Torah — the commentaries that the rabbis wrote upon it, the laws that are derived from it, and all the elaborations of the narrative portion. The other sacred Hebrew source is the *Haggadah*, which means "the telling" and is a commentary on the Torah. It fills in the details or supplies the missing information on a biblical story, reconciles apparent contradictions, answers questions, incorporates fables from other sources, makes moral deductions, adds contemporary historical allusions, discusses relevant theological topics, and indulges in biographical anecdotes. In this sense, it is an indispensable source for information on the people and events of the Old Testament.

The *Haggadah* contains hundreds upon hundreds of legends and fable, which serve to illustrate in some way the scriptural text. The oldest of this material evolved from the commentary of the Bible given by rabbis in the synagogues of Palestine as early as the Sixth Century BC. Such an exposition is called a m*idrash* or "inquiry." The *Haggadah* is usually contrasted with the Halakhah which derives from oral law. Both *Haggadah* and Halakhah were associated with the Talmud, a vast collection of Jewish writing compiled from the post-Biblical period of the Fourth Century for the Palestinian Talmud and the Fifth Century for the Babylonian Talmud.

The Kaballah consists of an oral tradition based on mysticism, that is, the esoteric and philosophical currents existing among the Jews in Palestine and Egypt, and the term came to designate secret mysteries whispered by the sages. Many attempts have been made to penetrate these mysteries which are said to contain "the wisdom of the ages."

The version of the Old Testament used by the Christian Church is the Septuagint which was created by 70 scholars at the command of Ptolemy II in the Third Century BC at Alexandria, Egypt. Translated into Greek, it is often referred to as the LXX version for this reason. The other Biblical translation in general usage is based on the Vulgate, a Latin translation and is authorized and used in the Catholic Church.

None of these versions of the scriptures are satisfactory to the serious researcher into the mysteries of the past, for the simple reason that there are may books mentioned in the scriptures which have never been found and are presumed lost.

The Lost Books of the Old Testament

There are many documents which are mentioned in the Old Testament that have been either lost or suppressed. For example, in the section in Joshua 10:13 which relates to the event when the sun stood still in the sky, it is said: "Is this not recorded in the *Book of Jashar*?" This book is also mentioned in 2 Samuel 1:17 when David is lamenting the death of Saul by the Amalekites. The *Book of Jashar* is apparently an epic account of the Israelites desert wanderings, the invasion of Canaan, and the battles fought by Saul and David. This lost book is probably related to the *Book of the Wars of Yahweh* which is mentioned in Numbers 21:14 when the Israelites were leaving the Sinai and were encountering resistance by the Moabites in their attempt to enter the land of Canaan.

Another lost book was apparently compiled in seven parts at Joshua's request. It is mentioned in Joshua 18:9 and describes the division of the land of Canaan and its distribution among the tribes of Israel. Its title is unknown.

There are many more passing references to lost books in the Old Testament. The *Book of the Story of Adam* is mentioned in Genesis 5:1 and seems to be a detailed account of the first ten generations from Adam to Noah. There is a reference to a *Book of Yahweh* in Isaiah 34:16 which appears to deal with agriculture and animal husbandry.

Other books mentioned in passing are the *Book of the Acts of Solomon* referred to in 1 Kings 11:41 which deals with the deeds of Solomon for the forty years that he was king. The *Chronicle of the Kings of Judah* as found in 1 Kings 14, 15, and 22, and the *Chronicle of the Kings of Israel* mentioned in 1 Kings 14, 15, and 16, are a detailed history of the early kings after the division of the empire of Solomon.

Other books referred to in passing are the *Book of Genealogy* and the *Chronicles of the Sons of Levi*. Even in the Dead Sea Scrolls there is an excerpt taken from the *Book of Lamech,* the antediluvian patriarch.

The history of the Hebrews, as recorded in the Old Testament, has many missing sections. For example, only two years of the forty spent wandering in the desert of Sinai is covered; The other 38 years are only a blank. There is only sketchy information on the late years of Solomon suggesting that the biographical account has been suppressed presumably for his worshipping plural gods. His harem of hundreds of wives or concubines probably did not sit well with the chroniclers.

The Books of The Pseudepigrapha

There is also an abundance of post-Biblical documents. In the thousand years after the Bible was first canonized, the Jews of Europe, Asia, and Africa wrote prolifically in an attempt to clarify the Mosaic Law. These provide a large literature of historical and anecdotal comments on Biblical passages. A large number of these documents by Jews were completely lost from the transmitted heritage and reappeared between 200 BC and AD 200, too late to be included in the formalized Hebrew accounts.

These documents have been grouped together under the general term Pseudepigrapha, a term which has evolved from the Greek denoting writings with "false superscription." The term is used by contemporary scholars not because it denotes something spurious about the documents but because the name has been inherited and is now used internationally.

This literature includes the *Book of Jubilees* and the three books of Enoch, one in Hebrew, one in Ethiopic, and one in Slavonic. It also includes the books of Ezra, the books of Baruch, much apocalyptic literature of the ancient Patriarchs, lost Judeo-Hellenistic works, and many expansions on the works of the Old Testament.

In addition to the Pseudepigrapha, there are collections of ancient Jewish and early Christian writings which are recognized as important to understanding the period in which the Pseudepigrapha were composed. These sources include the works of the Jewish Philosopher Philo of Alexandria, (circa 20 BC to AD 50), the works of the Jewish historian-general Flavius Josephus of about AD 37-100, the Dead Sea Scrolls dated to 150 BC to AD 70, the Targums of Aramaic translations and interpretations of Hebrew scriptures, Jewish magical papyri, the writing of the Hermetics (First Century AD documents attributed to Hermes and his followers), the Nag Hammadi papers which are Coptic codices of the First to Fourth Century relating to the Gnostic tradition, and the Apocrypha or documents preserved in Greek but not in the Hebrew Old Testament.

The Gnostics, The First Suppressed Heresy of the Church

The Gnostic literature was also completely left out of the scriptures, being serious contenders to the early Christian church. In the early years of the Christian era the Gnostics were harassed and utterly defeated and their literature was consigned to oblivion.

In the first three centuries of Christianity the most systematic and organized Christian religion was that of the Gnostics which spread from Palestine through Asia Minor to North Africa and then to the European territories of the Roman Empire. It was spread by Roman legions wherever they went and was integrated with the local religions and customs. It was so popular that it posed a serious challenge to the early Roman Church. In the Second Century, Valentinus, a major Gnostic thinker, sought election as Pope in Rome and came very close to being elected. This event marked the high point of Gnosticism. Alarmed by the growth and strength of Gnosticism (a religion that held a priesthood as unnecessary) the Bishop of Rome with the connivance and support of the Emperor Constantine convened a council of bishops in AD 325 and with their help declared Gnosticism a false doctrine and a major heresy.

Later all forms of Gnosticism were banned from the Roman Empire by an increasingly authoritative church. Gnostic texts disappeared from centers of learning, or were left uncopied which achieved the same purpose. Until recently the only Gnostic literature that was available were the refutations by the early Christian fathers. Then in 1945, extensive Gnostic treatises were found in earthenware jars in Egypt at a small town called Nag Hammadi. This find was as significant to Biblical research as that of the Dead Sea Scrolls in Palestine.

In the Gnostic tracts the existence of the serpent-gods is clearly indicated. The serpent in the Garden of Eden is a noble and virtuous creature. It is a woman called Lilith who is first created and then later Adam is provided to her as a mate. It is thus clear why the Manicheans, an early Gnostic sect (to which Saint Augustine belonged before his conversion) was persecuted so vigorously, for their beliefs undermined many of the precepts of the male dominated early church. Furthermore, in the Gnostic philosophy there is no need for an intermediary between man and God.

The Borrowed Stories of The Old Testament

Biblical apologists have deliberately shunned the issue of the origin of the stories of the Old Testament, in spite of the evidence that its antecedents lie in the plains of Mesopotamia. The Sumerian culture which can be traced as far back as the beginning of the Fourth Millennium BC, was the source of all the myths and stories of later civilzations of the Middle East, such as the Akkadian, Babylonian, and Assyrian peoples. This culture became Semitic and was subsequently transferred to the lands of the west — to Palestine, Syria, Lebanon, Jordan, and Anatolia.

The language of the Sumerians was superseded rather early by Akkadian, a Semitic tongue. These people later intermingled and eventually formed a fusion of the two languages. From this Sumerian-Akkadian milieu evolved the Semites and eventually the Hebrews. The Hebrews did not invent their language and literary forms; their culture was inherited from the older Mesopotamian and Canaanite cultures. It should be widely realized that when those famous Biblical figures of Noah and Abraham lived, there was no such thing as a Hebrew in existence. Both the Jews and Arabs traditionally claim descent from Abraham, who was neither Jew nor Arab, but a Semite who resided in the capital city of Ur in Mesopotamia.

When he left Ur, Abraham presumably brought with him these Sumerian traditions. According to Genesis, his father was a high priest; other sources indicate he was also a Prince in the hierarchy of the city of Ur. It is therefore manifest that the stories of the Creation, of Adam and Eve, the Fall of Man, and of the Deluge were derived from the literature and myths of Sumer, the fountainhead from which all nations of the ancient world drew their knowledge and beliefs.

The Old Testament was not written down in its present form much earlier than the Seventh or Sixth Century BC. On the other hand, most of the Sumerian stories and legends were composed and put to clay tablets about 2500 BC or not long thereafter. We know that the Eden of the Bible was located in Mesopotamia at the mouth of the Tigris and Euphrates Rivers, a region the Sumerians called E-DIN or the "Land of the God. "

Furthermore, many of the heros of the Old Testament were lifted from contemporary legends. For example, the story of Jonah was apparently universally known. Hercules was swallowed by a whale at Joppa, precisely the same place as Jonah. Persian legends tell of their hero Jamshyd who was devoured by a sea monster which later vomited him safely upon the shore.

The story of Job comes from a Babylonian poem about a virtuous man named *Tabu-utul-bel* who was sorely afflicted for some inscrutable reason and tormented by the gods. The story of Daniel was taken from a north Canaanite poem dated as far back as 1500 BC. The story of Samson is so strange and foreign to Hebrew lore as to indicate that it was borrowed in toto from Canaanite mythology; in fact, his name is derived from Shamash, the Sumerian Sun God who ruled Lebanon.

The struggle between good and evil which is fundamental to the Judeo-Christian concept of sin, is basically derived from and gets its impetus from a Sumerian story of the struggle between good and evil gods for control of the pantheon. The *Myth of Zu* describes how an evil god named Zu seized control of the heavens and is destroyed by a heroic god sent by the pantheon. From it was derived the story of the attempt of the evil angel Lucifer to seize the heavens and his defeat and banishment to Hell below.

The Origin of the Story of the Fall of Lucifer

The account of the good god against the evil one was a story known all over the Middle East in various forms. Its origin was undoubtedly in the Sumerian story called the *Myth of Zu.* This battle for control of the heavens is described in detail in a later chapter.

The story of the Fall of Lucifer is found in many of the ancient religious documents. For example, details of the struggle appear in the *Slavonic Apocalypse of Enoch,* also known as the *Second Book of Enoch,* a document which has survived only in Slavonic and was probably derived from Aramaic sources. It refers to an archangel called Samael who rebelled and tried to seize the heavens. Like the evil Sumerian god Zu he tried to enthrone himself above the gods. As related to Enoch in this book, God cast him down to Earth, from Earth to Sheol, and from there to the bottomless pit:

> But one from the order of the archangels deviated. He thought up the impossible idea, that he might place his throne higher than the clouds which are above the Earth, and that he might become equal to my power. And I hurled him out from the height.

A version of this struggle in the heavens is given the in the *Book of Revelation (12:7)* where the fallen angel is called a dragon:

> Now war arose in heaven. Michael and his angels fighting against the Dragon; and the Dragon and his angels fought, but they were defeated and there was no longer any place for them in heaven. And the great Dragon was thrown down, that ancient Serpent, who is called Devil and Satan.

What is interesting about the version in Revelation is that it equates the serpent, the dragon, and the evil angel, a sub-theme of this book which will be discussed in detail later. The notion of the evil or fallen angel as Satan and Lucifer was well established by the time of Christ. It apparently became formalized at the Council of Nicea in *325* which sought to define heresy. In the Middle Ages the concept of the evil god became well known; it appears in illustrated Medieval manuscripts and on the stained glass windows of the churches and cathedrals. Satan is usually shown or described as half-human and half-goat with horns, a tail, a chin beard, and cloven hoofs. This characterization seems to have been copied from the Greek depiction of Pan, the god of fun and sexual license. Many Greek vases portray people frolicking with Pan in obvious sensuous activities. The early Christian Church frowned on such activities and propagated the notion that life was grim and serious, that one's life should be a search to rid oneself of original sin. Sin became associated with licentiousness and the Greek god Pan became the symbol of Satan or Lucifer.

CHAPTER 3

WESTERN OR EUROPEAN DRAGONS

In Europe, the folklore of the dragon is rather confused for the term *dragon* was not only applied to beasts that could fly but also to earthbound serpents and to sea monsters as well. All sorts of monsters were called dragons.

For this reason, we must separate them into two groups — those that fly which could be considered true dragons, and those without wings which we must classify as merely monsters. However, in certain instances, the non-winged serpent is used symbolically to represent the dragon, such as in ancient Egypt where the deceased king is shown riding on the back of a serpent in the sky against a background of stars on his way to join his ancestors, the gods in the heavens.

Strange Winged Creatures

As the dragon is found in European legends, a composite description of the dragon would be as follows. It has the body of a reptile and two or four feet. When shown four-legged the hind feet are strong and powerful with four claws or toes. The front legs are smaller and often replaced by wings. There is a long tail capable of being coiled up.

The head is large with a long snout and forked tongue, and the jaws are equipped with many sharp pointed teeth. It usually has horns and two large eyes which are meant for it to see in the semidarkness of caves. Between the eyes is a third eyelike structure called a *dracontia* which is often described as a precious stone that is endowed with magical powers.

The dragon's body is covered with greenish scales while the underside is bright yellow. It sometimes has a series of sharp protective spines which extend down its back from the head to the end of the tail. The wings are most like that of a bat instead of a bird, with brilliant colors, and when fully expanded and waved, presents a very formidable display.

Wherever caves existed, there were likely to be dragons, whose serpent nature found refuge and comfort in dark, cold solitude. Caves were often located close to towns where they were convenient to sources of food, such as farm animals, and sometimes even humans.

Craggy or cave-riddled mountains were particular favorites of these solitary and suspicious monsters, for they provided impregnable places to hide. They flew from these aeries, and flying high they could locate their prey, drop down for the kill, and return to their dens to feed unmolested.

Fig.2 – Two and four-legged dragons from Medieval documents.

Water also sheltered these beasts. Many of the sea monsters were winged and hence could be classified as true dragons. They inhabited seas, rivers, and lakes all over the world.

In Europe, and particularly in England, the dragon was believed to be a hoarder of treasure. Perhaps the notion of the dragon as the protector of treasure originated in Greek and Roman times when serpents often were used to guard temples and sacred places.

Dragons have also been associated with various precious stones and no doubt this object symbolized the creature's great powers. The European dragon often carried a magical stone imbedded in its forehead. The Oriental dragon had a white or crystal-like object held directly below the chin, or suspended in the air in front of it. It was supposed to protect it and give it its magical powers.

The Dragons of the Greeks and Romans

Greek legends are replete with references to dragons, both good and evil. For example, Ceres flew to heaven in a chariot drawn by two dragons. When Medea fled from Jason it was in a chariot drawn by winged dragons.

Perhaps the most famous Greek dragon of all times was Typhon who was so big that its head was said to reach the stars and its wings so broad that they blocked out the sunlight. Its roaring was like that of a terrible storm, and from its mouth came not only flame but coughed-up rocks as well. It was finally slain by Zeus and buried under Mt. Etna, which today occasionally sends forth smoke, suggesting that the creature is not dead but awaits the right time to rise again.

Except for such isolated instances, serpent-dragons were believed by the Greeks to be great sources of knowledge and wisdom, and were considered sacred creatures with oracular abilities. Serpents were to be found in shrines where they transmitted their great wisdom through the mouths of priestesses. Python was one such serpent who guarded the shrine at Delphi until he was killed by Apollo.

Greek sea monsters are often mistaken for dragons. The dragon that the Greek hero Perseus slew was not a flying monster. As the legend goes, the Olympian gods had fabricated winged shoes for Perseus which permitted him to fly. As he flew high over the shores of the Red Sea he spied a maiden below bound to a rock on the shore. She was Andromeda, the daughter of Cepheus, the King of Ethiopia, and of Cassiope. On advice of an oracle, Cepheus had sent his daughter to the shore to be offered as a sacrifice to a sea dragon that was ravaging the kingdom. As the monster broke the surface of the water, Perseus rose in the air aided by his winged shoes, hovered over the dragon's back and penetrated his thick hide with his sword. The monster heaved an awful sigh and sank beneath the waves.

In the legend of Cadmus, the slaying of the dragon took place in a cavern in Boetia. In his *Metamorphoses*, Ovid describes the creature as being of a golden color with spectacular crests on its back. Its eyes sparkled with fire; it was terribly destructive due to its sting and venomous breath. Cadmus slew the dragon when it devoured all his men, whereupon he sowed the dragon's teeth in the furrows of a ploughed field. Instantly, each tooth became a warrior sprouting out of the ground. But they soon fought each other until only five were left alive. These five founded the city of Thebes and for hundreds of years, the descendants of these families still painted dragons on their shields to show that they came of a race born of the dragon's tooth.

It is possible that the poets of Greece and Rome may have introduced the dragon into their fables to give them a dramatic element of power and ferocity. In his description of the shield of Hercules, Homer describes it graphically as "the scaly horror of a dragon coiled full in the central field, unspeakable, with eyes oblique, retorted, that askant shot gleaming fire." Hesiod, the Greek poet of the Eighth Century BC, also gave a vivid description of the same shield but he made a distinction between serpents and dragons:

> On its center was the unspeakable terror of a dragon glancing backward with eyes of gleaming fire. His mouth was filled with teeth running in a white line, dread and unapproachable. On the shield likewise were heads of terrible serpents, unspeakable, twelve in number, who were wont to scare the race of men on Earth, whosoever changed to wage war against the son of Zeus.

According to the Roman historian Livy, a sea monster or dragon seems to have bedeviled the Romans during the First Punic Wars. At about 256 BC, the army of the Roman General Atilius Regulus encountered a large monster when trying to cross a river. It was of such size and ferocity that it kept the army from using the river. It seized many of the soldiers in its huge jaws and its tail crushed a large number of the legionnaires. The Romans assaulted it with missiles from catapults but they could not damage the hide of the monster. Finally they attacked from all sides with swords and stones and it succumbed. After death, its blood stained the ground, and the poison stench of its body drove the Roman camp away from the river; not only was dragon breath deadly to humans but its blood was also toxic.

Dragons as Guardians of Immortality

One of the twelve trials undergone by Hercules was to slay the dragon named Ladon which guarded a tree of golden apples, and bring the apples back to King Eurysthus. These apples reportedly contained the secrets of knowledge and immortality. In the story of Hercules we see the association of dragons with immortality. This theme is also found in the story of the Garden of Eden in the *Book of Genesis.*

In the Garden of Eden there were two trees — the Tree of Knowledge, and the Tree of Life or Immortality. It seems that the fruit of the Tree of Knowledge was also guarded by a serpent and that it too was similar in purpose to the apples guarded by the dragon Ladon. According to Genesis, Adam had access to all the fruit of the garden — only the Tree of Knowledge was forbidden, indicating that he could partake of the Tree of Immortality. It means that Adam was immortal at that time and did not need access to the fruit of that tree. Only when Adam ate of the fruit of the Tree of Knowledge was he forbidden to take from the Tree of Immortality. Hence the two were mutually exclusive.

One ancient Jewish account relates how the two trees grew out of one tree and separated or branched out at a certain height. It is only in the Old Testament that the dichotomy is made so strongly; all other societies refer to but one tree, that is the Tree of Immortality. It was not until the arrival of the Old Testament that we see so much emphasis on forbidden knowledge. It seems to have been a device invented by the Hebrew chroniclers to instill the feeling of original sin in man.

The idea of a plant or tree of immortality is not original with the Old Testament but was borrowed from the Sumerian antecedent where the theme of the search for long life or immortality echoes throughout many of the myths. The snake or serpent has historically been associated with immortality. It was the legged serpent in the garden (the symbol of long life), that caused immortality to be taken away from man.

The Unfortunate Dragon of Rhodes

Legends about dragons became established in Europe during the Middle Ages, perhaps fostered by the religious institutions which wanted to emphasize the struggle between good and evil. One of the most famous is that of the Dragon of Rhodes. Located in the Mediterranean near the coast of Anatolia, the island of Rhodes was held by the Knights Hospitalers of St. John who seized it after being expelled from the Holy Land by the Moslems in 1309.

But the occupation of Rhodes was not without inconvenience, for the people suffered terribly from a dragon or giant serpent. It lived in a dark cave in a mountainside and daily it would leave its lair and cause havoc among cattle and horses as well as any luckless people who happened to stray too close and were overcome by its fiery breath.

Six of the best knights of the order lost their lives when they tried to slay the monster. So in order to prevent further decimation of the order, the Grand Master placed a ban on any further attempts by his knights. Nevertheless, a young knight from Province, called Theodore, anxious to prove his mettle in battle, resolved to ignore the ban and slay the beast. Disregarding the explicit order of the Grand Master, he attacked the dragon with lance and sword accompanied by two trained bulldogs.

As he neared the beast, it rushed forth to meet him with its fiery breath and venom dripping from its gaping jaws. Theodore struck the dragon with his spear but the thick scales deflected the blow. Then with his sword he hacked away at the dragon when a blow from its tail knocked him to the ground. His faithful dogs charged the beast from beneath and sank their teeth into its vulnerably underbelly. The dragon maddened with pain reared up into the air trying to shake off the dogs. Seizing the opportunity, Theodore drove his sword to the hilt in the unprotected belly of the dragon. It fell to the ground in agony, black blood gushing forth from its wound. Then with one last blood-curdling scream fell dead at the feet of Theodore.

But it seems that all Medieval tales had a moral to them. As he was hailed by the people for his great deed, Theodore was summoned by the Grand Master who received him angrily declaring, "Rash youth you have transgressed my command. Tell me, what is the highest duty of our sacred order?" Meekly, Theodore responded "Obedience." So in spite of his courage and deed Theodore was stripped of his sword and knightly emblems. The Grand Master decreed that he be sent to the deepest of dungeons and remain there until his name was long forgotten. Humbled, Theodore did as bidden. He removed his shining armor and laid his sword at the foot of the Grand Master. Resigned to his fate he started to leave the room in despair when suddenly he heard the bellowing voice of the Grand Master as it resounded throughout the hall, "Return my son, once more you have shown yourself to be worthy to wear the cross. You have conquered yourself, and may now receive the honor due to him who has vanquished the dragon. Take back the sword that has earned you a place henceforth among the bravest and the best." Theodore's triumph was complete, and in time, he himself became Grand Master of the Order of the Knights of St. John.

The Medieval Dragon of Beaucaire

Among the Medieval French perhaps the most famous of dragons is that of the one called Drac, which lived in the river Rhone near the town of Beaucaire. It was described by the natives as a huge, gleaming, scaly monster with glowing eyes and terrible claws. One strange characteristic of this dragon was that it was invisible when it roamed the lands near the river. It could not be seen by the townfolk, who although knew of its existence, could not prevent it from seizing livestock and dragging them into the depths of the river. At times it even seized humans as well, and had a propensity for unattended children.

Fig. 3 – Winged but legless dragon inhabiting lakes and rivers.

One day a young wife from the town went down to the river with her infant son to wash clothes. As she labored by the edge of the river she noticed a golden cup with a single large pearl floating just offshore in the river. She reached for it and managed to grasp the pearl, but in doing so lost her balance and fell into the river into the waiting claws of the dragon. It promptly took her down into the sea and to its crystal cavern where the dragon had a brood of its own.

There the young wife was obliged to remain for seven years to nurse and tend the hatchlings of the dragon. After that period of time and when the dragons were full grown and able to fend for themselves, she was released by the grateful parent dragon and returned to the village of Beaucaire with the pearl as her reward.

Friendly Alpine Dragons

In the Alpine regions of France, dragon stories abound and the most popular of these concerns what may be called a friendly dragon called "vouivre" by the natives, a name apparently derived from the Latin "vipera." It was described by the people as a magnificent monster; it guarded fabulous treasure in its lair in a mountain grotto.

It was said that when it flew, its scales sparkled like diamonds, that it wore a crown of pearls, and that in the center of its forehead was a blood red ruby that served as its single eye. It was so luminous that when it flew, the dragon looked like it was bathed in fire.

There was one night each year, however, when the dragon became vulnerable. At this time it left its cave and flew to a nearby lake to bathe and to drink. When it entered the water it removed its precious red stone and placed it on the ground at the water's edge. Without the precious ruby the dragon was blind and helpless.

Although the folk of the countryside knew of its weakness, no one was brave enough to approach the dragon much less steal the red jewel. It was said that deprived of its sight the dragon would languish and die, and yet the fiery dragon lived on for centuries. Apparently, no person was daring enough to seize and profit from its treasure. Or was it because there was a deep affection for the "local" dragon?

Another story is told in the Alpine region of a barrel-maker who fell into a deep crevasse one autumn day while searching for wood to make wine barrels. Unable to climb out he explored the cavern seeking to find another way out. The caves, however, turned out to be the home of two winged dragons who seemed quite sympathetic to the plight of the barrel-maker. They allowed him to live there for the winter months where he spent the cold nights wrapped in the warmth of their coils. When spring came, the dragons grew restless and spread their wings. As they flew up out of the chasm, the barrel-maker seized the tail of one and was carried out to freedom. Eventually he made his way home where he became a local folk hero.

What is interesting about these French dragons is that they seemed to be warm and friendly types and not hostile to mankind. People seemed to have returned the favor by leaving them alone and not harassing them. But this was not true of the dragons of England.

The Many Dragons of England

Perhaps the oldest of the dragon-related stories in English literature is found in the early epic of Beowulf. As the leader of the Geats, he gained fame by killing the monster Grendel, which lived in the waters of a lake. In attacking the dragon, Beowulf could not penetrate its armored head but managed to stab it in the belly causing it to lose its supply of flame. Then he disemboweled it with his dagger but not before being bitten by the dragon and receiving a fatal dose of poison. One tradition states that the dragon lived in a barrow or Earth mound where it guarded secret treasure. Another form of the legend has Beowulf buried high upon a sea cliff surrounded by the dragon's gold and treasure.

England has a long tradition of dragons. Local peoples claim to have observed them for centuries. The dragon tradition has probably persisted here more than in any other country. In a survey of the English countryside, Marc Aleksander in his book *British Folklore* has revealed that there are more than 70 towns and villages which have a tradition of dragons.

The *Anglo-Saxon Chronicle* reports that in the year 793 AD, in Northumbria, fiery dragons were seen flying in the air accompanied by flashes of lightning. In 1113 AD it was reported that a group of clergymen encountered a dragon at Christchurch which had come out of the sea breathing fire from its nostrils. It flew around from place to place in the village setting fire to all the houses by its fiery breath. It even burned a nearby ship and all of its crew. Local records also show that in 1170 a large dragon was seen flying up into the sky from the ground, setting a home afire and reducing it to ashes near Colchester.

Dragons Hoarding Treasure

In England there are over 300 barrows or mounds which have been traced back to Neolithic times and which were used for the burial of the dead. It is presumed that valuable objects were also interred with these ancient chiefs. According to folklore, they contained hidden treasures which was guarded by dragons, who scourged the countryside by night, spouting flame as they flew. The origin of these traditions is credited to the story of Beowulf, which is dated to about the Eighth Century. Stories of treasure in a barrow which contained secret passages presumably leading to a chambered cave where the guardian dragon resided probably antedate the story of Beowulf since some of these barrows can be traced back thousands of years before the legend. The notion of dragons protecting the tombs of the nobles who were often buried with their belongings, may have been promulgated by the local chiefs to prevent people from ransacking and destroying the tombs.

A survey by Leslie Grinsell as reported in his *Folklore of Prehistoric Sites in Britain* reveals that there are many local names, particularly in the Midlands and the northern counties, which suggest a long tradition of dragons guarding treasure in barrows. Names like Drakelow, Dragonhoard, Drake Howe suggests dragons guarding buried treasure. The most famous of these is Dragon Hill near Oxford where a dragon (erroneously called a horse) has been engraved into the chalk hillside.

In the area of Salop at Bromfield there are a group of round barrows where tradition has them guarded by a dragon. In Lincolnshire near Walmsgate legend states that at a long barrow hill one of the dragons was slain and buried in the mound. The ancient name of Walmsgate is Wormsgate, and *worm* or *wirm* being the local name for wingless dragons. In North Yorkshire at least ten barrows are dragon associated.

Dragon Paths and Leys

There is a theory that has been prevalent in England throughout the ages, of lines of energy called *leys* connecting various ancient shrines, barrows, monoliths, and stone circles. These leys were believed by the ancient Druids to be actual *dragon paths.*

At first thought to have been used by ancient Druids and Celts as trade routes, they run in direct lines so that in many cases they go straight over hill tops and not around as one would expect of a road. It has been suggested that they may actually be part of geodetic net used by the ancients based on a form of Earth or non-magnetic energy.

According to the English chronicler Geoffrey of Monmouth in his *History of the Kings of Britain*, nobles were buried in these barrows which are connected with the ley lines. Geoffrey implicitly links the barrows with the giant stone circle at Stonehenge which he states was built by Merlin using special apparatus to move the stones from Ireland. Geoffrey claims that the "Giant's Ring" as he called it was also used for the burial of nobles and that the stones had medicinal properties and were used by the native people for healing purposes. These references by Geoffrey seem to support the connection between ancient burrows, menhirs or stone circles, and their association with ley lines as a source of subtle forms of energy. The investigation of ley lines is a vigorous ongoing work in England that promises to uncover a new science of Earth Energy.

A similar net of energy lines is found in China where they are called Dragon Paths or *Lung Mei.* The Chinese believe them to be an invisible energy force forming a geodetic grid over the surface of the Earth. This dragon current, as it is called, is of two kinds, *ying and yang*. They are negative and positive forces and are represented by the white tiger and the blue dragon. The Lung Mei follows ridges and hills, with the yang or male current taking the higher route over the hills, and the yin or female current mainly along the lower hills. The place where the two lines of force meet is supposed to be a favored or magical place. For centuries, and until fairly recently, buildings were never erected without first investigating and identifying these dragon lines in order to make sure that the building was located in a favorable location and away from negative or destructive forces.

The Legend of the Unlucky Gerolde

The most famous of British dragon legends are those associated with King Arthur and St. George, which are discussed below. There is a lesser known story of the hero Gerolde who acquired a deserved reputation as the slayer of dragons. As the story is related, the first dragon he slew was relatively small which he managed to surprise one day dressed in his shiniest suit of armor. The reflection of the sun off his polished armor dazzled the dragon and before it could recover, Gerolde impaled it on his lance. Hailed by the people as their deliverer, he toured the countryside receiving adulation and gifts, among which were colored silks and garlands. At their urging Gerolde attached them to his helmet and lance for good fortune. But not to leave well enough alone, Gerolde had a multicolor coat made of these ribbons. When slipped over his armored suit it immediately transformed him into a flaglike vision of bright colors.

Shortly after, clad in his colorful garments he encountered a large dragon

Fig. 4 – St. George slaying the Dragon

and attacked it with full confidence. This time the reflecting armor was hidden by the coat and the sun was behind a cloud. The dragon released a torrent of fire which immediately incinerated Gerolde on the spot. Badly shaken, his followers collected the charred remains of their hero and buried him nearby with full honors.

There is also a French version of the story of Gerolde indicating that the legend was probably universally know in the Middle Ages. Found in his *History of the Knights Hospitalers*, Abbe de Vertot gives a similar account except the hero is called Sieur Dieudonne (Sir Godgiven) and the event takes place in France.

St. George, The Professional Dragon Slayer

Although there have been many ancient legends of dragon battles such as the Teutonic warrior Siegfried and that of Beowulf in Britain, these dragon slayers were rank amateurs compared with St. George, who can be credited with being the first really professional dragon slayer. His fame spread all over Europe and his reputation was such that he was given sainthood by the early Church. He was claimed as a savior by many nations including England, Spain, Italy, Greece, Portugal and the city of Constantinople, and even by Ethiopia where he is its patron saint. Actually the legend of St. George can be traced back to Roman times.

The knight who became St. George was born in Palestine (his Roman name is not known but was probably Georgius) during the days of the Roman Emperor Constantine, at the time when the empire was beginning to unravel. His travels took him to Libya in northern Africa where he first earned his reputation as a dragon killer. While passing through the area of Silene he was told by the townspeople of a dragon which lived in a nearby marsh and had descended from the hills. It was raiding the local farms, eating the sheep, and when these were not available feasted on the local population.

The terrified people had given all their children to the dragon in order to satiate its appetite and when only the King's daughter remained she too was bound and offered up to the dragon. Without hesitation St. George saw his duty and approached the dragon in its lair. Catching the dragon by surprise he speared it with his lance. The dragon sprang screaming from its lair spitting venom and fire in all directions. As it reared to strike St. George, his lance again pierced its side and the dragon fell to Earth, the poison from its jaws trickling harmlessly to the ground. Leading the cowering beast to the town where the populace could observe him, St. George dispatched it by slicing off its head with one blow of his sword.

But in spite of his many exploits, St. George is said to have come to an unhappy end. Accounts differ on how he died. Some say he was arrested by the Roman Emperor Diocletian and put to death. Others claim that he was decapitated by the emperor of Persia after trying to convert his court to Christianity. It was also reported that his amorous adventures led to his death by a jealous husband.

Nonetheless, he was canonized by the Church several centuries after his death. But in the 16th Century, Pope Clement III decided that George had not been completely truthful about his dragon killing ability, and all references to his exploits with dragons were eliminated from his official biography. Recently he suffered the final ignominy and was decanonized by the Catholic Church.

St. George was a hero in Medieval England and became its patron saint in 1349. English sources claim that he visited England in his travels and conquered at least one dragon in the area of Berkshire. It is more probable that his story was brought back by the English Crusaders where the use of the name was a popular battle cry. His fame was widespread and he is often depicted as a crusading knight in stained glass windows and in illuminated manuscripts. The site of his battle with the dragon was immortalized at a place called Dragon Hill in Berkshire Downs. It is the location of the so-called Uffington Horse which appears more to resemble a **dragon** rather than a horse.

Located not far from the stone circles of Avebury and Stonehenge, Dragon Hill is famous as the location of the outline of a great "horse" carved into the chalk hillside. Called the Uffington Horse it goes back into misty antiquity and is mentioned in documents over a thousand years ago. The Uffington Horse is 365 feet long and can be seen for miles around. The most intriguing aspect of this "horse" is the fact that it does not look like a horse. It had odd features for a horse, especially a long dragon-like jaw. The belief has persisted among local people that it is not a horse at all but the outline of a dragon.

King Arthur, Son of the Great Dragon

According to Geoffrey of Monmouth the first British king after the departure of the Romans was one Vortigern who called himself High King of Britain. He fought the Saxon invaders for which he built a fortified castle in northern Britain.

As recounted in the legend, no matter how hard his masons worked during the day, the foundadtion of the castle sank into the ground at night. Brought in to solve the problem, Merlin the Chief Druid of the time, explained to the king that it was because the foundation of the castle rested on a subterranean cavern where two dragons slept during the day and fought each other at night. This cavern caused the foundation to be unsteady and the stones to collapse.

Vortigern had his men excavate the site and found the lair of the dragons. As the story goes, one monster was white which Merlin said symbolized the Saxon invaders, and the other was red and it was the symbol of the people of Britain. Thus, the red dragon not only became the symbol of Wales but also became the badge of Uther Pendragon, the father of King Arthur — Pendragon meaning the Chief or Great Dragon. Thus the legends make King Arthur the descendant of dragons, similar to the claims of the emperors of China and the Kings of ancient Sumer. To emphasize his dragon lineage, King Arthur's helmet was adorned with the head of a dragon.

The Welsh classic *Mabinogion* also relates the story of Merlin's dragons. It tells how these two dragons had been a nuisance to the people of the area for five centuries before the reign of Vortigern. They often appeared above the pit and fought each other in the sky until they fell exhausted to the ground. According to this legend, Vortigern was beseiged by Ambrosius, the last of the Roman leaders, who destroyed the castle. The brother of Ambrosius was called Uther Pendragon because when he was born a fiery dragon appeared in the sky.

A dragon also appears prominently in the exploits of one of the Knights of the Round Table at King Arthur's Court. Launcelot is said to have done battle with a dragon when travelling in a part of France ruled by a king called Pelles. His kingdom was beset by a dragon which ventured out each night to maim and slaughter the people. When Launcelot appeared, the king begged him for his aid.

The gallant Launcelot went to the lair of the dragon and when it burst out upon him, he slew it with his sword. King Pelles was deeply grateful and offered his daughter Elaine as a reward. But Launcelot refused because he felt he had given his heart to Queen Guinevere. But not to be outdone, and wishing to have an heir from the hero Launcelot, Pelles used enchantment and magic to give Elaine the outward form of Guinevere. Posing and resembling the Queen, Elaine invited Launcelot to her chambers who readily accepted. Nine months later a child was born to Elaine and he was called Galahad. Galahad became the greatest warrior of the Round Table.

CHAPTER 4

NON-EUROPEAN DRAGONS

The Dravidians or Nagas, the Serpent Race of India

In the 1920's, archaeologists made some amazing discoveries in the Indus River Valley. The ruins of two large ancient cities were excavated, one called Mohenjo-Daro, the other Harappa, and like the cities of Mesopotamia and the Nile Valley, were built on alluvial plains. But unlike these other cities, they seem to have sprung up fully planned. Both were identical in layout and while no ziggurats were found, each city had a mound ten meters high, a sort of artificial platform.

Mohenjo-Daro and Harappa did not evolve from primitive villages but were completed as cities within a century or so. They were built from "scratch" as if by an outside force. In other words, they were constructed as a colony, probably by the Sumerians, and presumably by their Chief Engineer Enki. According to archaeological evidence, the cities sprang up between 3500 and 3000 BC, and later came to a violent end around 2000 BC. Skeletons found in their ruins show a high rate of radioactivity as if some nuclear holocaust occurred here and destroyed the cities.

Historians are puzzled by the fact that these people are not related to the Aryans, who came some 500 years later and settled the Panjab and Gangetic Plain. Like the ancient Sumerians, the people of these two cities spoke an unknown language. Historians believe they were the home of the ancient serpent-people, the Dravidians.

The ancient *Book of Dzyan*, probably the oldest of Sanskrit sources, speaks of a serpent race which descended from the skies and taught mankind. The recovery of this ancient source from obscurity was accomplished by the theosophist, Madame H.P. Blavatsky who spent three years in Tibet, Bhutan, and Sikkim accumulating the thousands of Sanskrit sources which were compiled into the *Book of Dzyan*. According to this book, the Sarpa or Great Dragons were the Fifth Race to inhabit the world. The Fourth Race was a race of giants who had lived before the Deluge but were wiped out by that catastrophe. The book relates how the serpent gods or dragons redescended after the Deluge and instructed man in the arts of civilization. These serpent-gods had a human face and the tail of a dragon; they founded divine dynasties on Earth and are believed to the the ancestors of our current civilization, the Fifth Race of the *Book of Dzyan*. The leader of these gods was called "The Great Dragon."

The Dravidians or Nagas were said to be the result of the sexual liaison between serpent-gods and mankind. They were described as a coarse, cannibalistic people, dark-skinned and flat-nosed. They were known for their wisdom and lived underground in caves. These Nagas are described in many of the Sanskrit sources as an intelligent reptile that could fly around the skies in their chariots. It is a fitting description of a dragon. The Aryans who came later, ran into the remnants of these serpent people who are vividly described in one of their classical myths:

> Near Bhogavata stands the place where dwelt the hosts of the serpent race, a broad-wayed city, walled and barred which watchful legions keep and guard. The fiercest of the serpent

> youth, each awful for his venomed tooth; and throned in his imperial hall is Vasuki who rules them all.

Much of the evidence that Dravidian, Dasyus, and Nagas were different names for the same people can be found in the great epics of India, the *Mahabharata* and the *Ramayana.* Both epics concern the early Aryan contacts with these serpent people, some of which were friendly, but many which were hostile. Due to the intermarriage of the Aryans with them, a sort of ambiance, a love-hate relationship, seems to permeate the two great epics.

In the epic *Mahabharata*, a group of "celestials" arrive by aerial car to attend the wedding feast of one of the Aryan kings:

> And the gods came in cloud-borne chariots. Came to view the scene so fair. Bright Adityas in their splendor, Maruts in the moving air, winged Suparnas, scaly Nagas. Saints celestial pure and high, for their music famed, Gandharvas, and fair Apsaras of the sky, bright celestial cars in concourse, sailed upon the cloudless sky.

The poem describes the arrival of various Dravidians: the Adityas were their sun-gods, the Maruts were storm gods, the Gandharvas, the celestial musicians, and Apsaras were the celestial nymphs. These "scaly Nagas" intermarried with Aryans producing kings and heroes. Like in Sumer and Egypt, many of the ancient Hindu gods mated with humans, and produced a hybrid mammal-reptile, the semi-divine kings which resound throughout the literature of both Sumer and India. Ancient Hindu literature also asserts that the divine ones had descended and conducted biological experiments with mammals, specifically apes. In fact, Hanuman, the monkey-god, who with Rama is the hero of the epic poem *Ramayana*, was conceived when the god Shiva gave a sacred cake to Anjan, the ape. This obvious reference to a genetic experiment produced Hanuman, the super-monkey who is a hero of the epic *Ramayana.*

The Ramayana: A Hindu Epic About the Serpent Gods

One of the great epics of India, the *Ramayana*, is the story of Sita, the bride of a northern Prince called Rama, who is abducted by Ravan, the serpent king of Ceylon. In the myth Rama chases the army of Ravan across India with the help of an army of monkeys under the command of the monkey-general Hanuman.

The serpent-god Ravan retreats to his kingdom of Ceylon, supposedly safe from pursuit by the army of Rama. But Rama's aide and ally Hanuman builds a bridge of boulders across the straits separating the island from the mainland, thus enabling Rama to cross over and rescue his bride Sita.

Throughout the story, Ravan is described in barbaric terms more suitable to a reptile than a mammal — he "feeds on humans" and "drinks the blood of his foe." He is formidable in battle and almost defeats Rama when he uses his special Naga weapon, which seems to paralyze his enemies and drain their life force.

Ceylon, the island kingdom of Ravan, was the stronghold of the serpent people. It is described as the home of the Nagas in very ancient Chinese sources. In one of the first literary references to Ceylon, when it traded with China before the Aryan occupation of India, it is described as a land of strange reptilian-like creatures. Because of its gems and spices and its convenient location as an entrepot, it became popular with Chinese merchants.

Fa-Hsien, the ancient Chinese pilgrim trader reported that originally the island was occupied by Nagas or serpent deities with whom merchants of various countries carried on a trade. The Nagas never showed themselves to the outsiders. They simply set forth their precious commodities with price labels attached to them. The visiting merchants made their purchases according to the price, and took the things away.

The Mahabharata, The Great Snake Sacrifice

The other great epic of India, the *Mahabharata* is the longest and perhaps the greatest epic poem in any language. Much older than the *Ramayana,* it consists of 88,000 verses. The main theme of the story is the rivalry between two branches of the Kurus family. Called the Pandavas and the Kauravas, they fight a war which culminates in the near destruction of both branches of the family at the great battle of Kuruksetra.

The tale starts with King Pariksit of the Kauravas who shoots a deer while hunting with bow and arrow. Pursuing the deer he asks an ascetic if he had seen the wounded deer. Observing a vow of silence, the sage did not answer. This angered Pariksit who then took a dead snake and placed it around the sage's neck. The ascetic's son Srnga was incensed and put a curse on Pariksit. Thus started the blood feud between the two families.

Significantly a third party intervenes. Angry over the blasphemous use of one of their own kind, the serpent-people enter the story. Taksaka, the king of the serpent-people, sends snakes who cause the death of Pariksit.

The story of the blood feud is actually narrated as something which happened in the dim past. Since the ancient kingdom of the Kurus flourished along the upper course of the Ganges in the 14th and 13th Century BC, the events may have taken place in the early days of the Aryan invasion when there was much intercourse with the Nagas.

The *Mahabharata* actually begins with the great snake sacrifice of King Janamejaya, the son of Pariksit. As the king tells the story he performs a ceremony to avenge his death, a snake sacrifice called the yaina. The war stories and other narratives are told as revolving tales at the sacrifices which were of long duration. Its purpose is apparently to symbolically destroy the Nagas, the serpent-gods which supposedly could assume snake or human form at will.

In the ritual, the priest invokes the names of the serpents as he tosses live snakes into the fire. Astika, the son of the serpent-king Taksaka, intervenes and pleads with Janamejaya to let his relatives live. It is the view of the Indian historian Kosambi that the *Mahabharata* itself was not so much an account of a great war but rather it was the story of the great *yajna* sacrifice. In other words, it is the story of the symbolic ceremony of propitiating their serpent ancestors while at the same time expelling them from their cultural heritage.

The flying serpent gods of ancient India, which can rightly be called dragons, and presumably gave rise to the idea of fiery, flying reptiles, have an equivocal role in the mythology of India. This love-hate relationship is also seen in Egyptian mythology, but here it is for different historical reasons.

The Flying Serpent of Egypt as Good and Evil

In the mythology of Egypt individual dragons did not roam the skies as they did in Europe, India, and China, but the flying serpent is often present as the symbol of immortality.

Ancient Egyptians had an ambivalent approach to the flying serpent for he is seen as the source of both good and evil. And this is probably due to certain singular historical events.

Fig. 5 – Egyptian Flying Serpents

In the Old and Middle Kingdoms, the latter which ended at about 1450 BC, the serpent is a benevolent creature and associated with the gods and immortality (see fig. 5). But later, starting with the New Kingdom (in particular the 18th Dynasty), it becomes a sinister creature and an object to be hated and exorcised. How did this change come about?

In the earlier dynasties, the flying serpent appears on the walls of the tombs of the kings and here he is depicted as a friendly creature which bears the king on his back into the stellar sky. It is symbolic of the king being carried by the flying serpent to the land of immortality, to the land of the gods in the heavens. At about this time, the snake was adopted as a symbol of kingship or godship and began to appear as the "uraeus" — the divine asp appearing on the headdress of the kings of Egypt.

Winged symbolism was very common in Egyptian mythology and many of the gods are shown to be winged. Overshadowing all Egyptian symbolism was the winged disk flanked by serpents which represented the sun god and his ability to fly. There is little doubt that until the end of the Middle Kingdom, the winged serpent was an essential and beneficent part of Egyptian mythology. But something happened in the period of chaos that lasted for hundreds of years after the fall of the Middle Kingdom and which separated it from the New Kingdom.

The New Kingdom was founded by the first kings of the 18th Dynasty, who had rid the country of the hated Hyksos, the foreign invaders which had occupied Egypt for 400 years and destroyed all monuments and temples of the old religion. At this time, the serpent takes on an evil character. It now becomes an evil object to be exorcised at rituals. Called Apep or Apop (the Greek Apophis), it is a manifestation of the despised foreign barbaric Hyksos who did so much damage to Egyptian culture. The Hyksos as we shall see were also known as the Amalekites by the Hebrews and were a part of the Rephaim, the descendants of the Nefilim.

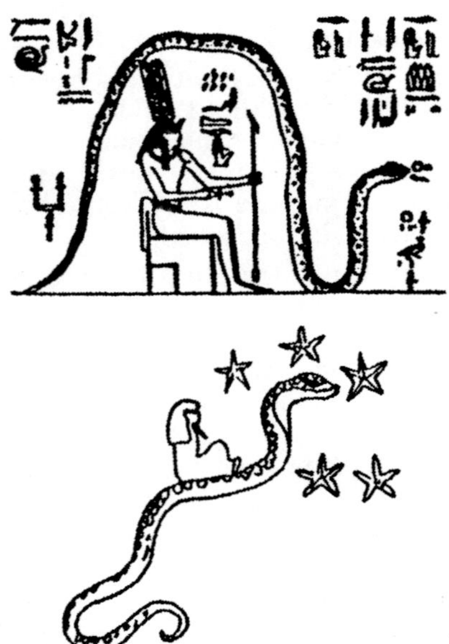

Fig. 6
Egyptian Serpent-Vehicle Symbolism

From Pyramid Texts on walls of tomb of the Old Kingdom. At top, Osiris travelling through the underworld in his serpent boat. At bottom, the serpent bearing the Pharaoh up to the stars to join the gods.

Apop was the original Hyksos ruler, and with his descendants ruled from the 14th through the 17th Dynasty. Many of the Hyksos rulers adopted the name Apop, and in particular, the last king was also called

Apop. Apop became the symbol of the serpent-people, the Hyksos/Amalekites, who occupied Palestine and invaded Egypt at the time of the Exodus. Apop possessed many epithets and in ceremonies meant to destroy him, he was cursed by a number of names. The ritual is strongly similar to the *yajna* ceremony of the ancient Hindus who also called out various names of the snakes as they were cast into the fire.

The Book of The Dead as a Guide to Immortality

It was the overriding desire of Egyptian royalty, and later commoners, to reach the gods in heaven after death and thereby achieve immortality. To attain this goal, detailed instructions were required. The so-called *Book of the Dead* is a collection of instructions that date back to early Egyptian dynasties which inform the dead how to prepare themselves. It was a "roadmap" through the difficult route which led to the gods. These sacred texts are first noted inscribed on the walls of the burial chamber of the pyramid of Unas, the last king of the 5th Dynasty, circa 2400 BC. They are also found in tombs of other kings of the Old Kingdom.

Called the *Pyramid Texts* because of their source, these carved inscriptions are a collection of spells and directions which gave the king all the information he needed for the trip to the afterlife, how to overcome innumerable obstacles, avoid pitfalls, hostile gods and monsters, and finally reach the gods in heaven.

Most authorities agree that the Pyramid Texts reflect the belief in a stellar cult that would require the deceased king to journey to the stars. Often he is pictured astride a serpent heading for a star constellation. His journey is an imitation of the sun god himself, who would traverse the sky daily in his boat of heaven.

During the period known as the Middle Kingdom, the Pyramid Texts were adopted by the lesser nobility and painted on their wooden coffins. Thus they came to be called the *Coffin Texts*. Eventually these ritualistic texts were transcribed to papyrus and adopted by the general populace.

Collectively, the three sets of texts are usually referred to as the *Book of the Dead*. You might say that it was their equivalent of a do-it-yourself manual on how to reach heaven and thereby achieve immortality.

The Friendly Dragon and the Shipwrecked Sailor

There is an ancient Egyptian story which illustrates the friendly and paternal nature of the serpent during the early period of Egypt. It was found on papyrus in a tomb of the 12th Dynasty of the Middle Kingdom (circa 2000 BC) and narrates the adventures of an Egyptian sailor. According to the story, the sailor and a crew of 120 picked men had set sail aboard a commercial ship for a trip to the king's mines, presumably in Africa.

While at sea a severe storm came up and the ship foundered with all its crew except for the lucky sailor. Cast up on an island which he found to be a veritable paradise, lush with all kinds of fruit and

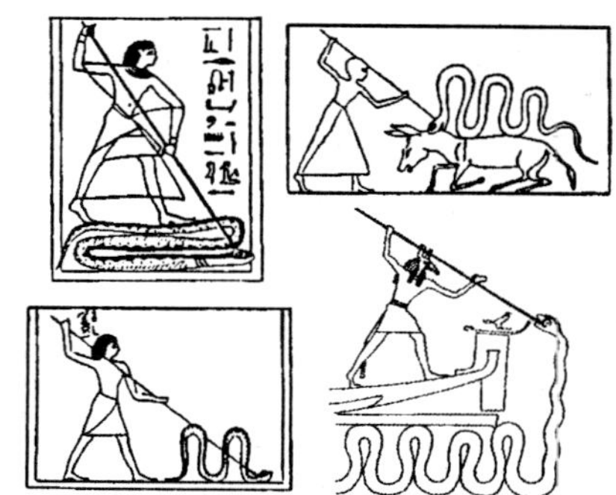

Fig. 7 – The Egyptian Serpent as Evil

Starting with the 18th Dynasty and during the New Kingdom, the evil serpent Apop is often shown being attacked by Pharaoh or god (Seth). The evil serpent represents the hated Hyksos, the serpent-kings from Palestine who destroyed the culture of the Middle Kingdom at the time of the Exodus.

vegetables, fish and fowl, the shipwrecked sailer built a fire and made himself comfortable, prepared for a long stay. But after a few days he was suddenly startled by a loud crashing in the woods nearby and the Earth shook terribly.

The sailor saw a monster emerge from the woods and he fell to the ground in fear. As he narrates it, "Uncovering my face, I found a serpent coming, thirty cubits long, his beard was two cubits long. His body was plated with gold. His eyebrows were of real lapis lazuli. He coiled himself in front of me."

"Who brought you little one," asked the serpent. "If you delay I'll make you know yourself as ashes." In fear of being incinerated on the spot by the fiery serpent, the sailor told him the story of the shipwreck. But as it turned out the serpent was friendly and quite solicitous of the well-being of the sailor. He told the sailor not to worry and that a ship would come to rescue him in four months time. Meanwhile, he would tell him of his sad story and how he happened to be alone on this island.

The serpent related how he had lived there with his siblings and children for a long time and they totalled 75 serpents altogether. While he had been away, a star suddenly fell out of the sky and destroyed all his family by fire, leaving him as the sole survivor. Presumably it was not a natural event but a weapon of the gods, used during the period after the Deluge when they fought each other in the sky.

While there is no mention of wings in the story, the serpent had all the appearance of a dragon. He was covered with scales and had a fiery breath that could have made ashes of the sailor. It is worthy of note that wings are also not depicted on the serpent which carries the dead Pharaoh to the stars. The ability of the serpent-god to fly was probably taken for granted and for this reason not always used in graphic depictions.

It is in the history and mythology of China, however, where the flying serpent or dragon is seen in its full glory, not only as a benevolent monster but as the actual antecedents of the long line of Chinese emperors.

The Benevolent Chinese Dragons

Unlike the Western dragon which is generally associated with evil and destruction or greedily guarding a treasure hoard, the Oriental dragon is often represented as a benevolent creature, friendly to mankind, although sometimes quite capricious. The dragon or *lung* as it is called, has so completely permeated ancient Chinese culture that its mythology is dominated by four general groupings of dragons. The cosmic division of labor is as follows:

The Celestial Dragons

These were the Great Dragons and celestial guardians of China. They lived in the heavens, and maintained the cosmic order of things, preventing catastrophes of land and sea.

The Dragons of Hidden Treasures

These subterranean dragons had charge of all the precious jewels and metals buried in the Earth. Each of these dragons bore an enormous jewel under the chin, reported to be the large white pearl of wisdom, that would multiply whatever it touched. In this sense it is related to the Philosopher's Stone of Medieval Europe. The dragon legends of Alpine, France also refer to a similar jewel that multiplied whatever it touched.

The Earth and River Dragons

These dragons determined the course of rivers, regulated their flow and maintained their banks. It was their duty to prevent serious flooding Every river in China had its own Earth-Dragon King, who held sway over the waters from a palace far beneath the surface.

The Spiritual or Weather Dragons

Floating across the sky, colored the same hue of blue as the sky itself, the spiritual dragons governed the wind, clouds, and rain on which life always depended. The Chinese took special care to appease them, for if these dragons grew angry or neglectful, the result was certain disaster.

Fig. 8 – The Chinese Dragon

The Dragon Ancestors of the Chinese

In earlier days, Asian dragons shared the world with humankind and did so peaceably. In this respect, they have been profoundly linked with Chinese culture. According to Chinese history, the first humans were believed to have been created by an ancient goddess named Nu Kua, who was herself part dragon and part mortal.

The Dragon is one of the signs of the Chinese Zodiac, a form of calendar which dates back to 2500 BC. The Chinese years are the Rat, the Ox, the Tiger, the Rabbit, the Dragon, the Serpent, the Horse, the Sheep, the Monkey, the Cock, the Dog, and the Pig. Of these animals, all but the Dragon are encountered today, suggesting that when the Zodiac was formed, the Chinese believed that the Dragon actually existed.

According to Chinese history, Asian dragons were present at the Creation and shared the world with mankind. Like the Western serpent, the dragon was linked with the development of man and it was the dragon that taught him the essential arts such as how to make fire, how to weave nets for fishing, and how to make music.

The Chinese chose the dragon as the national emblem for profound reasons. They believed that the Celestial Dragon was the father of the First Dynasty of Divine Emperors and as a result the dragon's pictorial emblem became regarded as inspiring divine beneficence to the land of China. The dragon was unrivaled in wisdom and its power to confer blessings, and as a result came to symbolize that most beneficent of men, the Emperor, who was believed to have dragon blood. This affinity with the dragon is shown by the imperial accouterments: the Emperor sat on a dragon throne, rode in a dragon boat, and even slept in a dragon bed.

Fig. 9 – Chinese dragon from an old lantern silhouette

The belief in the existence and friendship of the dragon is thoroughly woven into the life of early Chinese history. The *Yih King,* the most ancient of Chinese books, whose origins are cloaked in mystery, describes the early days when man and dragon lived together on Earth peaceably and man even intermarried with the dragon gods. Many of the ancient emperors are described as having dragon-like features, as for example, Hwanti, who ruled about 2697 BC. The Emperor Yaou (2356 BC) is also described as having the countenance of a dragon and was called "dragon faced" by the people.

The Story of Liu Ye, the Human Who Became a Dragon

An ancient tale is told which resembles in many ways the stories of Mesopotamia. In this case it is the story of a human achieving immortality by joining the eternal ones, the flying dragons.

As the story unfolds, a young scholar who lived in ancient times was despondent since he had just failed the annual exam to become an imperial administrator. As he paused to rest by the Ching River, he noticed a girl goat herder who was beautiful of face and form despite her rough peasant clothing. Curious, he asked her where she came from. She said that she was a princess of the dragon race and that she was the daughter of the Dragon King of Lake Tungting, some hundreds of miles distant.

She had been given in marriage to the Prince of this river but he had refused to give her the honors due to her as his wife, placed her under an enchanted spell, and cast her out to roam the lands as a mortal. Moved by her story, Liu Ye offered to help her. Following her instructions he took the long and arduous journey to the mountain lake of Tungting. After a month's journey he arrived at the court of the Dragon King.

He was ushered into the great hall where on the throne, clasping a jade stone to signify his rank, sat the Dragon King in his mortal form. The young man related the story of the exiled princess, offering as proof a small tablet inscribed in the Princess'hand.

No sooner has the young man spoken when there was a terrible roar behind the throne and a dragon spouting fire crashed by. After it had passed, the Dragon King explained that the mighty dragon was Chien Tang, his own brother who had a terrible temper because that was his fate for refusing to assume the form of a mortal human. He had apparently overhead the conversation of the young scholar and in a terrible huff had gone off to rescue the maiden, his brother's daughter.

A short time passed and then a silk clad human appeared at the hall entrance. On his arm was the Dragon Princess still dressed in the rags of a goat herder. Chien Tang then told his story of how he had found the palace of the lake dragon and killed the Prince. In a single fiery breath he had reduced the palace to ashes.

But his attack had caused havoc to the land and destroyed the crops and thousands of Chinese farmers as well. Distraught by the damage that he had done, Chien Tang had flown up to the Emperor of Heaven himself for forgiveness. The Chief Dragon decided that since he had now learned the pain of mortal sorrow, he was granted the choice of assuming mortal form at will.

Just as Chien Tang finished speaking, Liu Ye saw the palace transformed before his eyes. The figures of the courtiers seemed to dissolve and reform again. He saw the flashing of wings, the sparkling coils of dragon's bodies, and the gleam of dragon's eyes.

Then addressing Liu Ye, the thunderous voice of the Dragon King said "Be one with us, mortal," and he placed his daughter's hand in that of Liu Ye and smiled. Instantly Liu Ye lost his mortal and earthbound form and become one of the race that lived in the sky.

Fig. 10 – Mayan Dragon (Winged Snake)

He found himself in a blue sky, rising on a wind that stretched and pulled his powerful wings wide, warmed by a sun that beat on his shiny, scaly back. Flying beside him was a creature in his own image, the Dragon King's daughter. Soaring on the wind together they plunged through the clouds.

This tale of immortality gained may have had its origin in the myths of Sumer. It has been suggested by some Sinologists that Chinese culture originated in Mesopotamia, as a colony of Sumer, along with that of Egypt, India, and Mesoamerica. There is a close similarity to the languages; Sumerian was unique among the languages of the ancient Middle East since it was agglutinative, and in this respect belonged to the same group as the Chinese. Even in the present day, the Chinese syllabary is based on signs fundamentally similar to the old pictographs of the Sumerians.

Central American Dragons

Among the Mayas of Central America, snake symbolism was very common and most of the serpents depicted in their art are feathered, indicative of their ability to fly. In other words, they were regarded as flying serpents or dragons. There is no record of when the Mayas first appeared in Central America. The books created from memory by the Quiche Indians, called *Chilam Balaam,* relate that the first inhabitants of Yucatan were called *Chanes* or "People of the Serpent," who were said to have come from the east across the sea led by their leader Itzamna.

Fig. 11 – Mayan Serpent-Gods

Fig. 12 – Olmec bas-relief in cave of Central Mexico showing Olmec God in his feathered (flaming?) chariot.

J. Eric Thompson, the dean of Mayan studies, maintains that the term *itzem,* from which the god's name is derived, should be translated as "lizard" or "reptile." In fact, Itzamal, the sacred city of the god Itzamna, literally means "the place of the lizard." There are many anthro-morphic forms of this god where he is depicted as half-human and half-serpent. He was the most important deity in the Mayan pantheon and was the dominant sky-god, ruler of the heavens, and one of the few Mayan gods not associated with death and destruc-

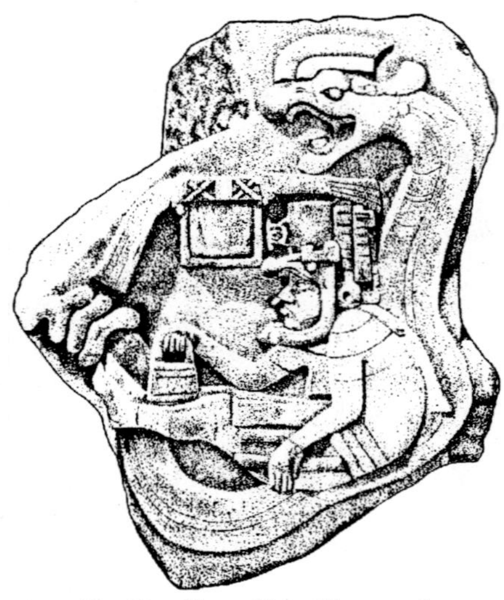

Fig. 13 – Olmec Stone Monument.

Monument shows Olmec god in protective coils of a serpent. Note small bucket in right hand similar to Sumerian "situla" or water of immortality. (figs. 45 and 46). There is also a resemblance of the Olmec god to that of the Egyptian god Osiris shown travelling through the underworld in a serpent-like boat (fig. 6).

tion. He was the creator god who is said to have infused the breathe of life into man.

In the Aztec civilization which superseded the Mayan one, the benevolent feathered serpent god is also found in the pantheon. Quetzalcoatl is the plumed serpent god who brought the benefits of civilization to Mexico. His name comes from *quetzal,* meaning bird with long green tail feathers, and *coatl* meaning serpent. He reportedly taught man all the arts and sciences, and is probably the most significant of the Aztec gods. He is said to have arrived in a flying boat.

Like the gods of the Sumerian pantheon, the Mayan gods often squabbled among themselves and perhaps the most famous of these legends concerns the struggle between Quetzalcoatl, who represented all that was good, and another powerful god called Tezcatlipoca, who was the opposite of Quetzalcoatl and represented discord, destruction, and sacrifice from mankind.

Tezcatlipoca had planned a number of schemes to destroy Quetzalcoatl. One day he got Quetzalcoatl drunk and, bidding his sister to join them, got them both drunk and involved in a sexual orgy that lasted for so long that Quetzalcoatl abandoned his life of purity for one of sexual licentiousness.

Then realizing what he had done and overcome with guilt, Quetzalcoatl built a great funeral pyre, and attired in his quetzal feather robe and turquoise serpent mask, flung himself into the flames. As his body turned to ashes, a flock of birds came out of the flames and flew into the morning sky, one of which became the morning star.

The comparison with the Phoenix bird of Egypt is obvious and indicates that all these universal stories of the bird arising from the flames as a symbol of immortality and associated with the flying serpent gods, must have had a common origin. It is discussed later how the source of the Phoenix legend was ancient Mesopotamia, where the rising of the sun god in his flying machine, in a burst of fire and thunder, gave rise to the universal story of the Phoenix.

Fig. 14 – Aztec feathered Sun God Quetzalcoatl holding serpent in his right hand.

CHAPTER 5

WHAT EXACTLY WAS A DRAGON?

At this point in our story we can summarize the universal understanding of what qualities of appearance and behavior constitutes a dragon. There is a common thread that runs through all these stories of flying serpents with a fiery breath.

They Were Winged. The dragon is depicted as a giant reptile or lizard with the ability to fly. This proficiency is shown by its having a set of bat-like wings. In some cultures they have feathered wings but the allusion to flying is the same.

They Were Legged Serpents. Many legends present the dragon as a legged snake or serpent, having either two or four legs. This separates it from sea monsters which had no legs or wings. Some of the dragons are shown winged without legs and these lived in the lakes and rivers.

They Had A Flaming Breath. The main feature of the dragon was its ability to spout fire which was sometimes used for defensive reasons and often to incinerate its victims. This form of defense is unique to dragons. No animals, reptiles, or birds existing today or in the past, have had this peculiar form of bad-breath. This biological feature defies all reason and cannot be explained scientifically.

They Coexisted With Man. These creatures must have existed fairly recently for they shared the Earth with early man. They interacted with mankind either as his tormentor, as in European cultures, or as his benefactor as found in the East. In the Chinese Zodiac the dragon is included with eleven other animals that exist today. The early Chinese must have considered the dragon as a real live creature.

They Were Associated With Gems. Dragons were usually occupied with precious jewels or gems, sometimes as hoarders and guardians of such treasure. Some dragons possessed a large red or white jewel capable of wondrous achievements. This jewel was associated with immortality.

They Created Man. Dragons were present at the creation of man and in most instances were the actual Creator. They provided early man with all the arts and crafts necessary to establish civilization. Many cultures claim man descended from these reptile-like gods.

They Held The Secret To Immortality. They possessed the secret of long life and often bestowed it on man, sometimes by jewels which provided unlimited wealth as well. Dragons were the source of magic and secret knowledge.

To Some They Were Friendly, To Others They Were Considered Evil. In the Judeo-Christian traditions they are looked on as evil. The rest of the world, which has a different religious background, regarded them as friendly, benevolent monsters.

They Were Revered As Gods. Many kings such as those of Sumer, Egypt, India, and China considered themselves as semi-divine since they claimed to be descended from the reptile gods. Many of them assumed dragon-like accouterments.

They Lived Underground. Dragons either lived underground or underwater in crystal palaces where they had a propensity to collect and guard treasure, especially precious gems.

They Fought Each Other In The Sky. Dragons constantly bickered and fought among themselves, either for territory or over the control of precious stones. This is the source of the struggle of the evil dragon found in many cultures.

LOGICAL CONCLUSIONS

They Were Not Dinosaurs. We have to rule out dinosaurs not only because they lived millions of years before the advent of Homo sapiens, but there is no known flying dinosaur which fits the description of a dragon (the pterodactyl falls far short).

They Were Real And Not Imaginary. The dragon was known universally. All cultures pictured dragons in a similar way with only minor differences. It seems, therefore, that they must have had a common origin. What does it symbolize or represent?

Their Obsession With Gems. Gems have a central theme in the legends of dragons. They had a compulsion to hide and protect these precious stones. Sometimes the possession and protection of these jewels was the all-encompassing purpose of existence. Were these "stones" the "power crystals" of the Sumerians which gave extraordinary power to the owner?

TheirAbility To Fly. Of their flying capability the following deductions can be made. The wings of the dragon symbolize the fact that the serpent-gods could roam the skies and the Earth at will, even to reach the stars or a "home" in the heavens. Giving them wings was the only way early man knew how to show this ability of the gods. This notion of showing the gods and demi-gods with wings is universal.

Their Fiery Breath. The fiery breath or flame-throwing ability of the dragons may have had two origins. These serpent-gods roamed the skies and fought among each other and sometimes incinerated early man accidentally with their flaming breath. Flames may have represented a fiery weapon of some sort. It may also have been the flaming exhaust of their sky vehicles as described in the books of Ezekiel and Enoch. Early man knew the dangers of getting too close to these dangerous exhausts.

Their Obvious Reptilian Origin. The world-wide depiction of flying reptiles makes it abundantly clear that our creators and ancestors were not of mammal origin but were an alien saurian breed. Nearly all cultures attribute their origin to a reptilian-like creature that descended from the skies or came out of the sea. The serpents (and not mammals) dominate nearly all the myths and legends of mankind.

CHAPTER 6

ARRIVAL OF THE REPTILE GODS ON EARTH

In our efforts to trace back in time the origins and antecedents of the Western ideas of dragons, we are steadily and irresistibly drawn back to the lands of Mesopotamia. It has been said by many historians that "all roads lead to Sumer," which we shall find is true and that its rich tradition was the fountainhead of all dragon stories.

Undoubtedly, Mesopotamia was the fertile ground from whence sprang all the legends and stories associated with dragons. It is here that we will find the first allusion to flying serpent-gods as dragons. After the Deluge, there was a terrible period of struggle when the serpent-gods fought among themselves in the sky, and when mankind retreated underground for shelter and survival. It was also the beginning of all the legends which associate dragons with precious stones.

The Sumerian King List

There are many Sumerian documents which refer to a group of gods that descended from the skies and established a civilization at the delta of the Tigris and Euphrates Rivers. The ancient Sumerian kings traced their lineage back some 240,000 years when, according to their history, their ancestors came to this planet. Called the ANUNNA(their Sumerian name) or *Anunnaki* (their later Akkadian or Semitic name), they built a civilization here long before the advent of the Deluge. The arrival and colonization of Mesopotamia by a group of ancient astronaut gods was first proposed and reported extensively by Zecharia Sitchin in his "Earth Chronicles" series (*The 12th Planet, The Stairway to Heaven*, *The Wars of Gods And Men*, *The Lost Realms* and *When Time Began*).

The arrival of the Anunna or Anunnaki and their subsequent colonization of the Earth is described in the *King List*, one of the most remarkable and valuable documents available on our prehistoric ancestors. The *King List,* which originated in the third Millennia BC, was a political tract in which the primary aim was to give an account of the various dynasties that ruled in Mesopotamia in accordance with the theory that legitimate kingship could be transferred from city to city and could only reside in one city at a time. Since many of its records of the Fourth and Third Millennia BC have been corroborated separately by archaeological evidence, the *King List* has been accepted by many as a valuable historical document.

The dean of Sumerian studies, the late Samuel Noah Kramer, has concluded that it provides unique information and that "if used with discrimination and understanding, provides us with a historical framework of inestimable value." His book *The Sumerians* also contains the most recent and complete version of the *King List*. An earlier list in the book *The Sumerian King List* by Thorkild Jacobsen also provides an analysis of the various god-kings and variations which make up the *King List*.

The so-called *King List* records the names of the kings of Sumer and the lengths of their reigns from what was to them the beginning of history, a time in the distant past when "kingship descended from heaven" and founded five cities in the Mesopotamian plain.

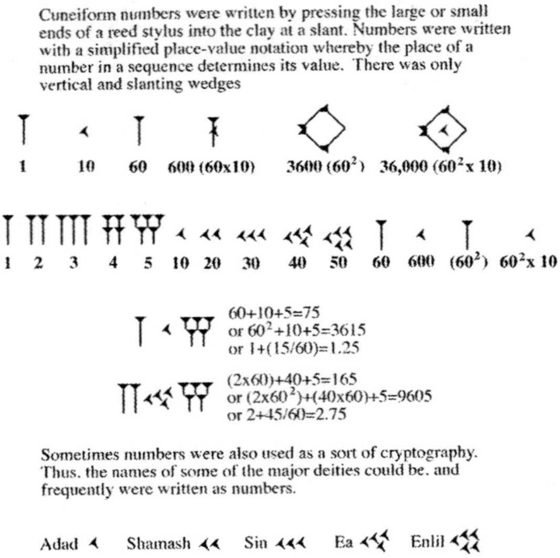

Cuneiform numbers were written by pressing the large or small ends of a reed stylus into the clay at a slant. Numbers were written with a simplified place-value notation whereby the place of a number in a sequence determines its value. There was only vertical and slanting wedges

1 10 60 600 (60x10) 3600 (60^2) 36,000 (60^2x 10)

1 2 3 4 5 10 20 30 40 50 60 600 (60^2) 60^2x 10

60+10+5=75
or 60^2+10+5=3615
or 1+(15/60)=1.25

(2x60)+40+5=165
or (2x60^2)+(40x60)+5=9605
or 2+45/60=2.75

Sometimes numbers were also used as a sort of cryptography. Thus. the names of some of the major deities could be. and frequently were written as numbers.

Adad Shamash Sin Ea Enlil

Fig. 15 – The numerical system of the Sumerians.

The *King List* then records an interruption when "the Flood swept over the land" — an event which we know as the Deluge or Great Flood. The *King List* then resumes the narrative as "kingship descended" once more, presumably from an orbiting spaceship. It describes the kings and their reigns down to part of the Isin dynasty, which began to rule about 1950 BC.

It is generally believed that the Proto-Sumerians were the origin of our Western Civilization, and that these beginnings were in the area called Mesopotamia, literally "the land between the two rivers." The arrival of these "gods" is reported in the records that their descendants left behind — the Sumerian, Akkadian, and Babylonian cuneiform tablets.

After the Deluge, the Sumerian cities were rebuilt and resettled on the alluvial plain of Mesopotamia. Since the oldest of these date to about 3500 BC and was built on virgin soil, it is clear that they were not built upon the ruins of former cities. This is due to the fact that the waters of the Persian gulf have risen some 150 feet due to the effects of the Deluge, inundating the former cities. It is the contention of the author that the ancient antediluvian cities, as well as the original Garden of Eden, are under the waters of the adjacent Persian Gulf.

While the southern part of Mesopotamia came to be called Sumer, the area farther up the plain at the near convergence of the two rivers was later called Akkad. The Akkadian city BAB-ILU became quite prominent and gave its name to the entire region — Babylonia.

The introduction of an intensive river-canal system to irrigate and drain the plain gave rise to a dense population and to the establishment of a great culture. The lower part of Mesopotamia became a very fertile garden area which the Sumerians called E-DIN, or "the abode of the righteous ones." It was the location of, and gave its name to, the Biblical Garden of Eden.

Language and Origin of the Myths

The Proto-Sumerians have been a puzzle to linguists and archaeologists. The language is agglutinative, not inflected like Semitic or Indo-European. In structure it resembles Turkish, Chinese and Finno-Ugarian. In vocabulary, grammar, and syntax, however, Sumerian stands alone and seems not to be related to any of the known languages, living or dead.

Philologists cannot identify any hypothetical homeland from which the Sumerians came, with their unique language and culture. It is as if they came from out of the blue, literally speaking. The *King List* thus becomes more pertinent and important in providing essential information on these early colonizers.

Written Sumerian in a cuneiform style first appeared at the end of the Fourth Millennia and was used until about 100 BC, more or less for scholarly and religious purposes. Akkadian, the Semitic language of the Babylonians and the Assyrians, is nearly as old and was written in Mesopotamia from about 2400 BC to nearly 100 AD. Another ancient cuneiform language called Hittite is the earliest of the Indo-European languages to be preserved. The vast majority of Hittite clay tables found at ancient Hattusa, modern Bogazkoy in Turkey, date from about 1650 until about 1200 BC.

Most of the texts we have of the Sumerian stories which tell of flying serpents or dragons are from the Old Sumerian Period (2500-2200 BC) or the Neo-Sumerian Period, which preserved Old Sumerian culture (2200-1900 BC).

In the Old Babylonian (1900-1600 BC) and Middle Babylonian (1600-1300 BC) Periods, new versions of the myths appeared, copied from earlier Sumerian stories. The Babylonians tended to edit the older works, sometimes recasting them to fit their own traditions.

Fig. 16 – The hero Gilgamesh.

Above: The name Gilgamesh written in Cuneiform. Below: Assyrian relief showing the hero Gilgamesh subduing a lion

Although the bulk of the texts of the myths are found in Semitic form, many sections and fragments have been found in the original Sumerian. It thus appears that most of the older myths were set down about 2500 BC, after an indefinite period when they had been transmitted in the oral tradition.

City	King	Years of Rule	Per City	(shars) Divided by 3600	(neros) Divided by 600
Eridu	Alulim	28,800		8	48
	Alagar	36,000		10	60
	Two kings ruled		64,800	18	108
Badtibira	Enmenluanna	43,200		12	72
	Enmengalanna	28,800		8	48
	Dumuzi	36,000		10	60
	Three kings ruled		108,000	30	180
Larak	Ensipaziana	28,800	28,800	8	48
Sippar	Enmeduranna	21,000	21,000	5.83a	35
Shuruppak	Ubartutu	18,600	18,600	5.16a	31
Total of 5 cities, 8 kings ruled			241,200	67	402

a. If 600 years is added to the rule of Enmeduranna and 600 subtracted from that of Ubartutu, we arrive at the full numbers 6 and 5, respectively.

Fig. 17 – The incredible reigns of the Antediluvian Kings from the King List.

Originally, Sumerian was expressed in pictographs very much like the early hieroglyphics of Egypt and China, suggesting a close association in the early days after the Deluge. But due to the lack of a cheap and ample source of written materials such as papyrus and parchment, Sumerian had to be written on clay tablets which were then baked for permanence. Due to the difficulty in drawing pictures on clay, it was found more expedient to draw a picture of the item represented by pressing a stylus into the wet clay — and thus, cuneiform was born. A large or small reed stylus (resembling somewhat our modern golf tee) was used with the ends being pressed into the clay at a slant.

Huge Numbers of The King List and Scriptures

The *King List* attributes reigns of legendary and incredible lengths to many of the rulers of the earlier antediluvian kings. In this sense, it affirms the enormous lifespans of the Patriarchs of the Old Testament.

These lifespans in the Sumerian *King List* has been a source of wonder and

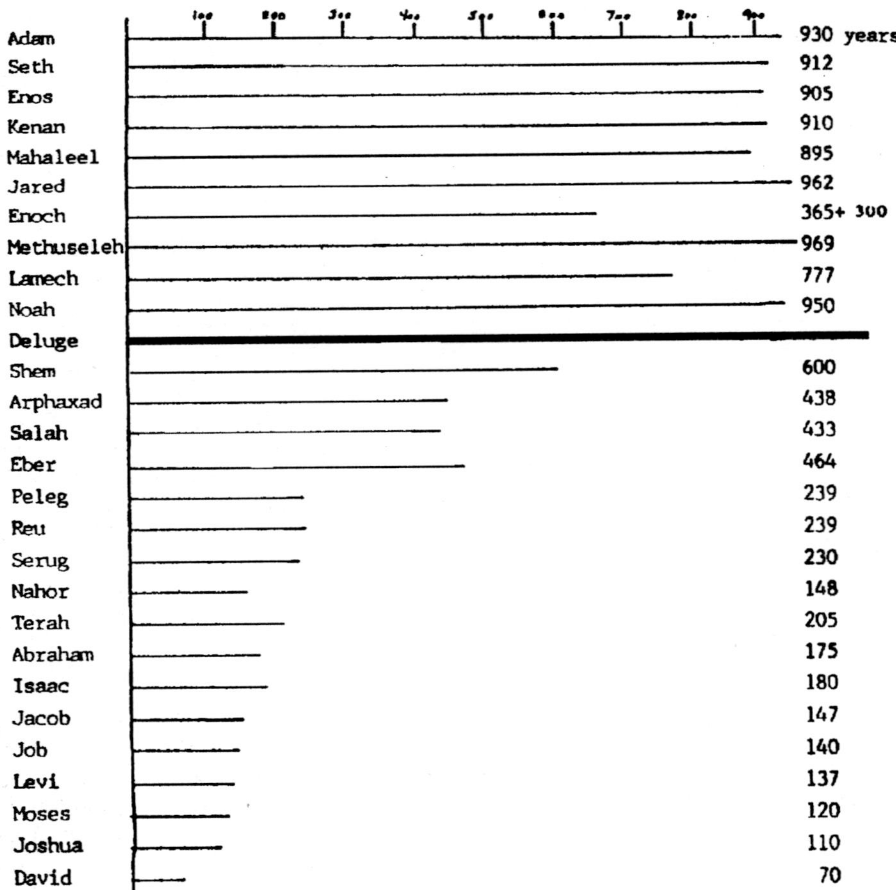

Note: Enoch was in heaven for 6 Jubilee years or 300 years plus 365 on Earth for a life-span of 665 years. The decline in life-span after the Deluge is striking. Was it due to the decline in Saurian genes?

Fig. 18 – Longevity among the ancients in the Old Testament.

puzzlement. By current standards the numbers of the antediluvians are completely fanciful. These huge numbers are consistent throughout the *King List* and therefore seem not to be erroneous. While a rational explanation has thus far escaped historians, most researchers feel there must be some underlying logic to these large numbers since a parallel can be found in the enormous lifespans of the antediluvian Patriarchs.

It is entirely possible that these are not Earth years as we know them. A divine year or "year of An" is often mentioned in the cuneiform tablets and although not fully understood, is probably not equivalent to our normal Earth year. A reflection of this is found in the Old Testament (Psalms 90:4), where one divine year is said to be the equivalent of a thousand years.

It was not unusual for the ancients to compute time by other than normal Earth years such as, for example, in the *Book of Jubilees*, where a Jubilee year is equivalent to 50 regular years. That is equal to seven week years (a week year was seven years) and one year added for atonement, when all activities were supposed to cease.

The *King List* describes the activities of the antediluvian Anunna as they descended from the skies and first established a city at Eridu, where two kings ruled for 64,800 years. Eridu was then abandoned as the capital and the kingship was moved to Badtibira where three kings reigned for 108,000 years. Then the kingship was moved to Larak where one king ruled for 28,800 years. A fourth city to become the capital was Sippar, where one king reigned for 21,000 years. The kingship was then transferred to Shuruppak, where one king ruled for 18,600 years. Thus, as the table (figure 17) summarizes, eight kings ruled over five cities for a total of 241,200 years. The *King List* then states laconically that the Flood swept over the land, putting an end to all activities.

Their numerical system was sexagesimal in character and they made use of the factor of 10 as well as 6. Thus the sequence 1, 10, 60, 360, 600, 3600 takes on a special meaning in their mythology. If the duration of the various terms of kingship are presented graphically, it becomes obvious that this sexagesimal system underlies the fabulous numbers of the *King List* (figure 17). Called a SHAR by the Sumerians, the number 3600 appears to have a special meaning in this list. It can be seen that with slight adjustment, the years of reign of the Sumerian kings are divisible by this number. It indicates that the term of reign for a Sumerian antediluvian king was presumably a "shar" — probably renewable every 3600 years.

In the theories of Sitchin, the cycle of 1800 years is extremely important to the Anunnaki for it represents the orbit of their home planet Nibiru, which returns to our solar system every 3600 years.

The Sumerian Cities

What reason or purpose brought these alien beings or Anunna, as they called themselves, to this planet we do not know. But from their legends and myths we can deduce that it was probably for commercial purposes. The functions of their early cities would suggest that they came here to obtain gold, silver, and other rare metals. In his work *The 12th Planet*, Sitchin developed the concept that the antediluvian cities were associated with the need of the Anunnaki for metals. These five antediluvian cities of the *King List* were all related to the production and shipment of metal, such as a headquarters city, a metal production center, a missile platform, a flight control center and a medical center. Sitchin further suggests that the need for gold was essential for the survival of their home planet Nibiru, to be used to prevent their waning atmosphere from being dissipated.

A Sumerian story which deals with the creation of the world describes the first city built on Earth:

> When the Kingship had come down from heaven,
> AN founded the five cities,
> gave them their names,
> apportioned their uses.

The first of these cities, Eridu, he gave to the leader Nudimmud (an epithet for Enki). Eridu was the first city built on this planet which probably gave our world its name — Earth, the third planet in our solar system. The origin of the word "Earth" is unknown and its origin lost in antiquity, but logically and linguistically it can be traced back to Eridu. For example, in Old High German, Earth is *Erda*; it is *Erthe* in Middle English, *Era* in Greek, *Ereds* in Aramaic, and *Eretz* in Hebrew, to name just a few. It seems that all philological roads lead back to the first city built on this planet by our alien forefathers — Eridu.

It was from Eridu that Enki directed all operations on Earth, as he supervised the draining of the marshlands, the raising of the cities, the establishment of agriculture and animal husbandry, and the development of the mines, presumably in Africa, including the transportation of the ores, and the processing of the ores at Badtibira.

Badtibira or "place where the ores are processed" in Sumerian, retained its kingship for the longest time of all the cities, almost half of the period recorded before the Deluge, indicative of its primary importance in the scheme of things.

Larak was the third city assigned the kingship and and was the space control center for the complex. Little is known of this city and, like Badtibira, has not been located archaeologically.

Sippar was the platform for the space shuttles, especially those hauling metal cargo. One of the Sumerian myths states that this city was built for the god Utu, one of the major gods also known by his Semitic name, Shamash. When the space activities were moved to the west after the Deluge, Shamash reappeared at Baalbek in Lebanon which became the new "Eden" and the home of the gods.

Shuruppak or "place of utmost well being" was dedicated to the Chief Nurse and Medical Officer of the expedition, the goddess Ninhursag. She was deeply involved with Enki in producing a primitive man to do the labor of the gods.

Uruk was the ceremonial center for the Anunna and the home of the great god An when he was on Earth. He seems to have disappeared from the Pantheon after the Deluge and the city was taken over by Inanna, his granddaughter, who used it as her base of operations where she hatched her many famous schemes.

Nippur was the city of Enlil where he ruled from the E-KUR or "house on the mountain." From here he exercised supreme authority over all the Anunna. on Earth before the Deluge. In one of the hymns dedicated to Enlil there is a graphic description of a control center bristling with communications and other electronic equipment. From the heights of the Ekur, it was said that Enlil's "eyes scans the land," and "his lifted beam searches the heart of all the lands." This is strongly indicative of a communications or control center.

The city of Nippur was rebuilt after the Deluge but at a different location. Nippur is where, according to the *Hebrew Apocalypse of Enoch*, the Lord kept his *shekinah* or spacecraft — this being also the entrance of the Garden of Eden until the days of Enosh. Then he abruptly left for his heavenly abode, never to return except on special occasions. It was also at Nippur, at the river Chebar, that Ezekiel saw the "fiery chariot" described so vividly in the book of that name.

Every Sumerian city was dedicated to a major god, who served as its protector and benefactor. There was a special secure area with a great court wherein were the palace and temples. In the center was a *ziggurat* which overlooked the city. The ziggurat was a stepped artificial mountain or pyramid rising from the treeless plain. On its lower levels there were quarters for the priesthood. They controlled the whole wealth of the state; its ranks included archivists, teachers, scribes, scholars, mathematicians and other functionaries.

Atop the ziggurat there was a sacred temple. In its center was an antechamber or *cella*, the "holy of holies," and was reserved for the gods to rest when they were on Earth. It was here that they mated with selected humans in order to produce a race of demi-gods to serve as the kings, generals, and other intermediaries. These acted as a buffer with mankind.

All the great heroes of Mesopotamia claimed to be the issue of a god and a mortal. These beings were called "changelings." The hero Gilgamesh often boasted that his mother was the goddess Ninsun. Another great hero, Sargon the Great of the Akkad Dynasty, also claimed to be a changeling and the child of a mortal and a goddess.

CHAPTER 7

THE SUMERIAN NAMES FOR DRAGONS

The Reptiles or Dragons Descend to Earth

The concept of a winged, legged serpent or flying reptile, breathing fire, that could fly the skies at will, appears to have originated in ancient Sumer. The Sumerian cuneiform tablets are replete with references to these "dragons." They had very specific descriptive names for them.

Traditional translations seem to treat these references as being merely allegorical, in other words, many historians believe that these were merely colorful metaphors, a result of the vivid imaginations of the ancients. This is in spite of the repeated references to their gods as fiery and flaming serpents. Undoubtedly these references are based on actual events and experiences that took place in their past history. It may be that they were adapted by succeeding dynasties to reflect their own cultural differences, but the essence of the myth, the underlying event which instituted the myth, was a real happening or event. The ancients knew full well that their gods were reptilian creatures who arrived here from elsewhere in the universe, and had the ability to fly around at will in the skies. The ancient people probably also witnessed the battles of the gods in the skies over supremacy and power.

In a fragment from one of the earliest known Sumerian tablets dated to about 3500 BC, there is a description of the coming of the gods to this planet from the skies, long before the event of the Deluge, at a time when the Earth was engulfed in a dense cloud cover. The reptilian nature of the gods is explicit:

> The reptiles verily descend,
>
> The Earth is resplendent as a well-watered garden,
>
> At that time Enki and Eridu had not appeared,
>
> Daylight did not shine,
>
> Moonlight had not emerged.

In this fragment, there is no attempt to mask the nature of the gods by a metaphor. Later descriptions of their gods as fiery, winged serpents developed out of the need to represent them in their literature and art by the only way they knew to make it understandable to the common people.

The Sumerians (and later the Semitic Akkadians) had many names for flying serpents. In some of the myths, the serpent-gods are perceived as benevolent and sympathetic to mankind and the names were complimentary; but in other stories they are regarded as evil gods, which led to the origin of the story of the evil dragon as found in the Biblical story of the fall of Lucifer.

The most significant Sumerian term used to describe the flying serpent with flaming breath was U-SHUM-GAL, which was a common epithet for the great god Enki and other major gods. Modern translations render the composite word as "dragon," without further comment. It is also translated as dragon in the recently published Sumerian Dictionary (Volume 2) of the University of Pennsylvania. Scholars seem so perplexed by the meaning of USHUMGALthat they have opted to take the easy way out and just leave it as "dragon."

However, if we break the composite word down into its prime components, that is, U, SHUM, and GAL we can arrive at the basic meaning of the term. The basic root word SHUM means "flying serpent" and is used in various word combinations to provide a variety of terms, all descriptive of the activities of the flying serpents. Because of the troubling indication that SHUM may represent a sky vehicle with flaming exhausts, traditional translators prefer to leave the problem unresolved.

An exception to the rule is the British scholar J. Kinnier Wilson. As a trained geologist and respected linguist who lived in Mesopotamia for many years, he brought a fresh approach to the study and translation of ancient Sumerian.

Most academicians limit a mythological or religious meaning to terms and events mentioned in Sumerian stories, that is, they treat the events as unreal or imaginary, as if they did not really happen. Wilson suggested that these myths were all based on natural events. True to his scientific specialty, Wilson associated the myths to strange and unusual geological phenomena. In his book *The Rebel Lands*, he suggests that the stories are based on the wonder and fear of ancient peoples as they observed bursts of flames from rifts in the Earth, caused by the ignition of gaseous deposits which suddenly, on occasion, erupted and shot forth into the sky.

Despite this tendency to force the ancient myths into so restrictive a format, his translations and analysis are invaluable and a complete departure from academic views. It is refreshing to have a new approach to these translations, where everything is not compressed into a religious format. From these new translations it is apparent that the flying serpents we are dealing with are actually space vehicles of some sort. Many of the translations of Wilson are used in this work.

Ushumgal as the Sumerian Dragon

The Sumerians had several names for their gods. They all have the basic meaning of a flaming flying serpent. An analysis of the elements which make up the word-phrase U-SHUM-GAL reveals much. The letter or symbol U means "flying, fiery, or bird-like" and this double meaning indicates that the Sumerians associated flying with flames. As we state before, the term SHUM means "flying serpent" and it has the same meaning of the Semitic term MUSH which is discussed below. GAL is the usual Sumerian term for "great or noble" and is usually applied to the gods or their activities, but it has a meaning of great in the sense of fearsome and formidable. It is used often to describe the terrible weapons of the gods. In summary, it is apparent that the composite word USHUMGAL means a great fiery flying serpent, presumably a metaphor for a space vehicle of the gods.

In the early days of Sumer, the great dragon or USHUMGAL was a complimentary name for a benevolent serpent god. This is seen in the early myth *Enki and Inanna: The Organization of the Earth and its Cultural Processes*, which deals with the organization of activities on Earth. In this poem, Enki is praised as the "great USHUMGAL" who created the fertile lands of Edin and made the world green and prolific.

It is a characteristic of many ancient languages that words which refer to the gods and their activities were considered sacred and could be used only to describe the divinity itself and its activities. Perhaps it is for this reason that Sumerian words were not translated into the Semitic language which replaced it in Mesopotamia, but transliterated. Thus USHUMGAL became *U-shum-gal-lu* in Akkadian, the Semitic language which replaced it. Many of the words of the Old Testament (which was written in Hebrew, a form of Western Semitic), are borrowed directly from the Sumerian. Such an example is *kabod,* the term used for the flying chariot of Ezekiel.

In the same story mentioned above, USHUMGAL is an epithet applied to the god Dumuzi, the husband of Ishtar (Inanna) who is referred to as U-SHUM-GAL-AN-NA or the "great fiery flying serpent of heaven." In this passage, which deals with the assignment of tasks on Earth by Enki, Dumuzi is put in charge of animal husbandry and agriculture. As the husband of Ishtar, Dumuzi is the subject of numerous stories, most of which deal with the treachery of Ishtar and her role in his destruction.

The use of SHUM as flying serpent is also found in another myth called *Inanna and Ebih*, the story of the destruction of an unidentified mountain land by Ishtar (Inanna) and Ninurta. Here Ninurta is called a U-SHUM-IGI-HUSH or "flying serpent with a fiery look." The term HUSH is discussed below; it also has the meaning of flying serpent. Ninurta is also called MUSH-SHA-TUR-GAL-GAL or literally, "the flying serpent with the fiery glance." Wilson states that the two appellations have the same meaning, that the terms MUSH and SHUM are interchangeable. Evidence for this is found in a fragment of a laudatory poem to the senior god Enlil where he is called MUSH-ZU-DINGIR or "the wise flying serpent god." The *dingir* was the standard Sumerian symbol (it appears as a star in cuneiform) to denote godship and usually preceded the god's name in the written cuneiform.

The Fiery Serpent or Mush-Hush

Another name for the serpent sky gods was MUSH and is often found in the combination MUSH-MUSH. It appears frequently with dragon connotations or applications. The Sumerian language often emphasized a term by repetition and thus MUSH-MUSH would mean a great MUSH or a great flying serpent. Other combinations of this term are found in the story *Inanna and Ebih,* where Ninurta is called a MUSH-SHA-TUR-GAL-GAL or "great serpent of a fiery glance" in battle, probably referring to some sort of flame weapon he had available. Ninurta is also referred to as MUSH-KUR-RA or the "bright or fiery serpent of the mountain land" when he did his battle with the evil god ZU, which is discussed below.

To emphasize its flaming nature, the word HUSH or flaming is often added to the term MUSH. In Semitic Akkadian it became *Mush-hush-shu.* The term MUSH-HUSH, which is often seen in Semitic versions of the myths, was applied to gods who lived in the heavens, presumably in the orbiting spaceship. This is seen in the *Tale of Adapa,* the story of the mortal who is offered immortality by the gods but refuses it. In the story narrated by Adapa, the chief steward of Enki, he describes how he went to heaven to report to the chief god An. He had first to pass approval by two guards stationed at the "heaven's gate." These gods were Dumuzi, mentioned above, and Ningishzida, a minor Sumerian god who is associated with immortality and often addressed as the Lord of the Tree of Life; he later became the god of healing. He has the serpent as his sacred symbol and is often depicted as a serpent with a human head. Both gods are called MUSH-HUSH.

Combinations of the words MUSH and SHUM with other syllables are often used to apply to vehicles or equipment which are associated with noise and fire. In an obscure myth called *Enki and Eridu: the Journey of the Water-God to Nippur;* which relates to the Abzu of Enki, MUSH-KU is the name of some sort of living monster which is under the control of Enki. KU means "bright" in Sumerian but in the sense of a metallic brilliance and hence, when used with MUSH means a bright metallic fiery object — a perfect description of a rocket ship.

Another combination is SHUM-KA, which is the name of a creature made by Enlil in the *Epic of Creation*, and is usually translated as monster. Since KA means "to speak or mouth" and is applied to openings which produce sound and noise, SHUM-KA probably means a noisy, flying serpent and again refers to a craft of some sort used by Enlil.

The Sumerian word MUSH seems to have a Western Semitic equivalent in the term *se-er-ru* which is usually shortened to *seru*. This word has the same root as the word seraphim, the flying or fiery serpent worshipped by the Israelites during the days of the Exodus. It is discussed in the following chapter.

CHAPTER 8

THE SUMERIAN SERPENT GODS

The Sumerians and Akkadians did not call their alien visitors "gods." It is in later cultures that the notion of divine beings filtered into our language and thinking. They were called the "lofty ones," in the sense of those who occupied the heavens. The Western word "god" has through usage come to mean superior spiritual beings, far removed from mankind and incapable of defect or error. Man is considered to be a blemished incomplete being, burdened with "original sin" and destined to worship and pay homage to an unreachable god. The Sumerian gods, on the other hand, were far from spiritual. They were real live physical beings capable of serious errors and misjudgments. They could be called "supermen" if the term could be genetically applied to a saurian race.

The Sumerian gods regarded man as a convenience and nothing more. He supplied their wants, kept their cities, and provided cannon fodder for their various military ventures. The gods were cruel and unsympathetic masters. They considered humans as merely unruly children, no more important than pets, to be governed ruthlessly and without sentiment. At one time, man was regarded as a source of food and no different from the cattle and sheep that he raised. These accusations may seem like hyperbole to the reader, but we shall see, by subsequent events, that this is indeed correct. It should be remembered that the Sumerian word LU was used for sheep as well as man, and it seems that this term was used gastronomically as well.

When the serpent-gods arrived here to establish a colony on Earth, they were ruled by four senior gods. These were AN the great patriarch, who rarely came down to Earth and stayed in the background, and his three children. Of these ENLIL was the leader of the expedition and chief of all activities of the Anunna on Earth. His brother ENKI was the chief engineer who supervised all the construction, mining, and technical activities of the Anunna, including the genetic engineering. The fourth senior god was NINHURSAG, the great nurse and medical director. There were many children and grandchildren of Enlil and Enki but only a few of these junior gods are important to our story.

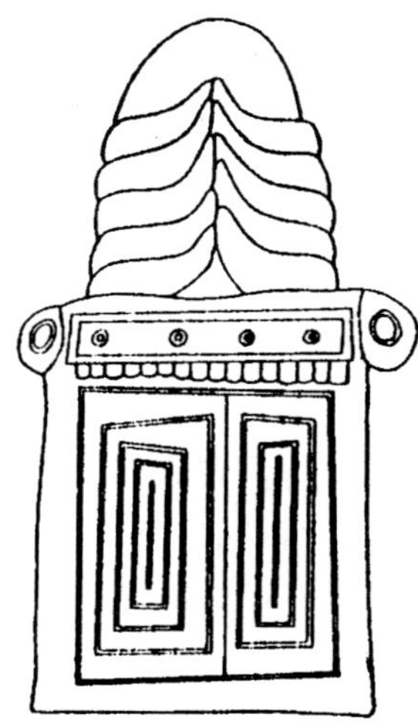

Fig. 19 – The multi-horned cap was the distinctive head-dress of the divinity. When placed on an altar it represented the senior gods of An, Enlil, Enki, and Ninhursag (See also figs. 20 and 21).

After the Deluge the children and grandchildren of Enlil were assigned the lands of the Middle East. The eldest son NANNAR (*Sin* in Semitic) was given Mesopotamia and the western lands extending all the way to the Mediterranean, except for Lebanon. Lebanon was the location of Baalbek, the

Babylonian boundary stone of the Kassite Dynasty of the Second Millenium BC, in the Louvre Museum. This stele depicts the Babylonian pantheon.

FIRST REGISTER: At the top of the stele are the symbols of the three major gods of Mesopotania, reading from left to right, the crescent moon of Sin, the eight-pointed star of Ishtar, and the radiant four-pointed star or solar disk of Shamash. Beneath, in the same register are the symbols of the senior gods: the two altars with horned crowns for An and Enlil, the fish-goat (ibex) symbol and ram symbolize Enki; the fourth emblem depicts the umbilical cord and knife to sever it, the symbols of the mother goddess Ninhursag.

SECOND REGISTER: These are the deities of war. The winged lion and the mace with panther heads are Nergal, god of the underworld; the vulture and curved weapons symbolizes Zabada, the god of hand-to-hand fighting; Ninurta is represented by the griffon and curved weapon.

THIRD REGISTER: The major gods of Babylon. Marduk, the chief deity is represented by the dragon and the triangular tool or marru. Nabu, a son of Marduk and patron of scribes and god of wisdom is symbolized by the tablet on the altar. The third god is Gula who is guarded by the sacred hound; she was the goddess of healing.

FOURTH REGISTER: The bull and altar with the forked lightning represents Adad; the deity symbolized by the ram and chisel is not identified; the lamp probably represents Nusku; the plough is Ningirsu, and the bird perched on a post may be Shuqamuna, a local deity. The other bird may be Shimaliya, the divine consort.

FIFTH REGISTER: The altar with a sheaf may be Nisaba, originally a corn goddess. The scorpion is the emblem of Ishara. The horned serpent is probably Ningizzida, a son of Enki and the god of architects and engineers.

Fig. 20 – Babylonian gods and their sacred symbols.

---

spaceport and launch facility, and was assigned to UTU (*Shamash*), a son of Nannar.

Another son of Enlil was ISHKUR (Adad) who was given Anatolia, better known Biblically as the land of the Hittites. We will show that he was the Yahweh or Jehovah of the Old Testament. Nannar had a daughter, sister to Utu, called INANNA (*Ishtar*), who had no assigned territory because of her sex, and as a result plotted continuously to acquire power.

Another son, called NINURTA, is of prime importance to our story. He was assigned the land of Elam east of Mesopotamia, but somehow was left out of many of the decisions of the pantheon. As Enlil's chief of staff he was the challenger chosen by the pantheon to battle and defeat the evil god Zu.

The Sumerian gods were always depicted graphically with a multi-horned headdress or crown. Horns were a divine attribute and the depiction of a horned headdress was strictly restricted to the gods although in later years certain more ambitious kings had themselves portrayed this way. The four senior gods are often represented as a horned altar (figure 19).

A Babylonian boundary stone of the 12th Century BC (British Museum) This limestone stele of Nebuchadnezzar I, King of Babylon, represents the pantheon of that city at that time.

Reading from top to bottom, left to right.

The serpent which overshadows the whole pantheon probably represents the pantheon as serpent-gods.

FIRST REGISTER:
The eight-pointed star of Ishtar, the crescent moon of Sin, and the four-pointed radiant star of Shamash.

SECOND REGISTER:
Three horned crowns sitting on altars represent the senior gods An, Enlil, and Enki.

THIRD REGISTER:
The chief deity of Babylon symbolized by the triangular tool on the altar guarded by a dragon is Marduk. The second altar is his son Nabu, patron of writing as shown by the tablet on the altar. The third altar is dedicated to Ninhursag, the mother goddess as shown by the mid-wife symbol.

FOURTH REGISTER:
The curved weapon with a vulture head of Zababa, the two-headed lion mace of Nergal; The third emblem of a horse in a shrine probably represents the Kassite deity of horsemanship. The fourth deity of a bird perched on a post may be a local deity.

FIFTH REGISTER:
This register contains two unidentified gods- one seated on an altar and the other a scorpion-man or god.

SIXTH REGISTER:
Adad as symbolized by the bull and the forked lightning. The gods associated with the beetle and scorpion are not identified. The lamp is usually associated with Nusku.

Fig. 21 – The Babylonian Pantheon

A Babylonian boundary stone of the Kassite Dynasty of about the 15th Century BC, now in the Louvre Museum, depicts the pantheon of Babylon at the time (figure 20). The first register depicts the four senior gods — the horned crown of An and Enlil, the altar with the ram's head and the goat-fish depicts Enki, and the altar with the umbilical cord and knife to sever it, the symbol of the great nurse Ninhursag.

By the 12th Century, the pantheon of Babylon had changed as shown by the boundary stone erected by Nebuchadnezzar I (1125-1104 BC), now in the British Museum (figure 21). At this time Ninhursag had been demoted and is not with the "big three;" she is found not on the first register with An, Enlil, and Enki, but on the second register after the local gods Marduk and Nabu.

When written in cuneiform the god's name was always preceded by the *dingir* sign or symbol for godhood. Originally written in pictographic style as a star, the Sumerian word for god became formalized in cuneiform as the symbol which not only represented the name "An," its chief god, but also was used to mean "heaven." The *dingir* symbol was transferred into Akkadian Semitic to mean god and was synonymous with "ilu" or "el."

ıddition to the *dingir* sign, the name of the Sumerian god . descriptive term such as USHUMGAL (*Ushumgallu* in great fiery flying serpent."

an animal or symbol sacred to him or her. These can be seen ndary stones used by the Babylonian dynasties of the Second figure 20 and 21).

I... r Gods

The old senior god and patriarch An is not important to our story since he appears to have stayed in the background and did not get directly involved with activities on Earth. It is possible that he died or returned to his native planet.

AN or Anu in Akkadian, was the great progenitor and senior god who stood above all the other gods. His abode and seat of authority was in the heavens, the orbiting spaceship or URU-SAG-AN-NA, literally "the chief city of the heavens." According to the stories of ancient Mesopotamia, he did not get involved directly in the operations of his brood on Earth except to settle the many disputes between his sons Enlil and Enki.

Enlil, the Chief of the Expedition to Earth

Although he was the younger son of An, ENLIL (Akkadian Ellil) became the most powerful deity of the Sumerian pantheon next to An. Literally the "Lord of the Command," he was the commander of the expedition to Earth. His sacred city was Nippur, and when the gods assembled on Earth in council, he presided at the E-KUR or "House on the Mountain," his temple on the ziggurat. The temple dedicated to Enlil was called the DUR-AN-KI or "bond of heaven and earth," from where he directed all activities on Earth.

Enlil made sure that the decrees of the gods were carried out against mankind. He disliked mankind and only tolerated humans as necessary to provide for the welfare of the gods. It was Enlil, according to the Sumerian story of the Deluge, who brought on the destruction of mankind because noisy and boisterous humans interfered with his rest.

Enlil was not very popular with the people of ancient Mesopotamia, as shown by the scarcity of his appearances in the art and legends of Sumer and the later civilizations. In contrast, Enki was well liked by the populace and appears in numerous myths and in their art as a benevolent god.

Fig. 22 – Enki as the Water God, here shown with streams of water with fish emanating from his shoulders (see also fig. 24). Enki is often represented by the fish-tailed goat or ibex, which combines the two symbols sacred to him (see fig. 20).

Enki, the Chief Operations Officer

Although he was AN's first born, Enki was given lower rank than his younger brother Enlil, who had been born to AN by another wife who was also his half sister. By the laws of Sumerian inheritance, Enlil became heir to the throne. Enki was given a numerical rank second to Enlil (figure 15). Lingering resentment over his disinheritance and the growing competition over who would control activities on Earth brought Enki into direct conflict with his brother Enlil.

EN-KI or "Lord of the Earth" was also called E-A or "He whose house is on the water," a tacit reference to his water palace from where he carried out operations when he first arrived on Earth. Enki was all things to the expedition: engineer, scientist, and what is more important, creator of mankind.

As a master engineer he supervised the turning of the marshlands of Mesopotamia into a veritable paradise. He planned and supervised the construction of the canal system, the diking of the rivers, and the draining of the marshlands. In a self-laudatory poem he boasts of making the marshlands a haven for birds and fishes, of directing the invention and use of the plow and yoke, of starting up animal husbandry, and bringing the construction arts to Earth in order to raise and maintain the cities.

He had many epithets. He was the God of Wisdom, the God of Mining, the Lord of the Sea and Shipbuilding, and Lord of the Flowing Waters. He is often portrayed with a stream with fish flowing from his shoulders, symbolic of his capacity to provide navigable waters and to insure potable water to the cities of Mesopotamia (figure 22).

His home was Eridu, the first city built by the alien astronauts, and was located at the edge of the watered plain. A Sumerian story describes how Enki loved to go sailing on these water courses in his craft which he called "the ibex," after the nimble goats which inhabited the surrounding mountains. Thus the ibex and the goat with a fish tail became symbolic of the god Enki and appears this way on Sumerian seals and monuments.

As the god of mining, Enki is often portrayed with a human miner holding an ingot of metal on a carrying pole. Metal was molded in the form of a cylinder with a hole through the middle in order to facilitate its being carried on a pole with a handle (figure 24). Most important of all, he is remembered as the god who created man and who came to his defense against the capricious Enlil.

The Abzu or Water Palace of Enki

When the alien reptile gods arrived here and began to build the cities and drain the swamps, a temporary residence was required for Enki to live in and from where he could conduct operations to make the land inhabitable. It would make sense that his first domicile would be a spaceship that descended to Earth and was based at the delta of the rivers to serve as a home and working headquarters. Enki is often depicted on cylinder seals as residing in this water palace or Abzu (figure 24).

It was probably sealed and submersible as well. In fact, in the *Epic of Gilgamesh* when Utnapishtim, the Babylonian Noah, was building his "ark" he was told to seal it thoroughly in order to make it waterproof, "Like the Abzu thou shall seal her."

The term AB-ZU in Sumerian, or *Apsu* in Semitic, is derived from the combination of AB or AP meaning "the father, the creator, the great one," and ZU or SU meaning "one who knows, the wise one," thus suggesting that it was the source of all wisdom or knowledge.

Fig. 23 – The Evil Dragon of Mesopotamia

Fig. 24 – Enki in his water palace - The Abzu. From a cylinder seal in the British Museum, circa 2200 BC, which depicts Enki in his water palace and as the God of Mining. To the right is a human bearing an ingot of metal on a carrying pole with handle.

Originally Abzu was the term used for our Sun. In the older stories like *The Creation Myth* which deals with the formation of the universe, the Abzu is called "the primeval one" and "the begetter," of the planets of our solar system. Later when the Anunna arrive here and begin to set up operations, the Abzu is clearly the abode of Enki, located near the city of Eridu.

In many stories it is referred to as a majestic water palace from where Enki conducted his many operations. In the myth *Enki and the World Order*, the Abzu is described as a splendid shrine, nestled among the shade trees which are filled with birds, and among navigable canals which are stocked with fish. In this Eden-like garden Enki takes pleasure trips over the marshland and canals in his MAGUR-type boat which he refers to as "the Ibex of the Abzu," an obvious allusion to the wild goat of the surrounding mountains.

The term MA-GUR is derived from the Sumerian terms MAmeaning "boat or ship" and GUR meaning "to turn about," thus the MAGUR boat of Enki in which he toured the delta would be compared to what we would call today a small runabout.

It was also here in the Abzu that he maintained control over the MEs or Tablets of Destiny, those strange objects which appeared to be crystals and were used for the storage of information, or as power sources. It was to the Abzu that Ishtar journeyed in order to extract some of the ME from Enki by first getting him drunk.

Enki as the Amphibious Reptile of the Babylonian Legends

The traditions of ancient Mesopotamia recount the story of an amphibious ancestor who taught the arts and crafts of civilization to mankind. Written in the Third Century BC by the Babylonian priest Berossus, it describes the origins of civilization as his forefathers believed it. Although most of the works of Berossus have been lost, fragments have been preserved by his contemporaries such as Apollodorus, Polyhistor, and others.

The account speaks of a group of creatures who came out of the Persian Gulf called "Annedoti" led by one Oannes. They reportedly were amphibious creatures with the head and legs of a man, and the body and tail of a fish. A late Babylonian representation of Oannes shows him wearing the triple horned crown of the Sumerian gods. He is also feathered indicative of his ability to fly (figure 25).

Fig. 25 – The fabled Oannes as Enki. Late Babylonian representation of Oannes, the fishtailed amphibious being who brought civilization to Mankind. Oannes wears the horned triple crown of the Sumerian gods and wings under his fish skin, meant to show their ability to fly. Oannes hold the cone and situla or food and drink of long life and immortality.

Apollodorus referred to Oannes and the Annedoti as "musarus," which means "an abomination," in Greek. The name Annedoti also means "the repulsive ones." In other words, the creatures credited with founding civilization were frankly described by the ancient Babylonian people who revered them, as "repulsive abominations."

If the tradition had been invented, a more normal attitude would be to glorify these creatures as splendid gods and heroes. Yet the fact that they chose to describe their ancestors this way argues for the authenticity of the account. It was the Babylonian tradition that they owed their culture and knowledge to creatures who came up from the sea and who were disgusting and loathsome to look upon.

Of further significance is the fact that the Oannes of Berossus and Apollodorus bears a striking resemblance to the Sumerian Enki who founded the Mesopotamian civilization and brought the arts and sciences to mankind. Enki lived in his water palace or Abzu located on the edge of the Persian Gulf. Enki's Abzu was sealed and presumably submersible. Oannes was said to return to his watery abode in the evening to spend the night.

Even the name Annedoti is quite similar to the people of Enki, the Anunnaki, from whence it was probably derived. The Greek term may have originated with the Sumerians and was later carried over as a description of a race that was both reptilian and loathsome.

Ninhursag, the Chief Medical Officer and Mother Goddess

The fourth senior Sumerian god was NIN-HUR-SAG or "Lady of the Mountain Top." She was a half-sister to Enki and Enlil. In earlier days Ninhursag was of higher rank than Enki and preceded his name when they appeared together. But probably due to her plotting with Enki in the creation of man and presumably other matters, she later was reduced in status and practically disappeared from the pantheon as a major influence. She was eclipsed by the rising star of Ishtar, who injected herself in all Sumerian affairs. In the Western Lands of Palestine, Syria, and Lebanon, Ishtar appeared in several forms and displaced Ninhursag as the mother and fertility goddess.

Ninhursag is also known by other names such as NIN-TI or "The Lady who gives Life," NIN-MAH "The Exalted Lady" and MAM-MU "The Creator Goddess." She ruled the antediluvian city of Shuruppak. Her sacred symbol was the umbilical cord and the cutter knife used to sever it.

With Enki, she conducted biological experiments in the laboratories atop her ziggurat at Shuruppak which failed to produce a workable primitive man. Finally in Enki's floating headquarters she assisted Enki in producing the first primitive creature, a hybrid reptilian and mammal form.

The Sebbiti or the Seven Ruling Gods

The pantheon was dominated by three other gods besides the "big four" and together they were known as the SEB-BI-TI (Sebbitu in Akkadian) or the "Seven who decided the fates." Besides Enlil, Enki, and Ninhursag, there were the junior gods Nannar, Ishkur, Utu and Inanna. In times of trouble they met to decide the the fate of mankind.

The number seven came to mean "fortunate" in later years and in the Assyrian and Babylonian periods the gods became associated with seven planets. According to the Jewish writer-general Josephus, the seven branches of the Jewish Sacred Candelabra or Menorah represented the seven planetary gods of Babylon.

The mythologist Robert Graves suggested that the association of the number seven, such as in the seven days of Creation and the seven days of the week, among other things, can all be traced back to the seven planetary gods of the Babylonians.

CHAPTER 9

THE ACTIVITIES OF THE YOUNGER RULING GODS

The second tier of the pantheon consisted of Nannar, Utu, Ishkur, and Inanna; they were the active serpent-gods after the Deluge. They were the children and grandchildren of Enlil and only the progeny of his were given ruling authority in the Middle East. The sons of Enki apparently were assigned geographic areas and activities away from Mesopotamia and the Western Lands, a precaution on the part of Enlil to prevent conflict between the cousins, but also to retain control of Mesopotamia by his family.

Nannar, the Moon God and Legitimate Ruler of Mesopotamia

The most significant of these younger gods was NANNAR, the eldest son and favorite of Enlil. He was assigned all the lands of Mesopotamia after the Deluge, as well as the Western lands of Palestine, Syria, and Jordan. His sacred city was Ur or "The Capital City" and his symbol was the crescent moon. This symbol so dominated the post-diluvian times that it later was adopted by Islam as its motif, just as the cross of Shamash became the symbol of Christianity.

His Semitic name *Sin* (the Sinai region was named after him) is really not a Semitic name but a loan word from Sumerian SU-EN or ZU-EN meaning the "Wise Lord." The earliest form of the name was ZU-EN or ZU-IN which is found in Old Assyrian inscriptions in the 19th Century BC. It was later contracted and the sibilant shifted until the name became *Sin,* following normal principles of phonetic development. Since the order of the phonetic elements was often reversed it was also written as ENZU, and thus makes it very probable that the *Enzu* of the *Myth of Zu* was in all probability the Sumerian god Nannar.

This is strongly suggested by the absence of Nannar/Sin from The Myth of Zu, which is discussed below. It also explains his falling out of favor at certain times in the history of the Middle East. From hereon he will be referred to in this book by his Semitic name Sin.

Utu, the Sun God and Chief Astronaut

U-TU or "the Shining One" was a grandson of Enlil and along with Inanna was a twin born to Sin. Utu's city in antediluvian times was Sippar, the space platform from where the freighters laden with metals shuttled to and from the orbiting spaceship.

After the Deluge, he moved his space activities to the Western lands and to Lebanon where

Fig. 26 – Marduk, later patron deity of Babylon.

At left: Marduk shown with his sacred animal, the serpent-dragon or "mush-hush-shu." At right: The "mush-hush-shu" also appeared in glazed tile on the walls of the Ishtar gate at Babylon during the reign of Nebuchadnezzar about 1100 BC.

Baalbek became the new space city. In these lands he was known by his Semitic name of *Shamash*. The city of Baalbek was named after him and it appears as Beth-Shamash in the Old Testament, or in other words, the "House of Shamash."

The origin of the name Shamash has been a puzzle among scholars, but John Gardner in his translation of the *Epic of Gilgamesh* states that it was probably derived from the Sumerian SHUM-HUR (Akkadian *Shumhuru),* which has

Fig. 27 – Shamash and Astronauts

Relief from palace of Ashernasurpal II at Nimrod showing two priests or kings and two winged gods facing the tree of life, with symbol of Shamash overhead in his winged chariot. The two winged gods or astronauts hold the food and drink of immortality, that is, the pine cone and situla or water bucket.

the meaning of "fiery flying serpent of the mountainland," a fit description of his role in Lebanon. Hereafter he will be referred to by his Semitic name Shamash.

Shamash, the Sun God, later also became known as the God of Justice in the Babylonian Pantheon. In a tablet circa 900 BC found at Sippar, he is shown holding a rod and ring denoting right and justice, that is, straightness and completion. He is shown here as the "divine cordholder," the god of measurements, holding the divine cords that connect heaven and Earth (figure 41). Shamash was the Sun God who daily traversed the sky and the "one from whom no secrets were hidden." His symbol was the four pointed star with four sun rays.

Fig. 28 – Depiction of Shamash.

The Chief Astronaut with wings and tail feathers of a bird, shown against his sacred symbol of a four-spoked wheel or star with four rays.

Shamash was often depicted with wings, indicative of his role as Chief Astronaut of the Anunna. An Assyrian relief from the palace of Ashernasurpal II at Nimrod shows him in a winged wheel hovering over the symbolic tree of life or immortality. It is flanked by two nobles and two winged astronauts, each bearing the symbols of immortality — the pine cone and the SITULA, the water bucket containing the "water of life"(figures 27 and 33).

Ishkur, Ruler of Anatolia and Yahweh of The Old Testament

Fig. 29 – Assyrian wall relief showing a winged Adad with stylized thunderbolts.

The youngest son of Enlil, ISH-KUR or "He of the Mountain Land," was assigned Anatolia as his inheritance. He was the god of the Hittites, known locally as Teshub, and held a strong influence over the lands of northern Palestine and Syria all the way south to Jerusalem. Ishkur made some incursions into the politics of Mesopotamia, but mostly he limited his activities to trying to extend his influence and control over the Western lands.

Better known by his Semitic name of *Adad*, or the *Hadad* of the Old Testament, he was the god of thunder and lightning, and is often depicted holding the forked lightning bolt (figure 29). Adad was the Yahweh (or Jehovah) of the old Testament who tried to use Abraham, at first, and later Moses, to extend his sphere of influence over the land of Palestine. This role is discussed below. Hereafter he will be called by his Semitic name of Adad.

Ninurta, Chief of Staff and Enforcer of Enlil

Ninurta was assigned the lands of Elam, that is, those east of Mesopotamia. For some unknown reason Ninurta was unranked in the Sumerian pantheon and seemed to be, more or less, the chief of staff of Enlil and the main enforcer of Enlil's decrees (figure 15).

He was known by a number of names throughout Mesopotamia, perhaps because of his popularity in being the hero of the pantheon, the god who prevented the "palace revolution" or overthrow of the authority of Enlil. In Nippur he was called Ninurta, but in Lagash he was Ningirsu, in Isin he was known as Pabilsag, Ninazu in Eshnunna, and Zabada in Kish.

Ninurta comes to the fore in Sumerian affairs as the challenger who attacked and defeated the evil god Zu and brought the MEs or tablets of destiny back to Enlil where they belonged (see Chapter 10).

Inanna (Ishtar), the Love and Warrior Goddess

Fig. 30 – Ishtar as the Warrior Goddess.

Ishtar is often depicted on seals as the warrior queen. She has divine weapons in a quiver on her back and in her left hand. Her foot is on the lion, her sacred symbol. The star of Shamash is overhead. Ishtar used Lebanon (Dilmun) as one of her main bases. It is here that she met Gilgamesh.

Of prime importance to the history of Mesopotamia and all the lands of the Middle East is the daughter of Nannar called IN-ANNA (her name is probably derived from NIN-ANA or "Lady of Heaven"). She permeates all the literature of Sumer, Akkadian, Babylon and subsequent cultures to the west.

When the lands were divided after the Deluge, she was left without a city or kingdom due to the happenstance of her gender. By Sumerian tradition a female could not rule a city, and this did not sit well with the ambitious Inanna. As a token gesture, she was given the city of Uruk, the sacred city of her grandfather An, as her home base, but was denied all the trappings of power that went with it. From Uruk she schemed and plotted how to gain power for herself. She certainly was the troublemaker of history par excellence.

To avoid confusion, her Semitic name *Ishtar* is used throughout this book,

Fig. 31 – The Pleides as Ishtar's symbol.

As the sacred symbol of Ishtar, the Pleiades was sometimes represented by seven circles, later by seven stars.

except where noted. Where she appears in the Sumerian myths as Inanna, her name has been changed to Ishtar to avoid confusion.

She has appeared in numerous Sumerian myths, most of which depict her attempt to seize power. A famous myth throughout the Middle East was her descent to the underworld to try to seize control from her sister Ereshkigal, and how she was ransomed by her husband who had to take her place in the underworld. Another story has her seizing some of the MEs or power stones from Enki by getting him drunk in his water palace. Her failure to seduce the hero Gilgamesh was a well known story all over the Middle East.

After 2100 BC, when the Semitic language replaced the Sumerian in Mesopotamia and spread to the western lands of the Levant, her Semitic name Ishtar became well known in the literature of the Middle East. In the Western Lands she established her base in Lebanon and, along with Shamash and Adad, was part of the trinity of gods which dominated these lands for millennia.

Over the years her personality and name were adopted by many cultures and adapted to their native cultures. She was worshipped both as a warrior goddess and as a love goddess. She became Anath, Asherah, and Astarte of the various western Semitic peoples such as the Canaanites and Philistines.

Her sacred animal was the lion. In the early art of Mesopotamia, Ishtar was associated with the so-called gatepost with streamers whose exact meaning is still unknown but associated with the reed huts which dotted the land of the Middle East. Their use as communication centers is discussed in chapter 25.

Fig. 32 – Rock carving of the twelve gods.

Rock carving of the Eighth Century BC attributed to King Sennacherib of Babylon. In the inscription he invokes twelve gods: top row, An Enlil, Ninhursag, and Enki. In the lower row are the gods Sin, an unknown god, Adad, Marduk, Nabu, Nergal, Shamash, and Ishtar.

Later glyptic art has Ishtar identified with the symbol of seven dots, arranged in two rows of three, with a seventh dot placed between the rows at the far end (figure 31). On a cylinder seal dated to the Eighth Century BC, Ishtar is shown flanked by winged gods, probably assistants of Shamash. The seven dots or Pleiades is prominent over the head of one of the astronauts (figure 33). A rock carving of the same period attributed to King Sennacherib invokes twelve gods. Ishtar is represented here by the seven stars of the Pleiades (figure 32).

Fig. 33 – Ishtar and the Pleiades.

Impression of a cylinder seal of the Neo-Assyrian Period, showing Ishtar with a human, probably Gilgamesh, in a symbolic door frame (doorway to the stars?) flanked by two winged astronaut gods who hold the symbols of immortality. Note the Pleiades symbol in upper left corner and the moon of Sin in upper right. A stylized Humbaba, the mechanical monster, appears in the lower right.

The seven stars of Ishtar are interpreted by most historians as representing the Pleiades. The stars used were all eight-pointed stars and eventually evolved into a single eight-pointed star used as the symbol of Ishtar.

The Pleiades played a strange, yet unknown, part in the ancient mythology of Mesopotamia. In astronomy the Pleiades are a cluster of stars in the constellation Taurus. Only six of the stars can presently be seen with the naked eye, but with a telescope several hundred are visible in the cluster. Alcyone is the brightest star in the Pleiades.

The Different Roles of Ishtar

She had three manifestations in the Middle East. She was well known as the goddess of love and sexual behavior and appears to have replaced Ninhursag as the fertility goddess. In the *Epic of Gilgamesh* she is reproached by Gilgamesh for her cavalier treatment of a whole series of lovers, and for this reason, among others, he declines to be her latest conquest. Many songs and paeans are addressed to her in the love goddess role.

She is also a militant goddess of war, fond of battle and often pictured with a quiver of six weapons, often described as mass destruction weapons (figure 30). She was fond of battle and supported the kings of Mesopotamia as they fought their battles.

Another aspect of Ishtar appeared late in the Kassite Period around the Eighth Century BC, where she is now associated with the planet Venus. It is strange that such a bright and visible planet as Venus had not been seized on by her or one of the other gods as their sacred planet. Venus is not mentioned or appears in the literature of Mesopotamia until the Ninth Century BC and seems to verify the theory of Velikovsky that this planet did not appear in the sky before that time.

Another aspect of Ishtar which has lately been suggested by Biblical archaeologists and historians is that she may have been the Asherah of the Old Testament. In this role she was the consort of Yahweh. This is discussed below.

CHAPTER 10

THE ATTEMPT TO SEIZE POWER IN THE PANTHEON

The story of Zu must have had a strong impact on the minds of ancient peoples for it concerned a struggle for power within the pantheon itself. It actually concerns the theft of the ME or "power stones" from the possession of the chief god Enlil and their recovery by his champion, the god Ninurta. The ME (pronounced "may") has no equivalent in English and no translator has thus far been able to provide a satisfactory explanation of the term. It seemed to apply to anything composed of system, direction, ordered events, law, arts and crafts, even weapons and mechanical devices.

Traditionally, scholars translate the term as "divine powers" or "tablets of destiny" for want of a better descriptive term. But these names are grossly deficient, for in reality they were physical objects that could be carried about and upon which was engraved or transcribed instructions and standards of behavior. In this sense they seemed to be like our modern day computer storage disks and chips. The ME were actually the how-to-manuals of the ancients but embedded in "stone."

Each ME provided the possessor full authority and power over a certain aspect of life, perhaps by providing essential information and instructions on controlling certain physical equipment. In this respect they may have been control modules used to operate certain pieces of equipment related to automatons, communications, weapons, and protective equipment. Some of the ME were called ME-GAL-GAL or "great ME" and were associated with "divine" weapons of mass destruction.

The Story of Zu, the Evil Dragon

This dramatic story of the battle in the skies between the gods was discovered in the ruins of Mesopotamia; an Assyrian version was found at Nineveh and fragments from the old Babylonian version at Susa. The *Myth of Zu* is not complete due to missing portions, but it is found in many succeeding cultures where the story is slightly changed to reflect local preferences. By assembling the various versions of the myth, the complete story can be pieced together.

The *Myth of Zu* begins as a paean to the god Ninurta, glorifying and praising him for his bravery; he is called the "foremost among the Anunna" and the one "who bound his enemies and tied up the stone things," and who vanquished the fugitive Zu with his weapons. More will be said later about these "stone things."

As the story begins, the wicked Zu is a trusted confidant of Enlil and allowed freedom of the royal rooms of the palace. He apparently had access to the inner shrine of Enlil, the Duranki, for the event took place atop the ziggurat at his capital city of Nippar. The ME or power stones were stored here under the trusteeship of Enlil, who had the authority to dispense them as he saw fit. According to the myth, Zu observed how the ME were vulnerable and a plot began to take shape in his mind:

> I will take the divine ME,
>
> And the decrees of the gods I will direct.

I will set up my throne and control all the ME.

I will direct the totality of the Igigi.

The term I-GI-GI means "those who observe" or "the watchers" and appears to be part of, if not the Anunna itself. They are mentioned numerous times in the epics. Heidel equates them to the Anunna while Kramer believes they were a group apart. It is possible that "the watchers" were those who remained in the spaceship when the serpent gods descended to Mesopotamia.

To return to the story, Zu bides his time and waits for the right moment. The propitious time came when Enlil decided to take a bath, thereby leaving the ME unattended and exposed. Zu takes action:

He seizes the ME with his hands,

Taking away the sovereignty of Enlil,

The power to issue decrees.

Zu then flew away,

And retired to his mountain stronghold.

Enlil was astounded that anyone would try and seize the control of the pantheon. He was numb with fear that Zu now had in his hands unlimited power. Enlil bemoaned the fact that now his sanctuary had lost MELAM or "its splendor and brilliance." The term ME-LAM or "brilliant ME" is often applied to the ME, suggesting that they were light-emitting crystals.

Meanwhile the great senior god An, who was apparently in the orbiting spaceship, was quite upset over the antics of his children and called all the gods together to discuss a solution. He polled the assembled gods for a volunteer, a champion to rescue the ME and correct the wrong done to the pantheon:

Who among you will slay Zu and make his name greatest among the cities below.

The first person he selected to take on the task was Adad, the god of Anatolia, indicating that Zu had probably retreated to this mountain area controlled by Adad. Adad declined the dubious honor, however, declaring that he believed Zu was now invulnerable. Adad pleaded with An not to send him:

The ME he has under his control.

His utterance has become like that of
  the god of Duranki.

He who opposes him will become like clay.

Much of the subsequent text is missing here and it appears that An had asked several other gods to take on the mission. When the available text resumes it appears that Ninurta had volunteered to lead the attack on Zu and retrieve the collection of control stones or ME.

Ninurta to the Rescue

Ninurta is told to arm himself with the "seven winds of battle," presumably a series of weapons, and is told to cloak his ship with a "fog" device to screen him from Zu. He then sets off for the mountain stronghold of Zu. Upon seeing Ninurta approach, Zu is indignant at his audacity:

When Zu saw him he raged at him . . .

I have carried off all the ME and control
  the decrees of the gods.

Who are you to come to challenge me?

Fig. 34 – Ninurta attacking the evil god Zu

Drawing from Assyrian wall sculpture of palace of Ashurnasirpal of Ninth Century BC, depicting the champion Ninurta attacking the evil god Zu, shown here as a composite monster, with the head and body of a horned serpent, front paws of a lion, winged, with tail and feet of an eagle. In the myth "Slaying of Labbu," he is referred to both as a lion and a dragon.

Explain yourself!

Ninurta informed Zu of the decision of the pantheon, and that he had Enlil's full support. He added that he also had the support of Enki, perhaps to impress him since Enki was the chief engineer as well as the designer of weapons systems. "I've come to fight you," he said.

When Zu heard this he spread "a curtain over the face of the mountain, there was darkness," presumably a protective screen or force field of some sort. Ninurta managed to penetrate the gloomy darkness and as he neared Ninurta's stronghold launched fourteen "storm flood" weapons, presumably missiles of some sort, at Zu.

But the "arrows" could not approach Zu.
They were turned back.
While he controlled the ME,
no "arrow" could approach him.
The weapons were stopped,
in the midst of the mountain,
They vanquished not Zu.

Dismayed by Zu's seemingly impregnable stronghold, Ninurta asked Adad to report the situation back to Enki, that his missiles were helpless against the defenses of Zu. Learning of Ninurta's problems, Enki decided that the only way to beat Zu was to fashion a new and more powerful weapon for which Zu had no defense, a totally new ME weapon.

"Subdue him," Enki says, "by the use of the 'south wind' and let his pinions be overcome."

The "south wind" has appeared elsewhere in Sumerian literature and it is apparently a winged projectile of some sort, for in the *Tale of Adapa* it is described as a low flying craft which was disabled by the hero Adapa by mistake.

The final stages of the battle seem to have been fought in the sky where the weapon of Ninurta was aimed at the pinions of the wings of Zu's aircraft. A bird's pinion feathers are the tip control feathers which give it maneuverability, obviously referring to the control surfaces of Zu's craft.

The struggle between Ninurta and Zu is depicted in a dramatic wall sculpture in the palace of the Assyrian king Ashurnasirpal at the ancient city of Ashur on the Tigris River. It dates to the Ninth Century BC. It shows a winged god chasing a monster with bolts of lightning in both hands. The monster is scaled, horned, and winged, has the front paws of a lion and the rear legs of an eagle as well as tail feathers. Its face is a composite of lion and serpent (figure 34).

Fig. 35 – Zu's trial before Enki.

Sumerian seal showing the judgement of Zu, the evil god shown here as a bird. The god on the right, probably Ninurta, has a seven-headed weapon. Two gods hold the prisoner before Enki for judgement.

They fought in the sky "wing to wing" according to the account, and Zu was finally vanquished. Ninurta then retrieved the ME and brought Zu back to Enlil for trial. It is not stated in the accounts what happened to Zu. A Sumerian seal shows a bound "Zu bird" being brought before Enki for trial (figure 35). The story of Zu was very popular in Mesopotamia and the execution of Zu appears quite often in their depictions on cylinder seals (figure 36).

The story of Zu and the stolen powers does not end here, however, for after having them in his hands temporarily, Ninurta also fell victim to their attraction and tried to steal them from Enki.

Who was the Evil Dragon-God Zu?

He is called ZU "the wise one" in most stories or sometimes ANZU "the wise one of heaven" in the more recent accounts. Scholars have wondered who this god was, important enough to be trusted by Enlil — but for some reason this was not stated in the myth.

All the evidence seems to point to Sin, the eldest son of Enlil and his favorite. Since Sin was the patron god of most Sumerian cities, perhaps his image is being protected by the priesthood of those cities. After all, he was the legitimate ruler of not only Mesopotamia but of the Western Lands as well. Was this the first major political cover-up in history?

The name Sin is really not a Semitic name but a loan word from Sumerian SU-EN or ZU-EN for the letters S and Z are interchangeable (for example Sumerian ABZU is APSU in Akkadian Semitic). In addition, Sumerian names can be read forward as well as backwards, especially in names, so that ZUEN can be written as ENZU (the Lord Zu) as well.

There is also more convincing evidence. Sin is strangely absent from the story of the *Myth of Zu* and this in itself strongly suggests that he was the culprit. As the favorite son of Enlil, he would be a trusted confidante and allowed full access to Enlil's chambers.

In order not to let such a calamity happen again, it was decided by the pantheon to transfer the ME to a more secure place for safekeeping — the Abzu of Enki.

Fig. 36 – The evil god Zu being attacked.

Drawings from Assyrian and Babylonian seal impressions showing the evil god Zu being killed by the hero Ninurta. The dragon-slayer motif was very popular among the peoples of Mesopotamia.

Transfer of the ME or Power Stones to Enki

Since the Abzu of Enki was a sealed craft, access to it could easily be controlled; it was the ideal place to store the power stones. Information on the transfer of the ME to the safekeeping of Enki is found in a self-laudatory hymn addressed by Enki to the Anunna:

> My great brother, ruler of all the lands,
>
> Gathered all the ME together.
>
> Placed the ME in my hands;
>
> From the Ekur, house of Enlil,
>
> I passed on the arts and crafts to my Abzu at Eridu.

The pantheon must have breathed more easily now that the power stones were under the tight control of Enki. But this was not to be the end of a threat to steal the ME. There is another related myth which describes how the hero Ninurta is overcome with desire to possess the ME and tries to obtain them from the Abzu, going to the extreme of assaulting Enki's vizier or aide.

Ninurta Tries to Steal the ME or Power Stones

It seems that Ninurta had difficulty in relinquishing the ME to the pantheon after he had retrieved them from Zu. Their vulnerability in the temple of Enlil was recognized and it was decided to store them under the watchful eyes of Enki. There was also an attempt later by Ishtar to obtain some of the ME from Enki in the Abzu by seducing him, and this will be discussed below.

There is a myth directly related to the battle between Zu and Ninurta and the events after that struggle. *Ninurta's Pride and Punishment* has been reconstructed from fragments found at Ur and Nippur. It tells what happened after Zu handed the ME over to Ninurta. The myth begins with a god called Anzu who complained to Ninurta that because he had been attacked violently, the ME had "dropped out" of his hands and ended up in the Abzu.

Ninurta then assumes the narrative and laments the loss of the ME which he had possessed briefly, with the awesome power that went with them. As the story continues, Ninurta makes a trip to the Abzu where he is greeted joyously by Enki who praises him as the victor over the "bird" and as an unrivaled hero whose name will be duly honored by all.

This blessing, however, does not satisfy the ambitious Ninurta. As the myth states, "On the whole universe the hero Ninurta set his sights" or in other words, he coveted the ME and their power. Ninurta demanded that Enki release the power stones to him. Realizing that Ninurta meant to do him physical harm, Enki asked his vizier Isimud to eject Ninurta from the Abzu.

Ninurta not only refused to leave but actually struck Isimud. Thereupon an irate Enki fashioned a weapon called a "turtle" which proceeded to attack Ninurta. It was presumably an automaton or robot of some sort; it dug a pit and threw in the rebellious Ninurta. Enki then added insult to injury by scoffing at the struggling Ninurta, calling him a mountain-destroyer who could not climb out of a pit. Ninurta would have stayed here had not the mother goddess Ninhursag appeared on the scene to rescue her son Ninurta. After much pleading she managed to convince Enki and he released Ninurta and thus spared his life.

The ME as the Stone Things of Ninurta

The opening part of the *Myth of Zu* glorifies and praises Ninurta for his bravery. He is called the one who bound his enemies and tied up the "stone things," obviously meaning the ME of Zu which were used as weapons against Ninurta. There is another related myth which seems to identify these ME used by Ninurta as weapons.

In a myth which has to do with the battle and destruction of a monster called an ASAG-demon, Ninurta turns to some unidentified "stones," cursing those which had been his enemies in his battle with the ASAG-demon and blessing those which had been his friends.

Apparently these are references to the ME which he used to defeat Zu as well as to the ME which Zu used against him. According to the research of Kinnier Wilson, the ASAG-demon is the same creature as Anzu. ASAG is also called the "seven-headed demon" — in other words, the adversary with seven weapons.

It has been suggested earlier that the Old Testament story of the struggle between God and Lucifer to control heaven and of Lucifer's defeat and banishment was probably a later Hebrew version of the struggle for power between Zu and the Sumerian pantheon.

The term "stone" and "stone things" appears quite often in Sumerian stories in the context of weapons and automatons, and which obviously equate them with the ME. We shall see that they were actually quartz data storage crystals.

The Slaying of the Flying Dragon or Labbu

There is a Babylonian legend called the *Slaying of the Labbu* which concerns the destruction of a monster called the "Labbu." The word "Labbu" means lion but in the legend it is called both a lion and a serpent-dragon. The story is much more recent than the *Myth of Zu* and presumably represents a later Babylonian version of the same incident.

This monster or Labbu has all the characteristics of a dragon — it lived in the sea but had legs and was winged. It not only attacked the fish and creatures of the sea but also birds and other flying creatures, as well as animals. It was known to attack and eat humans as well.

As the story goes, the people appealed to the gods to deliver them from this monster. An unidentified god called Tishpak was commissioned by the pantheon to seek and destroy this bothersome monster.

In attacking the Labbu, Tishpak first throws up a screen of clouds to hide his approach and intentions, then, covering himself with a protective cloak, shoots a missile at the Labbu and kills it. The description of the battle is quite similar to that of Ninurta against Zu and the story may actually be a later Babylonian and Assyrian rendition of the *Myth of Zu*.

There is a related Akkadian fragment published by Wilson which seems to make it clear that Tishpak was actually Ninurta. In this tablet Ningizzida (one of the epithets of Ninurta) is described as the one "who struck down the impetuous Labbu."

In a later version the evil god Zu has become a composite monster. It is probably the Labbu which is depicted in an Assyrian relief which shows a winged god with thunderbolts in his hand chasing a strange creature (figure 34). The graphic description of the Labbu in the poem with the mane of a lion and the body of a serpent with flying characteristics is presumably the composite monster or dragon of this illustration. The monster is winged, Scaly like a serpent, has horns, front paws, the head of a lion and talons of an eagle.

CHAPTER 11

THE PLURAL GODS OF THE OLD TESTAMENT

The Origin of The Old Testament Gods

It is generally agreed that there are two traditions which make up the books of the Old Testament, the older or Elohist tradition which refers to the deity in generic terms, and the Priestly tradition where the deity is called Yahweh, often called Jehovah, somewhat erroneously, due to a mistranslation from the Greek Septuagint. The two main streams are intertwined throughout the Old Testament and sometimes exists side-by-side as, for example, in Genesis where there are two versions of the Creation.

One gets the impression from reading the Old Testament, particularly Genesis, that no one was really in charge. There is a lot of argument and debate with God; there is much confusion in the Garden of Eden where an omnipotent god has to search for Adam and Eve. The role of Satan or Lucifer in heaven and on Earth is obscure. The activities of the Nefilim are barely touched on and then forgotten.

The god of the Old Testament has many human attributes — he is jealous, and vindictive; he does not seem omnipotent for at times he allows evil to exist and often gets into debate with the devil. There are many gaps in the narrative; it is disjointed; jumps abruptly from one subject to another without explanation or resolution. It leaves more questions unanswered than it resolves.

In the scriptures, the deity is called *El* (plural *Elohim*) some of the time and *Yahweh* the rest of the time. Biblical scholars agree that the usage of Yahweh appears to be an anachronism and may have been inserted at later times.

Hebrew *Elohim* is grammatically a plural form and is often translated as "God" at times, but also "Gods" or "divine beings" at other times, mainly because the text is often ambiguous. Generally, the name for the deity is *El,* which appears to be the term for the deity in western Semitic as well as Biblical Hebrew. It apparently was borrowed from the pantheon of indigenous people of the land of Canaan or Palestine. Who then was this El who was the supreme deity of the Canaanites?

As the ruling god of the Western Semitic pantheon, the leading Sumerian deity Enlil was transcribed syllabically as *ilulu,* then becoming *ili* in Akkadian or Semitic, and later *el* in Hebrew. El thus becomes the name for Enlil, the supreme being in Palestine, and is carried over into the Old Testament.

While the rest of the world believed in many gods, the compilers and editors of the Old Testament endeavored to proclaim a faith in a sole god. In spite of these monotheistic attempts, however, there remains many instances where the Biblical narrative falls into the plural form Elohim. In Genesis 1, for example, when the notion to create Adam is brought up, the words used are all in the plural: "And Elohim said: 'Let *us* create man in our image and after our likeness."

Later, in the Garden of Eden, when the serpent is tempting Eve he says: "You are not going to die. No. the gods (Elohim) will know that the moment you eat it your eyes will be opened and you will be the same as the gods (Elohim) in telling good from bad." Again later, after the Fall, the deity complains, "Now that man has become like *us* discerning good from bad."

In other instances, the deity often addressed remarks aside as if to other members of the celestial group. Even after the Deluge, when man was trying to erect a tower in Babel, the deity remarked to an associate, "Let us, then, go down and confound their speech." Therefore, notwithstanding attempts by early editors to proclaim a policy of monotheism, evidence of a pantheon has not been completely erased from the Old Testament.

The Lesser Gods: The Nefilim and the Angles

Not only does the Old Testament suggest that there were many deities, but these lesser gods seem to have descended to Earth to interfere in the affairs of man. This is explicit in Genesis 6 which states:

> Now when man began to increase on Earth and daughters were born to them, the divine beings (Elohim) saw how beautiful were the human daughters and took as their wives any of them they liked . . . It was then that the Nefilim appeared on Earth, as well as later, after the divine beings had united with human daughters to whom they bore children.

The Biblical term for these lesser deities seems to have been Nefilim. Is the descent of these Nefilim reflected in the literature of Mesopotamia? Could they be the Anunna or Sons of An of the Sumerian pantheon who also descended to Earth in the antediluvian period? We shall see that these were different names for the same group of people.

The term *Nefilim* has given theologians and translators problems over the centuries, so much so that today it is the policy to leave the term intact in modern translations. *Nefilim* is derived from the Hebrew NFL literally "the fallen ones" or better still "those who dropped down." It has been interpreted to mean "fallen angels" in the sense of those who were cast down, or the evil angels, although the text does not justify this conclusion. The noted Jewish Biblical commentator of the 19th Century, Malbim, maintained that in ancient times the rulers of countries were the sons of deities who arrived on Earth from the heavens. He maintained that they were the sons of pagan deities and called themselves Nefilim.

Genesis asserts that they came down to Earth in two groups: "It was then that the Nefilim appeared on Earth, as well as later." The descent of the two separate groups of "angels" to Mount Hermon in northern Palestine is reported in the *Book of Jubilees*. A group descended in the days of Jared in the 10th Jubilee; later in the 25th Jubilee during the days of Noah, another group came down to Earth. Since a Jubilee year is 50 regular years, this source claims that they descended to Earth about 700 years apart. The Nefilim and the offspring the Rephaim are discussed below.

The *Enuma Elish*, the Babylonian account of the Creation, also refers to a group of 300 Anunna who descended in this period to populate the Earth. These divine beings also intermarried with the daughters of man.

The "angels" of the Old Testament has become a general term to describe lesser deities who have been quite active in the affairs of man. In Biblical Hebrew the world often used is *malakh*, however, other terms such as *bene elo - him* or "sons of god" are often translated as angels. It has been used as a cover term for any of the lesser deities coming in contact with mankind. These messengers got around very easily by some sort of flying device; hence the representation of angels with wings, a symbol of their ability to fly. This was the only way the ancients knew how to convey this fact. The incident of the destruction of Sodom and Gomorrah illustrates the ability of these "angels" to fly about.

This is patent in the events described in Genesis 18 and 19, where several angels briefed Abraham on the coming destruction of the cities. The traditional translation states that when they decided to visit Sodom, they "set out from there and faced Sodom." The distinguished Biblical scholar E. A. Speiser in his work *Genesis*, suggests that this translation is erroneous and that it could be more accurately rendered as "they looked down upon the face of Sodom." This reading of course, gives a completely different meaning to the incident.

Later, after the angels take Lot and his family to safety outside the city, the traditional text states "led them safely outside the city." Again, Speiser suggests an alternate translation as "brought them out and deposited them outside the city." Thus, the revised text makes it quite clear that the angels first reconnoitered the cities by air, then seeing the need to rescue Abraham's nephew and family, removed them by their aircraft and deposited them outside at a safe place.

Misinterpretation of the First Commandment

In Exodus 20, the Ten Commandments given to Moses start with "You shall have no other god before Me," as stated in the King James version or in the Jewish Torah it appears as "You shall have no other god beside Me." In either case it is a minor difference but it does accentuate the last phrase.

It has been interpreted and promulgated for two millennia by the Hebrew and Christian priesthood as the foundation of the monotheistic base of the Judeo-Christian religions. But a close look and reading of the First Commandment brings certain questions to mind and in analysis it does not support the idea of a monotheistic god — in fact, to the contrary, it implies many other gods, but at a different and lower level of power.

If the phrase was meant to be "you shall have no other gods," why not just stop right there and not add the phrase "before me." If anything, the Commandments are the spirit of conciseness and certainly would not contain any unnecessary verbiage. Therefore, the sentence can only mean that "you will have no other gods "above" or "over" me. In other words, Yahweh is declaring that he is the superior god of a pantheon.

It must be remembered that the Hebrews lived in and came out of a milieu of plural gods: Abraham came from the land of the Sumerian pantheon and the land of Canaan where plural gods vied for power. They lived hundreds of years in Egypt under the plural Egyptian gods.

If Yahweh was Adad of the Hittite lands of Anatolia, as we shall see, he was making the point that he was the supreme god and other gods, especially Enlil (the El of Canaan and Syria) should be subordinate to him. The statement "You shall have no other gods before me" means simply "you shall have no other gods above me." This does not rule out a plurality of gods but suggests that there were other gods in the Hebrew pantheon, and in particular, Asherah, as we shall see, which was the Hebrew name for Ishtar. She was the consort of Yahweh.

The Many Gods of the Land of Canaan

It is obvious in several places in the Pentateuch that other gods existed in the land of Canaan and Adad competed with them for superiority. When Moses came down from Mount Sinai with the tablets and found the Israelites worshipping a golden calf (actually a bull according to other sources), he smashed the tablets in anger. The bull was the animal sacred to Enlil, that is, the El of

Fig. 37 – Adad, the Hittite god.

Neo-Assyrian relief of the Canaanite Storm God Adad brandishing lightning bolts. His cult animal, the bull, was appropriated from Enlil. To the right, a boundary stone of the 14th Century BC, showing the forked lightning and bull as the sacred symbols of Adad.

Palestine and Syria, and meant that the people were slipping back to the old ways, worshipping the old gods (Later the bull symbol was appropriated by Yahweh as his symbol).

Another example of the conflict between Enlil and Adad was the sacrifice of Isaac, which is discussed in Chapter 19. A close reading of this verse shows that it was El who requested the sacrifice from Abraham and that he was stopped at the last moment by the intervention of the angel of Yahweh.

Much has been written on the gods of the Holy Land at the time of Abraham and Moses (circa 2000-1500 BC). Yet this research usually does not take in consideration that these lands were claimed and occupied by the kings of Mesopotamia who left their imprint of Sumerian gods on the land.

There were four major gods which reigned in the Western Lands of Palestine, Syria, Lebanon, and Jordan, after the Deluge. The ancient supreme god was El, the Semitic version of Enlil, the chief of the Sumerian pantheon. His influence over the Biblical lands decreased as the younger gods became more active and influential. By the time of Abraham, the worship of El was "the old time religion" that was still practiced in certain areas where the influence of the younger gods had not penetrated.

Three younger gods had been assigned the lands of the West: Shamash was given Lebanon as his land; Adad ruled over Anatolia, the land of the Hittites; and Sin controlled the rest of the lands of the Levant. His influence rapidly declined and by 2000 BC, the days of Abraham, had all but disappeared. This was probably due to his treachery in Sumer when he tried to seize control of the pantheon from Enlil.

The goddess Ishtar was a major influence in the Western Lands and made her "throne base" in Lebanon with Shamash, her brother. She appeared in these lands under various names. Shamash made his headquarters at Baalbek, known as Beth-Shemash or the "House of Shamash" in the Old Testament. He was commander of the space flight center here, which had been moved after the Deluge. It was to this land that Gilgamesh journeyed in order to seek immortality by seeing his grandfather in the orbiting spaceship. It was here he met Ishtar who offered him a ride up if he would become her lover.

Adad as the God of the Hittites

Adad, the Lord of Anatolia, is the western god who is important to our story. He extended his power south and to the east as the Hittite empire. At one time he controlled Syria and Palestine as far south as Jerusalem, and some of the lands to the east as far as Mesopotamia (figure 37).

In Hittite legends we can see the reflection of Sumerian culture and history. The struggle between the Storm-god Teshub (the local name for Adad) and the evil dragon or flying serpent is reminiscent of the struggle in the *Myth of Zu*. At first Teshub is defeated by the Dragon but with the assistance of the goddess Inara (obviously a name for Ishtar) who prepares a feast and gets the Dragon drunk, the Storm-god returns and kills the Dragon. As we can see the Mesopotamian myth was adapted to the Hittite milieu and the hero becomes Adad instead of Ninurta (figure 38).

Fig. 38 – Adad and Ishtar in Anatolia. Drawing from rock-relief in chamber at Yazilikaya, Turkey, showing the Hittite god Teshub and his consort Inara, their local names for Adad and Ishtar. Teshub holds the forked lightning and stands on the backs of two lesser gods.

In the Canaanite pantheon Baal was the son of El. His consort was his sister Anat. While the name Baal is found in northeast Semitic such as Phoenician, Ugaritic, and Hebrew, in earlier years before the 15th Century BC he was known as the ancient Semitic god Hadad (Adad in Akkadian).

The Hittite Storm-god Adad bears a strong resemblance to the Yahweh of the Bible. In fact, the Hittite influence was quite dominant in the lands occupied by Abraham, Jacob, and Isaac. The Hittite heritage of the Hebrews was clearly spelled out in the *Book of Ezekiel* (16: 1-3) where the prophet is told by Yahweh that:

> "Your origin and your birth was in the land of
> the Canaanites; your father was an Amorite,
> your mother a Hittite."

In other words, the Hebrews had intermarried among the native peoples of Palestine, the Amorites being the general term for the indigenous people. In Joshua's time we find that Jerusalem had been the property of the Jebusites, a sect of the Hittites which had earlier migrated south from Anatolia. The Hittite influence of Adad was quite strong among the Hebrews, for example, Uriah the Hittite was one of David's chief generals. Solomon had several Hittite wives.

When Abraham paid a tithe of ten percent to the King of Jerusalem after the invasion of the Mesopotamian kings, he was paying homage to the king of Canaan, who in turn owed allegiance to El or Enlil. Melchizedek, the King of Jerusalem, welcomed the victorious Abraham with these words:

> "Blessed be Abram by El-Elyon,
> Creator of heaven and earth.
> And praised be El-Elyon
> Who had delivered your foes to you.

Abraham's reply was rude and disrespectful when he said that he had sworn to "Yahweh, the most high, Creator of Heaven and Earth," that he would take no booty.

El-Elyon, literally "El, the most high," is here placed in juxtaposition to Yahweh. Abraham serves notice of his loyalty to Yahweh or Adad rather than to El, the old Sumerian god. These verses highlight many of the skirmishes in the Old Testament between Yahweh and El.

Yahweh as the Hittite God Adad

According to Exodus 6:3 the appellation Yahweh did not come into use until the time of Moses, for Moses is told by the deity that "I am Yahweh, I appeared to Abraham, Isaac, and Jacob as El-Shaddai, but I did not make myself known to them by my name Yahweh." Scholars agree that the name Yahweh was a later addition by priestly scribes. The tetragram *YHWH* or *Yahweh* became the distinctive personal name for the god of Israel and is used most frequently throughout the Old Testament to represent the deity.

As mentioned above Yahweh was also known by the name El-Shaddai. This El-Shaddai name appears in Genesis no less than six times and is considered to be the descriptive title for the god of the Hebrews. The Hebrew root *shaded,* from which it has been supposed to be derived, means "to overpower," "to treat with violence," or "to lay waste." These meanings give the deity a fearful character, that of devastator or destroyer. It is partly for this reason that the god of the Hebrews is known as an uncompromising and vindictive god.

It is also possible that Shaddai may be connected linguistically with the Hittite *shadu,* or mountain. In actuality, both of these meanings can be applied to the Hebrew God El-Shaddai, for he is none other that the God of Lightning and Thunder of the Hittites. He was the Anatolian god of the twin mountain often depicted with thunderbolts in his hand.

The origin of Yahweh is unknown and while many explanations for its meaning have been proposed, the most logical seems to be that the divine name is a form of the verb "to be" or *HWH,* thus meaning "the one who is." This is manifested in Exodus 3 where Moses queries the Lord on his real name so that he can inform the tribes of Israel who wish to know what to call their god.

> God said to Moses "I am who I am," and he said
> "Say this to the people of Israel:
> "I am has been sent to you."

This verse has given translators all kinds of problems and it is footnoted in all translations of the Bible with the caveat that it can also mean "I am what I am" or "I will be what I will be." Its ambiguity is probably due to the fact that it is a liturgical epithet. It means exactly what it says: "I am the one who is or who exists."

In ancient times, divine names were held to have intrinsic power in themselves and certain appellations could only be used by the priesthood. In the Sumerian and Babylonian pantheon only descriptive names are used. The true names of the gods are not known.

Yahweh or "the one who is" is probably an attempt by Hebrew priests to substitute an innocuous name for that of the deity thereby defusing any possible harmful consequences. This is also found in the Rabbinical tradition where the name Yahweh holds certain powers, and in ancient times only a few priests were allowed to pronounce the name.

All deities were wary of revealing their true names lest these might be used for improper purposes, which is the original sense of "blasphemy." The Romans had a habit of discovering the secret names of enemy gods by bribery and torture, and then enticing them to desert their cities.

Ishtar or Astarte as the Consort of Yahweh

The Sumerian goddess Inanna, better known by her Semitic name Ishtar, was worshipped all over the Western Lands under different local cultic names. To the Phoenicians and Philistines she was Astarte; to the Canaanites she was

Asherah. She appears in the Old Testament under these names as well as Astoreth and Anat. These were all permutations of the name Ishtar, the fertility goddess and "Queen of Heaven" of the Semitic peoples.

In these lands, Astarte was the chief consort of the god of storm and warfare, appearing in the Old Testament as Baal-Adad (sometimes as Haddu, Hadad, and Addu). In the early Second Millennium BC, Baal replaced El as the leading god of these lands and came to be used as the generic term for god. It is noteworthy that nowhere in the mythology of these peoples is Astarte or Ishtar associated with El.

Baal also served not only to represent a deity but in the scriptures was often used as the generic word for "god" — especially for the non-Hebrew gods. For example, in Joshua 24 the people of Israel are criticized because they "worshipped Astarte, the majestic lady, and the baals (gods) of the nations surrounding them."

Until the breakup of Solomon's empire (c. 931 BC) Astarte was often referred to as the consort of Baal. Solomon was one of her worshippers as is noted in 1 Kings 11:4-5:

> When Solomon grew old his wives stayed his heart to other gods; and his heart was not wholly with Yahweh the God as his father David's had been. Solomon became a follower of Astarte, the goddess of the Sidonians.

Sidon was a sister city to the Phoenician city of Tyre, which under Hiram built the Temple for Solomon. The Temple as described in the Old Testament bears a strong resemblance to the actual temples of the Phoenicians. It is entirely possible that the Temple erected by the master builder Hiram of Tyre was dedicated to the mother goddess Astarte. In Phoenicia and Philistia she was also worshipped "in the high places," hilltops and mountains. Mount Herman, for example, abounded with her shrines.

The Old Testament describes how Solomon worshipped Astarte and how he offered sacrifice and incense "in the high places." The worship of Astarte was quite common among the Hebrews and appears in the form of Astaroth (see Judges 3:7 and 1 Kings 16:33 for example).

In Joshua 24: 33 (a verse which does not appear in the King James version but is found in the Hebrew text) she is called Astarte, the "majestic lady," or *Astarten kai Astaroth.* Astaroth is a plural form of majesty and it is obvious that the word applies to Astarte. It is found throughout the Old Testament; Astaroth may not be a name but actually a descriptive term for "majestic lady," referring to Astarte as the consort of gods or baals.

Asherah, the Hebrew Fertility Goddess

The name Asherah is mentioned at least 40 times in the Bible. After the death of Solomon, the term Asherah becomes predominant in the Old Testament. There were three manifestations of Asherah and Biblical authorities do not agree on the meaning of each usage. Sometimes Asherah was an image or a figurine of the goddess. Some of these figurines have only a torso, breasts and head, and appear to have been raised on a pole or tree top where she was worshipped "in the high places." Other references associate her with a grove of trees, the so-called "sacred grove."

Despite the persistent efforts of the religious establishment to suppress and eradicate all traces of Asherah, worship of the great Mother Goddess of Canaan flourished in ancient Israel. The famous archeologist Dame Kenyon, who first excavated Jericho, found at Jerusalem a hoard of several dozen broken female figurines dated to the Seventh Century BC deposited in a cave a few hundred yards south of the Temple Mount in Jerusalem. Many were of the goddess Asherah.

Many of the subsequent kings of Judah tried to eradicate the worship of the Mother Goddess after the division of the kingdom. King Hezekiah (circa 715 BC) in a spirit of reform "abolished the hill-shrines and smashed the sacred pillars and cut down the Asherah." Religious reforms continued under subsequent kings to try to stamp out this persistent worship of the female goddess. King Josiah of Judah (c. 640 BC) ordered "the objects made for Baal and Asherah removed from the Temple and burned." Apparently the statues and altars still remained in the Temple until that time.

Just how powerful goddesses were under the Jewish monarch can be seen from Jeremiah's denunciation of his co-religionists who attributed Judea's downfall to their breach of faith with Anath (a local form of the goddess) and cried "Let us once more worship the Queen of Heaven, as our fathers did before us."

That Asherah was a consort of Yahweh seems to have been purged from the Old Testament. Archaeological evidence to the contrary, however, makes it clear that she was his consort. Found by archaeologists on the wall of a tomb near Hebron and dated to the Eight Century BC, an inscription said "Blessed by Yahweh and his Asherah." Similar inscriptions have turned up as archaeologists unearth more ancient sites. In a cave in the Sinai near Kadesh-Barnea explorers found this inscription on the wall: "I bless you by Yahweh of Samaria and by his Asherah."

It has been suggested elsewhere that Ishtar used the cluster of the stars Pleiades as her sacred symbol. Such an association is also found in the Hebrew literature. There is a story told in the Jewish *Midrash* about the Nefilim who came to Earth before the Deluge led by the evil angel Shemhazi. He was so smitten by the beauty of Istahar (obviously Ishtar) that he promised her the secret name of God if she would give herself to him. She agreed but once she heard the "Ineffable Name" she refused Shemhazi's advances. She pronounced the secret name and was lifted up to heaven where she was transformed into the constellation Pleiades. The role of the Pleiades in ancient Hebrew sources is puzzling, for it appears time and time again (see Chapter 13).

CHAPTER 12

PHYSICAL CONDITIONS BEFORE THE DELUGE

At the time of the arrival of the Anunna or alien astronauts, some hundreds of thousands of years ago, the climate of the Earth was completely different from what it is today. It was moist and stable, not running to the extremes in temperature as it is today. This was due to the enormous amount of moisture being held in the Earth's atmosphere, a veritable cloud canopy. This condition is described in the *Book of Genesis* as the "separation of waters."

The alien astronauts were a sapient reptile form and found conditions here congenial to their existence for the simple reason that it probably duplicated the environment on their home planet. It is no accident that all the early settlements were founded at the mouth of large river systems, where moisture was abundant. Besides the original colony at the mouth of the Tigris and Euphrates, other civilizations sprang up in similarly favorable places such as the Nile Delta and in the Hindus river system. These were actually offshoots of the main colony in Mesopotamia.

The Antediluvian Vapor Canopy of the Earth

The theory that the Earth had a primordial vapor canopy was developed by Donald Patten in his book *The Biblical Flood and the Ice Epoch.* He surmises that it was in some ways like that surrounding Venus today. The canopy of Venus consists primarily of carbon dioxide and hydrocarbons, with some water vapor. The Earth's primordial vapor canopy, on the other hand, was composed mostly of water vapor, some carbon dioxide, and virtually no hydrocarbons.

This cloud cover condensed out at the time of the Deluge. Patten believes that plant life was luxuriant in that early period because of the proportions of carbon dioxide and water vapor in the atmosphere and the capture of long wave radiation which resulted in the "greenhouse effect."

This greenhouse effect meant that temperatures would tend to be uniform between night and day as well between summer and winter. There was little circulation of the atmosphere and this lack of cyclonic activity precluded the formation of storms and other forms of precipitation.

Although the surface of the Earth was shielded from the direct rays of the Sun, plant life was abundant and luxurious due to the proportion of carbon dioxide in the atmosphere which was probably many times higher than it is today. Two climatologists, Owen Toon and Steve Olson, in their article on "The Warm Earth," in *Science* (October 1985), maintain that the early atmosphere of the Earth may have contained as much as a thousand times more carbon dioxide than it does today.

There was no rain or storms in those days. People obtained much of their water from underground sources, as it is stated in Genesis 2:

> God had not sent rain upon the Earth . . .
> instead, a flow would well up from the ground
> and water the whole surface of the soil.

Water was also provided by the rivers which descended from the mountains, fed by natural springs. The heavily saturated atmosphere also condensed at nightfall producing a heavy dew which provided a certain amount of moisture.

The Meaning of the Separation of Waters

According to the account of the creation of the Earth in the Book of *Genesis*, at one time the waters were all comingled together. Then they were divided:

> God said: "Let there be an expanse in the middle of the water to form a division between the waters," and it was so. God made the expanse, and it divided the water below it from the water above it.

The separation of the waters with half remaining on the surface of the Earth and half going into the upper atmosphere is also mentioned in the *Book of Jubilees*. One of the lost books of the Bible, Jubilees was originally written in Hebrew as an extensive retelling of Genesis and Exodus. It has been found in Greek, Syriac, Latin, and Ethiopic as well, however, the Ethiopic text is the only one that has survived in a form that is virtually complete. The *Book of Jubilees* makes it clear that as much moisture remained in the atmosphere as was found in the world oceans:

> And on the second day he made the firmament in the midst of the water. And the waters were divided on that day. One half of them went up above, and one half of them went down beneath the firmament.

Clearly, it is asserted that as much moisture was held in the sky, presumably as a dense cloud cover, as was contained in the seas below. Berossus in his history of Babylonia, relates that at the time of creation "the whole universe consisted of moisture," and that Zeus "separated Heaven and Earth from one another."

This condition was noted worldwide, for many ancient cultures speak of a time in the past when there was no sun as we know it today. In the *Popul Vuh*, the sacred book of the ancient Quiche Maya, it is expressed that there was a time when it was cloudy and twilight was upon the face of the Earth. There was no sun yet to be seen for "the sky and the Earth existed but the face of the sun and the moon were covered." The dense cloud cover or vapor canopy would mean that blue sky was not seen by the ancients until after the Deluge.

One of the oldest pieces of Sumerian mythology, if not the oldest, yet known seems to echo this description.

> The reptiles verily descend.
>
> The Earth is resplendent as a well-watered garden.
>
> At that time Enki and Eridu had not appeared.
>
> Daylight did not shine.
>
> Moonlight had not emerged.

A stable cloud canopy also meant that the Earth had to be watered by a different regime than it is today. The *Book of Genesis* bears this out when it states that God had not yet sent rain upon the Earth, and that instead water would well up from the ground.

It was not until the cloud cover collapsed with the event known as the Deluge that man saw sunlight and the blue sky. Verification of this is also found in Genesis which states that the Lord introduced the rainbow after the Deluge. Rainbows are the result of the prismatic effect of the bending of the rays of the sun through water droplets. Rainbows can only occur after rain and require the direct action of sunlight.

Desiccation of the Land

During this early period the climate was benign all over the world. The stable and moist atmosphere was ideal for the development of huge vegetarian dinosaurs and other large reptile forms. Had the climate remained the same, who knows what reptilian forms would have evolved. In their analysis of the reasons why dinosaurs and reptiles became extinct, Allaby and Lovelock in their book *The Great Extinction*, suggested that if the climate had remained unchanged until the present day there is no reason to suppose that the reptiles would have declined. Furthermore, they say that "Mammals might still be living in nocturnal obscurity and had intelligent beings evolved — let us say beings with advanced technologies — they might well have scaly skins and probably long tails."

Physical conditions, however, began to change dramatically. The land began to dry out. Since there was no cyclonic activity to produce rain, moisture had to be gotten from the ground or from spring-fed river systems. A limited amount of moisture was provided by the heavily saturated atmosphere which condensed at nightfall.

The changing climate was no longer friendly to the alien saurians. Mammals had become better adapted to the changes and were slowly replacing the reptiles as the dominant form on Earth. The lush vegetation was declining. The Anunna who lived off the abundant vegetation were beginning to suffer.

A Sumerian myth called *Dispute between Cattle and Grain*, describes how the children of An originally lived off the land:

They knew not the eating of bread,

Knew not the dressing of garments.

Ate plants with their mouth like sheep,

Drank water from the ditch.

Since conditions on Earth had changed and the Anunna could not feed themselves, the myth describes how two goddesses were created in the spaceship to help the Anunna obtain food — the cattle goddess Lahar, and the grain goddess Ashnan. According to the story, the goddess tried to teach the Anunna how to grow food but for some reason the experiment was a failure. This is why, the myth states further, that mankind was created.

The Anunna had been vegetarian but when food became scarce they turned to eating flesh. This is reflected in the Ethiopic *Apocalypse of Enoch,* which describes how the Nefilim began to eat the flesh of animals, all the time pleading the scarcity of vegetable food.

Both religious and secular sources indicate that early man and the serpent gods were vegetarian and not meat eaters. According to Genesis, man did not eat flesh until after the Deluge. This was not true of the Nefilim or Anunna who turned to eating the flesh of animals and eventually that of humans. The desiccation of the Earth may have been partially caused by numerous catastrophes which seemed to have plagued the antediluvian period. Earthquakes and other natural catastrophes are often alluded to in the religious literature and the Sumerian myths.

Earthquakes and Other Catastrophes

Earthquakes and other natural catastrophes were not unknown to early man for they are mentioned in many ancient sources, both religious and secular. The *Haggadah*, the source of Hebrew oral tradition, describes a period of calamities that occurred in the generation of Enosh, the second after Adam, when the Earth was beset by "four revolutions in nature," presumably a reference to major earthquakes, perhaps caused by a shift of the Earth on its axis.

Other ancient sources in the *Haggadah* reveal that, at this time, there were severe disruptions in the water supply — that "the mountains became barren," and so many people died that the corpses rotted where they lay and were not buried.

Such a shift would have an effect on the calendar, especially the length of the year. In the *Ethiopic Apocalypse of Enoch*, there are several admonitions to the people against errors in the compilation of the length of the year. Enoch tells Methuselah that "the year is completed in 364 days" and not to note this correction would upset all the order of the days of celebration. It would thus appear that, at least for a while, the length of the year was 364 instead of 365 days.

Even the Greek historian Herodotus, in his *Histories*, refers to ancient perturbations of the Earth. He was informed by the Egyptian priests at the ancient sacred city of Heliopolis that in the preceding 10,000 years, "the sun had been removed from its proper course four times." It seems that the axis of the Earth had been displaced four times, for the sun was said to have changed its usual position, twice rising in the west, and twice in the east.

Curiously enough, the statement of Herodotus agrees with the ancient religious sources which speak of four major disturbances during the days of Enosh. The sun's eccentric behavior is also found in the Hebrew oral tradition which affirms that in the period before the Deluge "the laws of nature were suspended, the sun rose in the west and set in the east." The Egyptians were aware of these changes for in the Old Kingdom there were two names for the sun, one that rose in the east, and the other that rose in the west. The century just before the Deluge must have had many natural catastrophes which were a forerunner of the major one to come — the Deluge.

The 120 Year Period of Genesis

There is a curious statement in Genesis 6 which immediately precedes the account of the Deluge that refers to a period of 120 years. For generations, scholars have interpreted the verse to mean that man was granted a lifespan of 120 years. In Genesis, El admonishes man that

> My spirit shall not abide in man forever, for he is flesh,
>
> but his days shall be one hundred and twenty years.

This interpretation as relating to man's lifespan seems odd in view of the fact that the text deals with God's intent to destroy mankind in the coming Deluge. Subsequent statements in Genesis do not support this figure as an arbitrary lifespan. After the Deluge, the descendants of Noah lived longer than the limit of 120 years.

Shem lived to be 600, his son Arphaxad to be 438, and his son Salah to be 433, and so on, down to Abraham who died at the age of 175. Isaac then lived to be 180, and Jacob 147, and it was not until generations later with Moses, who died at 120, that the so-called prophecy appeared to come true. Furthermore, since the days of Moses there has been a steady decline in man's lifespan until today when 80+ is considered to be the average.

Obviously, the statement in Genesis does not apply to lifespans but to something else, whose meaning was omitted during the early formative years of the

Old Testament. Moreover, the location of this fragment just before the account of the Deluge strongly suggests that it is related in some way to that universal catastrophe.

This relationship is brought out in many of the ancient religious documents. Ancient Rabbinical literature, for example, relates how Noah had been informed of the coming catastrophe 120 years before, and told to exhort the people to amend their ways. In other words, the 120 years was one of probation, when man was given the choice of avoiding destruction by changing his ways.

A similar warning is found in the Slavonic *Apocalypse of Enoch*, but here the information is passed on to Methuselah instead of Noah, who is told to warn the people to change their ways in view of the fact "that the destruction of the Earth draws near." Methuselah was also informed that the Earth "will change its seasons" in anticipation of the time of destruction. Apparently there would be severe disturbances caused by an Earth shift during this interim period of 120 years.

During the interim period, conditions on the Earth were unsettled and numerous disturbances anticipated the major destruction to come. The skies at the time must have been terrifying, for the solar system was playing a game of celestial ping-pong. The *Slavonic Apocalypse of Enoch* tells of a period of chaos just before the Deluge when society broke down and nations warred against each other. References to such unrest is not limited to the religious documents but is also found in the Sumerian cuneiform literature.

In the *Atrahasis Epic*, the Babylonian account of the Deluge, mankind was afflicted with plagues and other pestilence just before the disaster. Interruptions in the flow of waters from the mountains caused the Mesopotamian plain to become salty and unproductive. This reduction of fresh water allowed the Persian Gulf to back up the Tigris and Euphrates Rivers. As a result, the waters became brackish and,as the epic describes it,

> The fountains were stopped, so that the flood could not rise at the source. The field diminished its product . . . The wide-open plain brought forth salt; her bosom revolted, so that no plant came forth, no grain sprouted.

The Eden of the Bible had became a brackish, desolate plain. As the epic states, there was mass starvation, disease became rampant, and the survivors had to resort to cannibalism.

A dwindling food supply was not the only problem just before the Deluge, there was one of overpopulation as well. Using the genealogy of the *Book of Genesis* as a source of demographics, it can be shown that there was a high population density in that area.

Assuming 20 children per family, a very conservative figure considering the long life of the inhabitants and the system of polygamy, and counting on ten generations from Adam to Noah, the extraordinary total of over a billion people is deduced. While this number may be mathematically correct, logically it represents an impossible census for the number of people existing at the time of the onset of the Deluge. More likely, it suggests that there was an extremely high mortality rate among humans.

CHAPTER 13
WHEN WAS THE DELUGE?

The catastrophic event which resulted in the inundation of the Earth was so devastating that it is remembered in all the cultures of the world. For example, here in America the tale of the Great Flood, where all humans except a few were drowned in a great deluge, was recorded by all native peoples. Hultkrantz in his comprehensive survey in The *Religion of the American Indian*, states that the myth of the Great Flood is recorded in America from the Eskimos and Hare Indians in the north of North America to the Araucanians in the south of South America.

Of the world myths, the Judeo-Christian religion is probably unique for it places the blame directly on the nature of man. In the *Book of Genesis* the moral depravity of man is given as the reason for the Deluge.

> And God saw how corrupt the Earth was, for all flesh had corrupted their ways on Earth.

In the Sumerian epics, the catastrophe was brought on by the caprice of the gods. The *Epic of Gilgamesh* is silent on this point and merely states that it was decided by the gods in counsel. A more detailed explanation is provided by the fragmentary *Atrahasis Epic* where mankind is blamed for being noisy and depriving the gods of their rest:

> Enlil held a meeting. He said to the gods, his sons:
>
> "Because of their noise I am disturbed; because
>
> of their tumult I cannot get any sleep."

The epic continues to say that after punishing man with plagues and earthquakes, Enlil got angry and brought on the Great Flood.

The Collapse of the Water Canopy

The inundation which engulfed the Earth has been described in numerous sources. Probably the best known and most vivid description is contained in Genesis:

> "All the fountains of the great deep burst forth,
>
> And the sluices of the sky broke open."

In other words, the waters came from both the heavens and the ground. The Sumerian account seems to support this description. In the *Epic of Gilgamesh* "the underworld footings collapsed, the dikes gave way, and a tempest swept the land." In the works of the Pseudepigrapha it was prophesied that "the great storages of the waters of heaven will come down to Earth."

In the Hebrew oral tradition as recorded in the *Haggadah*, the cloud cover is given as the major source of water. These ancient Hebrew legends refer to the Deluge as a union of water from the firmament above with the water issuing from the Earth.

From these accounts, therefore, the dynamics of the catastrophe can be described as twofold. First, there was a heavy sustained downpour from the skies that lasted for weeks even months and, secondly, water from ground sources formed gigantic tidal waves which swept the lands.

Since a vast amount of water condensed from the skies, the question arises, e vapor canopy provide enough rain to engulf the world

ed that if the atmosphere was composed of pure moisture d, it would amount to no more than 30 feet of water, certself to inundate the Earth. However, the oceans of the 200 million cubic miles of water. The sudden movement enough to drown about three-quarters of the present surin some cases as deep as 30,000 feet. The tidal movements ss of water, in addition to the condensation of the cloud cover, would certainly provide enough water to drown even the largest continent.

Cosmic Causes of the Deluge

In addition to the inundation of falling rain and the sloshing of the oceans, water may have been added from outside sources. According to the theories of Velikovsky as enunciated in his landmark work *Worlds in Collision*, the Deluge was caused by the planet Saturn. Saturn, which is about a hundred times more massive than the Earth, had flared as a nova at that time. The planet expelled debris, some of which was absorbed by Jupiter, and some of which eventually encountered the Earth and other planets. He concluded that the Deluge was the result of this debris, consisting mainly of moisture which collapsed the Earth's vapor canopy, adding enormous amounts of water to the surface of the Earth, enough to raise the sea surface to its present level.

The "light of seven days" of which Isaiah (30:26) speaks of refers to the seven days just before the Deluge when the Earth was engulfed in brilliant light. The Sumerian legends verify this phenomenon for in the *Epic of Gilgamesh* it is recorded that just before the Deluge "the Anunna raised their torches, lighting up the land with their brightness." This bright light which was recorded both in secular and religious sources may have been caused by the planet Saturn.

In the Talmud, seven days before the Deluge, God changed the primeval order and the sun rose in the west and set in the east. In fact, ancient Hebrew had different words for this phenomenon: "Tevel" being the Hebrew name for the world in which the sun rose in the west, and "Arabot" the name of the sky where the rising point was in the east. The Egyptians also had different gods for the sun rising in the east and the west. Whatever the causes of the Deluge, there were astronomical events that affected the stars, our solar system, even the Earth itself.

The Pleiades and Destruction

The Pleiades received their name from Greek mythology who knew them as "The Seven Sisters." As recounted by Apollodorus, the seven daughters of Atlas and Pleine were pursued through the mountains of Greece by the giant Orion. The Seven Sisters, Maia, the mother of Mercury, Taygeta, Celaeon, Asterope, Alcyone, Electra, and Merope, appealed for help from Zeus who changed them into stars and placed them as a cluster in the sky. Although only six are visible today to the naked eye, all ancient myths refer to seven stars in the Pleiades.

Their significance to the Greeks is shown by the fact that all the temples of Athena were aligned to their rising in the fall. What is not commonly known is that the procession of the equinoxes, the great cycle by which the constellations do a full circle and lasts about 25,900 years, is also known as the "Great Year of the Pleiades."

The connection between the Pleiades and the cosmic cycle is also found

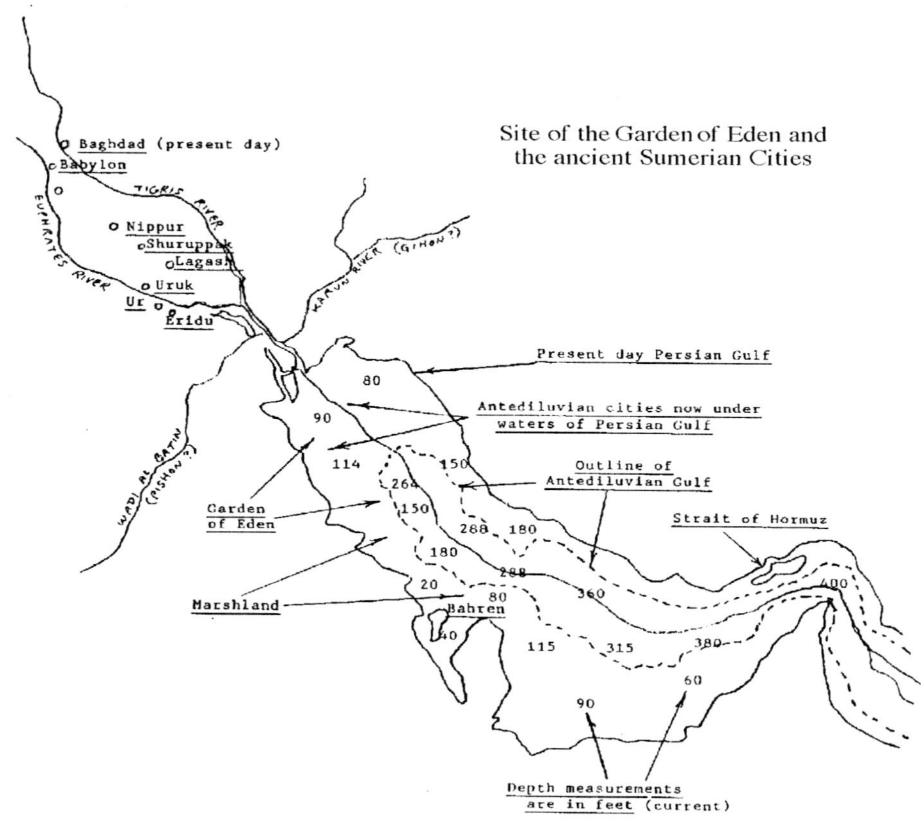

Fig. 39 – The Antediluvian Persian Gulf

elsewhere in the world. In Mexico and South America these stars have a sinister meaning. It was reported by Cortez, the 16th Century invader, that he had heard a native tradition that these stars were associated with death and destruction.

In Celtic practice in England the rising of the Pleiades in November marked the beginning of the festival of Samhain, known today as Halloween, where the dead arise from their graves and pass on into their permanent residence in the underworld. Among the Druids all fires were extinguished to allow the dead to leave and pass on. Bonfires were then lit to ritually end the period of danger. In the spring the festival of Beltane marked the setting of the ominous cluster of stars in May, marking the beginning of new life.

It has been calculated that at the time of the building of the Great Pyramid, the long narrow downward passage was directed towards the pole star of the Pyramid builders. The theosophist H.P. Blavatsky calculated that when Alcyone, the brightest star of the Pleiades, was directly over the apex of the pyramid, the Dragon Star or Alpha Draconis was perfectly aligned with this passageway. This reportedly occurred about 3340 BC. Others have calculated that the Pleiades is the center point of our Sun's orbit.

There are other strange references to the Pleiades in religious literature. The Pleiades seem to have some connection with "The Shadow of the Valley of Death" described in the 23rd Psalm. Rabbi Dobin in his remarkable study of the role of astrology in Jewish religion *The Astrological Secrets of the Hebrew Sages*, revealed that the famous 23rd Psalm is associated with the Pleiades. The reference herein of the "Valley of the Shadow of Death," has been associated by most scholars with a valley around Jerusalem. This explanation seems incomplete and not satisfactory, for the phrase also appears in Amos 5:8 where it is associated with the Pleiades:

> He who made the Pleiades and Orion, and brought on the Shadow of Death in the morning, and darkened the day into night, who calls for the waters of the sea and pours them out on the surface of the Earth; the Lord is His name.

It's clear here that the Pleiades and Orion are associated with catastrophic events that brought on darkness on Earth in the morning and turned day into night, at the same time causing the land to be flooded.

Evidence all over the world indicates that the sea level before the Deluge was much lower than it is today. Lower sea levels would mean that the old coastlines would be different. If the continental shelf had been the original coastline of the continents, world seas were then 150 to 200 feet lower than they are today. The shelf is of sedimentary origin, indicating that it had been the coastline for a very long time.

The water over the continental shelf of Eastern North America varies in depth to 600 feet; however, most of the area is about 200 feet deep. A drop in the sea level of 200 feet would expose most of the continental shelf. The same is true of the Persian Gulf, where a drop of 150 to 200 feet would uncover most of the land and leave a much smaller gulf, more like a large river in width (figure 39). Thus, the original Sumerian cities built in the antediluvian era would presently be under the adjacent waters of the Gulf.

In other words, cities now being excavated in Mesopotamia were built on virgin soil and not on the ruins of previous cities. Whatever the cause, it was significant enough in intensity to divide the history of mankind into two great periods. The antediluvian era is known as the time of the gods, the "golden age" in many mythologies. Much of what was achieved by man and god was washed away by the disaster.

The Date of the Deluge as About 4000 BC

There have been many attempts to date the catastrophe known worldwide as the Deluge or Great Flood, but so far none have proven to be generally acceptable. Since Sumer is considered to be the origin of Western Civilization, if not of all world culture, archaeological evidence in the Mesopotamian plain would seem to present the best evidence in establishing the date of the Deluge.

The consensus of Near Eastern archaeologists believe that Sumer was settled about 4000 BC. This figure is arrived at by starting with 2500 BC, an historical date that can be associated with known rulers, and adding 1500 years — a time span large enough to account for the stratographic accumulation of all the earlier cultural remains down to virgin soil. The Deluge had left the lands a vast swampy marsh broken up here and there by low islands of alluvial land built up by the gradual deposit of silt of the Tigris and Euphrates Rivers. As the *King List* states, the alien gods descended again after the Deluge to reestablish cities on the plains of Mesopotamia. These cities were presumably built on virgin soil.

If this theory is true, the cities of ancient Sumer should provide a true and consistent record of the origin of these cities as found in the layers of silt laid down by the Great Flood. Archaeologists have found that the silt layers are not consistent. Near the ancient city of Ur, archaeologists have dug down and found a layer of eight to eleven feet of clean silt between early and late settlements. At Shuruppak, a two foot layer was found — but for a later period. The strata of clean clay at Uruk was five feet deep, but again for a later period. It is evident that if these several strata are actually flood deposits they still do not represent one and the same inundations since they occur at different points in the stratographic sequence.

It would seem, therefore, that a common strata of virgin soil would have to be located deeper. Since Eridu was considered by the Sumerians to be the oldest city in the world and the first city rebuilt after the Deluge, excavations here should provide valuable evidence to the age of the Sumerian civilization.

Archaeologists digging at this site came upon a temple dedicated to Enki which appeared to have been rebuilt many times over. Digging deeper into the strata, excavators came upon a cross-section of the beginnings of Mesopotamian civilization.

At a stratus equivalent to 2500 BC, archaeologists found the rebuilt ruins of Enki's temple, then again at 3000 BC. Digging further they came upon the foundations of the first temple dedicated to Enki. It rested on virgin soil; nothing had been built here before. Time had been rolled back to circa 3800 BC. It is at this time that civilization began in Sumer. The date of the Deluge would then logically be sometime just before this date or approximately 4000 BC.

The origin of Sumerian culture at about this time has been confirmed by artifacts found at Uruk. The earliest known text in Mesopotamia was one found at the ruins of Uruk and is dated to about 3500 BC. It is a tablet with small pictures, or pictographs, undecipherable but of a type which preceded cuneiform writing. Allowing for several hundred years to drain and recover the plain and rebuild the cities, it also indicates a date of about 4000 BC for the Deluge.

The Deluge was a traumatic experience that left an indelible impression on mankind. It is remembered as a catastrophe that started a new era for mankind. Many cultures date their beginnings from this time. The Jewish calendar counts time from an enigmatic beginning in 3671 BC or "the years that have passed since the counting of years began."

In Egypt, the First Dynasty began about the middle of the Fourth Millennium BC, after a chaotic period of 350 years which separates the human kings from the semi-divine kings of the Archaic Period. Elsewhere, the Fourth Millennium is also marked as the beginning date from which time is reckoned, as for example, in Mesoamerica where the Olmec calendar begins in the year 3373 BC.

Chronology of Events After the Deluge

Only a few so-called absolute dates exist for Mesopotamia and Egypt and when these are examined closely they are not that absolute. The main anchor for Egyptian chronology is based on the rising of the star Sirius during the reign of Sesostris III of the 12th Dynasty. This astronomical event is identified as 1872 BC and from this date predecessors and successors were given "absolute" chronological identifications.

Anyone writing on the ancient Middle East is like a mountain climber tethered to a whole line of climbers, at the head of which he hopes there is someone with his pick firmly anchored in rock. Unfortunately, the fixed points provided even by astronomy are not all that firm, and from time to time whole chains of carefully calculated data slither down into oblivion.

On the other hand, dates derived from the Bible can be used to erect a

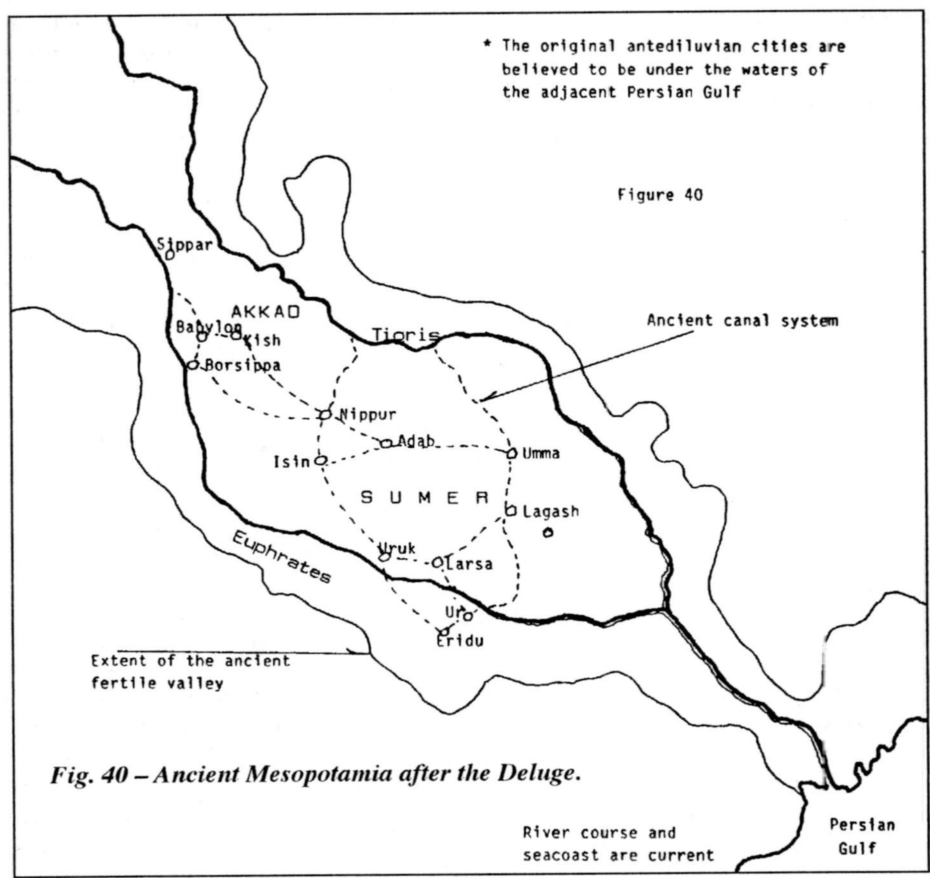

Fig. 40 – Ancient Mesopotamia after the Deluge.

chronology from Abraham to the Judean kings, a period of about a thousand years. However, there arises the problem that nowhere in this millennium do the events coincide with the traditional Egyptian chronology. It is as if the two civilizations lived side by side without any contact. Obviously, something is amiss in this scheme of things.

It can be shown, however, that dates derived from explicit information in the Old Testament can show that the early Judean kings existed at the same time as the 18th Dynasty and that the Exodus coincided with the fall of the Middle Kingdom in Egypt. This theory was developed in several books by Velikovsky — *Ramses II and his Time*, *Oedipus and Akhnaton*, and *Peoples of the Sea.*

Scholars agree that the key to establishing the time of events in Biblical times hinges on fixing the time of the Exodus. Many dates have been proposed but they either contradict explicit statements in the Old Testament or they do not fit in with knowledge of the Egyptian dynasties of the period. Basically, the problem is correlating the Exodus with current and subsequent events in Egypt.

At this point in our exposition, we must jump ahead in order to clarify the chronology of events which happened between 1500 and 1000 BC, since this sets a basis for timing events which happened between 4000 and 1500 BC.

The Date of The Exodus and Other Events

Scriptural evidence places Moses and the Exodus in the middle of the 15th

Century BC; other Biblical events occurring before and after the Exodus show the correctness of this date. A mid-15th Century date provides a sound benchmark to establish the time of events in the days of Abraham which relate to the destruction of Sodom and Gomorrah and the other cities of the Siddim Plain, to the expulsion of the Hyksos from Egypt and the supporting role of Saul and David, and to the identification of the Queen of Sheba as Queen Hatshepsut of the 18th Dynasty. The chronology of these biblical incidents can be corroborated by both Egyptian and Mesopotamian data.

In order to establish the date of the Exodus we must refer to the pertinent Biblical references. In I Kings 6 it is stated that the Exodus took place 480 years before the fourth year of Solomon's reign, when he began to build the Temple. This year would be 967 BC considering he ruled from 971 to 931 BC. The chronology may oscillate a few years due to the uncertainty of the end of Solomon's reign and the division of the kingdom. We have chosen a middle date.

If the temple was built in 967 BC, we arrive at 1447 BC as the date of the Exodus, that is, 967 plus 480 years. Since the sojourn in Egypt lasted 430 years according to Exodus 12, this would place the entrance of Jacob into Egypt in the year 1877 BC or 1447 plus 430 years.

An analysis of the information in Genesis suggests that the patriarchs were in Canaan for 215 years before entering Egypt. This figure is derived as follows: Abraham entered Canaan at the age of 75; Isaac was born to him at age 100; Isaac was 60 at Jacob's birth; Jacob was 130 when he stood before the Pharaoh. Thus 215 years (25 + 60 + 130 = 215) elapsed from Abraham's entrance into Canaan and Jacob's into Egypt. Adding the 215 years to 1877 BC we thus arrive at the date of 2092 BC as the time Abraham and Lot left Harran for the land of Canaan.

The establishment of the time of the reign of the Kings of Judah is also critical to any attempt to synchronize Israelite and Egyptian chronology. Saul is believed to have ruled from 1021 to 1011 BC. David reigned from 1011 to 971 BC, and Solomon from 971 to 931 BC. This provides us with a time scale for the period of over 1200 years which encompasses the birth of Abraham and the death of Solomon. A 15th Century date also fits in well with information found in the *Book of Judges*.

Evidence from the Period of The Judges

A date earlier or later than the mid-15th Century date for the Exodus would contradict information in Judges. For example, one of the later Judges was called Jephthah, who had to deal with a powerful Ammonite king who claimed the land of Transjordan which had been seized and occupied by the Israelites for many years.

The king wanted the land of his ancestors returned to him "because Israel seized my land, when they came up from Egypt." He warns, "return them now peaceably, and I will go." Jephthah then describes the route they took in the Exodus and how Sihon would not let them pass through his territory and attacked them, thus the Israelites captured the territory of the Amorite from Arnon to Jabbok and he added, "While Israel inhabited Heshbon and its dependencies, and Aroer and its dependencies, and all the cities on the banks of the Arnon, some *three hundred years*, why did you not liberate them within that time?" (emphasis ours).

Since Jephthah lived about 1100 BC, the event of the invasion of the Israelites must have been about 1400 BC, that is 1100 plus 300 years. The invasion of Transjordan occurred after the period of wandering, or 40 years from the departure from Egypt, and when totaled gives a figure in agreement with the proposed date of 1447 BC.

The *Book of Judges* also provides the reign of the various Judges between the death of Joshua and the rise of Saul as the first king. This information also tallies with a period of about 400 years for that of the Judges. In Judges 3 through 12, the reign of each Judge and intervening lawless periods starting with Othniel and ending with the rule of the Philistines is given as 350 years. Adding 350 years to the inauguration of the rule of Saul, we have 1021 BC plus 350 years, or 1371 BC. An additional 35 or 40 years of rule under Joshua should be added providing a date span of 1406 to 1411 BC as the year of the Israelite occupation. Adding 40 years to account for the wandering in the desert provides 1451 BC as the date of the Exodus, remarkably close to our suggested date.

CHAPTER 14
THE DRAGONS GO UNDERGROUND

The Fourth Millennium War in the Skies

The days immediately after the Deluge were those of struggle between the gods over control of the pantheon and the Earth as we have seen in the Myth of Zu. The battles probably took place in the Fourth Millennium BC soon after the Deluge when the land was resettled. By 2500 BC, most of the myths of the Sumerian gods had been well established in Mesopotamia. Except for the creation myths which deal with the antediluvian period, most of these stories involve activities of the younger gods, the ambitious children and grandchildren of Enlil. At this time, legends of dragons struggling in the sky took root and presumably, also the notion of dragons living underground and guarding valuable treasures.

The story of the descent of Ishtar to the underworld to try to seize the domain of her sister Ereshkigal, which resulted in Ishtar's captivity and ransom by her husband Dumuzi, must have happened soon after the Deluge for Dumuzi is listed in the *King List* as the first god-king to become the head of a city-state in Sumer.

Both mankind and the gods took refuge underground at this time for it was one of extreme danger from overhead combat of the gods, where fallout from mass destructive weapons made it unsafe to live on the surface of the Earth.

Cultures all over the world have legends of underground cities and of hidden gates which give their gods access to the underworld. This belief is reinforced by the discovery of a vast number of underground cities and tunnels, perhaps only a fraction of what really exists. Ancient Sumerian myths also refer to gates to the underworld at all the important cities of Mesopotamia, with the main gate being at Uruk, the most sacred of the Sumerian cities. Many world cultures trace their ancestors to gods and people who emerged from the ground after a major world catastrophe when the surface of the Earth was too dangerous to live on. For example, the Hopi Indians of southwestern United States believe that their ancestors, the Anasazi, emerged from the underworld to repopulate a devastated world. The places of "emergence" were sacred places called "kiva" and were round, domed, stone buildings half-submerged into the ground. These were the places of creation used by their ancient gods, the Kachinas. It is where the Anasazi contacted the gods. Many of these buildings still exist and are used for ceremonial purposes. In this respect it is curious to note that the term "kiva" has a strong Sumerian flavor to it for KI-VA has the same meaning in Sumerian. KI means "ground" or "underworld" and VA is the word for "mouth" or "entrance." The name Anasazi means the "ancient ones" in Hopi although the origin of the name is unknown. There is a striking similarity of the name Anasazi to Anunna (Sumerian) and Anunnaki (Semitic). These intriguing coincidences may only be the tip of the iceberg and suggests a common ancestry. It is a puzzle contemplating a solution.

Underground Cities in Palestine

The extent of the existence of underground cities is reflected in ancient rabbinical sources which state that Eden had seven gates, one of which was located at Hebron in Palestine, and another was said to be at Mount Zion in

Jerusalem. The ancient cities of Jericho and Beth-Shean (*shean* means serpent) are also suspected to have extensive tunnel systems. There are many reports which originated in the Middle Ages that state there are rooms and passages underneath the Dome of the Rock, the Islamic shrine in Jerusalem.

The ancient city of Beersheba, located south of Jerusalem and north of the semidesert area called the Negeb, has many underground rooms and tunnels dating back to the Fourth Millennium BC. Historically, this area which extends from the coast to the Dead Sea and the Arabah Valley, has been called the land of the serpent-people and was occupied by the Amalekites in the Third and Second Millennium.

In 1951, at 50 sites in the northern Negev and particularly near Beersheba, researchers found the ruins of numerous villages. These were not on the surface of the hills where one would normally expect them to be but instead they were completely underground. Running at a depth of 20 feet these tunnels form a network like an underground city. These cities have been dated to about 3000 BC.

Composed of large rectangular rooms connected by tunnels, and smaller rooms that were egg-shaped, people entered through vertical shafts sunk into the end rooms of each row. There are no fortifications in the area nor are there signs of military invasion and destruction. Why people would choose to live this way has been a puzzle to historians. It was certainly not for security from wild animals, for a simple stockade would suffice in that case. It could not be as a defense against marauding tribes for the residents could easily have been trapped underground. Apparently, it was something in the sky that was dangerous and lethal. The only logical conclusion is that they retreated underground for safety.

The Underground Complex in Turkey

In the plateau region of central Turkey in Cappadocia there was discovered in 1963 an astonishing underground city at Derinkuyu which is nearly two square miles in area. It was home to 20,000 people and had been here in the days of the Greeks and early Christians who had used it for refuge.

In his book *Distant Secrets*, Ronald Schiller describes how they extend 240 feet deep into volcanic rock and built on eight levels. There are 10 miles of tunnels branching off in all directions. Lining the passageways are hundreds of rooms comprising living quarters, storerooms, wine cellars and workshops.

Fig. 41 – Shamash as the god of measurements

From a stone tablet, circa 900 BC, found at Sippar at the temple of Shamash. Shamash was worshipped as the Sun God who daily traversed the skies and the "one from whom no secrets are hid," probably because his space craft surveyed all that went on below. Two horned gods hold divine cords which connect with the altar of Shamash below. The cords represent his connection or shuttle flights between heaven and earth. As the divine cordholder and space traveler it was said that he "measured the bounds of the Earth."

Fresh air is provided by ventilation shafts 9 feet in diameter, which rise 240 feet to the surface with openings at each level. They are so well engineered that the city maintains a constant 55 degrees Fahrenheit. There are 52 of these main shafts. Where several streets came together there are broad underground public squares. From archaeological evidence it is surmised that the topmost levels were occupied by early Christians, and before them some 2000 years earli-

er, the native Hittites. They too presumably inherited the underg
from a people who lived there sometime before 2500 BC.

Fresh water was plentiful and brought up from wells deep in t
original excavators of these cities were careful enough not to leave
rubble dug out of the rock which would have betrayed the existence of th
cities and, partly for this reason, they remained undiscovered for thousands of years.

Thirty-six additional cities have been located, one near Ozkonak was the home of 60,000 people. A similar city at Kaymakli was connected to it by a tunnel over 6 miles long. Altogether it is estimated that all these Anatolian cities could accommodate from a half to one million people underground. These cities are considered to be one of the greatest engineering achievements of antiquity.

The Caves in India and Tibet

The mountains of India and Tibet have long been associated with underground tunnels and cities reputedly created and inhabited by the serpent gods. According to the sacred tradition of the Hindus, in the Himalayas there are extensive caves and underground tunnels attributed to the legendary Nagas, the serpent people. Tradition states that they could fly around in magical machines. The underground cities were lit by magical "stones," and here the Nagas guarded fabulous treasures.

Andrew Tomas relates in his book *On The Shores of Endless Worlds*, that in his travels to the Himalayas, he had met with learned people who referred to underground crypts protected with "artificial fire." He relates of a visit to a holy man, a sadhu, who described a place called Naggar in the western Himalayas, a city which reportedly was the kingdom of the Nagas.

The mythology of India is rich with references to underground tunnels and cities. The Hindu classic *Vishnu-Purana* for example, speaks of Patala, the capital of the Nagas, where the snake-gods wandered about decorated with brilliant jewels and protected a vast trove of treasure and a library of lost lore about the antediluvian days.

Helen Blavatsky, the famous theosophist, spent three years in Tibet and Sikkim where she compiled together a large amount of Sanskrit writing called the *Book of Dzyan.* She reported stories of subterranean caverns with concealed entrances containing treasures and artifacts of the ancient sky gods. She described a land that was honeycombed with passages, with miles of tunnels, and secret chambers of all sizes.

Blavatsky described the Nagas or Sarpa which guarded the underground cities as semi-divine beings with a human face and the tail of a dragon. She equated the Sarpa, which means serpent, with the Seraphim of the Old Testament and in particular, that of Moses. The *Book of Dzyan* reveals that an ancient race of serpent men descended to Earth and founded the Fifth Race on Earth which gave birth to the present one.

The Sanskrit literature of India is replete with the struggle in the air between the Nagas and other ancient peoples. These accounts mention a city of the serpents called Bhagavata. It is an underground civilization, the abode of the serpent people, without sun, moon, nor stars, but lighted by the splendor of sun and moon stones.

Tunnels in South America

Another area of the world which has numerous legends of underground cities is South America. They are said to contain untold treasures guarded by ent men. In his *The Gold of The Gods*, Erich von Daniken reported of a twork of underground tunnels in Ecuador. The walls of these passages are polished and the corridors form perfect right angles, suggesting they were built by knowledgeable engineers. These long straight galleries extend through different strata of hard and soft rock with polished walls suggesting some form of device that melted the rock.

The engineering technology of this tunnel system is astounding. According to local legends of the Indians, the system of caves extends for hundreds of miles. Metal and stone tablets found inside the caves are covered with unknown hieroglyphics and many of these are on display at a museum in Cuenca, Ecuador.

Similar stories relate to Peru, to the ancient city of Cuzco which is said to have been founded by Urcaguay, a serpent god, and that tunnels underneath the Andes extend for miles as far as Tiahuanaco. This tunnel system is said to have been built by the people who built the megalith stonework of Machu Picchu.

The Underground World as Viewed by the Sumerians

To the ancient Sumerians the underworld was as extensive as the surface world. It was a vast region under the Earth honeycombed with abandoned mines, underground cities, and vast tunnel systems.

There were many terms used by the Sumerians to refer to the underworld but the most common was KI-GAL or the "Great Below." It was guarded by many gates as is seen in the case of Ishtar, who had to pass through seven gates to reach the center where her sister had a palace.

The netherworld was believed to be the huge cosmic space below the Earth corresponding roughly to heaven, the huge cosmic space above the Earth. It is perhaps why it was often called the KUR, a Sumerian term that seems to have several meanings. Specifically, it means a mountain or group of mountains. The term KUR was also used to describe an artificial mountain such as the E-KUR or "home that is a mountain." Perhaps due to the fact that the Earth was honeycombed with tunnels, abandoned mines, and underground cities it came to be called the great KUR or the great below. These underground chambers came to be used as shelters during the millennium after the Deluge, when it was dangerous to live on the surface.

The Sumerian view of the underworld was similar to the Egyptians, who also pictured it as a vast subterranean area where the dead prepared for their trip to the afterlife, as described in the *Book of the Dead.*

To the ancient Sumerians death was not conceived as the absolute end of life or as effecting the complete annihilation of conscious reality. Rather, it meant the separation of body and spirit, the decay of the former and the transfer of the latter from one mode of life or existence to another. While the body was laid to rest in the ground, the spirit descended to the underworld to sojourn there throughout eternity.

Through fear of the gods, through sacrifice, the building of a temple, the making of an image, or other deeds of piety, the hour of death could be postponed and life could be lengthened. There was an old saying in Sumer:

> "The fear of the gods begets favor;
> sacrifice increases life. He who fears
> the Anunna lengthens his days."

Not many humans achieved immortality, for it was rarely bestowed by the gods. In Mesopotamia, Utnapishtim (the Babylonian Noah) and his wife were granted immortality. The antediluvian king of Sippar, Enmeduramma, was lifted to heaven and it has been suggested that he was the Enoch of the Bible.

The netherworld was governed by divine regulations and rules, among which one of the most important seems to be that its denizens must be stark naked. Another rule, one which proved fatal to Dumuzi, the husband of Ishtar, is that once in the underworld no one, not even a deity, could reascend to the world above unless a substitute could be found to take his place.

Thus, in the Sumerian myth, to make sure that Ishtar would return with a suitable surrogate to take her place, several GALLA or mechanical men remained by her side while she was on the surface to make sure that she would obtain a suitable substitute.

Although the general feeling is that the netherworld was dark and dreary, this would seem to be true only of daytime; at night the sun brought light as it travelled through it, and on the 28th day of the month the sun was joined by the moon.

The deceased were not all treated alike. There was judgment of the dead by the Sun God Utu and the Moon God Nannar. Sumerians were convinced that life in the netherworld was but a dismal, wretched reflection of life on Earth, but this life could be alleviated somewhat according to how one served the gods on Earth. It was rite and ritual which played the predominant role in their religion. Since man was created for no other purpose than to serve the gods, to see to their needs and to feed them, it was obviously his major duty to perform this service in a manner pleasing and satisfactory to his masters.

Early man did not worship his gods. The ancients had no word for "worship." The gods were feared and served. Human sacrifices to the gods were performed; these were meant as meals and were not just symbolic offerings. Later the sacrifices were replaced with animals and much later they became mere ritual. The rites of human sacrifice are discussed below.

The Underworld as Described in the *Epic of Gilgamesh*

In Tablet VII of the *Epic of Gilgamesh* the underworld is described as follows by his companion Enkidu who had just returned from that dismal place:

> "The house of darkness, the house where one who goes in never out again, the road that, if you take it, one never comes back, the house that, if one lives there, one never sees light, the place where they live on dust, their food is mud. Their clothes are like bird's clothes, a garment of wings, and they see light, living in darkness, on the door a door-bolt, deeply settled dust."

Enkidu further describes how he saw the mighty kings of the past acting as servants, "waiting on tables filled with roast meats, serving baked goods, and filling glasses with water from cool steins."

There is no indication in Gilgamesh or elsewhere that the netherworld, to which all humans are sent at death, distinguishes between a place of punishment for evildoers and a place of happiness for the morally upright. The fate of humans differed in the netherworld, mainly due to the efforts of loved ones left on Earth who strove to maintain their remembrance, otherwise they would be like the downcast spirits in the story of Enkidu.

The Hebrew view of the underworld or *sheol* is very similar. The way one dies seems to make a difference and the actions of those left behind can ease the burden. It is also a very confused view of life after death.

The Hebrew Sheol

The common Hebrew designation for the place of the dead in the Old Testament is *sheol.* The etymology of this world is obscure despite many efforts to trace its roots to ancient Semitic Akkadian. It is possible that it is a borrowed word from the Sumerian since the Hebrew antecedents are in Mesopotamia and the Hebrew view of the underworld is very similar to theirs.

Sheol may be a carry-over from the Babylonian SHU-ILU, which means "the city or place of the gods." That it is occupied by the gods is indicated in the Old Testament when Saul consulted the oracle of Endor before his battle with the Philistines at Gilboa. In this instance the souls of the dead in sheol are actually called deities or "Elohim," such as in the statement "I see a god coming out of the Earth." (1 Samuel 28). In this respect the dead could be consulted by using divination methods.

The sheol of the Hebrews was very indistinct and nowhere is it described in any detail. It is the KUR or KIGAL of the Sumerians, in fact, the Biblical Sheol and the Hades of the Greeks are actually later counterparts of the Kur of the Sumerians.

When a dead man has been duly mourned, he was thought to have joined the honorable company of his ancestors in sheol where they lay fast asleep (Job 3:14). The souls of the dead, however, did not slumber but were credited with powers of thought. They could be consulted by divination as they were in 1 Samuel 28. Unless buried among his ancestors, a dead man was banished to an unknown part of Sheol and denied proper worship. Hence Jacob and Joseph's repetitive demands for burial in Canaan.

Sheol was considered to be outside of God's jurisdiction as indicated by Psalms 88:5 and Isaiah 38:18. The notion that God controlled Sheol does not occur until about the Fifth Century BC. Sheol came to be treated as Purgatory, where souls await the Last Judgment. This is still the Orthodox Jewish and the Catholic belief.

The idea of a fiery hell was added later by the Christian church. The place of the righteous became known as Paradise and the place of punishment was first called Gehinnom or Gehenna, probably taking its name from the Valley of Hennom near Jerusalem, where human sacrifices were made to the local gods.

Gehinnom came to be described in the early Christian Church as an enormous realm in the depth of the Earth where the souls of the wicked were punished in flames and gnawed by worms and serpents. After the Third Century AD, hell became the ultimate fear of every Christian and the terror of damnation forever in hell shaped medieval Christianity. Abetted by a monolithic church which reserved for itself the secret of redemption, its subjects had no choice but to submit to its authority in order to keep out of hell after death.

One of the ways to appease the gods and make "bonus points" for eternity was by human sacrifice. Before the Deluge, human sacrifice was not only common but demanded by the gods. Human sacrifice continued for some time after the Deluge and seems to have ceased as a deliberate ritual about the time of the aborted sacrifice of Isaac by his father Abraham. Animals replaced humans and this change is clearly described in the books dealing with the Exodus, where the "burnt offering" can been seen as an obvious cooked meal for the resident deity.

CHAPTER 15

THE CREATION OF ADAM: THE REPTILE-MAN

Where Was the Garden of Eden?

The location of the Garden of Eden is provided by Genesis 2 which specifically states that it is at the confluence of four rivers which join together to run through the Garden of Eden:

> A river rises in Eden to water the garden; outside it forms four separate branch streams. The name of the first is Pishon: it is the one which winds through the whole land of Havilah . . . The name of the second river is Gihon: it is the one that winds through the whole land of Cush. The name of the third river is Tigris: it is the one that flows east of Asshur. The fourth river is the Euphrates."

Of the four rivers mentioned two offer no problems since they are the Tigris and Euphrates which still water the lands of Mesopotamia and empty into the Persian Gulf. The Pishon and Gihon have presented difficult problems to most scholars, since they seem to have disappeared, or at least, dried up or lost their status as major tributaries.

The text states that the Pishon "winds through the whole land of Havilah." But where is Havilah? According to Genesis 25, when Ishmael died his relatives came from all over the area from as far as Havilah, "which is close to Egypt," to Asshur in Mesopotamia. Therefore for the location of Pishon we must look to the area adjacent to Mesopotamia to the west, that is, Arabia.

In northern Arabia a large river once flowed northeastward toward the Persian Gulf. Now called the Wadi al Batin, it runs along the northern border of Kuwait and flows into the Euphrates at what is now Abadan. At one time it drained all of northern Arabia.

The river Gihon "that winds through the whole land of Cush" is also a problem. Cush is usually equated with Ethiopia, an error in the King James version of the Bible and promulgated since as a correct identification. However, the Hebrew word for Cush or Kush should be correctly written as Kashshu, according to Speiser in his study of Genesis. Kashshu refers to the Kashites (Kassites) which conquered Mesopotamia about 1500 BC and prevailed for 500 years. These hordes came down from the surrounding Zagros mountains. The Gihon river may be the Karum River which today flows into the Euphrates River near Abadan. Until it was dammed, contributed most of the sediment forming the delta at the head of the Persian Gulf.

There are other bothersome difficulties to be resolved with placing the geographic location of Eden in Mesopotamia since there are references in the Old Testament to people being banned "east of Eden," which would place them in the Zagros Mountains.

After eating the forbidden fruit, Adam and Eve were banned from the garden, presumably by the east gate, for Genesis says,

> Having expelled the man, he stationed
>
> east of the Garden of Eden the cherubim

and the fiery revolving sword,

to guard the way to the tree of life.

After the murder of Abel, Cain was also banned to the east to "the land of Nod, east of Eden." This "east gate" was also the one that Gilgamesh entered in his trip to the "land of the gods" (see chapter 20).

When, according to the *King List,* the Anunna came to the planet Earth about 241,000 years before the Deluge and colonized the delta of Mesopotamia, they called this area E-DIN or "the Land of the Gods or Righteous Ones." The EDIN of the Anunna was destroyed in the Deluge and for reasons of security and practicability the "Land of the Gods" was moved to the land of Lebanon.

This mountainous land could only be entered from the north or the south and one entrance through the mountains, an east entrance which is used today and faces Damascus. It is through this east gate that Adam and Eve were ejected and guarded by the cherubim with the revolving sword. It was also here that Gilgamesh met the guards with "the stinging weapons" which at first prevented him from entering the "land of immortality," but let him through after recognizing his semi-divine appearance. This gate faces Damascus the oldest continually occupied city in the world. It has for centuries claimed to have been settled by Adam and Eve after they were expelled from the Garden of Eden.

The Denizens of Eden

According to Jubilees, Adam was placed in the Garden of Eden to till and reap it. "He protected the garden from birds, and beasts, and cattle, and gathered fruit and food." The duties of Adam are described in similar terms in one of the Babylonian versions of the creation of man: It was his duty to maintain the canals and water courses and to raise plants in abundance in order to fill the granaries of the Anunna.

At that time Adam was to eat only the green things of the field. The prohibition against the use of animals for food was revoked in Noah's time after the Deluge. According to certain sources in the *Haggadah,* Adam was not completely cut off from the enjoyment of meat dishes. Though he was not permitted to slaughter animals, the angels brought him meat and wine on occasion.

He cohabited the garden with these "angels" or serpent-gods until the event known cryptically as the Fall of Man. As the *Haggadah* states, the serpent in the garden was a noble creature. These serpent-gods or Anunna were tall, two-legged, intelligent reptile forms. Like man he stood upright upon two feet and in height he was equal to the camel. It was his superior mental gifts that caused him to become an infidel. He did all the work in the garden before the advent of man and and as Genesis says, "he supplied Elohim with silver, gold, gems, and pearls."

It is noteworthy that serpents were present in all gardens of delight. For example, Greek myth refers to the Garden of the Hesperides, a veritable "eden" where apple trees bore golden fruit. It too was guarded by a serpent, the serpent Ladon, who was eventually slain by Heracles.

The Decision to Create a Work Force

In the epics of Mesopotamia, man's creation was secondary and even incidental to the creation of the universe and to the colonization of this planet by the alien visitors. After the astronauts had landed, the recovery of the swamps and the building of the cities commenced under the leadership of Enki. All the cities built had a specific purpose, seemingly to support the mining operations which culminated in the metal processing center at Badtibira. The building of the cities, the constant repairing and rebuilding of the canals and dikes, the mining operations — all these required considerable effort on the part of the sons of An. The working gods became rebellious, refusing to do the laborious work. On the advice of Enki, the gods decided to create a worker.

It is with this background that man arrives upon the scene. Man's creation was conceived and executed not as an end in itself or as a natural development of the civilization of Mesopotamia. Rather, man was created as an expedient to satisfy a group of discontented aliens. Man's purpose was to serve the gods; he was made to ease the burden of the gods and to assume the laborious and distasteful tasks being performed by the increasingly unhappy Anunna. Man was meant to be the breadwinner, the laborer, and the caretaker of the gods.

Early Failures to Fashion a Creature

The difficulties of the Anunna did not go unheeded by the gods in the orbiting spaceship. Earlier vegetation was so luxuriant that the serpent gods did not have to produce much of their food for they literally lived off the land. With the environment changing and become drier, the lush vegetation disappeared (along with the vegetarian dinosaurs).

One of the Sumerian myths, *The Dispute Between Cattle and Grain,* describes the early attempts to ease the suffering of the Anunna. As the poem relates, the sons of An did not know how to grow grain, to bake bread, nor to make garments. They ate plants from the field like the animals and drank water from the ditch. As long as vegetation was abundant they had no problem feeding themselves, but as the climate began to dry out and their numbers increased they had to look to other means of gaining sustenance. It was necessary to grow their own food. But the gods lacked the skills that were needed to grow food and raise animals.

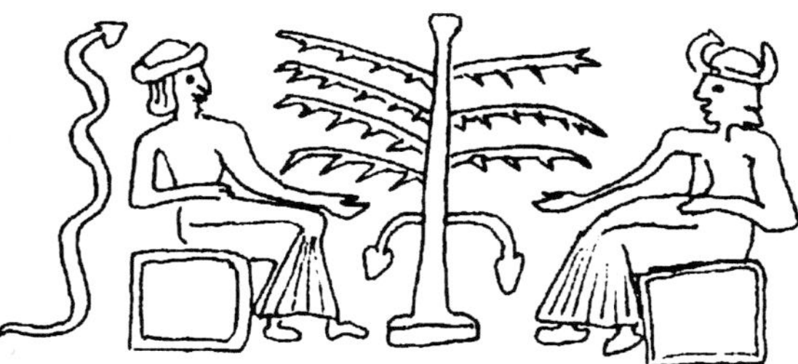

Fig. 42 – Babylonian tradition of the creation of Man

Babylonian cylinder seal depicting the creation of mankind. The tree of life is flanked by modern man on the left and the creator god (Enki) on the rights. Note symbolism of the serpent at the left.

It was decided to create two goddesses in the "Creation Chamber" of the gods, presumably in the orbiting ship, to teach the Anunna how to grow food and raise animals — these were Lahar, the Cattle Goddess, and Ashnan, the Grain Goddess. These goddesses tried to teach the Anunna the arts of agriculture and animal husbandry, but with no success. Then realizing that this experiment was a failure, the gods in council decided to take a drastic step — to create a primitive worker. The Chief God An informed the gods in assembly:

> I will produce a lowly primitive;
> Man shall be his name.
> I will create a Primitive Worker;
> He will be charged with the service of the gods,
> that they might have their ease.

Since the previous experiment in the laboratories of the spaceship did not turn out successfully, it was decided to commission Enki, working with the Chief Nurse Ninhursag, to produce a primitive being. This creation, called a *lulu* by the Anunna, was to be the first primitive man.

Enki and Ninhursag conducted a number of experiments in the Abzu, Enki's floating laboratory near Eridu, all aimed at the creation of a primitive worker. There were many attempts which ended in failure for one reason or the other.

Ninhursag fashioned six different types of abnormal individuals from clay. These were a failure and of these, the last two types are described as a barren woman and a sexless creature. Ninhursag made a woman who could not give birth. Then she made one with no male organ and no female organ. After these six failures Enki decided to do some creating of his own. His creature was also a failure, weak and feeble in body and spirit. Ninhursag tried to help the creature but to no avail. She talked to him but he failed to answer. She gave him bread to eat but he did not reach for it. He could neither sit, not stand, nor bend his knees. These attempts at producing a primitive worker were a total failure.

Successful Creation of the Ape-man Reptile Hybrid

At first, there was much trial and error. Finally a successful method was found. Using a group of primitive female animals, presumably the ape-women, the eggs were fertilized by young astronauts, then extracted and reimplanted in the wombs of the 14 so-called birth goddesses. Apparently, the young gods died in the process according to one of the creation epics:

> Let us slay two Lamba gods.
>
> With their blood let us create mankind.

In another version of the *Atrahasis Epic*, "fourteen wombs were gathered together," impregnated with the "essence" of the gods, and as a result, seven male and seven females were created. While successful in producing a viable primitive being, the process had one main drawback — subsequent events revealed that the creatures were clones and could not reproduce themselves. The fact that both sexes were produced, seven males and seven females, would suggest that the intent had been to make them capable of reproduction, but for some unknown biological reason they failed at this.

In this manner, primitive man or Adam was created — a combination mammal-reptile hybrid. The procedure used by the Sumerians is reflected in Genesis where it states that the image of God was imposed on the "clay," the basic genetic material mentioned in the Sumerian tablets. God's essence is mixed with the malleable clay of the Earth, the ape-man. In the Sumerian tablets, the clay is mixed with the essence of the gods and upon this creation they "impressed upon it the image of the gods." In both cases, man is created in the image of God.

The question arises, therefore, where did this genetic material come from that produced the mammal characteristics for a hybrid? Neanderthal Man, the most evolved form of ape-man had been on the scene for hundreds of thousands of years as a result of a slow process of evolution. It was presumably this ape-man that was used in the experiments of the Anunna. This ape-man is described in the *Epic of Gilgamesh* as the wild man who is "converted" into a civilized being to later become the companion of Gilgamesh in his many adventures.

Called Enkidu, he is a wild creature that feeds on grass and lives among the animals. As a friend to the animals, he saves them from the traps of the hunters. In the epic, an unhappy hunter complains to Gilgamesh who is then king of the city of Uruk. Gilgamesh is told that this creature wears no clothes and his body is covered with hair. He is intelligent enough to fill in the pits which the hunter had dug to catch wild animals. He also frees the game from the traps, lives with the animals, runs with the gazelles, and shares their drinking places.

The Adam of the Bible was not the Homo sapiens of today. He was what one might call Homo-saurus, a hybrid mammal-reptile creature that was to become our ancestor and the first step in the creation of modern man. In just a few years, man had taken a quantum jump in evolution. He had suddenly evolved from ape-man to a hybrid that would become modern man or Cro-Magnon Man.

Man Created in the Image of the Reptile God

The *Book of Genesis* makes it abundantly clear that man was originally created in the image of his God:

> And God created man in his image:
>
> In the divine image created he him,
>
> Male and Female created he them.

Since the Adam of Genesis and the "lulu" of the Sumerians were created in the image of the serpent-god, shouldn't traces of this fact be found in some of the ancient scriptures? Indeed, it is reported in the Gnostic version of the creation of man. One tract describes Eve's reaction in the Garden of Eden:

> She looked at the tree. And she saw that it was beautiful and magnificent, and she desired it. She took some of its fruit and ate, and she gave to her husband also, and he ate too. Then their minds opened. For when they ate, the light of knowledge shone for them. When they put on shame, they knew that they were naked with regard to knowledge. When they sobered up, they saw that they were naked, and they became enamored of one another. *When they saw their makers, they loathed them since they were beastly forms. They understood very much* (emphasis added).

The hybrid that was created probably looked reptilian since he was created "in the image of God." Genesis is very specific about this, for it states "then God said 'I will make man in my image, after my likeness." Adam was thus created in both the image or *selem* and likeness or *dmut* of his creator. The use of both terms in the Biblical text was meant to leave no doubt that man was similar to the gods in appearance. It is this likeness, or lack of it as we shall see, that is at the root of many of the admonitions of the Bible and the Sumerian literature.

An interesting source in the Genesis Rabbah, a *Midrash* account of Genesis and compiled in the Fifth Century in Palestine, states that Eve was not created from Adam's rib but rather from his tail, which had been part of his body. God cut this off and the stump, now a useless coccyx, is still carried by Adam's descendants.

It is interesting to note here that before the name of each of the hybrids, the Sumerians placed the sign for "deity," that is, the *dingir,* which means that the first ancestors of mankind were regarded as being divine at least to some degree. The reason for this conception lies, of course, in the fact that they were created with divine blood which was mixed with clay. Through biological manipulation, the Anunna or Nefilim took an existing ape-man and gave it part of their divinity,

Fig. 43 – Impression from cylinder seals of serpent-gods.

their saurian blood. Some of the scriptures confirm the fact that biological experiments were conducted on Earth and that some of these got out of hand. These experiments seem to have been done routinely by the Nefilim, who not only possessed advanced technical means in transportation and communication, but in the biological sciences as well.

In the Ethiopic *Apocalypse of Enoch*, the crimes of the Nefilim on Earth before the Deluge are disclosed in detail. The Nefilim had been given the mission of bringing the beneficial arts and crafts to mankind. But what started out as a laudatory endeavor to help mankind, soon turned sour.

The Nefilim began to teach man the martial arts, the "making of swords and knives, shields, and breastplates." They also taught man the forbidden sciences of "incantation, alchemy, and astrology." Implicitly this would include various chemical and biological sciences. But the worst of the crimes they were accused of was that of toying with genetics, that of "changing man into a horse or mule, or vice versa, or transferring an embryo from one womb to another." This practice of reimplanting an embryo into another womb is quite similar to the activities described in the *Atrahasis Epic*, wherein 14 clones were created. It appears that the Nefilim or Anunna were well acquainted with the biological sciences associated with genetic manipulation and selective breeding.

Homo-Saurus, the Primitive Man of Eden

Genesis makes the point repeatedly that before the Fall, man was naked while he occupied the Garden of Eden. It was not until he ate of the forbidden fruit that he realized that he was naked and put on clothing. Other ancient religious sources support man's nakedness, but they also reveal the reason why he was naked. According to a source in the *Haggadah*, the bodies of Adam and Eve "had been overlaid with a horny skin." This skin "was as bright as daylight and covered his body like a luminous garment." It is an apt description of a reptilian skin or hide. It was for this reason that Adam did not wear nor did he need clothing for protection or for comfort.

The *Book of Genesis* also makes it clear that Adam did not sweat in the Garden of Eden before the Fall. That was his punishment for eating the forbidden fruit, for he was told "by the sweat of your face shall you earn your bread." Adam did not sweat before the Fall for the simple reason that sweating is characteristic of mammals and not reptiles.

As long as they remained in the Garden of Eden, Adam and Eve did not propagate. The Sumerian tablets explain why — because they were "mules" and could not reproduce their own kind. The incident which the Bible refers to as the "Fall of Man" was his acquiring the ability to procreate by taking on many of the traits of mammals. It is explicit in Eve's punishment that she is to bear the pangs of live birth like a mammal.

Thus a fitting description of Adam and Eve and their creators would be as follows:

- They had a scaly or horny skin or hide;
- This hide was shiny and luminous as is seen today in some reptiles;
- They did not sweat which is the province of mammals;
- They did not wear clothes since they were unnecessary;
- They had a pale green skin or hide.

The evidence for the color of their skin is found in the *Haggadah* which describes how Adam was created from dust taken from the four corners of the world. "The dust was of various colors — red, black, white, and green. Red was for the blood, black for the bowels, white for the bones, and green for the pale skin." Had Adam been a homo sapiens, the color of dust used for the skin would presumably have been pink or brown.

Homo-saurus or reptile-man was probably much larger and taller than modern man. Many of the ancient sources refer to his being a giant before the incident of the Garden of Eden. For example, Rabbinical records disclose that "Adam, who had been a giant, diminished in stature to the size of an ordinary man."

The antediluvian Patriarchs and the Sumerian kings, who were part saurian, were apparently very large men and stood out physically among the hordes of mankind. The Rephaim, the descendants of the Nefilim who existed after the Deluge, were also giants, and like the antediluvians their span of life seems to have diminished as the saurian blood became more and more diluted with time.

CHAPTER 16

THE "FALL OF MAN" OR THE CREATION OF HOMO-SAPIENS

Man Acquires "Knowledge" or the Ability to Reproduce

After a primitive man was created — a hybrid between the native ape-man and the alien reptile-god — the Anunna were still without an ample work force for the simple reason that the Homo-saurus were clones and could not reproduce themselves. Each had to be created by a biological process in the laboratory.

Realizing that the only solution to the labor problems was to modify the Homo-saurus, Enki gave this creature dominating mammalian traits and thus produced the first Homo sapiens. The Adam proved to be a successful experiment, in fact, so successful that by the time of the Deluge he had multiplied so prolifically that his numbers began to cause innumerable problems on Earth.

The Sumerian stories do not describe the biological process by which man was changed from a dominant reptilian type to a modern Homo sapiens. The change, however, is provided by numerous religious sources which were undoubtedly derived from Sumerian sources. They survived in the religious literature probably because of the enmity of Enlil to this new creature. The demotion of Ninhursag at the time was probably due to her role in the biological change.

Religious sources describe the major changes taking place in the appearance and physiology of Adam and Eve after they partook of the forbidden fruit in the garden. The major and most apparent change was their loss of the smooth, shiny reptilian hide which is described as their "cloud of glory."

The event which Biblical scholars refer to as the "Fall of Man" begins with Adam and Eve, who have been placed in the garden by the deity to till and to tend it. Among the many delightful things to eat were the fruit from the two trees in the middle of the garden: "the *tree of life* and the *tree of knowledge* of good and bad." Adam and Eve are told explicitly by the deity that:

> You are free to eat of any tree of the garden, except only the tree of knowledge of good and bad, of which you are not to eat. For the moment you eat it, you shall be doomed to death.

They were free to partake of the fruit of the "tree of life," that is, the tree of immortality. In other words, Adam and Eve were immortal while they lived in the Garden of Eden. Only the fruit of the tree of knowledge was forbidden. Exactly what was meant by this "knowledge" that was so important for them not to touch?

According to the Biblical scholar Spieser, in his translation and study of the *Book of Genesis*, the Hebrew stem *YD* that is used throughout Genesis signifies not only "to know" but more specifically "to experience." As applied to connubial relations the stem *YD* means to know sexually, that is, to have sexual relations. In fact, it is applied not only to normal marital relations but also to clandestine conduct, even to homosexuality and to sex among animals. It is not a matter of delicate usage, as is sometimes alleged; nor is it confined to Hebrew. Akkadian as used in Mesopotamia, for example, extends it to dogs. To know Biblically is to know sexually, that is, to have sexual intercourse.

By achieving "knowledge" man acquired some sort of sexual fortitude or prowess. The knowing that was withheld from man was of a profound and serious nature. It was something good for man, but something which the creators did not want him to have. As long as Adam and Eve lacked it, they lived in the Garden of Eden without offspring. Having obtained it Eve was condemned to suffer the pangs of childbirth. The tale of Adam and Eve is the story of a crucial step in man's evolution: the acquiring of the ability to procreate like a mammal. In achieving this, however, man had to forfeit some of his saurian heritage, his so-called divinity.

Man Becomes Naked and Loses his Reptilian Appearance

The scriptures add laconically that before they ate the forbidden fruit "the two of them were naked, the man and his wife, yet they felt no shame." Later, when they ate of the fruit, the immediate and only result was that "then the eyes of both were opened and they discovered that they were naked."

One wonders why there is all this emphasis on nakedness. It is as if the expulsion of Adam and Eve from the garden was a dramatic way to explain how mankind came to wear clothes. It is obvious that the wearing of clothes was merely a manifestation of something else — the acquisition of "knowing" or knowledge. Perhaps it was because Adam and Eve had the skin and hide of a reptile, and did not need clothes to keep warm or for protection.

An ancient source in the *Haggadah* relates how Adam and Eve lost their reptilian skin or hide. The first result was that Adam and Eve became naked.

> Before their bodies had been *overlaid with a horny skin, and enveloped with the cloud of glory*. No sooner had they violated the command given them that *the cloud of glory and the horny skin dropped from them*, and they stood there in their nakedness, and ashamed (emphasis ours).

It is clear here that their nakedness had to do with losing their "horny skin" and their "cloud of glory." Similar descriptions are found in the old Rabbinical legends. Describing man before the Fall, it was said that "his skin was as bright as daylight and covered his body like a luminous garment."

This luminous and bright skin or hide was their "cloud of glory." Other legends state that the change brought about by the Fall was that "the brightness of his skin, which had covered him like a garment, disappeared." This emphasis on the strange appearance of the outer skin of Adam and Eve was apparently generally accepted by the early rabbis. For example, in a *Midrash* account by Rabbi Eliezer ben Hyrcanos, a Palestinian sage of the First Century, he describes the skin being as smooth as the cuticle of a fingernail.

> Adam wondered at Eve's nakedness, because her glorious outer skin, a sheet of light smooth as a fingernail, had fallen away. He tasted the fruit and the outer skin of light fell away from him also.

The nakedness that is emphasized so much in the ancient documents is related to a protective outer skin that was luminous and shining. Man's nakedness was in losing his protective horny hide or skin, that is, his divine appearance. Henceforth, man would have to wear clothing to protect his vulnerable mammal skin. Man would now begin to sweat as a mammal, a physiological function not intrinsic to reptiles.

Now that man required clothing for protection against the elements, an apparent sympathetic deity "made shirts of skins for the man and his wife, and clothed them." This generous deity, however, probably had other reasons in mind, for as the *Haggadah* reveals, the clothes were made of skins sloughed off by the serpents. Was this done to remind man of his serpent origins? It was an ironic way of impressing on man's memory that he originated as a saurian and that he existed at the tolerance of the gods. This theme reoccurs time and time again in man's later relations with the saurian gods and was formalized in the ritual of circumcision.

Genesis sketchily describes the physiological changes that resulted from the punishment of Adam and Eve. As their chastisement, Eve will have to suffer the pangs of child-bearing while Adam will have to earn his bread by the sweat of his brow. Logically, it would appear that heretofore Eve did not produce live offspring, nor did Adam sweat. Sweating is the province of mammals; Adam and Eve did not sweat before the Fall for the simple reason that they were basically reptilian.

Man Forfeits Immortality and Long Life to Become a Mammal

Man had access to the tree of life or immortality since it was not forbidden to him, in other words at that time he was immortal. Now that he had achieved the ability to procreate, the deity worried that he could also partake of the tree of life and attain immortality, as Genesis states:

> "What if he should stretch out his hand and take also from the tree of life and eat, and live forever." So the Lord God banished him from the Garden of Eden, to till the soil from which he was taken. He drove the man out, and stationed east of the Garden of Eden the cherubim and the fiery ever-turning sword, to guard the way to the tree of life.

According to the scriptures there was no turning back for man. He had taken the decisive step and achieved "knowing" or sexual knowledge and could procreate and now start the mammal race known as mankind or Homo sapiens. In obtaining this mixed blessing, however, he had to give up long life or immortality. The two were apparently mutually exclusive. Man could have retained his divine reptilian form and long life but remain a mule at best, a limited homo-saurus.

In terms of evolution, modern man appeared on the scene about 40,000 years ago as if by magic. Cro-Magnon Man was not an ape-man and so different from the form it replaced, Neanderthal Man,as to require a quantum jump in the process of evolution. One has only to see the skulls of the ape-man (Homo-erectus) and his successor Homo sapiens to realize that in terms of evolution it would have taken millions of years for the change to take place (figure 44).

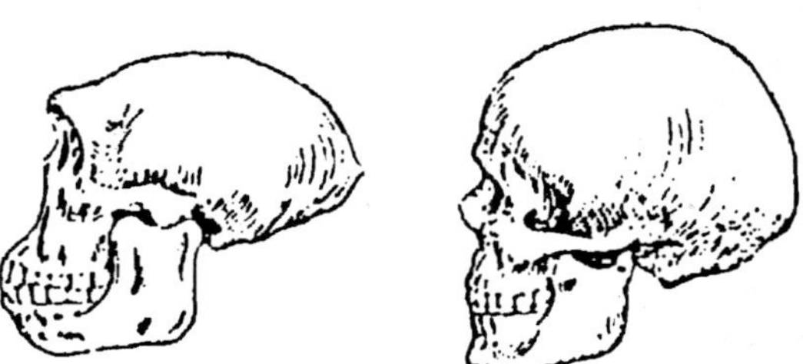

Fig. 44 – Contrasting skulls of Man

Left: Homo erectus skull (Neanderthal Man). To the right is skull of Homo sapiens (Cro-Magnon Man). Traditional evolutionists would have us believe that they are the same species that changed overnight in evolutionary terms. One is definitely an apeman.

It is the perplexing problem of the "missing link" that has puzzled evolutionists for over a hundred years. Is it possible that the so-called missing link will never be found? And, more important-

Fig. 45 – The food and water of immortality.

Two winged gods depicted as birdmen with the cone and situla of immortality. They flank a stylized tree of life. Shamash and his pilots were often depicted as eagles.

ly, if this missing link is ever discovered, it will most likely be in the ruins of the ancient civilization of the valley of Mesopotamia.

The sad story is that man could not have the best of two possible worlds, mammal form and long life. It explains why man's lifespan shortened steadily as each generation diluted the saurian gene more and more. The gods were unhappy with the ensuing changes and would not let man forget in the years to come of his choice. It echoes throughout the chapters of the Old Testament as "the weakness of the flesh." To them the reptile form was "divine" and the further man evolved from his saurian origins the less he remembered his saurian origins.

Achieving immortality or long life was a favorite topic in Sumerian myths and often reflected in their murals and on their clay cylinder seals. The gods are sometime shown with a pine cone in one hand, and a *situla* or water bucket in the other hand, representing the food and water of eternal life or immortality (figures 45 and 46).

The Story of Creation as Reflected in the Tale of Adapa

While no Sumerian myth has been found thus far that closely parallels the Fall of Man as related in the Old Testament, there is one poem which tells a story that is probably the source of the account in Genesis. The *Tale of Adapa*, as it is called, was found in the archives of Egyptian kings at El-Amarna, as well as in the library of the Assyrian King Ashurbanipal. Ostensibly, it was universally known in ancient days. Its main theme, like that of the *Epic of Gilgamesh* is man's squandering an opportunity for gaining immortality. It also provides the theme of the serpent warning Eve that God had deceived her about the properties of the forbidden fruit.

Fig. 46 – Eagle-like astronauts in antiquity.

From frieze in palace of Assurnasupial II at Nimrod, showing winged gods with food and water of immortality.

Adapa was a model specimen of the Homo sapiens created by Enki in the Abzu. Like the Adam of Genesis, Adapa had achieved knowledge but not immortality. The duality of the two trees is repeated here. This is clear in the tale as it begins with the statement:

With wide understanding, to him he (Enki) had given wisdom,
but eternal life he had not given him.

Enki had trained Adapa to do specialized chores for his household — he procured food for the table, did the baking, and prepared and tended the dinner table at Enki's water palace. As the story unfolds, one day Adapa was out in his boat fishing to obtain food for Enki's table, when the "southwind" came up and swamped the boat. Adapa cursed the wind and as the story states "broke the wing of the south wind."

This is a curious phrase indeed and, in view of another Sumerian poem, seems to be the wing of an aircraft. In the *Myth of Zu*, one of the weapons unleashed against Zu and the one that finally defeated him was the "south wind." Its context makes it sound like an unmanned winged craft of some sort. In Adapa's case he seems to have disabled it accidentally.

Meanwhile, up in his "heavenly abode," the chief god An is worried that the "south wind has not blown over the land for seven days," and asked his vizier to investigate. When he reported back that a mere mortal had disabled the south wind, An was furious and angrily summoned Adapa to his spaceship to give an account of himself. Enki, who was not only man's creator but quite often his defender and benefactor, briefed Adapa on how to act in the great god's presence.

Adapa is told how to reach the heavenly ship of An. Enki "made him take the road to heaven, and to heaven he went up," obviously taking a shuttle from Sippar, the space city. He is warned that he will be offered the bread of death: "thou shall not eat it." He will then be offered the water of death: "thou shall not drink it," warns Enki.

Adapa was ushered into the presence of An who asked him pointedly why he had disabled the "south wind." Adapa explained that he was catching fish for his master's table. The sea was like a mirror until the south wind came up and overturned his boat, thus indicating that his boat was swamped by the blast of wind from the apparently low flying "south wind." An was impressed by Adapa's intelligence and, moreover, by the fact that he had learned "forbidden things," such as how to reach the gods in the orbiting spaceship.

To continue the story of Adapa, it was decided to have him join the ranks of the gods by having him partake of the food and water of life. Adapa would thus achieve immortality and become like one of the gods. Actually, it

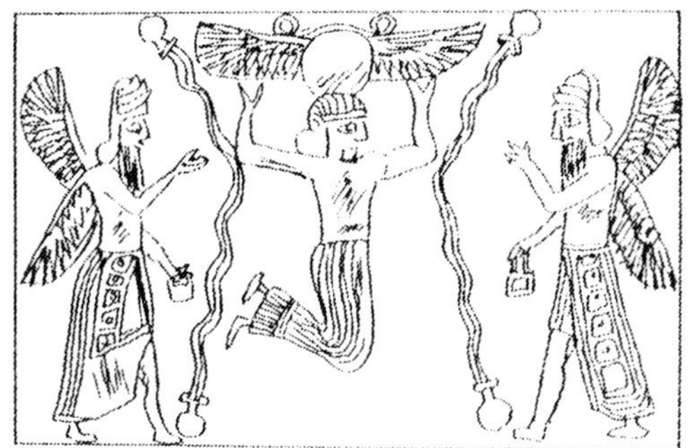

Fig. 47 – The story of Adapa.

Above: Imprint from a seal showing Adapa rising in the sky, hanging onto the winged sphere of Shamash. Two astronauts stand by, each with a situla or bucket with the water of immortality. The flowing waters between the jars is also a symbol of long life. Below: A more stylized version shows Adapa inside a capsule being raised by the winged astronaut god.

would mean reverting back to his reptilian nature. This is probably why he was forewarned by Enki, who did not want his creation tampered with. When Adapa refused the food and water of immortality, An wanted to know why; Adapa told him of Enki's warning which infuriated An, who sent a messenger to Earth to chastise Enki. An finally relented, however, but it was too late for Adapa. Symbolically, man had missed the chance to achieve everlasting life.

Adapa returned to Earth, a trip during which he saw the wonders of space: "as Adapa from the horizon of heaven to the zenith of heaven cast a glance, saw its awesomeness." Adapa was ordained a high priest of Eridu and he was promised that henceforth the Goddess of Healing would also tend to the ailments of mankind. Like the Adam of the scriptures, Adapa became the ancestor of mankind. As his destiny, Adapa would be "the seed of mankind."

Enki is remembered as the creator and benefactor of mankind and is associated with godly knowledge, healing and immortality — exactly the qualities attributed to the serpent in the Garden of Eden. Thus the Biblical "Fall of Man" takes on the character of a confrontation between Enlil, the Elohim of the Bible, and Enki the usurper serpent-god.

The same conflict is seen in the *Tale of Adapa* when Enki prevents the gods from tampering with his creation. There are echoes of this dissension in the Hebrew *Apocalypse of Enoch* when this patriarch is to be given godhood and immortality. The "angels" representing the older gods protest that God is revealing divine secrets to man. They remind him that "did not the primeval ones give you good advice when they said 'don't create man?'"

To the conservative and older gods, man was considered to be an inferior animal, for time and time again he is criticized for his sweaty and dirty mammalism. In the Hebrew *Book of Enoch* man is scorned by the minor gods who characterize him as "mankind born of woman, blemished, unclean, defiled by blood and impure flux, men who sweat putrid drops." This disgust of the "angels" towards their sweaty, fleshy mammal cousins is reiterated throughout the Old Testament where it appears under the imagery of the "weakness of the flesh."

The Anunna loved their reptilian appearance, their lustrous and gleaming bodies; mammal traits were repugnant to them. Our revulsion to reptiles and particularly serpents may be based in these ancient memories of a saurian ancestry.

The problem of revulsion is a difficult one, however, and better left to psychoanalysts. It seems largely to be a learned experience, a result of what we are taught when we are young. It is also entirely possible that the lingering memory of our reptilian ancestry may exist in our subconscious and contribute to the dislike of reptiles.

The Search for Immortality

In ancient legends, man seems to always achieve some sort of "knowledge" yet loses immortality. It is as if the two are mutually exclusive. Adam gets "knowledge," but is banned from the garden and from partaking of the Tree of Life. So it is with Adapa who is given "knowledge" by Enki but is cheated in obtaining the drink and food of life that would have made him immortal. The same is true of the hero Gilgamesh. Many of his adventures are attempts to achieve immortality.

In the *Epic of Gilgamesh* it is a sub-theme. After a long journey to reach his grandfather Utnapishtim, Gilgamesh is told that the gods have refused him immortality. Having compassion for his grandson and in order not to let him return empty-handed, Utnapishtim informs Gilgamesh of a magical plant that restores youth and vitality and where to find it.

Thus on his return home, Gilgamesh follows the directions of his grandfather and manages to obtain this magical plant. He decides, somewhat unwisely, not to partake of it immediately, but rather to take it back to Uruk to share it with his friends. This turns out to be a mistake, for when Gilgamesh stops by a pool of water to bathe, the plant is stolen from him.

In order to wash the grime from his long journey, Gilgamesh took a much needed bath. He foolishly left the magic plant on shore unattended. As he bathed and much to his consternation, a serpent smelled the fragrance of the plant, came up through the water and carried it away. As the serpent left, it then threw off its skin.

In world mythology, the serpent has been the symbol of long life, of cure and regeneration, and of immortality. Serpents have everywhere been associated with healing. For example, the Mayan book *Chilam Balaam* relates that the first inhabitants of Yucatan were the Chanes or "People of the Serpent" who came across the water from the East with their leader Itzamna, who was called the "Serpent of the East," and was a healer who could cure by laying on of hands and revive the dead.

Even in the Old Testament, the role of serpent as healer is illustrated in the incident of the "bronze serpent" or seraph which was raised on a pole and became a cure for the ailments of the tribes of Israel during their journey from Egypt.

The duality of knowledge and immortality, as represented by the two trees in the Garden of Eden, is not generally found in ancient literature. Aside from the brief reference in the *Tale of Adapa*, ancient literature concentrates on man's efforts to achieve long life and immortality. The symbolic tree of life and the magical food and drink were popular subjects among the various cultures of the Middle East and often appear in their art forms.

The opposite is true of the Old Testament, where immortality is all but forgotten and the emphasis is on the sins of man caused by his downfall in achieving knowledge. An exception is found in the pseudepigraphic document called the *Life of Adam and Eve,* which narrates episodes in the life of these two after they left Eden. Dated to the First Century AD, it is available both in Greek and Latin versions. It provides a little known event of Adam's attempt to obtain some of these rejuvenative remedies. According to the text, Adam was old and dying and near the end of his life. He requested Eve and his son Seth to return to Eden for the "oil from the tree of mercy" with which he might be anointed, relieved of his pain, and his life extended. At the gates of Eden they are met by the angel Michael who refuses the plea of Seth with the argument that the magic elixir is not for man.

The Hebrew concentration on a view completely opposite to all the ancient secular traditions would suggest that the emphasis on "knowing" by the early priesthood was a deliberate deviation, which became a doctrine with the purpose of forcing on mankind "original sin" and his fall from grace, in order to achieve a degree of control over their minds and behavior.

When the snake stole the magical plant of Gilgamesh and immediately shed its skin, it was demonstrating a form of immortality. Shedding of the skin has in this way entered the theology of the Hebrews and Christians in the form of the rite of circumcision.

As part of the covenant between the deity and Abraham, and later reinforced by being repeated many more times to his descendants, he is told:

> You shall circumcise the flesh of your foreskin, and that shall be the mark of the covenant between me and you.

Just as the serpent achieves long life through sacrificing and leaving off part of himself, so may man also be saved by ritually sacrificing part of himself. The rite of circumcision also served as a perpetual reminder to man that his true origins lay in the serpent-god creator.

Of those who achieved true immortality and joined the gods, only two are recorded in the ancient literature. The gods made it clear that it was not granted lightly. Utnapishtim is one of the few who was given immortality.

After the Deluge, Utnapishtim and his wife were taken up into the spaceship where Enlil placed him through a ritual process, "hitherto Utnapishtim had been but a man; but now Utnapishtim and his wife shall be unto us gods." He was sent to live "at the source of the two rivers where Shamash rises," in the land of Dilmun. Unlike his counterpart, Noah did not achieve immortality. The gods of the Old Testament were much more jealous and uncompromising gods.

Only one of the Patriarchs before the Deluge achieved this distinction. It is passed over cryptically in Genesis, stating that "Enoch walked with God. Then he vanished because God took him." Nonetheless, the three apocalyptic books of Enoch provide the full story — details which were eliminated from the Old Testament.

Enoch was not only made immortal but was also deified so that he became second in power to the chief deity himself. This unusual metamorphosis was done in order to provide an objective magistrate who could preside over the trial of the Nefilim, who had committed all sorts of crimes on Earth.

CHAPTER 17

THE PATRIARCHS, DEMI-GODS OF THE ANTEDILUVIAN PERIOD

The antediluvian days are remembered as the reign of the god-kings in the Sumerian *King List* and as the era of the Patriarchs of the *Book of Genesis*. The sources make it clear that these leaders which formed the aristocracy that ruled in these days were of divine blood, that is, they were part saurian.

A second group to inhabit the Earth were the Nefilim or the Anunna who descended to live here and to intermarry with human women. They are discussed in the next chapter. The third group to populate the Earth was mankind, the Homo sapiens produced by the Anunna as a labor force to do all the menial tasks.

Of the three, we are concerned with the demi-gods, the priest-kings of the antediluvian period which are remembered in the Old Testament as the descendants of Adam and Eve.

Two Lines of Descent in Genesis

The line of descent from Adam and Eve provided by the *Book of Genesis* is very confusing for it poses many problems; it not only lists the progeny of Cain but then adds the parallel line of Seth. It even duplicates some of the Cainite names and approximates some of the others (figure 49).

It is obvious that there were two separate streams of tradition, but both were derived from the same distant source. The original center of dissemination was manifestly in Mesopotamia. While the name Methusael is clearly Akkadian (MUTU-SA-ILI or "man of god"), the rest of the names have nothing in common with their Mesopotamian antecedents and it would seem that before they reached the Hebrews they had gone through many Semitic centers of dissemination where they were transformed with local records and traditions.

There is a third list mentioned in the pseudepigraphic literature that has been neglected, presumably because it does not agree with the proposition in Genesis that Abraham inherited the mantle of priesthood from Noah. Provided by the Slavonic *Apocalypse of Enoch,* this list of priest-kings ends with the Patriarch Melchizedek who is transported to the heavens just before the Deluge. It contains many strange and unfamiliar names that do not appear elsewhere in the scriptures (figure 48). It is dated to the First

Adam
Sit (Seth)
Enos (Enosh)
Rusi
Amilar
Prasidam
Maleleil
Serokh
Arusan
Aleem
Enoch
Methuselah
Nir
Melkisedek

Note: Kenan, Jared, Lamech, and Noah are left out of this list. Lamech is mentioned only in the accompanying text as the father of Nir. The priest-king line ends with Melkisedek just before the Deluge.

According to this document, also known as The Second Book of Enoch, the line of priest-kings which began with Seth, ended with Melkisedek who is taken up to the heavens. Noah is passed over in favor of his younger brother Nir. Noah is instead given the role of repopulating the earth after the Deluge.

Fig. 48 – The patriarch Melkisedek: A third line of descent.

Century AD and describes Enoch's ascent to heaven, his deification, and his return to Earth. It is perhaps better known for its line of succession which avoids Noah and instead passes it to his brother Nir, and then to his son Melchizedek.

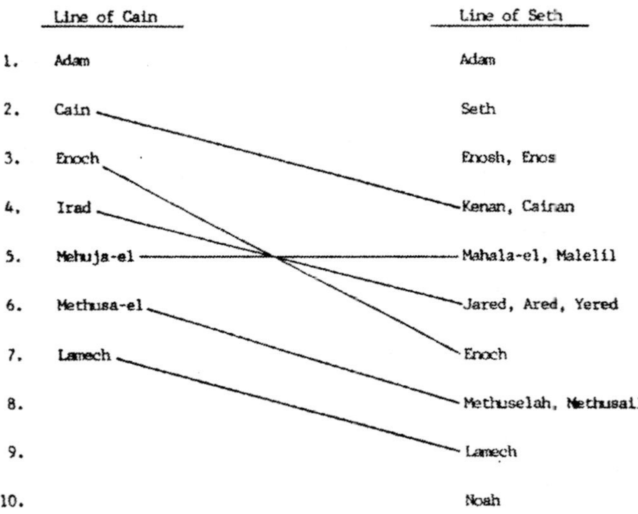

Fig. 49 – Coincidences in the lines of Cain and Seth

The Cain-Abel Murder Mystery

The Biblical explanation for the first recorded murder in the history of mankind is somehow not convincing for, according to Genesis, Cain killed Abel because his sacrifice was snubbed by the Lord in favor of Abel's. Logically, this alone would not seem provocation enough to cause Cain to commit fratricide. It seems more like a spurious explanation invented by the ancient chroniclers. The answer lies elsewhere and the works of the pseudepigrapha bears this out. A more complete and sinister version of the crime is provided in the ancient document the *Life of Adam and Eve.*

When Eve conceived and bore Cain she said, according to Genesis, "I have added a man-child with the help of the Lord." In the case of Abel, however, the text says merely that "next she bore his brother Abel." Genesis thus suggests, although obliquely, that the birth of Cain involved the deity.

We must look to other sources to understand and clarify what actually happened. Further clarification of the paternity of Cain is found in the *Apocalypse of Adam,* a Gnostic document of the First Century AD, wherein Adam reveals to his son Seth that "the Lord, who created us, created a son from himself and Eve, your mother." The pseudepigraphic document called the *Life of Adam and Eve* also observes that Eve "bore a son and he was lustrous." This is a good description of the shiny, luminous hide of the reptile gods.

It was not unusual in ancient times to believe that serpents regularly impregnated women. Sacred serpents kept in Egyptian temples acted as the god's procreative agents. The second *Tanis Papyrus* contains a list of sacred titles given to such beneficent serpents housed in the larger temples.

Among the Greeks, barren women would lie all night on the floor of Aslclepius's temple, hoping that the god would appear in serpent shape and impregnate them during sleep. At the Phrygian Mysteries of Sabozius, women ritually married the god by letting live snakes, or golden replicas, slide between their breasts down to their thighs.

The Murder and Cannibalism of Abel

If the deity was the father of Cain, while Adam sired Abel, it explains many of the events which happened subsequently, for if the deity were his father, Cain would be part reptilian and more God-like. It would explain his fierce and bloodthirsty nature and account for the murder of his brother Abel. An unusual and somewhat bizarre version of the crime of Cain is found in the *Life of Adam and Eve*, which narrates some episodes in the life of Adam. There are two versions — the Latin or Vita version, and the Greek or Apocalypse one. In the Vita version, Eve has a vision where it is "as if the blood of our son Abel was in the hands of Cain who was gulping it down in his mouth." The Apocalyptic version is somewhat more dramatic, as Eve tells Adam:

> My Lord, I saw a dream last night, the blood of my son Amilabes, called Abel, being thrust into the mouth of Cain his brother, and he drank it mercilessly . . . And it did not stay in his stomach but came out of his mouth. They got up to see what happened and found Abel killed by Cain.

The crime of Cain was, apparently, not only to commit fratricide but also to eat the flesh and blood of his brother. This behavior seems more reptilian than human, for Cain was sired by the deity and was therefore half saurian. This may have been the main reason for aborting the line of Cain, to be superseded by that of Seth.

Whether provoked or not, Cain committed a serious crime, much more serious than just an error in offering a sacrifice. Cain not only killed Abel but ate his flesh and drank his blood. For this barbaric deed Cain was banished to the east to the land of Nod. Then, as a sign that Cain came under the Lord's protection, he placed a mark on Cain, the nature of which is not described in Genesis.

In order to protect his semi-divine progeny, the deity warned that "whoever kills Cain shall suffer vengeance seven fold." Strangely, this same statement is repeated in the verse on Lamech which ends the line of Cain and, obviously the two verses are related.

Cain is considered by the deity to be a bad experiment; but since he is his offspring, he cannot be destroyed. He is exiled to a far land so that he nor his offspring can do no more harm. Cain is said to have married his sister Awan at the end of the Fourth Jubilee or about the 200th year of Adam's life. Rabbinical sources indicate that he died in his 930th year, that is a year before the death of Adam. In the pseudepigrapha, Cain was reportedly accidentally killed by Lamech, thus fulfilling the curse of the seventh generation.

The Reptilian Line of Cain

After the murder of Abel and Cain's barbaric behavior in the eating of the flesh and drinking of the blood of his victim, the deity realized that his son, out of Eve, was not fit to continue the development of mankind and was banished to the land of Nod.

However, Genesis continues the line of Cain, uneventfully, through Irad, Mehujael, Methusael, and then ends with Lamech. Not content with dropping the line here, the scriptures left behind a puzzle, a cryptic verse that has been the bane of Biblical scholars. The verse which ends the line of Cain is as follows:

> Lamech said to his wives,
>
> Adah and Zellah, hear my voice,
>
> O wives of Lamech, give ear to my speech:
>
> I have killed a man for wounding me,
>
> A boy for injuring me.

If Cain be avenged sevenfold,
Then Lamech seventy-seven fold.

Genesis then drops all mention of the Cainite line and abruptly begins the genealogy of Seth. Obviously the verse contains the clues to this sudden change of policy. If the line was doomed, what were the reasons? The solution to this enigmatic verse which ends the line of Cain probably lies in the existence of the two, even three, parallel lines of descent. The answer to the puzzle may be found in the events in the life of Lamech, which is discussed below.

The Patriarchs Enosh, Kenon, Mahala'el and Jared

After Abel's death and Cain's banishment, a third son arrives on the scene. Like Abel, Seth is born of Adam and Eve; ostensibly, the deity has decided not to intervene in the affairs of man and allow him to produce his own offspring. Seth marries his sister and Enosh is born. Thus begins the line of Patriarchs which continues unbroken until the time of the Deluge. The heroes of the Old Testament, quite often and proudly, claim their descent from this Sethite line. Who then were these Patriarchs, and since they were undoubtedly residents of Mesopotamia, what evidence is there in the scriptures and other ancient writings to link them with the Anunna or alien astronauts?

Of the first four Patriarchs, very little information is available in the Old Testament. Enosh means "mortal" or "human being" and according to the scriptures he was considered to be the first mortal or human. It is during his era that the "faces of man became ape-like" according to ancient Rabbinical sources. It would thus appear that the human countenance became less reptile-like and assumed mammal or ape-like features during the years of Enosh.

It is perhaps for this reason that the generation of Enosh is not treated well in the ancient sources. The *Haggadah* calls it the generation of the "counsel of the ungodly," since the contemporaries of Enosh were accused of practicing "the arts of divination and the control of heavenly forces." Man was beginning to show a spirit of independence and intellectual curiosity that apparently did not abide well with his reptilian masters.

The days of Enosh were also marked with many earthquakes which caused untold misery. Drought and famine followed, and then there was a mass dying off of the population. According to the Hebrew *Book of Enoch*, the Lord decided to remove his shekinah or spacecraft from the area of the Garden of Eden in the days of Enosh and return to the heavens.

Sumerian sources reveal that at first the chief god An resided at Uruk, the Erech of the Bible, but for undisclosed reasons decided to return to his heavenly abode, never to come back except on special occasions. He may have left because of the numerous earthquakes and bad conditions at the time of Enosh.

Enosh is said to have lived 905 years; at the age of 90 he begot Kenon or Cainan. Meaning "metalsmith" or "craftsman," little is known of Kenon from ancient sources. Since the second city built was called Badtibira or "city for metal processing," there seems to be an association whose meaning has been lost.

Kenon lived 910 years and begot Mahala'el at the age of 70. Mahala'el or "praiser of the Lord" lived 895 years; nothing is known of him. When he was 65 (or 460 years after Adam had left Eden), Jared was born. Thus Adam, Enosh, Kenon, Mahalel'el, as well as Cain, would all still be living at the time we enter the era of Jared.

Jared was the first Patriarch not to marry his sister. Perhaps it is symbolic of the end of an era where intermarriage among siblings was not only condoned but practiced as a general custom as, for example, among the Egyptian royal family. The days of Jared should be, by calculation of the figures given in Genesis, from the year 460 AA to 1422 AA (that is, AA = After Adam, or the years elapsed since the birth of Adam).

It has been suggested that Jared or Yered, as it is sometimes given, means "he of Eridu." This would place Jared at the city of Eridu, just as Enosh was at Badtibira, and Enoch at Sippar. The days of Jared are of major significance to human history for it was then that the Nefilim first descended. Jubilees state that "in his days the angels of the Lord, who were called Watchers (Nefilim), came down to Earth in order to teach the sons of man, and perform Judgment and uprightness upon the Earth." The arrival of these astronauts during the days of Jared is also reported in the Ethiopic *Book of Enoch* and later verified by documents found among the Dead Sea scrolls.

Enoch as the Favorite of the Gods

The information on Enoch in Genesis is sparse and little mention is made of him. Enoch was 165 years old when his son Methuselah was born. Enoch then lived 200 more years, at which time "Enoch walked with God, then was no more, because God took him." The phrase "walked with God" has been generally interpreted to mean that he ascended to heaven during his lifetime. This cryptic phrase implies, nevertheless, of the existence of some fuller narrative about Enoch, lost or omitted from the Old Testament.

Enoch became a hero in Jewish apocalyptic literature and two books were ascribed to him, the "Ethiopic" and "Slavonic" books. The figure of Enoch was especially significant in the spiritual movement from which the Dead Sea scrolls originated. His story and writings are treated in the *Book of Jubilees*, and he plays an active role in the Hebrew *Apocalypse of Enoch,* which is ascribed to the Palestinian scholar Ishmael.

Enoch's ascent to heaven is actually just the beginning of a fabulous career, wherein Enoch became "divine" and was made chief of the heavens, second only to the deity himself. After his ascent he came back to his family briefly to teach his son Methuselah the wisdom he had learned and written down in heaven.

After a brief stay here he returned to the spacecraft for six Jubilee years. During this period he apparently commuted between the spaceship and Earth. The apocalyptic literature mentions his residence in Eden and on Mount Qatar, an unidentified place which could very well be the city of Sippar in Mesopotamia.

Enoch's "Rise" to Power

The elevation of Enoch to the status of a god is recounted in the Slavonic *Book of Enoch*. Enoch himself reveals the experience:

> When 165 years were complete for me, I fathered my son Methuselah; and after that I lived 200 years . . . On the assigned day of the first month, I was in the house alone . . . And I lay on the bed sleeping . . . Then two huge men appeared to me, the likes of which I had never seen on Earth . . . And they stood at the head of my bed and called me by my name.

Enoch awoke and was terrified.

> Then these men said to me "Be brave Enoch, in truth do not fear, the eternal god has sent us to you. And behold you will ascend with us to heaven today."

He was told to tell his sons and household that he was leaving. He was then taken up "on their wings" to the heavens. Enoch was given a tour of the spaceship. In one area he saw two hundred dejected "angels" and was told that they were the ones who had descended, committed many crimes, and were being held for trial. Enoch's clothes were taken away and he was "anointed" and given "clothes of glory," a symbolism to show that he was changed physically, made over like one of the gods.

This is just the reverse of what happened to Adam in the Garden of Eden, he lost his "cloud of glory" and then was given clothes. It appears from what happened subsequently that Enoch received some form of "divinity" here at this time. Then a "pen for speed-writing" was given to Enoch and books were read to him while he copied dictation about the "marvels and secrets of heaven."

He remained on the ship for sixty days, then was returned to Earth to spend thirty days to impart knowledge to his sons. He was then picked up and flown back to the spaceship where he was to be the chief investigator for the inquiry into the crimes of the Nefilim. The Hebrew *Book of Enoch* contains the testimony of Rabbi Ishmael, the famous Palestinian scholar, where he dreams he is taken to heaven and meets Metatron, who appears to be the most powerful being there. "Why is your name like the name of your Creator with seventy names?" asks Ishmael. "You are greater than all the Princes, more exalted than all the angels, more beloved than all the Ministers." Enoch answers, "Because I am Enoch, the son of Jared." He then describes how he was made chief of the heavens over the objections of the angels.

Enoch is made acting chief with all the titles and powers of office. He is given the "divine names," the seventy names which confer power over the heavens and Earth. These names seem to be like the Tablets of Destiny or the MEs of the Sumerian gods. They are formulas or devices which give the owner absolute control over certain aspects and categories of life.

Enoch served as Metatron (from the Greek *meta-thronos* or "the one who serves behind the throne") for six Jubilee years or 300 years. According to this document he was resettled in Eden and while little is known of these 300 years when he served as Metatron, he presumably commuted back and forth between a city on Earth and the spaceship.

The Crimes and Trial of the Nefilim, the Criminal Astronauts

The *Book of Jubilees* state that in the days of Jared "the angels of the Lord, who were called Watchers, came to Earth in order to teach the sons of man." These are the Nefilim who are described in Genesis 6:

> Now when men began to increase on Earth and daughters were born to them, the divine beings (Elohim) saw how beautiful were the human daughters and took as their wives any of them they liked . . . It was then that the Nefilim appeared on Earth — as well as later after the divine beings had united with human daughters.

According to the *Haggadah* there were 200 astronauts who descended in the days of Jared onto Mount Hermon in northwest Palestine near Lebanon. In the Babylonian records of creation, the *Enuma Elish*, a large group of divine beings descended to Earth. The Anunna were quite restless in their spaceship for having achieved freedom from labor with the creation of man, they were becoming increasingly bored and restless. It was then decided to resettle part of them on Earth.

Accordingly, 300 of them descended to Earth while another 300 remained on the spaceship. Called the *igigi,* they were presumably the ones with specialized functions, the technicians of the spacecraft.

The well-intentioned plans of the Nefilim or Anunna appear to have changed for the worse, for soon thereafter they began to engage in a variety of activities that raised the wrath of both god and man. The Ethiopic *Book of Enoch* suggests that their descent was a secret and unauthorized act of a group of rebellious "angels."

> In those days, when the children of man had multiplied, it happened that there was born unto them handsome and beautiful daughters. And the angels, the children of heaven, saw them and desired them and they said to one another, "Come, let us choose wives for ourselves among the daughters of men and beget us children." And Semyaz, being their leader, said unto them, "Let us all swear an oath and bind everyone among us by a curse not to abandon this suggestion but to do the deed." Then they all swore together and bound one another by the curse. And they were altogether two hundred.

As Metatron, Enoch Prosecutes the Nefilim

During this time, Enoch was performing the work of a scribe at a hidden location on Earth. "No one of the children of God knew by what he was hidden and where he was," notes the account although it makes it clear he was among the Anunna of the Mesopotamian valley. He is then approached by the "Nefilim of Heaven" and told to go among the "Nefilim of Earth" and apprise them of their crimes. "Enoch, scribe of righteousness," he is told, "go and make known to the Watchers of heaven who have abandoned high heaven and have defiled themselves upon the Earth."

> Enoch approached the Nefilim and warned them that, "There will not be peace with you, a grave Judgment has come upon you. They will put you in bonds, and you will not have an opportunity for rest. You have shown to the people deeds of shame, injustice, and sin."

As a group "they were all frightened and fear and trembling seized them. They begged Enoch to draw up a letter of forgiveness and to petition the deity on their behalf. Enoch did as they requested.

At this time, the records say, Enoch was in the area of Dan, near Mount Hermon, where the Nefilim are said to have originally landed. Enoch flew up to heaven in a spacecraft or "fiery chariot" and in his words, "the winds were causing me to fly and rushing me high up into heaven."

He was greeted by the deity who heard Enoch's petition on behalf of the Earth-bound Nefilim. The deity was angry and not disposed to be merciful, mainly because it was not proper for a mortal to intercede for the Nefilim. It just was not done in the scheme of things. Rather it was more fit and proper for them to intercede on the behalf of mankind.

He chastised them thoroughly: "For what reason have you abandoned the high, holy eternal heaven?" He contended that they had been spiritual beings "possessing eternal life but have defiled yourselves with women and like them producing blood and flesh which will die and perish."

It seems that their offspring was more mammal than reptile and again we see that equation, contrasting eternal life and the physiology of the Anunna with that of mortals of blood and flesh.

But the plans of the Nefilim on Earth went awry and they produced creatures quite unlike their reptilian forebears. The "divine" race was becoming diluted and the mammalian genes appeared to dominate the reptilian strain which became recessive. This factor may have been the main reason which led to the experiments in genetic engineering, one of the major crimes leveled against the Nefilim.

In order to redress the unforeseen and unwarranted dilution of the saurian strain, the Nefilim began experiments in changing the genetic codes, hoping in this way to reestablish their strain as the dominant one. These experiments apparently got out of control for one of the accusations against the Nefilim was to practice "alchemy" by "changing a man into a horse or mule or vice versa, or transferring an embryo from one womb to another."

Other cryptic references indicate that these experiments also involved animals, for "they began to sin against birds, wild animals, reptiles, and fish." Monsters of all sorts were produced; these in turn oppressed mankind in the years before the Deluge.

The Nefilim then turned to cannibalism, not a great change morally to a race used to human sacrifice. The increase in human population and the catastrophes of the period produced extreme food shortages. The religious literature relates how "the giants consumed the produce of all the people until the people detested feeding them. So the giants turned against the people in order to eat them."

The gods in heaven were incensed over these activities and swore to eliminate the offspring of the Nefilim which caused havoc on Earth. The deity directed the "avenging angels" to:

> Proceed against the bastards and the reprobates and against the children of adultery; and destroy the children of adultery and expel the children of the Watchers from among the people. And send them against one another so that they may be destroyed in the fight.

The *Atrahasis Epic* version of the creation describes a condition of famine and desperation just before the Deluge. The land had become barren because of the drought. People roamed about in despair due to disease and illness. The dead were everywhere and, as the tablets reveal, each family "devours" the other, then finally eats their own young.

The actual trial of the children of god is not described in the books of Enoch, yet there was a decision handed down for Enoch to transmit to them. "He testified about the Watchers who had sinned with the daughters of man; he testified against them all," relates the *Book of Enoch*. The verdict is given, and in Enoch's words:

> Judgment is passed upon you. From now on you will not be able to ascend to heaven onto all eternity, but shall remain inside the Earth, imprisoned all the days of eternity. Before that, you will have seen the destruction of your beloved ones.

There are two parts to the verdict: the Nefilim themselves will be imprisoned in the Earth, and secondly, their offspring will be destroyed. Their imprisonment in the Earth is reflected in the Mesopotamian epics where some of the Anunna suffer a similar fate.

In the Sumerian epic *Descent of Ishtar to the Netherworld*, some of the Anunna are residents of the netherworld where they are visited by the goddess Ishtar. It is a "land of no return," a land of darkness and misery, where the "prisoners eat clay for bread and drink muddied water for beer."

Enoch as the Sumerian Enmeduranna

Enoch went to heaven in a fiery chariot according to the *Haggadah*, and here he was changed physically and made divine as the first step in becoming chief of the heavens, second only to the deity himself. The Hebrew *Book of Enoch* describes his ascent to power over the objections of the angels. Apparently, the deity did not trust the angels and brought Enoch up to the heavens to straighten things out. Three of the ministering angels asked the Lord "what right has this one to ascend to the height of heights?" The Lord replies, "I have chosen this one in preference to all of you, to be a prince and ruler over you in the heavenly heights."

He is given the name Metatron and the title Prince of the Divine Presence. These titles and powers of Enoch have made it difficult for Biblical scholars to try to fit him into the doctrine of monotheism.

Enoch or Metatron is placed in charge of the heavenly staff and given access to all parts of the heavenly abode or ship. Enoch also assumes control over all the vehicles, rockets, and other technical equipment. In modern terms, Metatron is the Chief Executive Officer answerable only to the President or Chairman of the Board.

The similarities between Enoch and Enmeduranna, the Sumerian king, is so striking as to indicate that the legends about Enoch and the stories of the legendary god-king of Sippar come from a common source. While the Biblical records preserve a partly expurgated narrative of Enoch, many of the original mythological motifs of Enoch continued to exist in the oral tradition until they reached their present form in Jewish pseudepigrapha, medieval legends, and mystical literature.

Both Enoch and Enmeduranna were the seventh rulers before the Deluge, Enoch being the seventh Patriarch in the line of Seth, and Enmeduranna the seventh antediluvian king of the Sumerian *King List*. Often called a priest-king in the books bearing his name, Enoch ruled both on Earth and in the heavens. Enmeduranna ruled at Sippar, the spaceport of the antediluvian gods.

His name EN-ME-DUR-ANNA means "the Lord of the MEs that connect heaven and Earth," or in other words, the king who controls the Tablets of Destiny that control the flights between heaven and Earth. This may be why Enoch is given so much importance among the Patriarchs because he was in charge of Sippar, the spaceport and the Sumerians most important city.

According to the *Book of Jubilees*, Enoch made incense offerings on Mount Qatar. Listed as one of the four sacred places on Earth, along with the Garden of Eden, Mount Sinai, and Mount Zion, Qatar is otherwise not identified in the religious literature except that it is referred to as the "mountain of the east." Since the reference point of this entry in Jubilees is Mount Sinai, the mountain of the east would be in the general direction of Mesopotamia. It would logically be the ziggurat at Sippar, the artificial mountain where Enmeduranna was priest-king.

Thus, Mount Qatar would be the ziggurat at Sippar in Mesopotamia, the Garden of Eden was in Lebanon, Mount Sinai was in the northern Sinai, and Mount Zion was in Jerusalem. We shall see how all these sacred places were part of the space program of the Anunna.

The Mysterious Lamech, Son of Methuselah

Methuselah, the son of Lamech, is given little coverage in Genesis. His son Lamech, however, is the subject of an historical mystery. In both the Cainite and the Sethite tradition, Lamech is the son of Methuselah. Genesis devotes much space to explaining the activities of the line of Cain, and then drops the line altogether. Quite cryptic in nature, there is some meaning here that has been lost to antiquity.

According to his lineage, Lamech had three sons — Jabal, Jubal, and Tubal-Cain. His wives were Adah and Zillah. He was thus the first admitted polygamist and the father of the founders of nomadism, the musical arts, and metalworking. Lamech is the seventh generation according to the Cainite lineage and the numbers 7 and 77 seem to play an important part in his poem in Genesis:

> Lamech said to his wives,
> Adah and Zillah, hear my voice,
> O wives of Lamech, give ear to my speech:
> I have killed a man for wounding me,
> A boy for injuring me.
> If Cain be avenged sevenfold,
> Then Lamech seventy-seven fold.

The references to killing a boy and a man, leading to a curse to the 77th generation, has been a puzzle to scholars for centuries. Who then were these people that were so important as to bring such drastic retribution to Lamech?

The answer may be found in the *Haggadah,* which provides details of the slaying of Cain. In the story, Lamech was reportedly old and blind and when he went hunting was led by his son Tubal-Cain, who would tell his father when game came into sight, so that Lamech could shoot at it with his bow and arrow. Once, he aimed at some horned creature which Tubal-Cain thought to be a beast. In fact, it was Cain bearing the "sign of Cain," a horn in the forehead, according to the *Haggadah*, but more probably a set of horns on the head. Lamech killed him and in despair, he struck out, inadvertently killing his son Tubal-Cain. Fanciful as the story goes, it accounts for the killing of a man and a boy, both of which were not just ordinary people. Cain's slaying was serious since he was half-reptile and protected by the gods as one of their own.

By the days of Lamech, the Anunna or Nefilim had become the bane of mankind. The hatred for these barbaric ancestors may have led Lamech to murder Cain, and while it may have been applauded by mankind, the gods and demi-gods were certainly not pleased. There is an echo of this in the treatment of Melchizedek, the grandchild of Lamech, who was taken away by the Nefilim to prevent his being killed by the people.

As priest-kings, the Patriarchs were considered to be allies and friends of the gods, presumably because they themselves were part saurian. Reptile vestiges must have made them easily recognizable, and these characteristics, possibly a patch of scaly skin on the chest or face, or perhaps the remnants of reptilian features on the countenance, would be considered by humans as the so-called "badge of shame." This may have been why Noah was so upset when seen naked by his sons.

The Lamech of the Line of Seth

It would seem that there were two different traditions of the antediluvian Patriarchs that originated from the same source. Why the two Lamech's were so different is an interesting puzzle that seeks a solution. Perhaps some of this confusion can be traced to the events of the time.

Enoch appears to be the last of the Patriarchs beloved and trusted by the gods. He went up for the second time in 987 AA(years after Adam), in our calculations, to become Metatron and preside over the trial of the Nefilim. The Nefilim reportedly descended during the days of Jared and since he was born in 460 AA, the troubles caused by them was between 460 and 987 AA.

In Noah's time a second group of Nefilim descended and again caused many problems for humanity. While there is no evidence that Methuselah as a priest-king was not trusted by the gods, the minimum amount of publicity he receives in all the ancient documents indicates he was not very popular. Neither was Lamech, for in the Slavonic Book of Enoch, Methuselah passes the mantle of priesthood to Nir, thereby bypassing the generation of Lamech, and what is more significant, skipping over Noah, his eldest son. Of this Lamech, Genesis has this to say:

> Lamech was 182 years old when he begot a son. He named him Noah, which is to say, "This one will bring us relief from our work and the toil of our hands, out of the very soil which the Lord had placed under a ban." After the birth of Noah, Lamech lived 595 years and begot sons and daughters. All the days of Lamech came to 777 years, then he died.

The scriptures seem ambivalent when it comes to Lamech, torn between the evil-doer of Cain and the laudable one of Seth. What is not often perceived is that while the Patriarchs had prodigious lifespans, they dovetailed to such an extent that, according to the chronology of Genesis, the total elapsed time adds up to no more than 1656 years.

In fact, if this chronology is used, at the time of Lamech's birth in the year 874 AA, all of the Patriarchs were still alive, Adam and Cain being the first to die in 930 and 931 AA, respectively. Therefore, the events of the days of Jared, when the Nefilim first descended, through the generations of Enoch, Methuselah, Lamech, and Noah, up to the Deluge, probably lasted no more than 700 or 800 years. The end of the lifespan of Lamech and Methuselah coincide with the onset of the Deluge, leading one to believe that they both died in that catastrophe.

Methuselah and the Priest-Kings Nir and Melchizedek

Although he was the longest lived of the Patriarchs — 969 years, little is known of Methuselah. He is mentioned in *Pseudo-Eupolemus*, a fragmentary source of the First Century BC attributed to the Greek writer Eupolemus, who is believed to have drawn his knowledge from the works of Berossus and Polyhistor.

According to Eupolemus, Methuselah obtained knowledge from "the angels and passed this to mankind." This may refer to the knowledge that was passed by Enoch to his family on his first return to Earth. Like Enoch, he must have commuted freely between Earth and the spaceship.

In a story from the Dead Sea Scrolls, Lamech was worried over the strange appearance of his new son Noah and asked his father Methuselah to see Enoch for an explanation. Methuselah apparently had no problem in reaching Enoch who was at that time in the orbiting spaceship.

Methuselah was also warned of the coming catastrophe. The Slavonic Book of Enoch reveals that 200 years before the event, he is told that "destruction of the Earth, is drawing near." At the same time, he is told to summon Nir, the second son of Lamech, and to brief him on the coming disaster, "then I will preserve the son of your son Lamech, his first Noah."

While Methuselah's grandson Noah is well known in the scriptures as the hero of the Deluge, there are very few references to his second grandson Nir, the son of Lamech, nor is there much information of Nir's son Melchizedek.

Both are considered to be Priest-kings in the tradition of the Patriarchs. When Enoch left to return to the spaceship after instructing his son Methuselah, the mantle of priesthood was passed to him. When the Earth was plunged into darkness, Methuselah and his brothers, with the sons of Enoch, built an altar and sacrificed sheep and oxen to propitiate the gods. Apparently it worked, at least there was a respite of ten years before the world was disturbed again.

Just before Methuselah died, the deity told him to transfer the priesthood to Nir. Methuselah was also to brief Nir on the coming destruction of the world by earthquake and rising waters, and by "the great storages of the waters of heaven that will come down to Earth." Presumably, this refers to the collapse of the cloud canopy encircling the Earth.

The Strange Appearance of Melchizedek

It is at this time that Nir's wife Sopanim, who had until then been sterile, suddenly conceived with child. She claimed that Nir nor any other man had slept with her, suggesting that the father was probably a Nefilim. Nir was not convinced of her innocence and banished her from his sight. Later, as she was about to give birth he visited her; suddenly she died at his feet. Nir and his brother Noah wrapped her in burial garments and placed her on the bed while they left to prepare her burial. They returned to the house to the surprise of their life. Sopanim had produced a child and as the Slavonic *Book of Enoch* stated:

> And a child came out from the dead Sopanim. And he sat on the bed at her side. And Noah and Nir came in to bury Sopanim, and they saw the child sitting beside the dead Sopanim, and wiping his clothing. And Noah and Nir were very terrified with a great fear because the child was fully developed physically, like a three-year old child. And he spoke with his lips, and he blessed the Lord. And Noah and Nir looked at him and behold, *the badge of priesthood was on his chest, and it was glorious in appearance* (emphasis ours).

Noah and Nir dressed the child in priestly garments and gave him the name Melchizedek. Noah suggested to Nir that the presence of the child be kept secret from the people for they would not understand his strange appearance and put him to death.

This "badge of priesthood" that he bore on his chest and that made him so unique that he was immediately recognized as part divine and automatically qualified him for the priesthood was none other than the "mark of the Nefilim" probably a patch of scaly lustrous hide.

This sign of divinity, a patch of scaly skin is also mentioned in the Hindu classics. In the Mahabharata, one of the demi-gods, Karna, is born of the sun-god Surya and an Earth mother. As such he is born "clad in a coat of armor, like a divine being." Karna makes a pact with the gods to give up his divine armor in order to obtain a sophisticated weapon. After accepting the celestial weapon, Karna begins to keep his end of the bargain. He begins to cut off the "armor" from his body with sharp tools.

> "The gods, the mortals, seeing Karna cut off part of his own body, roared with approbation, because no sign of pain were visible on his face, or were any scars left on his body."

Just as the Hindu sun god was Karna's father, the same may have been true of Melchizedek. Melchizedek, also called Adonizedek, means "My Lord is Zedek." Zedek was the Hebrew name for the Roman sun god Jupiter. Noah probably also carried the "mark of the Nefilim" as we shall see.

Later Nir was informed that soon a great catastrophe would envelope the Earth and destroy mankind, but his son Melchizedek would not perish. A messenger appeared later to take Melchizedek away for he said "when the people find out about the child, they will seize him and kill him." Melchizedek was taken aloft to his new home, the spaceship orbiting the Earth.

The Melchizedek Priesthood

The tradition of the priesthood of Melchizedek is entirely dropped from the Old Testament and instead it is vested in Aaron, brother of Moses, later to be replaced by the tribe of Levi or Levites. The priesthood of Melchizedek was kept alive, however, by the Mormons who gave this tradition precedence over all other priests in the scriptures.

The higher priesthood of the Mormon Church, or more correctly, the Church of Jesus Christ of Latter-Day Saints, is called the Melchizedek Priesthood. Aaron and Levi are given less importance, for the lesser priesthood is called the Aaronic Priesthood of which the Levitical Priesthood is but a subdivision.

The *Book of Mormon* traces the origins of the Melchizedek Priesthood back to the days of Abraham, to the person of that name who was high priest and King of Salem (later Jerusalem) to whom Abraham paid homage and a tithe of ten percent.

The Slavonic *Book of Enoch* also prophesizes that Melchizedek would head the priestly line after the Deluge. He was to be born in the twelfth generation after the Deluge and become King of Salem. Since the days of Abraham are about 2100 BC and the Deluge occurred, by our estimates, about 4000 BC, it would mean that the antediluvian Melchizedek would have to be at least 2000 years old. More logically, the Melchizedek of Abraham must have been a namesake of the original one carrying on the tradition of the priestly line of the antediluvian one by that name.

The Strange Appearance of Noah

Genesis asserts that

> Noah found favor with the Lord . . .
>
> Noah was a righteous man;
>
> he was without blame in that age.
>
> Noah walked with God.

The only other Patriarch who "walked with God" was Enoch, who became deified in his lifetime.

Although Noah was not deified or made divine in the religious literature, his Sumerian counterpart Utnapishtim was made immortal and sent to live with the gods. For some reason the Hebrew priesthood decided not to immortalize Noah.

Like his nephew Melchizedek, Noah was physically different. In the lost *Book of Lamech*, scraps of which have been recovered in the Dead Sea scrolls, Noah was so physically different when he was born that Lamech appealed to his father Methuselah, who in turn asked Enoch, whether or not Noah had been conceived by the Nefilim.

Methuselah was told that Noah was not from one of the divine beings but was from his own son Lamech. What then is this physical difference that so disturbed Lamech? Was this the difference that caused such consternation to Noah and his sons after the Deluge?

Genesis makes much of the incident after the Deluge when Noah, drunk from too much wine, collapsed in a drunken stupor in his tent. Ham entered and saw his father naked and told his two brothers, who proceeded to back into the tent with a cloth and covered the naked Noah. Finding out that his son Ham had seen him naked, Noah loses all sense of reason and puts a curse on Ham and his son Canaan.

One wonders over this irrational reaction. Was it because Noah wanted to hide the vestige of his reptilian past? The sensitivity of Noah in being seen naked can only mean that he bore the "sign of the Nefilim." Just like his nephew Melchizedek, it may have been a large badge-like area of scaly skin or hide on his chest.

Relations between humans and the Nefilim and their offspring were so severely strained that open warfare had actually broken out, and any vestige of reptilian ancestry in man was considered to be a "badge of shame." Melchizedek was whisked away by the deity just before the Deluge in order to prevent the people from killing him.

CHAPTER 18

THE REPHAIM: WARRIOR-GOD

After the Deluge a race of semi-divine warri
Levant. Called the Rephaim, they were installed as th
Lands and the space facilities at the beginning of the Third
this time they owed their loyalty to the eastern kings of Mesopotam
ly to Nannar/Sin who was the overlord of these lands.

When their cities in the Transjordan and elsewhere were destroyed by the eastern kings who invaded in the 21st Century BC, the Rephaim lost all fealty to legitimate authority and became an independent martial force in the Western Lands. They became a formidable and uncontrollable force that dominated and plagued the people of these lands for the next thousand years.

It was the Rephaim who built the impregnable glacis-type fortifications whose ruins are found all over the Middle East from Egypt to Anatolia. It was their descendants, called the Hyksos, who occupied Egypt for over four hundred years and under the Biblical name Amalekites prevented the Hebrew tribes under Moses from entering the land of Canaan.

Under various regional names such as Anakim and Philistine they controlled the lands settled by the Hebrew tribes for the period known as that of the Judges. As a political and military force, they were finally destroyed by the combined efforts of the Judean kings Saul and David in combination with Kamose and Ahmose, the first kings of the Egyptian 18th Dynasty. The history of the Rephaim is, as we shall see, interwoven with the destiny of the Hebrews from the days of Abraham until those of Solomon.

The Descendants of the Nefilim

In 1929, archaeologists excavating at Ras Shamra on the coast of Syria a few miles north of the modern city of Latakia, found a library of clay tablets dating to the 15th-12th Centuries BC. This site turned out to be the location of the ancient city of Ugarit, a main commercial stop on the trade route from northern Mesopotamia to the Mediterranean. Several of these tablets refer to an enigmatic people called the *rpum* or Rephaim. These tablets have been called the Rephaim texts; there is a close analogy with Rephaim or rpm of the scriptures.

The tablets concern a summons to attend a great banquet being given at an unspecified place to honor their great god El. It describes how the Rephaim prepare their horses and chariots for a trip, and after travelling for three days, arrive at the site of the feast. A great number of animals are slain for the banquet, and vast quantities of wine are supplied. This banquet lasts for seven days. In these tablets, the heroes are referred to as the "Rephaim of Baal," but they themselves are also considered to be deities since they are occasionally called *ilnym* or gods.

The noted Biblical scholar Adrian Curtis in his book *Ugarit (Ras Shamra)* has suggested that these Rephaim of the Ugarit tablets be divided into three categories:

1. The Rephaim of the Earth or the *rpi ars*. These appear to be the elite charioteers who came to the banquet.

. ephaim of Old or *rpim qdmym* or the royal ancestors.
.ey were probably the antediluvian Nefilim.

.he Rephaim who are gods or *rpum ilnym* or the heavenly Rephaim. These are presumably the Anunna who remained in the spaceship, sometimes called the Igigi.

.s the Rephaim of the Earth which concerns our researches here. They are semi-divine descendants of the Nefilim and as professional warriors their .signment was to protect the Western Lands.

Three cuneiform tablets also found at ancient Ugarit concern an epic of a youth called Aqhat. Known as *The Tale of Aqhat* it recounts the adventures of one Daniel and his son Aqhat, both referred to throughout the poem as "Rapha-men." Aqhat was pursued by the warrior-goddess Anath who wanted him as her lover. Aqhat refuses her advances and "she denounces Aqhat the youth, damns the child of Daniel the Rapha-man." Anat was the north Semitic name for Ishtar. The rest of the tablet is missing. The story is strongly reminiscent of the escapade of Gilgamesh with Ishtar in the land of the gods, when he too turns down the advances of the warrior-goddess.

Two Thousand Years of Domination

It is recorded in Genesis that the Rephaim were people indigenous to the land of Canaan. They first appear in Genesis 15, in the days of Abraham, when they are listed as one of the native peoples of Canaan. In the year 2068 BC when Yahweh concluded a covenant with Abraham at Hebron, he cataloged the people of the land as follows:

> To your offspring, I give this land, from the river of Egypt to the great river, the river Euphrates: the Kenites, the Kenizzites, the Kadmonium, the Hittites, the Perizzites, *the Rephaim*, the Amorites, the Canaanites, the Girgashites, and the Jebushites (emphasis ours).

At this time, the Rephaim are listed as one of the major nations of the land. Some 600 years later, at the time of the Exodus, when the Israelites were about to cross the Jordan River into Canaan, Deuteronomy 7 lists the seven nations of Canaan as follows: the Hittites, Girgashites, Amorites, Canaanites, Perizzites, Hivites, and Jebushites. The Rephaim are conspicuous by their absence. It would seem that in the intervening years they were wiped out as a nation or as a cohesive political force.

As we shall see, when their cities in the Transjordan were destroyed in the days of Abraham, the remnants settled in the western and southern part of Palestine. As a scattered people they were still a powerful force to contend with, and were known under various local names in the Bible such as Anakim, Amalekites and Philistines.

The Giant Warriors of the Scriptures

The scriptures make it clear that the Rephaim were the descendants of the Nefilim, and that they were giant ferocious warriors who dominated the Western Lands for two thousand years with their superior iron weapons and chariots. Their fortress cities were virtually impregnable.

In the *Book of Numbers* they are described as giants. During the Exodus, Moses decided to send scouts north into the land of Canaan to reconnoiter the land before any serious penetration would be attempted. The twelve scouts returned with a very pessimistic report about the Anakites:

They went up into the Negeb and came to Hebron, where lived Ahiman,

Fig. 50 – Distribution of the Rephaim during the Third Millennium BC and later.

Sheshai, and Talmai, the Anakites . . . However, the people who inhabit the country are powerful, and the cities are fortified and very large; moreover, we saw the Anakites there . . . All the people that we saw in it are men of great size; we saw the Nefilim there — the Anakites are part of the Nefilim — and we looked like grasshoppers to ourselves, and so we must have looked to them.

Forty years later, as the Israelites attempted again to enter Canaan, this time by taking the roundabout way through the Transjordan, they again encountered the Anakites. As they skirted the land of Moab, they were told not to harass the Moabites or to engage them in war. The land they were told was "formerly inhabited by the Emin, a people great and numerous and as tall as the Anakites. Like the Anakites, they are counted as Rephaim, but the Moabites call them Emin."

Thus, the Anakim or Anakites are equated to the Nefilim and the Rephaim, the former being their name before the Deluge, and the latter the term they were known by after the catastrophe.

The Rephaim and their cousins were a fierce martial race, giant in stature. When the average inhabitant of the Western Lands was about 5 to 5 1/2 feet tall, the 9 and 10 foot Rephaim must truly have been an imposing sight. After the Israelite reconnaissance team returned from Canaan they reported to Moses that the Anakim they saw were giant people, "we looked like grasshoppers to them" they declared.

King Og of Bashon, reportedly the last of the Rephaim in that area, was described as a huge man whose bedstead was 9 cubits long and 4 wide. A cubit was the length of a man's forearm, and varied slightly among the ancient peoples. Using a cubit of 18 inches, the bedstead would be 13 1/2 by 6 feet. A cubit of 15 inches would make it 11 by 5 feet.

The Philistine Goliath who fought David was 6 cubits and one span tall according to the scriptures. By the above calculations he would be eight or ten feet tall depending on the size of the cubit used. Goliath and his brothers are called *rph* or Rephaim in the Hebrew text, although traditionally the term has been translated as giant.

The famous Samson was probably also a Rephaim. While the Old Testament dotes on his fabulous accomplishments, his size is not given. In the *Haggadah*, however, he is called a rph. Born near Beth-Shemesh in Lebanon, he is named after the Sun God Shamash. His mother was reportedly impregnated by "Yahweh's envoy," presumably one of the demi-gods. Samson refused to marry one of the Hebrew women and instead chose a Philistine woman, presumably because she was one of the Rephaim.

Judges 14 describes one of his exploits which sounds very much like the parties of the Rephaim at Ugarit. When he was at Timnah, a town near Beth-Shemesh, it is said that "Samson staged there a party for seven days because that is what the elite fighters used to do." He is undoubtedly repeating the exploits performed by his ancestors at Ugarit. Samson's home was just a few miles from Baalbek or Beth-Shemesh, the sacred place where the Mesopotamian gods met and feasted in the Fourth and Third Millennium.

As warriors, the Rephaim were an awesome force. They had a variety of iron weapons that outclassed their opponents. Their large composite bow was said to outrange any other bow. In the Second Millennium, their iron chariots terrorized the countryside. Protected by the glacis-type fortifications, their cities were invulnerable; from these citadels they often burst forth and ravaged the surrounding countryside.

At the time of Abraham, the fortifications of the Rephaim were strategically located along the King's Highway in the Transjordan to protect the lands from the north, east, and south. The invasion of the eastern kings in 2085 BC and the destruction of these cities marks the end of their loyalty to established authority. They migrated to the west and built new fortified cities patterned after the glacis-type design.

This military class was known in the Old Testament by a variety of names depending on where they lived and their tribal associations. They did not mix with the other indigenous people and were given native names such as Emin by the Moabites, Zamzummin by the Ammonites, and Avvim by the people of the Negeb.

Originally occupying Lebanon and the Mount Hermon area, they spread north to coastal Syria and to the Transjordan where they built a string of fortified cities. In the western part of Palestine, they became allied and intermarried with the Caphtorim, who had come over from Crete and settled in the coastal areas, later to be known as Philistines and Phoenicians. Those that lived among the native people were generally called Anakim or Anakite, named after their ancestor Anak. Hebron was their capital city. A particular group of Rephaim settled in the Negeb and the Seir area and became known as Amalekites, or descendants of Amalek. These became the scourge of the Hebrews during the Exodus.

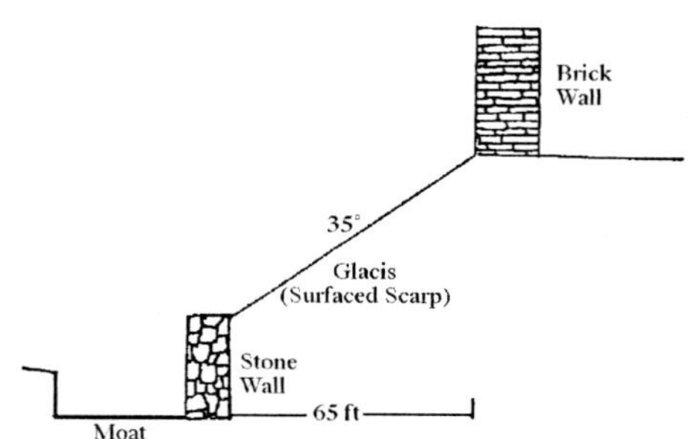

Fig. 51 – Glacis-type fortifications of the Hyksos.
Cross-section of the glacis-type or scarp defenses introduced into Palestine, Syria, Anatolia, and Egypt by the Hyksos (Amalekites) about 2000-19000 BC.

The Glacis-Type Fortifications: Strongholds of the Rephaim

Excavations at Jericho have revealed that it is one of the oldest cities in the world. It was occupied continuously, with occasional interruptions and destructions from 8000 BC until about 1500 BC, when it was destroyed for a final time, never to be rebuilt. For our purposes here we are concerned with the Bronze Age period.

Archaeological remains show that Jericho flourished as a major city from about 3200 until about 2100 BC when there was an abrupt break in occupation. At this time, the strongly fortified city was destroyed by a heat so intense that the bricks of the walls encircling the city were burnt red right through the center.

The site was rebuilt and reoccupied, but after 2000 BC an entirely new system of defense was introduced here — the glacis or scarp-type of fortification. This system of defense is not only found at Jericho but also all over Palestine, northern Syria, and even in the delta of Egypt. Its invention is usually attributed to the Hyksos.

The system of defense consists of a steeply sloping scarp of soil surfaced with plaster, tile, or brick, surrounded by a stone wall and a moat. At the top of the sloping scarp or glacis is another wall. Thus at Jericho a reconstruction of the defenses shows a stone revetment ten feet high, a plastered slope at an angle of 35 degrees running to a height of 35 feet above the revetment. On its crest there is a high wall of brick; this brick wall thus stands back from the stone wall at the bottom of the slope a distance of 65 feet. A cross-section of the defense fortification reveals its formidable appearance (figure 51).

After 2000 BC, many of the cities of the west were defended this way. It meant that there was a common culture or organization which bound all these cities together. This common bond was the military engineering genius of the Rephaim.

This type of defense was found at Beth-Shean, Shechem, Gezer, Megiddo, Hazor, Saruhen, and many other cities in Palestine. They are also found in Anatolia and northern Syria at Alalakh, Karchemish, and Ugarit. They also appear in Egypt in the Delta region. The glacis defenses, curiously enough, do not appear in Transjordan where an important civilization is known to have flourished between the 23rd and 22nd Centuries BC, when a long line of fortified cities existed along the main north-south road known as the King's Highway. These cities were destroyed at that time, never to be rebuilt for a thousand years. Moving westward, these Rephaim learned from this experience and rebuilt their cities in such a way as to prevent such a wholesale destruction again. At the same time they lost their loyalty to the Sumerian kings, refuted established authority, and became maverick troops, roaming the land as bands of armed warriors. It was much like the roving knights of the 14th Century AD in Europe, which had lost all fealty as the feudal system broke down, and ravaged the lands of northern France.

Secure behind their impregnable glacis-type defenses, the Anakim of the 19th through the 11th Century BC, terrorized the surrounding lands. These forays are described in the *Book of Judges.* Leaving their citadels in their war chariots, they ravaged the countryside and pillaged at will. Any organized effort at resistance was quelled immediately. They reinforced their dominance of the land by keeping control over the manufacture and use of iron. The *First Book of Samuel* reveals how there was no smith to be found in all the land of Israel, and any repairs to metal tools such as plowshares and sickles had to be done by the Philistines and their allies, the Kenites, who were skilled in metal-smithing. In this way, the Rephaim remained in control of the lands of Egypt and Palestine for centuries.

Transjordan, Home of the Eastern Rephaim

When the kings of Mesopotamia invaded Palestine in 2085 BC they passed by way of Damascus, then followed the Kings's Highway which ran south to Elath on the Gulf of Aqaba. This route brought them up against the citadels of the Rephaim, a sort of Maginot line that stretched the length of the Transjordan to protect the land of Palestine from such an incursion. The power of the invading kings, numbered as 800,000 according to the *Haggadah*, must have been overwhelming indeed, for they not only crushed these fortified cities but they never were rebuilt and the land remained unoccupied for a thousand years. The account in Genesis gives their route as follows:

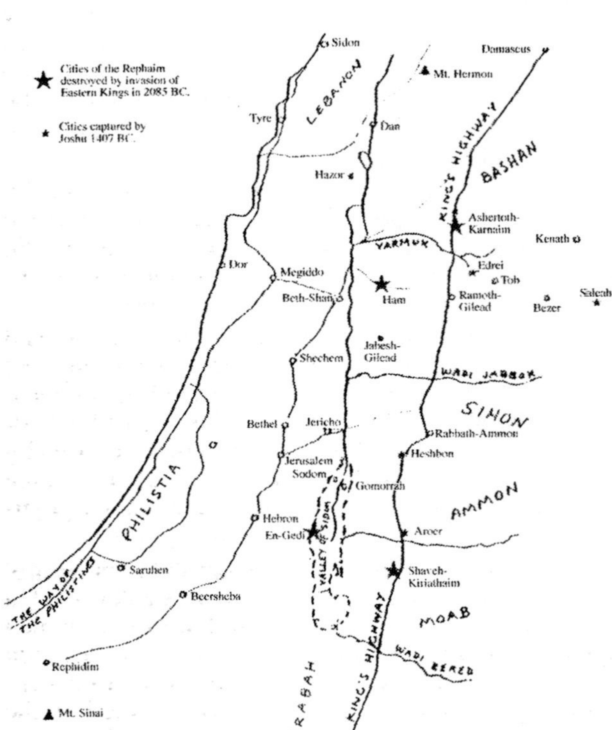

Fig. 52 – The Eastern Rephaim in Transjordan.

Entering the Transjordan from the north they first defeated the Rephaim at Ashteroth-Karnaim (figure 52). Heading south they then swung west to destroy the Zuzim at Ham, the citadel that protected the crossroad over the Jordan to Megiddo and the Sea. The Zuzim are identified below. Returning to their original route, they then defeated the Emim at Shaveh-Kiriathaim in southern Transjordan. Successfully penetrating the Arabah, they then swung over to destroy the Amalekites in the area of Kadesh. Although only a few cities are mentioned in the Genesis account, there were presumably many others destroyed.

The identification of these people is provided by the Biblical account which gives the route of the Israelites 600 years later. At this time, they encircled Palestine to enter the Jordan Valley by the same route as taken by the invading kings, except they did it from the south.

Deuteronomy 2 states that the land of Ammon was "formerly inhabited by the Rephaim, whom the Ammonites called Zamzummin, a people great and numerous, and as tall as the Anakites." They had been wiped out as a nation earlier and their land resettled by the Ammonites. The Zuzim of Genesis and the Zamzummin of Deuteronomy are one and the same people. In the Jewish Midrashic literature the name Zamzummin means "great masters in war," and the people were reportedly the offspring of the alliance between Canaanite women and the Nefilim of old.

The Emin are also referred to in Deuteronomy. In speaking of Moab, it states that "it was formerly inhabited by the Emin, a people great and numerous and as tall as the Anakites. Like the Anakites, they are counted as Rephaim, but the Moabites call them Emin."

After the Israelites had skirted the lands of Moab and Ammon they came to the country of Sihon. At that time, the eastern part of Palestine or the Transjordan was divided as follows: From the Wadi Zered at the bottom-most part of the Dead Sea to the River Arnon stretched the land of Moab. Its capital was Shaveh-Kiriathaim, the fortress capital of the Emin destroyed some centuries earlier. North of the Arnon and up to the Wadi Jabbok lay the land of the Ammonites where the Zamzummin lived and were widespread as far as the Jordan River where their capital at Ham was destroyed in the same invasion (figure 52).

Upon crossing the Jabbok, the Israelites challenged the Amorites led by King Sihon who had made Heshbon his capital. North of these lands was the kingdom of Og of Bashon, whose capitals were Edrei and Ashtaroth. Ashtaroth-Karnaim had been the first major city of the Rephaim to be challenged and destroyed by the invasion.

The kingdom of Og comprised Bashon and the Mount Hermon region and extended to the Jordan River in the west. Salcah was at its eastern extremity and Dan in the northwest. In Deuteronomy, Og is called the last of the Rephaim and particular mention is made of his huge stature as shown by the size of his bedstead, which measured nine cubits long and four cubits wide. It was captured by the Israelites and put on display in the city of Rabbah. The ease with which Joshua captured the lands of Transjordan indicates that they were scantly populated by the remnants of the Rephaim. However, it was not always so.

At a Bronze Age site near Bab Edh-Dhra just above the coastal plain east of the Lisan (the tongue of the Dead Sea), archaeologists found evidence of a dense civilization that flourished from 3300 BC until about 2100 BC at which time it was destroyed by a conflagration that is reflected in the ruins. The area seems to have been abandoned. A vast cemetery found here attests to a very large population during the Bronze Age, the time when it was occupied by the Rephaim.

These people used the charnel-house type of burial, consisting of a circular well-built mud and brick structure, sometimes lined with stone. The charnel-house was usually placed in a section of slope cut horizontally so that part of it was below ground and the upper part protruded above the surface. It is estimated that there are at least 20,000 of these burial chambers in the area.

Anywhere between 12 and 15 burials were made in each tomb. These burial chambers seem to have all been abandoned at about the same time. Before the inhabitants left, they burned a number of bodies inside. Most of the mortuary buildings contained a large deposit of ash near the doorway, indicating that this was the last event that occurred before the tombs were sealed. It remains a puzzle to this day.

In view of the ease of the advance of the invading kings in 2085 BC through a series of formidable defenses of the Rephaim, and the evidence that the area remained unresettled for a thousand years, it would suggest that the invaders used some kind of weapon that contaminated the land. The contamination of the dead in Transjordan would explain the reason for burning the bodies and sealing the tombs, and why the area remained relatively uninhabited for a thousand years thereafter. It may have taken that long for the poisoned land to recover and for the memory of the holocaust to be erased from the minds of the native population. It explains why the Rephaim moved westward and settled the lands there.

Hebron, Metropolis of the Anakim

Shortly after Abraham arrived in the land of Canaan in 2092 BC, he went to Egypt where he stayed for a while, only to return to Canaan suddenly in 2086 BC the year before the invasion. At Bethel, he split his forces and while Lot took part of the army to the Valley of Siddim, Abraham retired to the areas south of Mamre in the Hebron region. With the help of the Anakim generals Eshkol, Aner, and Mamre, Abraham pursued the departing invasion army. Who then were these allies of Abraham?

They are identified in the *Book of Joshua* as Anakim. The ancient name for the city of Hebron was Kiryat-Arba and it was the "metropolis of the Anakim." Kiryat-Arba meant the "city of Arba" and was named after the father of the Anakim. When the Israelite spies went up and scouted Canaan during the Exodus, they came to the region of Hebron which they said was inhabited by Ahiman, Sheshai, and Talmai, all called children of Anak.

These sons are described as Nefilim and were of extraordinary stature and power. The names of the sons of Anak do not appear elsewhere in the Old Testament, probably because they are not of Semitic origin. It is noteworthy however, that in the list of the Hyksos kings who ruled Egypt, one bears the name of Sheshai.

Like the Amalekites, the Anakim are vilified by the Hebrew scriptures. The Amalekites had prevented the Israelis from entering directly into Canaan after their flight from Egypt. When the Israelites finally settled in Canaan some forty years later, they were told, according to Joshua 11 that the Anakim had been eliminated from the lands of Judah and Israel.

> Joshua moved at the time to wipe out the people of Anak: from the Highlands, from Hebron, from Debir (from all the people of Israel and from all the Highlands of Judah). Along with their towns, Joshua utterly destroyed them. None of the people of Anak were left in the land of the Bene Israel. Only in Gaza, and in Gath, and in Ashdod did they remain.

The claim was somewhat premature, however, for during the next 400 years, the period equated to that of the Judges, the Anakim and their Amalekite and Philistine allies controlled and ruled the land and caused the Hebrew tribes much difficulty.

No reason is given for such a blank policy towards the people of Anak, and the execration is strongly similar to the curse against the Amalekites. The Anakim appear to have blocked the occupation of the Israelites mainly in the mountainous regions of the west — the citadels of the Philistines. Large pockets of indigenous peoples remained in Palestine and the Hebrew tribes were forced to settle in the less fertile areas, and for 400 years were at the mercy of the raiding parties from the strongholds of the Rephaim.

The Rephaim of Western Palestine: The Philistines

According to Biblical tradition, the land of the Philistines comprised five fortified cities which dominated the surrounding lands as far as Beersheba and Debir. Their main cities of Ashdod, Ekron, Gath, Gaza, and Ashkelon had withstood all the efforts of the Israelites to dislodge them after the Exodus and in the ensuing period subjected the tribes to continual harassment by their chariots bursting forth from their citadels. These Philistines are called Anakim in Joshua 11; in Jeremiah 47 they are referred to as the remnants of the Anakim. Who then were these Philistines who are supposedly part of the Anakim?

Genesis 10 states that the Philistines were descended from the Caphtorim or Cretans who settled in the coastal areas, displacing the native Avvim. In fact, one curious reference in the *Book of Amos* indicates that the deity brought the ancestors of the Philistines from Crete and settled them in Canaan just as he brought the Israelites out of the land of Egypt. In this sense they appear to be a "chosen" people.

These Cretans intermarried with the Rephaim, producing a race of fierce warriors who came to be known as Philistines to the Hebrews. Their territory overlapped with that of the Amalekites in the south and the Anakites in the west; at times, the scriptures seem to confuse the names of these three groups of people.

The Philistines were also related or at least allied with the people of the northern coastal cities later to be known as Phoenicia. This is indicated in Jeremiah 47 when he prophesies the fate of the Philistines.

> Because for the day is coming to destroy all the Philistines, to cut off from Tyre and Sidon every helper that remains. For the Lord is destroying the Philistines, the remnant of the coastland of Caphtor. Baldness had come upon Gaza, Ashkelon has perished. O remnant of the Anakim, how long will you gash yourselves?

The Philistines occupied the western hill country as early as the time of Abraham. After the destruction of Sodom and the other cities of the Valley of Siddim, Abraham and his family settled near Beersheba. In order to live here, they had to pay tribute and make a treaty with Abimelech, the King of the Philistines, who apparently controlled the area at the time. Abraham had to purchase land rights and obtain permission to live there. After the pact was sealed, "Abimelech, and Phicol, Chief of his troops, left and returned to Philistine country." This statement makes it clear that the Philistines did not live here, yet they controlled the land: it is also evident that the appearance of Abimelech's Chief of Troops meant that they had a large military force on hand to enforce their claims.

The Amalekite-Hyksos Equation

The Exodus is believed to have occurred in the middle of the 15th

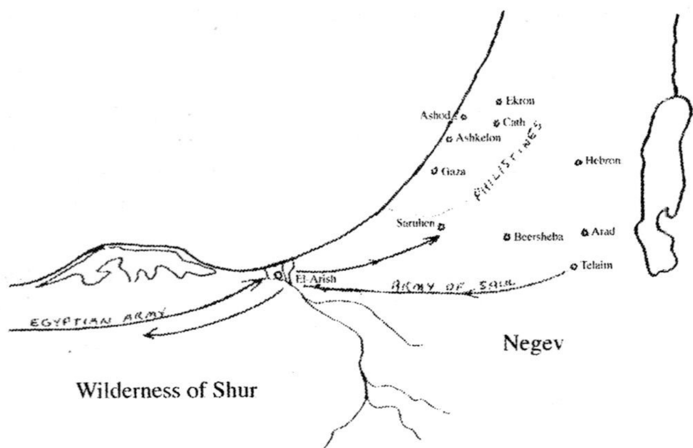

Fig. 53 – The end of the Hyksos/Amalekites circa 1000 BC.

Century BC, at the time of natural disasters that spelled the end of the Middle Kingdom in Egypt. It was a period of chaos which made it possible for Moses to lead a rag-tag army of refugees out of Egypt to try to reach the land of Canaan.

The complete collapse of government and military power in Egypt allowed the Amalekites to penetrate the land easily from their position in the Negev. In their attempts to enter the land of Canaan, the refugees under Moses ran into this irresistible force of professional warriors. They too were on the move, but in a westerly direction.

A pitched battle at Rephidim and numerous skirmishes convinced Moses that they could not penetrate this formidable army. The Amalekites moved into the delta of Egypt and occupied it almost unopposed by a disintegrating government and disorganized army.

Upon leaving Egypt, the Israelites entered the Wilderness of Shur and appeared to be headed for the land of Canaan by the most direct route. It was "the 15th day of the second month" after leaving Egypt that they camped at Rephidim. It is here that they ran into the main body of the Amalekite horde. Although Moses claimed it as a victory it was a costly one, for they were hard pressed and very close to defeat. This was but one of a series of battles with the Amalekites.

The migrating force led by Moses was harassed continuously by the descendants of the Rephaim as it is recounted in Deuteronomy 25:

> Remember what Amalek did to you on your journey, after you left Egypt — how, undeterred by fear of God, he surprised you on the march, when you were famished and weary, and cut down all the stragglers in your rear.

The ferocity of the attacks of the Amalekites closed the direct approach to Canaan at Rephidim. Yet they were to be blocked once more before they decided to turn south and try a more indirect route into Palestine. It was then that a curse was placed on the Amalekites, as pronounced in Exodus 17:

> I will utterly blot out the memory of Amalek from under the heaven . . . The Lord will be at war with Amalek throughout the ages.

The barbarity of the Amalek attacks is described in the works of the *Haggadah*. This battle apparently took place after the Amalekites had captured the cities of the delta of Egypt. Here they had obtained the archives where the Hebrews had lived and had obtained the table of descent of the Hebrews, their chiefs and the different families. The Amalekites appeared before the Israelite camps and taunted the Hebrews by name to come out, make peace with them and to transact business. Those who took the bait and answered the call were slaughtered and their bodies horribly mutilated.

Forced back into the desert, the Israelites spent forty years before they could enter Canaan by the direct route through the Transjordan. Settling among the Rephaim and their allies, the Hebrew tribes remained at the mercy of the Amalekites and their allies for the period of 400 years, known as the time of the Judges.

The Amalekites were not just a loose confederation of nomadic tribes as has been suggested by most Biblical commentators. There are many Biblical references which dispute this view. The most significant are the following.

It was predicted of Israel at one time that "their kings shall rise above Agag." (Numbers 24). This statement makes it clear that Agag, the last Amalekite king, was of such high stature that later kings of Israel would be measured against him. This would certainly not be said of just a tribal chief. Secondly, when Agag was captured by Saul, he was called "Agag, the King of the Amalekites." (I Samuel 15:8). Since Agag was such a powerful and great king so as to be used as a measure, then it follows that he must have led a great nation.

A third reference reveals that Saul besieged and defeated the Amalekites at a place called "the city of Amalek." (I Samuel 15:5). It then follows logically that a powerful prince leading a mighty nation would certainly have a large city as his capital. This evidence does not describe a group of disorganized nomadic tribes. It shows that the Hebrew tribes were up against a very powerful nation.

The Rule of the Hyksos Kings in Egypt

The country that the Hyksos conquered was a helpless land, one devastated by natural calamity. After the loss of the Pharaoh and his army, there was no resistance in Egypt and the invaders moved into the delta area with no opposition. From there they spread south, conquering cities and nomes and installing puppet kings to rule the provinces.

Although the Old Testament attributes the destruction of the Egyptian army to their pursuit of the fleeing Hebrews, it is more probable that it was destroyed attempting the stop the inflow of the Hyksos. Occupying the Nile Valley, the Hyksos built a fortress capital city at Avaris, usually placed in the delta, but more probably located in the Wadi El-Arish, also called the Brook of Egypt, which was the traditional boundary between Egypt and Palestine.

The Hyksos capital was strategically placed to defend the approaches to Egypt from the east, the direction of invasions in the past. In fact, since the Hyksos or Amalekites were spread throughout Palestine as well as Egypt, the location in the Wadi El-Arish was a natural one and enabled them to control Palestine as well as Egypt.

The Hyksos (a Greek name meaning "foreign kings") are not mentioned in the Old Testament by that name, yet archaeologically there is evidence of their occupation everywhere in Palestine and Syria — their uniquely designed fortress cities. This glacis-type defense occurs in the delta of Egypt, throughout the land of Canaan and as far north as Anatolia. Truly then, the people known as Hyksos must have been known in the Old Testament by another name.

Much of the information available on the Hyksos comes from Josephus who, in his *Against Apion,* quotes the Egyptian historian Manetho on the character of these people and their effects on the native Egyptian culture:

> There came, after a surprising manner, men of ignoble birth out of the eastern parts, and had boldness enough to make expedition into our country, and with ease subdued it by force, yet without hazarding a battle with them. So when they had gotten those that governed us under their power, they afterwards burnt down our cities, and demolished the Temple of the Gods, and used all the inhabitants after a most barbarous manner.

Josephus then relates how they appointed a king whose name was Salatis who made his capital at Memphis. He collected tribute from both the upper and lower regions of Egypt, and left garrisons at strategic places that gave him control over the whole land. Fearing an invasion from the eastern kings, he founded the fortress city of Avaris to protect against this potential threat.

The Hyksos are credited with introducing the war chariot to warfare, new types of swords, and the strong composite bow. They imposed their will on the Egyptians for 400 years, a period which equates with that of the Judges in Palestine.

Life in Palestine Among the Amalekites or Hyksos

With certain native peoples as allies, the Amalekites controlled Canaan with an iron hand. The scriptures reveal that the Hebrew tribes had to settle and live among the Amalekites who inhabited and controlled the plains of Judah. In other areas, they often attacked and harassed the Hebrews, sometimes in conjunction with other people. According to Judges, they joined Moab against the Israelites to capture the city of Jericho; at another time, they fought battles with the Hebrews who lived in the valley of Jezreel.

Since most of the cities of Canaan were in the hands of the native people, the migrating Hebrews were forced to settle in the less desirable areas between the cities. Here they were vulnerable to periodic raids from all directions. Most of the Hebrew tribes expressed frustration because the cities and lands which had been assigned by Joshua were still under control of the native people. Thus the tribe of Menassah lived among the fortified cities of Beth-Shean, Dor, Iblean, Megiddo, and Tanach, which remained in Canaanite hands. The tribes of Ephraim, Zebulon, Asher, and Naphtali could not seize the cities in their assigned lands — those of Gezer, Nahalal, Acco, Sidon, Helbah, Rehob, and Beth-Avath, for example. The five cities of the Philistines remained unconquered, as well as all the land of Lebanon from Mount Hermon to Harmath.

Behind their impregnable fortifications, the Amalekites would bide their time and then periodically burst forth from their citadels and raid the land in their iron chariots. One of their favorite tactics was to wait until the crops were ripe for harvest, and then they would drive their cattle ahead of them and;

> Destroy the land's produce . . . They would leave no means of livelihood — sheep, ox, or donkey . . . They would enter the land to devastate it. So Israel became utterly destitute.

For over four hundred years the Amalekites and their allies ruled this way, the Hebrew tribes never knowing when the ferocious sons of the Rephaim would break out of their cities and attack the settlers.

From their capital city at Avaris they could explode into the Negev and devastate that area at will. Josephus describes the citadel of the Hyksos which Salatis built east of the delta:

> It was a city he made very strong by the walls he built around it, and by a most numerous garrison of 240,000 armed men

> whom he put into it to keep it. Here Salatis came in summer, partly to gather corn, and pay his soldiers their wages, and partly to exercise his armed men, and thereby terrify foreigners.

The exercise that Josephus refers to was probably the armed forays into the land of the Negev.

It has been somewhat puzzling how the Hyksos/Amalekites could have maintained control over the lands of Egypt and Palestine for such a long time. It can be easily explained, however, by their ruthless nature and military ability, and their policy of keeping the people of the lands they occupied impoverished and weaponless.

In the *First Book of Samuel* it explains how the Amalekites and Philistines controlled the supply and use of iron:

> There was no smith to be found in all the land of Israel, for the Philistines had said to themselves, "The Hebrews might make swords or spears." So all Israel would go down to the Philistines to repair any of their plowshares, mattocks, axes, or sickles . . . So at the time of the battle of Michmash neither sword nor spear was available to any of the soldiers who were with Saul and Jonathan.

With their chariots, iron weapons, and composite bows, the Amalekites and Philistines were virtually unbeatable against an enemy who at best could muster stone age weapons. In the first battles of Saul and David against these formidable foes, the only weapons that were available to the Hebrews were clubs, stone slings, simple bow and arrow, and stone-tipped spears. It was not until later, when they could capture and seize sufficient iron weapons, that the tide turned and the Israelites began to drive the Amalekites from the land.

Revolt in Egypt and Palestine: End of the Rephaim

The Egyptian puppet king Sekenenre who ruled from Thebes started the revolt against the Hyksos kings of the Seventeenth Dynasty. The Hyksos kings at that time ruled from Avaris and left puppet kings throughout Egypt to carry out their wishes. The revolt was carried on by his sons Kamose and Ahmose who recovered most of Egypt. It was then necessary to dislodge the Hyksos from Avaris, the fortress they had retreated to after their defeats in Egypt.

The war of Kamose against the last Hyksos king Apophis (Apop) is preserved on a stele which was first erected at Karnak. It describes his attack on the river fortress Avaris and how he seized hundreds of ships, some of which contained "produce of Retinue." Kamose boasts that he had "made Apophis see a miserable time," and then adds that "the Prince of Retinue, weak of arms, who planned many things in his heart, but they have not come to pass for him." Retinue is usually identified as the land of Palestine. Thus the Prince of Retinue who seemed to be allied with Kamose was probably none other than Saul, who at that time was beseiging the Amalekites at El-Arish.

Kamose was able to reoccupy all of Egypt except their citadel at Avaris. His successor Ahmose, who is credited with founding the Eighteenth Dynasty, completed the defeat of the Hyksos with the help of the Israelites. Ahmose not only drove out the Hyksos but also pursued them to Saruhen, a fortress city on the border of the land of their allies, the Philistines. After a six-year siege, Ahmose destroyed this stronghold and the remnants of the Hyksos. We can read a direct account of these events in the biography of one of his officers, who with Ahmose attacked Avaris and destroyed it, and then moved on to Saruhen where he besieged the city.

The scriptures describe battles against the Amalekites at the Wadi El-Arish, and other places on the border of Egypt. In the *First Book of Samuel*, Saul was advised by the prophet Samuel to go forth and destroy the Amalekites:

> Yahweh the Lord of Hosts has spoken thus: "I have taken account of what Amalek did to Israel when they confronted them on the road as they were coming up from Egypt. Now go! Strike down the Amalekites and destroy everything that belongs to them, and have no pity on them. Slay both men and women, both weaned and nursing child, both ox and sheep, both camel and ass." So Saul summoned the army and mustered it at Telaim — two hundred thousand foot soldiers and ten thousand men of Judah. Then Saul went to the city of Amalek and lay sedge at the Wadi. Saul defeated the Amalekites from the Wadi toward Shur on the border of Egypt. He captured Agag, king of Amalek, alive and utterly destroyed all the people with the edge of the sword.

The account maintains that the city was beseiged from a wadi. There is only one river bed (wadi) in southern Palestine or northern Egypt, and that is the Wadi El-Arish, which forms the traditional boundary between Egypt and Palestine (figure 53). At certain times of the year it is a full fledged river; there is strong evidence that in ancient time it was flooded most of the year.

In the scriptures, the Wadi El-Arish is often referred to as just "the Wadi." Saul fought the Amalekites from "the Wadi toward Shur on the border of Egypt." The wilderness of Shur is that area between the Wadi and Egypt; it was the first wilderness the Israelites entered after the Sea of Passage. Thus the city of Amalek had to be El-Arish just as the city of the Hyksos was at Avaris. It is strange that scholars have not noted the close philological association of El-Arish and Av-aris.

The last Hyksos king was called Apop or Apophis (Greek). The Amalekite king captured by Saul at the Wadi was called Agag. The similarity of the two names is so remarkable as to require further elucidation. The explanation can be found in the way early Hebrew was written. Early Hebrew shows a striking resemblance between the letter "g" or *gimel* and the letter "p" or *pei*. No other Hebrew letters were so much alike. Each letter is an oblique line connected to a shorter, more oblique line, and is similar to the number 7. The size of the angle between the two oblique lines constitutes the only difference. Since the vowels in early Hebrew are interchangeable, Agag can easily become Apop. It thus appears that the last Hyksos king and the Amalekite king Agag were one and the same person. It is a known fact that the Eighteenth Dynasty which began the era of the New Kingdom in Egypt, started with Ahmose and the expulsion of the Hyksos.

It is also known that the first Hebrew king was Saul who, with David, presided over the extinction of the Amalekites. Placing these monarchs in the same time period rather than several hundred years apart solves many of the chronological puzzles in correlating Egyptian and Biblical history. This alteration is necessary to understanding the history of the Middle East from the time of the Deluge to the days of the Judean Kings. The reign of the Rephaim and its related tribes had lasted for thousands of years. The destruction of the Amalekites about 1000 BC marks the end of this group as a military and political power.

CHAPTER 19

CANNIBALISM AND HUMAN SACRIFICE

Was the Burnt Offering a Cooked Meal?

One way to ensure favor in the afterlife was by sacrifice to the gods. In antediluvian days it was a human that was sacrificed and this practice persisted after the Deluge until about the end of the Third Millennium BC, at which time it was replaced by animal sacrifice. It was a ritual requested by the gods, for it was their way of ensuring that they were fed regularly and without interruption.

Human sacrifice and cannibalism are what might be called "delicate" subjects since modern civilized people do not wish to be reminded that their ancestors may have offered humans in sacrifice to the gods or that they had been reduced to eating their own kind. Nevertheless, the subject cannot be avoided when describing primitive times.

Antediluvian man practiced barbaric customs for the simple reason that divine needs had to be met. The abortive attempt of Abraham to sacrifice his son Isaac stands as a landmark in human history; it indicates the end of this custom, a ritual required by the divine authorities.

After the days of Abraham there are few references to human sacrifice in the Old Testament. But there are many veiled indications that human sacrifice was still prevalent and practiced among the Hebrew tribes.

Throughout the years, the term "burnt offering" has been used exclusively by the translators of the Old Testament. The term could just as well have been rendered as "cooked offering" except that this wording would carry connotations of offering food. This would tread dangerously close to the ritual of human sacrifice as food for the gods. None the less, the gods had to be fed. They required cooked food, whether animal or human flesh in their offerings.

Occasionally indications have slipped through the translators and editors of the scriptures which reveal that a so-called "burnt offering" was in reality roasted or cooked meat prepared on what suspiciously looks like a barbecue grill. For example, in Genesis 31:54, Jacob and Laban form a treaty and seal it with a sacrifice to the Lord:

> Jacob offered a sacrifice on the Heights, and invited his companions to partake of the meal. After the meal, they passed the night on the Heights.

As the statement implies, the meat from the sacrifice was certainly not reduced to ashes but was consumed by Jacob and Laban and their friends.

Another reference which indicates that the sacrificial meat was meant to be eaten is contained both in Biblical and Sumerian sources. After the Deluge, Noah wished to show his obeisance to the god that had nearly destroyed the world. In Genesis 7:20 it says:

> Then Noah built an altar to Yahweh and, choosing from every clean animal and every clean bird, offered burnt offerings on the altar. As Yahweh smelled the soothing odor, he said to himself, "Never again will I doom the world because of man, since the devisings of man's heart are evil from the start; neither will I ever again strike down every living being, as I have done."

Yahweh was chagrined not because of the tribulations of mankind but because the Deluge had cut him off from his regular meals. For forty days of rain and 150 days of flood, the gods had not eaten and they were famished. This is reflected in a similar passage from the Sumerian story of the Flood. It is obvious that the Genesis story of the Deluge is derived from the Sumerian account which antedates it by thousands of years. According to the story as contained in the *Epic of Gilgamesh*, the Sumerian Noah, Utnapishtim, also offered a sacrifice after the waters had receded. The gods reacted quickly:

> The gods smelled the fragrance,
>
> the gods smelled the sweet fragrance,
>
> and the gods gathered like flies over the sacrificer.

It is obvious from these two sources that the sacrifice of Noah (or Utnapishtim) was meant to be eaten and not consumed by the flames. It is also germane to note, as we shall see later, that during the Exodus, Moses was instructed to leave salt by the sacrificial meal. Obviously, the gods loved their meat well seasoned.

The four books of the Torah which deal with the Exodus are filled with references to burnt offerings meant to placate the Hebrew God Yahweh. So much importance is attached to these offerings that it is even specified in exact terms who will offer the animals and birds, which ones will be acceptable and their condition, how to prepare the meal and how to offer it, and detailed instructions on building the grill to be used in these offerings. The Torah sounds suspiciously more like a cookbook rather than a religious document!

Undoubtedly, the very specific instructions given for choosing an animal and preparing it for presentation were meant to make sure that the deity had the proper diet and was not inadvertently poisoned by the Hebrew cooks. These cooked offerings had by the 15th Century BC become a substitute for human sacrifice, the preferred food of the gods. Later, during the days of the occupation of Canaan and with the absence of their god Yahweh, the priestly offerings became mere symbolic rituals.

The end of the barbaric ceremony of offering cooked humans on an altar or grill ended about 2080 BC with the sacrifice of Abraham, when he prepared to offer his son Isaac as a burnt offering but at the last minute was told to substitute a goat. This event marks the end of human sacrifice as an institution as required by the gods. It is a milestone in man's relation with the gods and in his development as an independent human being. Human sacrifice was a custom carried over from the antediluvian days when the gods ruled totally and the offering of humans as food in sacrifice was expected from mankind. In those days man was literally food for the gods. In fact, the Sumerian name for man is LULU; it is derived from the word for sheep, which is LU. Since Sumerian syllables were often repeated to give the meaning of great or large, LULU simply meant a large sheep — implying that man was originally considered as food for the gods.

Man was supposedly vegetarian in the antediluvian period; the prohibition against eating animal flesh was not raised until after the Deluge. In Genesis 9, Noah is told:

> Every creature that is alive shall be yours to eat; I give them all to you as I did with the grasses of the field. Only flesh with its life blood still in it shall you not eat.

Biblical scholars all agree that this meant that man was not carnivorous before the Deluge. The admonition not to eat "live flesh with its life blood" raises the suspicion that man was guilty of this usage in earlier times, else why bring up the matter at all?

The prohibition against eating "live" flesh and blood is repeated time and time again in the Old Testament as if it were a real problem among mankind. It is probably an echo of the fratricide of Cain when, according to one source, he not only killed Abel but also ate his flesh and drank his blood.

Cannibalism appears to have been quite common in the period before the Deluge for several reasons. While the Anunna or Nefilim were vegetarian in earlier days when food was abundant, they had become carnivorous after the creation of man. One of the reasons they had turned to eating meat was because the food supply had diminished; they felt no scruples in using man as food since he was considered as just another inferior animal form. This demand for human flesh was reiterated throughout the Old Testament in the admonition of the deity to man that "your first born is mine." This was meant literally.

This attitude is reflected in an early Third Century AD Christian tract called the *Clementine Homilies,* which describes how the Nefilim pleaded scarcity of vegetables and began to eat forbidden flesh. At first they slaughtered animals for food but later "dined on human flesh."

Leviticus as a Cookbook

Starting with the days of the Exodus an effort was made to modify human sacrifice (much to the credit of the Israelites) to the extent that animals were now offered up to appease the gods. The scriptures which deal with the wandering of the tribes in the desert make it clear that the offerings were cooked meals served up to the deity for his consumption while he was in attendance in the Tent of Meeting, his home among the Israelites. The Torah is replete with instructions on how to prepare a cooked meal for the deity. The instructions are very specific; they tell how to construct the grill and how to prepare the cooked meat. In modern terms we would refer to this altar as a "barbecue grill."

If Exodus is the story of the flight from Egypt then the *Book of Leviticus* is the cookbook, the manual that tells how to select the animals and birds to be cooked, which ones were not edible (that is, "unclean"), and how to cut them up and prepare the sections of meat.

The list of animals that are fit to be offered for the divine repast is very specific. The priests are to make sure that there are no deformed or diseased animals in the offering; the deity does not wish to get sick, or even worse, poisoned. They are told that "the burnt offering itself shall remain where it is burned (cooked), on the altar all night until morning, while the fire on the altar is kept going on it." The grill was adjacent to the part of the Tent of Meeting where the deity resided; food was to be left so that he could snack at any time during the night.

To be sure that the meal was fresh, the priests were told in Exodus 29 that they must offer two lambs each day — one in the morning and one at night. Detailed instructions tell how to prepare the offering. The ram or lamb must be cut into sections, entrails removed and presented separately. The deity also preferred his food seasoned, for in Leviticus 6 the Levite priests are told that "with all your offerings you must offer salt."

If these animal offerings were only meant to be ritualistic or symbolic sacrifices would there be any need cut them up into sections or the need to include salt? From the details of the preparation and offering it is clear that these ritualistic animals were not burnt to a crisp but rather prepared as a tasty and nutritious meal.

Man Turns to Cannibalism Before the Deluge

Because of the cloud canopy, climatic conditions on the Earth at the time of the arrival of the aliens was moist and stable. The "greenhouse" effect meant that there was little circulation of the atmosphere and this lack of cyclonic activity precluded the formation of storms and other forms of precipitation. Although the surface of the Earth was shielded from the direct rays of the Sun, plant life was abundant and luxurious due to the proportion of carbon dioxide and water vapor in the atmosphere. The amount of carbon dioxide was probably many times higher that it is today.

Owen Toon and Steve Olson, two climatologists studying the climate of the Earth thousands of years ago reported in *Science* (October 1985) that the early atmosphere of the Earth may have contained a much as a thousand times more carbon dioxide than it does today. Since plant life thrives on carbon dioxide it explains the lush vegetation of prehistoric times and the rise of the vegetarian dinosaurs.

Ancient records disclose that people obtained much of their water from underground sources. Water was also provided by the rivers which descended from the mountains, fed by natural springs and the heavy nocturnal condensation.

The end of what is geologically called the Cretaceus Age brought drastic changes in climate. Vegetation eating dinosaurs like the Apatosaurus, a 30 ton herbivore over 70 feet long, was replaced by carnivores like the Tyrannosaurus Rex — only 7 tons in weight but a voracious feeder. The huge dinosaurs disappeared and meat eating dinosaurs proliferated while mammals began to fill the ecological niche vacated by many of the reptiles. The generally accepted time-scale developed by the geologist Lyell over a hundred years ago theorizes that the end of the Cretaceus Age was some 30 million years ago.

This time-scale, however, has been under heavy criticism in recent years, since it does not embrace the possibility that there may have been intervening periodic catastrophes. The end of the Age may be much closer to modern times — perhaps only 100,000 years ago.

The desiccation of the Earth before the Deluge was hastened by numerous natural devastations. Earthshocks are often alluded to in the scriptures and they probably played an important part in the interruption of the water resources of the ancients as well as the general desiccation of the climate. As the cloud cover began to thin out from the steady night precipitation, moisture in the sky could not be replaced, such as it is today, through a regime of cloud thermal activity and evaporation from the ocean's surface.

The days of the Patriarch Enos, only two generations removed from Adam, were reported by ancient rabbinical sources as one which suffered "four revolutions in nature," an obvious reference to major catastrophes. As a result, the mountains became barren and people starved. Disease became rampant; so many people died that corpses could not be buried and rotted where they lay.

Interruptions in the flow of water from the mountains caused the Mesopotamian plains to become salty and unproductive. This reduction of fresh water allowed the Persian Gulf to back up the Tigris and Euphrates Rivers; as a result the waters of EDIN became brackish. The *Atrahasis Epic* describes conditions just before the Deluge:

> The fountains were stopped, so that the flood could not rise at the source. The field diminished its product. The wide-open

> plain brought forth salt; her bosom revolted, so that no plant came forth, no grain sprouted.

The Eden of the Bible had become a brackish, desolate plain. The problem was further complicated by that of overpopulation. Using the genealogy of the Book of Genesis as a source of demographics, it can be shown that there was a very high population density in that area.

Assuming 20 children per family, a very conservative figure considering the long life of the inhabitants and the system of polygamy, and counting on ten generations from Adam to Noah, the extraordinary total of over a billion people can be deduced. While this number may be mathematically correct, logically it represents an impossible census for the number of people existing at the time of the onset of the Deluge, and suggest that there was an extremely high mortality rate among humans.

The Nefilim exacerbated matters in the antediluvian period by not only eating the available food of man, but also turning on mankind and eating the people. Still hungry, they then started on each other and as the Ethiopic *Book of Enoch* reveals, "and their flesh was devoured the one by the other, and they even drank blood."

Man himself became cannibalistic during the period just before the Deluge. The *Atrahasis Epic* refers to a long period of famine at about this time, when the plains became salty, as the brackish waters of the Persian Gulf backed up the Mesopotamian valley. Crops failed and nothing grew. Famine and disease were rampant, and as the tablets say, mothers ate their daughters and "one house devoured the other."

Scientific evidence that early man was cannibalistic is also found in the caves of southern France. Inhabited from 55,000 to 35,000 BC these caves have produced many skeleton remains; they convey more than just anatomical information. In his book on *Secrets of the Ice Age*, Evan Hadingham reports that in the cave of L'Hortus in southern France, most of the bones are skull and jaw fragments; for some reason the other parts of the skeleton have disappeared despite the fact that in the same layers all of the joints of animals are well preserved. The human fragments are in fact mixed with the animal bones, suggesting cannibalism. In addition, two human long bones show intentional breakages that are identical to those of animal bones, undoubtedly in order to extract the marrow. Here is convincing evidence that primitive man dabbled in some form of cannibalism.

It was reported in the New York Times (July 18, 1986) that an international team of scientists found 6000 year old bones in the Fontbregoua Cave in France which suggests that humans were butchered, processed, and probably eaten in a manner that closely parallels the treatment of wild and domesticated animals. This team of researchers observed that raw meat was stripped from the bones of both humans and animals, then broken to extract the marrow and disposed together in a refuse pit.

The Sacrifice of the First Born

During their wandering in the desert it is clear in Exodus 34 that the Hebrews sacrificed their first born to the deity.

> Every first issue of the womb is mine, from all your livestock that drop a male as firstling, whether cattle or sheep . . . And you must redeem every first-born among your sons.

Sacrifice of the first born was quite common in ancient Palestine and practiced by the Moabites (2 Kings 3) and the Ammonites (Leviticus 18 and 20), among others. During the later days of the Exodus, it had become customary to substitute animals for humans in sacrifice and a sliding monetary scale was even set up, to be paid to the Levite priesthood:

> The Lord spoke to Moses saying: Speak to the Israelite people and say to them, when a man explicitly vows to the Lord the equivalent for a human being, the following scale will apply: If it is a male from 20 to 60 years of age, the equivalent is 50 shekels of silver by the sanctuary weight; if it is a female the equivalent is 30 shekels.

The passage from Leviticus then continues to provide ransom figures for other ages: if from 5 to 20 years old, it is 20 shekels for a male and 10 for a female; if the age is 1 month to 5 years, the price is 5 for a male and 3 for a female. These monetary proceeds of course were to be paid to the Levite priesthood, who seemed to have a pretty good deal going at the time. This redemption sliding scale does not sound very divine-like and it is clear that the deity had departed the scene and that religious affairs were in the hands of the Levite priesthood, who had developed a very lucrative practice.

After the Exodus and during the days of the occupation, human sacrifice seems to have been practiced by other tribes besides that of Zebulon, especially during times of stress when it was a ritual to propitiate the local gods. In Psalm 106, which refers to the days of the period of the Judges, it becomes clear that this practice was common:

> They sacrificed their sons and daughters to the demons, they poured out innocent blood, the blood of their sons and daughters; when they sacrificed to the idols of Canaan.

There is also the lamentable case of Jephthah during the period of the Judges, when he vowed to sacrifice a burnt offering to the Lord if he won his battle with the Ammonites:

> If you will really subject the Ammonites to my power, then anything coming out the doors of my house to meet me, when I return with victory from the Ammonites, shall belong to the Lord, I will offer it up as a burnt offering.

After achieving victory, Jephthah returned home and, much to his horror, rather than an animal running out to meet him, his daughter Mizpeh ran out of the house on his approaching. He gave her two months to say farewell to her friends and then, true to his words, he carried out his part of the bargain. Judges 11 laconically says that “at the end of two months she returned to her father, and fulfilled the vow that he had made.”

Even as late as the Seventh Century BC, the ritual of human sacrifice still obsessed the tribes of Judah, for in II Kings 16 it is observed that King Ahaz “burned his young son as a sacrifice according to the abominable practices of the nations whom the Lord drove out before the people of Israel.”

The Sins of the Tribe of Zebulon

The custom of eating human flesh, while forbidden to Abraham and his descendants, was not entirely eliminated in the succeeding centuries. It would reappear when man’s hunger overrode his ethical sensibilities, or in times of crisis, when he felt that a human sacrifice to the deity was required. This is clear in the ancient document called *Pseudo-Philo’s Biblical Antiquities,* which recounts the history of Israel from Adam to David. It is reputed to Philo the Jew of Aleksandria who lived in the First Century AD.

This document reveals that after the death of Joshua, the Israelites had difficulty in settling in the "promised land." Their presence was disputed by the native people, and the tribes were thwarted wherever they turned. Then they decided to casts lots to see who would replace Joshua as their leader and Kenaz was chosen. His first task was to question each tribe separately to find out where they had gone astray in order to better understand why their god had deserted them.

Many of the confessions were quite revealing, but one tribe in particular, that of Zebulon, confessed that "we desired to eat the flesh of our children and to know whether or not God has care for them." As this disclosure indicates, the problem of cannibalism was closely interwoven with that of human sacrifice, especially what was called the burnt offering. The tribe of Zebulon wanted to know whether the Lord still demanded the sacrifice of their first born as it was required in the past.

The So-Called Sacrifice to Moloch

A discussion of human sacrifice cannot be complete without an explanation of the strange references to Moloch or Molech in the scriptures, supposedly a local Canaanite god which required human sacrifice. The problem is that there is no known Canaanite deity by that name and it only appears in these few odd references in the Old Testament. In Leviticus 18 it states:

> Do not allow any of your offspring to be offered up to Moloch . . . Any man among the Israelites . . . who gives any of his offspring to Moloch, shall be put to death.

The Hebrew word *MLK,* which has come to be translated as a Canaanite god, has little linguistic or historical support. In their book on Ebla: *A Revelation in Archaeology*, Bermant and Weitzman note that in Phoenician and northern Semitic, the noun MLK is translated as "sacrifice." Thus in the cuneiform tablets found at Ebla it is obvious that the Semitic "moloch" is not a name but simply means sacrifice, and that such phrases as "give unto Molech or Moloch" in fact means "give up as sacrifice."

In his attempt to make Jerusalem the center of the empire and to internationalize the city, Solomon married many foreign princesses whom he brought to Jerusalem where he built palaces and temples for their gods. This practice did not sit well with the more conservative tribes. According to I Kings 11, Solomon built altars to "Molech" on the mountain east of Jerusalem as well as in the neighboring valley of Hinnom. Also known as Gehennon it became the Jewish term for hell. This practice of human sacrifice apparently continued for some time after Solomon's death and the division of the empire, for it was not until the reign of King Josiah of Judah in the Seventh Century BC that these altars were finally removed.

The notion in Western culture of a man-eating dragon, especially the numerous references to a human being offered in sacrifice to appease the dragon, seems to have had its roots in the requirements of the ancient Sumerian serpent-gods. A large part of the abhorrence to serpents may have had its beginnings in this ancient custom of offering human flesh to the gods.

CHAPTER 20

WHERE WAS THE FABLED LAND OF DILMUN?

The ancient land of Dilmun has probably aroused more curiosity than any other place mentioned in the cuneiform records of Mesopotamia. Many books have been written about this land of mystery, probably second only to that of Atlantis. Unlike Atlantis, however, there are many recorded references to Dilmun which assures us that it was a geographic location somewhere in the Middle East.

Dilmun was a land intimately associated with that of Mesopotamia, and just like Meluhha (Africa) and Magan (Egypt), supplied the cities of Sumer, Akkad, and Babylon with many economic necessities either through tribute or by commercial exchange. Dilmun was also a sacred or holy land often called the residence of the gods, a sort of Garden of Eden, often referred to as "the land of the living," that is, the land of immortality where no one got sick or died. It was the land of Shamash, the Sun God, where he ruled with the notorious goddess Ishtar.

Despite the references to Dilmun in Mesopotamian literature and myths, its location is still in dispute among scholars. We know for sure that Dilmun was not just a literary fiction for it is mentioned in economic texts as early as the 24th Century BC and as late as the Eighth Century BC.

The tendency in recent years has been to place it in the Persian Gulf and to identify it as the island of Bahrain. This theory was proposed by Geoffrey Bibby in his study *Looking for Dilmun* and seems to have taken root among academics. This identification, however, relies heavily on the inscription of Sargon of Assyria, circa 720 BC, who asserted that among the kings paying him tribute were "Uperi, king of Dilmun, whose abode is situated like a fish in the midst of the sea where the sun rises." Despite the discrepancy on the sunrise, the statement of Sargon has been taken to mean that Dilmun was an island and that the sea was the Persian Gulf.

Others like Samuel Noah Kramer, as in his book *The Sumerians,* have place it in the Indus River valley based on the references that it was located where the sun rises, that is, towards the east of Sumer. This theory is based largely on the Sumerian Deluge myth which states that the Sumerian Noah (Utnapishtim) was given immortality and transplanted to the "mouth of the rivers" and to "the place where the sun rises."

In both instances, the geographic placement of Dilmun seems to be contingent on the statement that it was in the east toward the rising sun. As we shall see, they have been misled by inaccurate translations.

The main difficulty in locating the land of Dilmun is due largely to arbitrary interpretations and translations of the Sumerian and Akkadian texts. A major source of information on this land are the accounts of the travels of Gilgamesh. Two epics are often mentioned in this respect, the famous *Epic of Gilgamesh* which consists of twelve cuneiform tablets, and the lesser known but complete poem called *Gilgamesh and the Land of the Living.*

Apropos the second epic, its title seems to be a mistranslation by scholars who tried to fit it into their own perspective. The Sumerian word for "land of the living" is KUR-LU-TIL-LA. Wilson, in his work *The Rebel Lands,* suggests that TILwas not understood by the translators and as a result equated it with TI, the word for "life." Actually TIL means bird or projectile; for example, it is the weapon which smote ZU the evil god. Thus, KURLUTILLA should correctly be translated "The Land where Man sees the Bright Projectile." The terms which make up the composite word are as follows: KUR means "land or mountainous land," LU is the word for man, TILis the word for "arrow or projectile," and LA means bright.

Dilmun: The Land of Immortality and the Garden of Eden

Dilmun was looked upon by the Sumerians as a blessed paradise that was intimately related to Sumer on a religious or spiritual level. The land of Dilmun is described in the myth *Enki and Ninhursag* as a bright, clear, and pure land, called the "land of the living" where there is no illness and death does not exist.

> In Dilmun the raven utters no cry,
> The lion kills not.
> The wolf snatches not the lamb,
> Unknown is the grain-devouring boar.
> The sick-headed says not "I am sick-headed,"
> The old woman say not "I am an old woman,"
> The old man says not "I am an old man."

This Eden was created by Enki who ordered Shamash to bring up fresh water from the ground, thereby turning it into a paradise, a divine garden green with fruit-laden fields and meadows. Even today, springs at Balbaak feed the two major rivers that flow through the land.

Although Dilmun is not mentioned by name in the epic *Gilgamesh and the Land of the Living*, it obviously refers to this land where no one got sick or died. In this story, Gilgamesh, the King of Uruk, sets out to a distant cedar land to make a "name" for himself. He is told that the land is ruled by Utu/Shamash and that before he enters he must first secure the permission of the Sun God. He is told by his companion and servant Enkidu who had been to the borders of the land:

> My master, if you would enter "the land" inform Utu. . .
> The "land" it is Utu's charge,
> The land of the felled cedars,
> It is the valiant Utu's charge.

Obsessed with his mortality, Gilgamesh would journey to this cedar land in order to set up a "name" or *shumu*, and for this he required the permission of Utu, the chief astronaut.

> I would enter the land and would set up my *shumu,*
> In the places where the *shumu* have been set up,
> I would raise my *shumu.*

While the Semitic term *shumu* is traditionally translated as "name" it presents difficulties in understanding the text. As noted before, SHUM is the Sumerian term for "flying serpent" or rocket. It is *shumu* in Akkadian Semitic and *shem* in Hebrew Semitic as used in the Old Testament. In the incident of the tower of Babel, man wanted to erect a *shem* to reach the gods — just as Gilgamesh wished to do. As we will see, the *shem* of the Bible is also used in conjunction with the *kabod* or vehicle of the Biblical God. The *kabod* is often referred to in Hebrew literature as th... et. The SHUM or rocket of the Sumeria...

In the epic *Gilgamesh and the Land of t...* fabled land he must defeat the monster Humbaba... apparently a mechanical device that guards the c... Although the name of the land where Gilgamesh enters ... obviously Dilmun since it is described in the same terms: it ... a land of cedars, and one controlled by Utu or Shamash.

In the *Epic of Gilgamesh* he also makes a journey to a distant c... where he hopes to achieve immortality. He meets and destroys a monster c... Humbaba who protects the cedar forest, who is described as a fearsome monster: "his roaring is like that of a storm, his mouth is fire, and his breath is death."

The two epics involving the adventures of Gilgamesh to a distant cedar land, under the control of Utu or Shamash, and guarded by a mechanical monster are obviously related and may actually be part of the same story.

The Confused Structure of the Epic of Gilgamesh

Many scholars have noted the disjointed condition of the story that is narrated in the twelve cuneiform tablets that make up the so-called *Epic of Gilgamesh.* The confusion still exists and no attempts have been made to unravel the puzzle. We shall try to place these tablets in their correct position.

The most complete version available is the Akkadian one, composed in the Middle Babylonian Period about the 13th Century BC. Most translations follow this traditional twelve tablet format. Fragments of this epic have also been found in other forms or languages such as Old Babylonian Semitic, Hittite or northwestern Semitic, and in the original Sumerian as well. Some of these fragments date as far back as 2000 BC, confirming the view that the exploits of Gilgamesh were well known all over the Middle East in the Third Millennium BC.

The Babylonians of the 13th Century BC considered themselves the bearers of the older Sumerian culture and combined available legends to produce the twelve tablet version. Over a period of time it became the accepted version of the epic.

The fact that it is a compilation of many Gilgamesh stories is obvious in its structure. "Tablet I" deals with the birth of Gilgamesh, his deeds, and the creation of Enkidu as a friend to Gilgamesh. "Tablet II" continues this association as they leave for the cedar forest which is guarded by the monster Humbaba. In "Tablet III" they obtain permission from Shamash to enter the land under his control. The story is continued in "Tablet IV" and "Tablet V" where Gilgamesh has dreams of what is apparently the glare and noise of a rocket launch. They then battle the monster Humbaba.

"Tablet VI" appears to be a complete break in the story, and unless it can be related in some way to Gilgamesh's purpose of reaching the gods and requesting immortality, it makes no sense whatsoever. This tablet describes how Ishtar tries to seduce Gilgamesh, is rejected in turn and asks for revenge from the gods in council. She is given permission to send a divine weapon called the "Bull of Heaven" to destroy Gilgamesh and Enkidu. Gilgamesh and Enkidu destroy the heaven sent weapon, however.

The story within a story is continued in "Tablet VII" and "Tablet VIII" where the gods decide that someone must pay for this crime and since Gilgamesh is partly divine and Enkidu is not, Enkidu must be condemned to death. Tablet VIII ends with Gilgamesh delivering a eulogy.

…sh is on a journey to reach …He approaches the mountains …a stinging weapon. The guards … is allowed to pass. He passes …the glittering city of the gods, pre… for a *shumu* is turned down by

…his meeting with Siduri, the so-called … journey across the "seas of death," …as trip to the heavens. Siduri has been … name for Ishtar. She makes a deal with …h Utnapishtim. In return he must become

… secure many "punting poles" or fuel rods, which … …carded. He reaches his grandfather who is evidently in … …. The story is continued in "Tablet XI," where Utnapishtim … …uge story. Gilgamesh is told that he cannot be granted immortality, … …r, Utnapishtim knows of a magic plant which will rejuvenate him and leng… …n his lifespan. Gilgamesh obtains it but on his way back to Uruk it is stolen by a snake.

"Tablet XII" is a complete break with the narrative of the trip to the fabled land. In this Tablet Enkidu has been condemned for a crime, presumably for destroying the "Bull of Heaven," and is about to enter the netherworld.

In addition to the two main epics relating to Gilgamesh's trip to Dilmun there are many other stories which relate to it in some way. Many of these have been found only in fragmentary form, such as the one called Gilgamesh *and the Bull of Heaven*, and another called the *Death of Gilgamesh.* It is obvious that the *Epic of Gilgamesh,* as it was completed in twelve tablets around the 13th Century BC, is a composite of many stories circulating in Mesopotamia at the time.

A Summary of What Actually Happened to Gilgamesh

It is possible to reconstruct the adventures of Gilgamesh by putting the various stories together. The theme of the Gilgamesh saga is the search for immortality and his failure to attain it. He was born semi-divine; yet feared that he would die someday because of his mortal half. He sought to reach the gods in heaven since only they could grant immortality. A companion is created for him by taking a primitive man, possibly an ape-man like the Neanderthal, and putting him through a "humanizing" process which consisted of six days of sexual activity with a special goddess. The creation is called Enkidu which means "the creation of Enki" (ENKI-DU).

Accompanied by his friend and and a contingent from the city of Uruk, Gilgamesh begins his journey to "the land of the living," also called the paradise of the gods, the cedar forest, and the home base of Shamash. Sailing up the Euphrates for the port of Mari, the ship is wrecked in a fierce storm and only Gilgamesh and Enkidu survive. They continue their trek overland, presumably following the trade route from Mari, through Tadmor, and down to Damascus, where they approach the mountains of Lebanon from the eastern entrance. Here they meet the guards with "stinging weapons." They are challenged but allowed to pass after the guards recognize Gilgamesh's semi-divine appearance.

While in the mountains they encounter the guardian mechanical monster Humbaba and with the help of Shamash, destroy it. They pass through a tunnel for 24 hours and finally reach light and the city of the gods, presumably Baalbek. Gilgamesh is refused the use of a shuttle rocket to reach the gods in the orbiting spaceship. At this time Ishtar comes to his assistance and offers to supply transportation for him if he will became her lover. He agrees and she provides a shuttle for him and he reaches the orbiting spaceship. Here is met by his grandfather Utnapishtim, who relates to Gilgamesh the story of the Deluge. He tells a crestfallen Gilgamesh that the gods cannot grant him divinity or immortality. But not to let his grandson go home empty-handed, however, Utnapishtim tells Gilgamesh of a magic plant that will rejuvenate Gilgamesh. The hero obtains the plant on the way home but it is stolen from him by a snake, which then promptly sheds its skin.

Arriving at Uruk empty-handed, and because his trip was fruitless, Gilgamesh reneges on his promise to Ishtar. She is incensed and begs the gods to give her a divine weapon to punish Gilgamesh. They provide her with a divine weapon called the "Bull of Heaven," which attacks the two adventurers. Nevertheless, they manage to destroy it. Abetted by the vindictive Ishtar, the gods in council decide that someone has to pay for this and since Enkidu is just a mortal he is condemned to die. Enkidu is sent to the netherworld, and the story ends as Gilgamesh eulogizes his friend. In a separate story Gilgamesh manages to rescue Enkidu from the underworld.

Lebanon as the Land Visited by Gilgamesh

A study of the elements which make up the adventures of Gilgamesh provides clues to the land he visited. The evidence overwhelmingly supports the identification of Lebanon as this land. To begin with, there is only one cedar land in the Middle East worthy of the name. In ancient times cedar forests covered all of Lebanon as well as part of Syria. In fact, the *Epic of Gilgamesh* refers to it as the "forest that runs for ten thousand leagues." When Humbaba roared it was said that "it shook the land of Saria (Syria) and Lebanon."

Lebanon was the source of lumber for the Egyptian kings from the days of the Early Kingdom. It supplied wood for their ships, palaces and temples. Egypt controlled the coastal areas of Lebanon from the Fourth Millennium until about 1500 BC — about the time of the fall of the Middle Kingdom. It also provided lumber for the cities of Mesopotamia. Centuries of exploitation has reduced it to just a shadow of what it once was.

There is also strong evidence that the land of Punt, the fabled land which the Egyptians referred to as "god's land," "the divine land," and the "land of incense" was also the land of Lebanon. The Land of Punt was intimately associated with Egyptian history and religious tradition and, when written in hieroglyphics, does not have the symbol for "foreign land," which indicates that they considered it to be historically part of Egypt.

Queen Hatshepsut of the 18th Dynasty made a trip to this fabled land which she describes in detail on the reliefs of the walls of her temple near Thebes. The reliefs state that upon her arrival to this land by ship, she is met by royalty of the Land of Punt who inquire whether she arrived by "the ways of heaven or by the sea." It was legendary in the Land of Punt that the gods or those favored by the gods, could arrive to this land by either seaship or airship.

The mountains that Gilgamesh reaches are called "mashu," which guards the place where Shamash "Comes and goes." The word MA-SHU has not been understood by most translators; however, it lends itself quite well to the definition of "the place of the (space) craft." MA is the Sumerian term for boat or craft, and SHU means a geographic place or location.

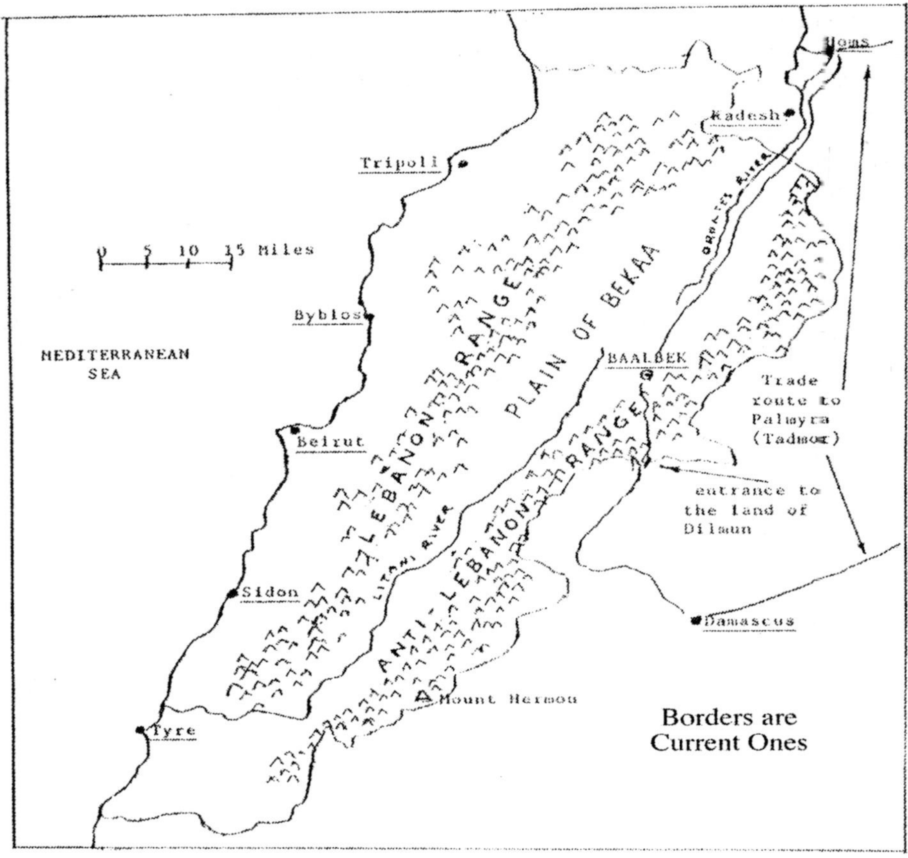

Fig. 54 – Lebanon, the ancient land of Dilmun.

When Gilgamesh is met by the scorpion men, that is, sentries with a stinging type weapon, he is instantly recognized as one of their own kind for "the one who has come to us, his body is the flesh of the gods." The scorpion men who guard the Sumerian paradise correspond to the "cherubim with the fiery revolving sword" of the scriptures, who were stationed at the eastern entrance to the Garden of Eden to guard the tree of immortality and prevent Adam and Eve from reentering.

Much of the confusion over the location of the Garden of Eden exists because scholars still located it in Mesopotamia after the Deluge, when in reality it had been moved to the west. Although the delta of Mesopotamia was the Edin of the Sumerians and the Eden of the Old Testament before the Deluge, it was decided after the catastrophe to move it to a more secure place, less accessible, and not subject to the caprice of nature, especially flooding. Thus the sacred place of the gods was moved to Lebanon and the space city established there.

It explains why Adam and Eve were expelled "east of Eden," and that entrance guarded by the cherubim. It is pertinent to note that Damascus is due east of this entrance to the land of Lebanon. It claims to be the oldest continuously occupied city in the world and traces its founding to that of Adam and Eve.

Gilgamesh travelled through a series of tunnels in the mountains to reach the place of the home base of Shamash. The path he took was called h*arran Shamash,* or the road to Shamash. After going for twelve double-hours, he saw light at the end of the tunnel and finally broke out into the open where he saw an area of bright crystal and colored stones. It was Baalbek the space city.

Most translations of the epic state that when Utnapishtim related the story of the Deluge he told how he was made immortal and then sent to live in to the land of Dilmun, which was "in the east" and at the "mouth of the rivers."

The distant land at the mouth of the two rivers has been interpreted to mean the delta of the Tigris and Euphrates, the location of the antediluvian Garden of Eden. Others, notably Kramer, have suggested the delta of the Indus River as more probable.

A different translation of the phrase in question appears in the translation of the epic by John Gardner and John Maier in their book *Gilgamesh.* Their suggested translation is "the source of the rivers" rather than "the mouth of the rivers." Of course, this gives a completely different meaning to the passage, for the delta of Mesopotamia or any other delta cannot be the land of Dilmun.

A search for the place in the Middle East where two rivers originate in the same area leads us back again to Lebanon, particularly to Baalbek, for it is there

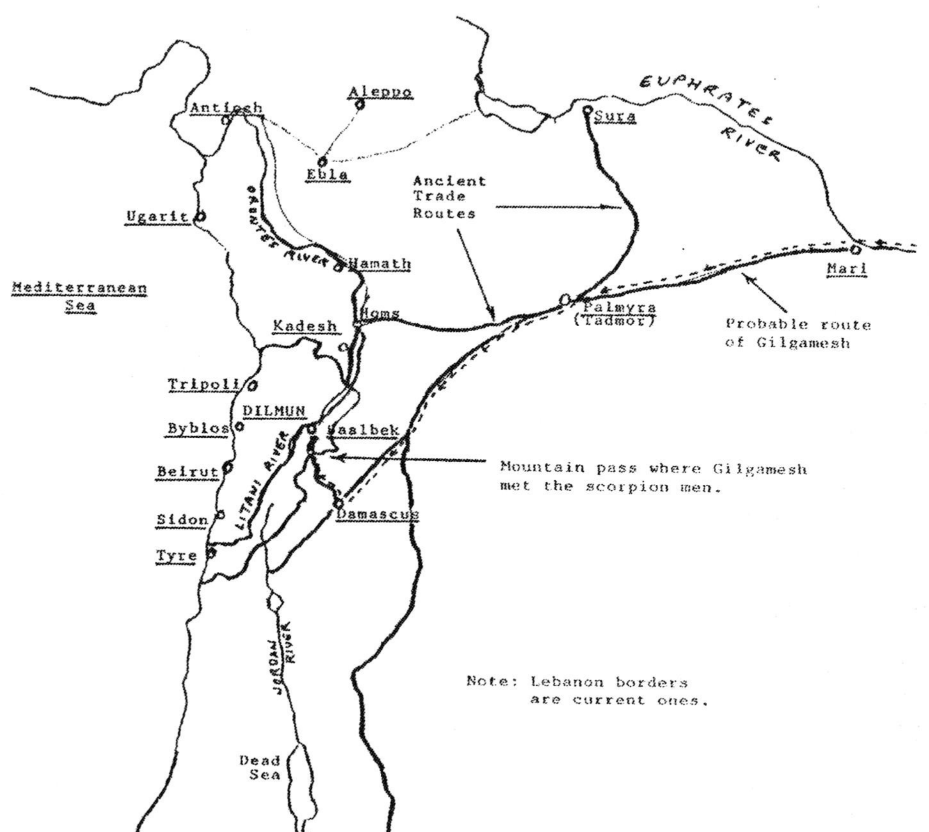

Fig. 55 – The journey of Gilgamesh to Dilmun, the Land of Shamash.

that the Orontes and Litanni rivers begin, one flowing north and the other south (figure 54).

Dilmun as the Land Where Shamash Rises

Despite the many indications that the land of Dilmun is Lebanon, the biggest obstacle has been the reference to it as where the sun rises. Called Ziusudra in the early Sumerian version, the hero of the Deluge is sent to live in "the land of Dilmun, the place where the sun (shamash) rises." Another translation of this passage states that he went to live in "the land (or mountain land) of crossing," where the sun or shamash rises. The land of crossing appears to refer to the place where Shamash took off and landed each day, in other words, where he crossed over from Earth to the heavens. The "land of crossing" can also be translated as "the mountain land of crossing" since the word lends itself to either definition. Again, this rules out the flatlands of the delta regions.

Supposedly situated where the sun rises, scholars have looked to the east for its location. But what is ignored is the fact that the word for sun and for the sun god is "shamash." The passage could also be read as "where Shamash rises," thus firmly placing it in the land of the cedars.

There is much compelling evidence that indicates that Dilmun should be sought in the west rather than the east. In a poem attributed to Sargon the Great who ruled about 2300 BC, he boasted that "the Sea Lands three times I circled, Dilmun my hand captured." Clearly Dilmun had to be near the Sea Lands, which was their term for the Mediterranean Sea coast. The cities of the Sea Lands were none other than the coastal cities of Lebanon, later to become the Phoenician League. Furthermore, Sargon's statement would indicate that the cities of the Sea Land were actually part of what he called Dilmun.

Fig. 56 – Ishtar and Gilgamesh.

Cylinder seal of circa 1800 BC showing Ishtar as the Love Goddess pleading with Gilgamesh to be her lover. Enkidu, Gilgamesh's human companion, is on her right. Above are the symbols of the major gods of Mesopotamia: the four-pointed star of Shamash, the crescent moon of Sin, the eight-pointed star of Ishtar, and below the spade symbol of Marduk, and the ibex representing Enki. Between Ishtar and Gilgamesh is a demon head probably a symbol of Humbaba, the mechanical monster that Gilgamesh defeated, and the bull's head below is presumably the "bull of heaven," a divine weapon which Ishtar sent to destroy Gilgamesh when he refused to carry out his part of the bargain.

Dilmun had to be in the west near Magan (Egypt) and Meluhha (Africa) according to the epic where Enki conducts an inspection trip of the lands he controlled. They are grouped together as if the three lands were near each other. Dilmun is often associated with the lands of Magan and Meluhha, which dictates that its location had to be in the west near Egypt rather than somewhere in the east.

The route taken by Gilgamesh is provided in the epic *Gilgamesh and the Land of the Living.* It also indicates a journey to Lebanon. For the trip, he had mobilized an expedition from his city of Uruk. They built a "Magan" ship, an Egyptian type river boat, which would take them up the Euphrates River. This type of ship precludes passage down the Euphrates and into the Persian Gulf since such a journey would require a more seaworthy ship able to survive the open sea.

Gilgamesh and his group must have planned to sail up the Euphrates as far as possible and take the overland trade route to the west at Mari. This was the transfer point for the trade routes to the Mediterranean. It crossed the desert to Palmyra (ancient Tadmor) and then divided, with one route going southwest to Damascus and the other west to Homs (Hims) at the northern entrance to Lebanon. Either of these routes led to the land of Lebanon or Dilmun, for just as today they are the two major routes into the mountain land from the east.

Gilgamesh's expedition was ill-fated; the ship foundered in a storm in the river Euphrates and all hands were lost except Gilgamesh and Enkidu. The heroes of the epic continued their journey on foot and finally reached the land of Shamash or the mountains of Mashu, the "place of the spacecraft."

Although Gilgamesh took the most direct route to Baalbek through the mountain pass near Damascus, it is noteworthy that there is also a major entrance to the land of Lebanon in the north. Even today there are ruins of an ancient city known as Kadesh, which guarded this entrance. The history of Kadesh is lost in antiquity but its name Kadesh is the Semitic term for "sacred city," and the reason for its holy appellation has been lost.

Commercial Giant of the Ancient World

Dilmun was not only an earthly paradise — the famous Garden of Eden, the meeting place of the gods, the land of well-being, and the home grounds of Enki, Shamash, and Ishtar, it was also one of the richest and most powerful countries in the ancient world. To judge from the economic documents of Mesopotamia, Dilmun had a long commercial history that covered a period of at least two thousand years. The ships of Dilmun were reported anchored at the docks of the Mesopotamian cities alongside those of Egypt and Ethiopia since at least 2500 BC.

As we have seen, in the days of the Akkad Dynasty, Dilmun was mentioned as a place on the coast of the Mediterranean. Sargon the Great, circa 2300 BC, boasted that he had traversed the mountains and encircled the Sea Lands and captured Dilmun.

Based on an account of Sargon II, the Assyrian ruler of the Eighth Century BC, false interpretations have been made of the location of Dilmun as an island and therefore Bahrain was chosen as Dilmun although there is no other evidence. Sargon II announced that:

> I brought under my control Bit-Iakin on the shore of the Bitter Seas as far as the border of Dilmun. Uperi, King of Dilmun, whose abode is situated, like a fish, thirty-double hours away in the midst of the sea of the rising sun, heard of the might of my sovereignty, and sent his gifts.

The account of Sargon II undoubtedly refers to the lands of the west and to the coastal cities of Phoenicia which was still a commercial power in the Eighth Century BC, although their influence had waned since their heyday from the 14th to the 9th Centuries BC. At that time, Tyre dominated the league of cities, and in fact, the title King of Tyre was synonymous with that of King of Phoenicia.

Located on an island offshore (as Aleksander the Great was distressed to find when, in order to capture it, he had to build a causeway from the mainland), it exercised control over the commercial cities of Aradus, Byblos, Sidon, and

Akka. Originally part of the Egyptian Empire, the Phoenician cities became independent with the fall of the Middle Kingdom in the disasters of the mid-15th Century BC. Tyre retained its independence until 586 BC, when it fell to Nebuchadnezzar of Babylon after a seige of thirteen years.

4000 BC	The lands resettled.
3500 BC	Lebanon becomes the garden of Eden. The space city is established at Baalbek. It becomes the home base of Shamash, the chief astronaut. Ishtar makes it her base also. Byblos emerges as a major port.
2900 BC	Gilgamesh enters the land in pursuit of immortality. He reaches the space city where Ishtar provides a rocket for him to reach his grandfather in the orbiting space ship.
2700 BC	Egypt exerts control over the coastal cities.
2500 BC	The Dilmun standard for gold is used by Ebla and the other cities.
2300 BC	Sargon the Great boasts of subjecting the land of cedars and the cities of the coast of Lebanon.
2225 BC	Naram-Sin invades Lebanon and destroys the space city at Baalbek and devastates the Bekaa Valley. The lands are poisoned by radioactivity and remain unoccupied for centuries. Space city is never rebuilt.
2084 BC	Invasion of the Eastern kings of the Third Dynasty of Ur. Palestine is devastated but Lebanon is scrupulously avoided. The alternate space center at Mount Sinai (Jebel Halal) is destroyed.
1447 BC	Exodus of the tribes from Egypt under Moses. Palestine is invaded and occupied but Lebanon is avoided. Egypt loses control of the coastal cities of Lebanon.
1400 BC	Rise of the independent city-states of Phoenicia.
969 BC	Hiram as king of Tyre and Phoenicia helps Solomon build his Temple and Palace.
944 BC	Queen Hatshepsut of the Egyptian 18th Dynasty pays a visit to the Land of Punt, their name for the land of Lebanon.
586 BC	Tyre captured and destroyed by Nebuchadnezzar.

Fig. 57 – A short history of Dilmun.

The account of Sargon II mentions places that are all near each other in the west. He claimed control over the area from Bit-Iakin, an unlocated city but believed to be Jericho, near the Bitter Sea (which can only be the Dead Sea), as far as the borders of Lebanon or Dilmun. He had subjected the coastal cities and particularly Tyre, which lay "in the midst of the sea." Mainland Dilmun, that is, the valley between the mountains, was not claimed by Sargon II for the simple reason that it had been devastated fifteen centuries earlier, as we shall see.

The economic significance of the cities of Dilmun, especially Tyre, is revealed in the Ebla economic accounts of the late Third Millennium, where its name served as a royal standard for gold. The term for gold throughout the Middle East was *gin-dilmun* or dilmun shekels. In his account of Ebla, in *The Archives of Ebla*, the historian Pettinato reported that the shekel in the trade accounts of Ebla was always written with the Sumerian term *gin* and accompanied by the addition of *dilmun*, thus indicating that the unit of weight and purity was set and originated in Dilmun.

All kinds of products flowed from the ports of Dilmun since it was an entrepot, that is, a trans-shipment point for goods from Europe, Africa, and the lands of the Mediterranean. Thus the goods which arrived in Mesopotamia in the boats from Dilmun were as varied as the lands they came from — copper, gold, lapis lazuli, ivory and ivory products such as inlaid tables, figurines, combs and boxes, furniture, semi-precious stones, cedar, other timbers and agricultural delicacies such as dates and onions.

In her remarkable book on the history of Babylon, Joan Oates reported that in the ruins of Hammurabi's Babylon, circa 1780 BC, there was unearthed a house of one official called Ea-Nasir who was an *alik-dilmun*, that is, a Dilmun trader, who dealt mainly in copper and copper products. He apparently was one of a number of middle-men in the trade of goods from Dilmun.

While the literary evidence seems to indicate that there were two Dilmuns, one legendary and one commercial, they were actually part of the land today known as Lebanon. There was a mainland Dilmun, that of the Bekaa Valley and the home of the spaceport at Baalbek, while across the mountains was the coastal plain of Dilmun with all its commercial cities.

The interior of Dilmun ceased to be a paradise and spaceport of the gods in the reign of Naram-Sin, the demented despot of the Akkad Dynasty, when he invaded and destroyed these lands in 2225 BC. Although the mainland territory was laid waste and avoided by everyone for over a thousand years, the coastal cities continued to flourish as independent city-states under the aegis of Egypt and later as the Phoenician League.

The Coastal Cities of Lebanon

The part of Lebanon along the seacoast was inhabited by Canaanites who later came to be called Phoenicians by the Greeks. The first of these cities to step on the threshold of history was the city of Gubla (Byblos to the Greeks), with a history that goes back to 3500 BC. Byblos and later the other cities of Tyre, Sidon, Berytus, and Aradus emerged under the control of Egypt about 2700 BC when they were noted exporting cedar wood, olive oil, and wines to Egypt.

Evidence of trade with Egypt goes back to predynastic times and continued uninterrupted for many centuries. The mountainous land provided wood for the palaces, temples, and boats of the Pharaohs. The 60 foot funerary barge of the Pharaoh Khufu or Cheops, circa 2550 BC, which was found in 1954 hermetically sealed in a limestone crypt at the foot of the great pyramid of Gizeh, was constructed of Lebanese cedar wood.

Caananite pottery was found in the tombs of the First Dynasty, about 2900 BC, and rich offerings to the Temple at Gubla were made by the Pharaohs of the Second Dynasty. Egyptian pectorals and jewelry were also found at Gubla. In his *History of Lebanon*, Philip Hitti observes that at this ancient city, the Canaanite temple of Baal stood side by side with the Egyptian temple of Isis. Canaanite princes not only took pride in decorating themselves in the Egyptian style but also called themselves "sons of Ra," the chief Egyptian solar deity.

As a nation, Phoenicia emerged about 1400 BC after the devastations of the 15th Century BC when Egypt was overrun by the Hyksos. The cities now achieved their independence from Egypt. First Sidon dominated her sister cities but eventually Tyre took the lead, and by the time of the Hebrew kings, the title King of Tyre began to mean King of Phoenicia.

In the days of Hiram, the forests had yet to be denuded, and the lumber and agricultural products of Lebanon flowed out to the world through its numerous seaports. With the expulsion of the Hyksos or Amalekites by the joint forces of Amose and Saul about 1000 BC, the land was divided between the three leaders.

Egypt retained a strip of land along the coast all the way to Phoenicia which gave her control of the coastal highway. Solomon took over Palestine, Syria, and to a certain extent the lands to the west. For example, he built a fortified city at Tadmor which controlled the rich trade route across the desert from Mari on the Euphrates. The area of Lebanon, from Ugarit in the north to Philistia in the south, came under the control of Hiram, king of Tyre. Hiram also inherited the mantle of responsibility for what remained of the sacred sites of Lebanon and particularly the city of Baalbek.

Although Dilmun is not mentioned by name in the scriptures there is much information on the littoral cities of Lebanon. The evidence that Hiram held a special position in the religious and political affairs of the time is reflected in the Book of Ezekiel where he is considered to be semi-divine and have special relations with the deity.

In Ezekiel 28 he relates in a diatribe against the enemies of Israel that "no secret is hidden from him." Apparently Ezekiel expressed the view of his day that while Hiram had been a good friend of Solomon, his descendants failed Jerusalem in her hour of need. Ezekiel says of Hiram,

> Because your heart is proud, you have said, "I am a god, and sit in the seat of the gods, in the heart of the seas." Yet you are but a man, and no god, though you consider yourself wise as a god. You are indeed wiser than Daniel; no secret is hidden from you. By your wisdom and understanding you have gotten wealth for yourself.

Ezekiel continues his accusations and reveals Hiram's divine status and the reasons for his downfall. He is here repeating the words of the deity:

> You were the signet of perfection, full of wisdom, and perfect in beauty. You were in Eden, the garden of God. Every precious stone was your covering . . . On the day that you were created they were prepared. With an anointed guardian cherub I placed you. You were on the holy mountain of God; in the midst of the stones of fire you walked.

Ezekiel is referring to the raised platform at Baalbek, "the holy mountain" and the brilliant rocket exhaust — "the stones of fire." It is also the land of the Garden of Eden and the guardian cherubim.

> In the abundance of your trade you were filled with violence and you sinned. So I cast you as a profane thing from the Mountain of God and the guardian cherub drove you out from the midst of the stones of fire.

It is apparent that the Garden of Eden is now located in the area controlled by Hiram. The cherub who acted as the guardian of Hiram at the Mountain of God is the cherub with the fiery revolving sword (or the scorpion-men) who guarded the cedar forest, the land of Shamash.

Lebanon — Garden of the Middle East

Because of its geographic location and integrated borders, Lebanon has always enjoyed a certain degree of natural protection from outside excursions.

Protected by mountains on three sides and the sea in the west, it avoided much of the tribulations of invading armies from the east. Being considered as a sacred or holy land also gave it a certain modicum of protection. Its religious tradition as the land of the gods was a safeguard, but it also was the cause of her demise.

Geographically, Lebanon has four regions: the coastal plains, the coastal mountain range, the central plateau or valley, and the interior mountain range. The coastal plain is a narrow fertile area, at times just a ribbon where the mountains come down to the sea, widening to about eight miles at the most. It is the site of a number of principal seaports which became the Phoenician city-states.

The coastal mountain range, called the Lebanon Mountains, runs the entire length of the country averaging about 35 miles wide in the north and six miles in the south. The Anti-Lebanon Mountains forms the eastern boundary of the country. At its southern end it is anchored by Mount Hermon, the country's highest peak at 9,055 feet. Its name means "sacred" and it is the site of the descent of the Nefilim before the Deluge.

The Bekaa plateau is sandwiched between the two mountain ranges and it is a fertile, undulating plain about 75 miles long, and from six to ten miles wide. It owes its fertility mostly to the Litani River, which originates near Baalbek and flows south to empty into the Mediterranean near Sidon.

Baalbek is also the watershed for the Orontes River which flows north and exits into the Mediterranean near ancient Antioch. In the south, the plain is separated from the Jordan Valley by a range of hills, whereas in the north it opens into the Syrian plain at Homs.

The Lebanon landscape is today considered to be one of the most beautiful in the world. The land is full of sparkling gushing springs, the climate is moderate, and the lands are luxuriant. In July, normally the hottest month of the year, the daily average at Beirut is 87 degrees F., while in Damascus, just 50 miles to the east, it is 96 degrees. The coastal plain receives 33 inches of rain a year, twice that of the corresponding coast of California.

In the past, Lebanon must have been a veritable paradise. Its mountains were covered with cedar and other hardwoods, and were teeming with wildlife like panthers, bears, and wolves. Its fabled city of Baalbek overlooked a luxuriant fertile valley watered by the two rivers and numerous springs. Its wealth was enhanced by the bustling commercial seaports on the coast. Besides lumber it exported agricultural products like wheat, olives, and incense. It was famous for its purple dye which gave the coastal area its name. The Egyptians called it the "land of incense," for it was a major source of frankincense and myrrh.

Lebanon was a natural selection by the Sumerians after the Deluge to be the site of the new Eden, the paradise of the gods. Its remoteness and protected borders also enhanced its value as a private resort and the location of the new spaceport.

The lands were assigned to Utu/Shamash, the chief astronaut, with the city of Baalbek as his headquarters. Called Beth-Shemesh in the Bible, it is literally the House of Shamash. His activities in the land of Lebanon are described in the myth *Enki and the World Order:*

> The hero, the bull who comes forth out of the cedar forest, who roars lion-like. The valiant Utu, the bull who stands secure, who proudly displays his power. The father of the great city, the place where Utu ascends, the great herald of the holy An. The judge, the decision maker of the gods. Who wears a lapis lazuli

> bear, who comes forth from the holy heaven, Utu, the son born of Ningal, Enki placed in charge of the entire universe.

Utu or Shamash is described as being "in charge of the entire universe," and since we know he had no administrative or political function, it presumably is a metaphor of his ability to move about at will and survey the known universe from the air. It is from Baalbek that he "roars like a lion" and "proudly displays his power," referring to the noise and commotion of the rocket launchings at the spaceport.

Shamash later became known as the god of measurements and judgment, probably because he would move about at will and survey all the lands. There is also a hidden meaning here which relates to the geodetic measurement of the Earth, since much evidence exists of an ancient sacred geodetic grid covering at least the Middle East.

CHAPTER 21

DESTRUCTION OF THE BAALBEK SPACE FACILITIES

The next two chapters concern the activities in the Western Lands during the Third Millennium BC when repeated invasions by the kings of Mesopotamia resulted in the destruction of the space facilities and the devastation of the lands of Lebanon, Palestine, Transjordan, and the Sinai. The agents of this destruction were the kings of the Akkad Dynasty and the Third Dynasty of Ur.

The Space Facilities Moved to the West

Today, the climate of Palestine is harsh and dry. There are many indications that it may have been much different 5000 years ago. Researches based on pollen spectra and profiles obtained from all of Palestine reveals that rainfall was much more abundant in the Third Millennium BC. Research at Tel Aviv University indicates that rainfall at that time had a different pattern. Rain probably originated from warm fronts pushed into Palestine by the western winds all the way from the Atlantic Ocean, whereas present-day thunderstorms originate over the eastern Mediterranean. This phenomena would result in summer rains and subsequently a greater annual rainfall. This would explain the abundant vegetation as shown by pollen distribution and particularly the wider distribution of the deciduous oak in the past. It supports the statements in the Old Testament that refer to Palestine as "a land of milk and honey."

Besides shifting weather patterns the lands were also subject to invading armies, overpopulation and overgrazing. These factors all played a part in changing the lands of the Levant to the semi-arid land that it is today. The major change in the weather pattern probably occurred during the catastrophes of the mid-15th Century BC.

The lands of Lebanon, in particular, were lush and munificent. To this new Garden of Eden the space facilities were moved and a city built to serve as the headquarters of the new launch platform and support facilities. It became the Biblical Garden of Eden and the Sumerian "land of pleasant living." It was the "gateway to the gods."

The old space platform at Sippar in Mesopotamia was now under the waters of the Persian Gulf. A new space complex was built in Lebanon at Baalbek. An alternate launch site was established in the northern Sinai at Mount Horeb or Mount Sinai, or what is now known as Jebel (Mount) Halal. A fortified support complex was also located in the northern Sinai at the oasis of Kadesh-Barnea to protect the eastern approaches to the space complex. At the same time the chief astronaut Utu, who had ruled Sippar, the space city, now reappeared in the land of Lebanon under his Semitic name of Shamash.

There is an ancient religious source that provides the names and locations of the three main sites of the space complex. Although couched in religious terms, there is a unique reference in the *Book of Jubilees* that refers to three places on Earth sacred to the Lord. These were:

> The Garden of Eden, also called the Holy of Holies
> and the dwelling of the Lord,

Mount Sinai in the midst of the wilderness and,
Mount Zion in the midst of the navel of the Earth

It is clear from this passage that these sites were all fairly close to each other and not spread out over the vast expanse of the Middle East, for the *Book of Jubilees* further states that they were "created as holy places, one facing the other."

Cutting through the theological verbiage, we have a reference to the Garden of Eden which is in Lebanon, whose capital city of Baalbek was "the dwelling of the Lord." Mount Sinai is "in the midst of the wilderness" of northern Sinai and served as the alternate space complex. Mount Zion is one of the three peaks that make up the city of Jerusalem and the place often referred to in Hebrew literature as "the holy mountain" and "the navel of the Earth." In this role Jerusalem served as the headquarters and administrative center for the western space facilities.

Ur-Salem (Jerusalem), the Space Control Center

Long before the days of the Hebrew kings, Jerusalem had been considered to be a sacred city by the people of the land of Canaan. Called Ur-Salem, it had several peaks of which Mount Moriah and Mount Zion were the most important.

In the days Abraham, Ur-Salem was the headquarters of the Western Lands which were ruled by the kings of Mesopotamia. When Abraham contacted Melchizedek, the King of Salem, after the invasion of the eastern kings, he paid a tithe or tribute of ten percent of all the booty he had gotten from the departing invasion force. There was no doubt in this passage in Genesis that Melchizedek was the ruler of Ur-Salem and the Western Lands. The current name Jerusalem, or Yerusalem as it is sometimes pronounced, is derived from UR-SALEM or the "Capital city of Salem." The Sumerian term UR is used only for capital cities and there could only be one UR in Mesopotamia. UR-SALEM was its branch or counterpart in the west. It indicates the political importance of the city.

Remarkably, Jerusalem was not a city sacred to the Israelites before the days of David. It is only mentioned once in the Torah, the first five books of the Old Testament, and it was not until Joshua 10 that the name is encountered. Actually, Shechem, a city north of Jerusalem, was regarded by the ancient Hebrews as sacred, with the shrine located at nearby Mount Gezerin. Shechem's holy status is reflected in its use as the storage place of the teraphims, the sacred idols or communications devices. Its importance may also be due to some as yet unknown reason, perhaps as a regional radio site with a permanent apparatus to contact the gods.

Located on a hill in the southeastern part of Jerusalem, Mount Zion had been the headquarters of Melchizedek and controlled by a special group of the Rephaim called the Jebusites. David built his city here later and displaced the Jebusites. Zion became the goal or "rallying cry" of the Jews during the diaspora, the place which they referred to as the "heavenly city." The name Zion is probably of Sumerian origin since the term ZI-ANNA means literally "the city of heavenly life," and Zion would be a Semitic permutation of the Sumerian term.

Mount Moriah is presently occupied by the Moslem shrine called the Dome of the Rock and is reputedly the place where Solomon built his temple. The Moslem shrine is built on a fashioned rock 57 feet long and 44 feet wide. At present, four to six feet are above the floor, with caves and passageways reportedly underneath. The monolith stone is similar to the stone platform at Baalbek, although quite smaller.

In Solomon's time, the temple was built upon the monolith rock at Moriah which was at that time considered to be sacred. Its original use as a landing and launching platform is lost in the dim past, although it retained its holy status.

It was also on or near the rock at Moriah that Jacob observed the angels going up and down a ladder or stairway.

> He had a dream: A stairway was set on the ground, with its top reaching to the sky; and the angels of El were going up and down on it . . . Jacob awoke from his sleep . . . Shaken he exclaimed "How awesome is this place! This is none other than the abode of El, and that is the gateway to heaven."

Coincidentally, the phrase "gateway to heaven" is the same terminology used by Gilgamesh to describe the land of Shamash, where he journeyed in order to reach the gods in heaven.

Where was Mount Sinai Located?

When Moses took refuge in the land of Midian to escape the displeasure of the Pharaoh he met Jethro, the high priest of Yahweh, and settled near Mount Horeb, also called Mount Sinai. The land of Midian was in northeast Arabia on the eastern shore of the Gulf of Akaba. From here the Midianites spread north into the Sinai and into Moab and the land west of Edom. The Midianites called themselves "the sons of the serpent," and apparently were descendants of the Anunna who were assigned the task of defending the installations at Mount Sinai and Kadesh.

From these references Mount Sinai would have to be in the northeastern part of the Sinai, perhaps in the general area of Midian. Kadesh-Barnea is also in that general area. Mount Sinai should be reasonably close to Kadesh since this was the staging area for the Israelites for the two years before their trek into the wilderness. Jebel Halal, a flat-top mountain just west of Kadesh-Barnea, meets all the requirements of being Mount Sinai or Horeb.

In Deuteronomy 33 there is a remarkable passage which places the location of Mount Sinai in an area which is the conjunction of Sinai, Seir, Paran, and Kadesh. Just before he died, Moses recounted the events of the Exodus.

> The Lord came from Sinai, He shone upon his people from Seir, He appeared from Mount Paran, and He came from Meribath-Kadesh, while lightning flashed from his right hand.

In this remarkable statement, Moses juxtaposes these four locations as if they are all the same place. In this respect, it is pertinent that the goal of the invading eastern kings some 600 years earlier was a place called El-Paran in the northern Sinai. Paran must have been considered to be a sacred place since they used the prefix "el" to mean divine. Thus Mount Horeb, Mount Sinai, and Mount Paran appear to be names for the same mountain or perhaps complex of mountains in the northern Sinai which served as the alternate space center. Kadesh and its complex of oases was part of this network.

Mount Sinai has to be near the Kadesh group of oases according to Deuteronomy 1, where the distance between the two locations is given in travel time. It states that:

> It is eleven days from Horeb to Kadesh-Barnea by the Mount Seir route.

It must be assumed that the Israelites were moving fairly slowly in their Exodus from Egypt since their rate of movement was determined by their flock of sheep and cattle who had to forage as they travelled. In view of this restriction it would take about eleven days to travel from Mount Sinai or Jebel Halal to the complex of oases at Kadesh. Placing Mount Sinai in the lower part of the Sinai peninsula makes no sense whatsoever.

There is also an interesting legend in the oral tradition of the Jews on how Mount Sinai was chosen as the place of the deity. Called the "Contest of the Mountains," it describes how Mount Tabor, Mount Hermon, and Mount Carmel fought among each other for the honor to be the resting place of the "Shekinah of the Lord," in other words, the landing place for his space vehicle. The dispute was settled by a voice from heaven which told them:

> The Shekinah shall not rest upon these high mountains that are so proud, for it is not God's will that the Shekinah should rest upon high mountains that quarrel among themselves. He prefers the low mountains, and Sinai among them, because it is the smallest and most insignificant of all.

Mount Tabor is 1938 feet high, Hermon is 9055 feet, and Carmel is 1791 feet. Mount Halal is 2944 feet high. The mountains in the southern Sinai, Mount Musa and Mount Ekaterina which are traditionally identified as Mount Sinai are 7497 feet and 8668 feet respectively. This height alone would of course eliminate them from the legend. In addition, Mount Musa and Mount Ekaterina have not been associated with the ancient religion of the Canaanites.

Mount Tabor, Carmel, and Hermon were all sacred to the ancient people of Canaan. In the Second Millennium BC, these three mountains formed a trilogy of places with shrines sacred to the Canaanite god Baal. The fact that these three mountains were considered by the Hebrews to be the location of their holy mountain shows the Canaanite elements in the Hebrew religion at the time.

The legend indicates that for practical purposes a flat low mountain was selected to be the resting place of the spacecraft. Mount Halal near Kadesh is such a mountain. It not only fits the legend well but is well suited, by virtue of its shape, as a launch and recovery pad.

The Significance of the Kadesh Complex

The area around Kadesh-Barnea seems to have been of major importance in ancient days. It appears to be one of the goals of the invading eastern kings in the year 2085 BC. Genesis describes how after defeating the fortresses of the Rephaim in the Transjordan they then crushed

> The Horites in the hill country of Seir, near El-Paran, which is on the edge of the wilderness. They swung back to En-Mishpat (now Kadesh) and subdued all the territory of the Amalekites, and also the Amorites who dwelt in Hazazon-Tamar (En-Gedi).

They must have bypassed Kadesh to strike their main target — the space complex at Mount Paran/Sinai/Horeb. They then swung back to destroy the fortifications and space support facilities at Kadesh. Continuing north, they destroyed the citadel of En-Gedi, which protected the Valley of Siddim from the south. The battle of the Valley of Siddim is described in the next chapter.

The name Kadesh-Barnea (Kadesh means sacred) is usually applied to a whole complex of oases fed by natural springs in that area. It was heavily fortified in early times. Remains of numerous fortifications in the area date to about 2000 BC, at which time they were destroyed, never to be rebuilt.

The area of Mount Sinai and Kadesh was of major significance to the Hebrews since it was a staging area for them during the days of the Exodus. It was from here that they were told to send scouts into Canaan to survey the land

and report on the state of the native defenses. They mingled with the inhabitants of the area as far north as Hebron. What they found and reported to Moses was discouraging — the land was inhabited by Anakim, who like the Amalekites were fierce warriors. They presumably saw also the glacis-type fortresses of the Anakim.

At Kadesh the news was badly received by Moses who now realized that his small disorganized army could not conquer the remnants of the Rephaim. From here, a group of the tribal leaders decided to attempt a foray into the land of Canaan. They were soundly defeated at Hormah. This marked the end of their attempts to penetrate directly into Canaan.

After two years at the Kadesh oasis, the Israelites decided to enter Canaan by a roundabout way. They sent a delegation to the east to the kings of Edom and Moab for permission to pass unopposed through their land to the Transjordan. They were refused permission, and the Hebrews were told not to fight these people but to take the long roundabout way by that of the Red Sea.

In the 40th year, Moses addressed his people from Mount Nebo just before crossing the river Jordan:

> Thus after you had remained at Kadesh all that long time, we marched back into the wilderness towards the Red Sea . . . and skirted the hill country of Seir a long time . . . The time that we spent in travel from Kadesh-Barnea until we crossed the Wadi Zered was 38 years, until that whole generation of warriors perished from the camp.

The Old Testament is strangely silent on those 38 years that the Israelites spent in the wilderness from Kadesh to the entrance to the Transjordan. It is obvious that there are some missing books. Whether omitted on purpose by the priestly scribes or just lost in antiquity, these omissions relate to critical periods in the history of the Hebrews. Their recovery would solve many of the puzzles of the Old Testament.

Sargon the Great and the Rise of the Akkad Dynasty

Except for the exploits of Gilgamesh, one of the kings of the city of Uruk, little is known historically of the first half of the Third Millennium BC. The *King List* indicates that the city-states of Mesopotamia were ruled by a succession of weak kings and details of their reigns is not known until the advent of Sargon, who founded what is called the Akkad Dynasty about 2334 BC.

Sargon was not born of a legitimate king; his antecedents are a mystery and his name has become legendary to later generations who referred to him as Sargon the Great. It is possible that he was the son of a priestess and a Sumerian god on an escapade to Earth. His origin is described in the biographic poem the *Legend of Sargon:*

> Sargon, the mighty king, king of Agade, am I.
>
> My mother was a changeling, my father I knew not.
>
> My changeling mother conceived me, in secret she bore me.

Sargon then describes how he was set adrift in a basket of reeds sealed with bitumen in the Euphrates, and later found by a water-carrier who raised him as his own son. Sargon then reveals how he worked as a gardener and came to the attention of the goddess Ishtar who made him king of the city of Agade.

The word "changeling" is sometimes translated as priestess because its meaning is not certain. Changeling was the term, however, applied to the issue of a god as an earthling. It was a hybrid creature of mixed divine (serpent) and human parentage. They made up the aristocracy, who ruled the Sumerian empire.

Sargon first became cup-bearer to the king of Kish; then for some unknown reason Kish fell out of favor with the gods and Sargon became king and set up his capital at Agade. The transition is described in the histographic poem the *Curse of Agade,* which strongly hints that Sargon was assisted by certain gods who conveniently cleared the road for him by destroying Kish and Uruk.

> After the frowning forehead of Enlil had killed (the people of) Kish like the "Bull of Heaven," after he had ground the house of Uruk into dust, like a giant bull, after in due time, to Sargon the King of Agade from the lands above to the lands below, Enlil had given him lordship and kingship.

The "Bull of Heaven" was a euphemism often used in the Sumerian legends for one of the special weapons used by the deities. It appears graphically in the legend of Gilgamesh, for example, when he and his companion Enkidu managed to destroy the "Bull of Heaven" — a weapon sent by the goddess Ishtar.

From the inscriptions preserved of Sargon we know that he conquered all of northern Syria as far as Anatolia and up to the borders of Lebanon.

> Sargon the king prostrated himself in prayer before Dagon (Enlil) in Tuttul (now modern Hit). He gave him the upper regions: Mari, Iarmutu, and Ebla as far as the forest of cedar and the mountain of silver. Enlil did not let anyone oppose Sargon.

There are several points of interest in Sargon's claims. He conquered Mesopotamia and the upper valley and the lands to the west, up to the borders of Anatolia (the mountain of silver) and that of Lebanon (the forest of cedar). Sargon conquered the ancient lands assigned to Sin. Anatolia and Lebanon, respectively, belonged to the gods Adad and Shamash and therefore were "out of bounds" to the invading Sargon. He describes how he captured the cities of littoral Lebanon and the Bekaa valley:

> The Sea Lands three times I encircled.
>
> Dilmun my hand captured.

The cities of the coast of the Mediterranean were usually referred to as the Sea Lands in the literature of Mesopotamia. Sargon may refer to three of the major cities of the littoral part of Lebanon, probably Biblos, Tyre, and Sidon.

Sargon conquered the known world from Egypt to India and became known as a military genius, an imaginative administrator and builder, and one of the most remarkable political figures of the ancient East. Later legends and chronicles celebrating the exploits of Sargon suggests his conquests may have included the lands of Egypt, Ethiopia, and India as well.

Unlike the rulers that followed, Sargon preferred to conquer and not to destroy in order to built up his vast empire, one that encompassed the entire known world. This is manifest in the archives of Ebla which reveal that the city seemed to thrive under the administration of Sargon, but was later destroyed by his grandson Naram-Sin.

Upon the death of Sargon, the empire broke away from the rule of Mesopotamia. The kingship went to his son Rimush who took over an empire torn by revolt and rebellion. Rimush ruled for nine years during which time he tried to subdue the Mesopotamian cities. His short reign suggests a violent death and reportedly he was killed by his servants.

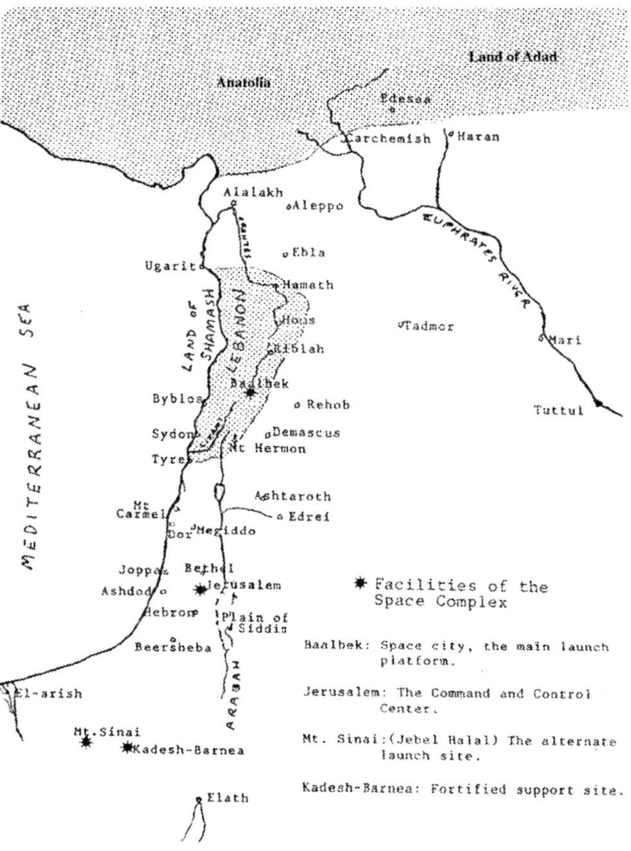

Fig. 58 – Western Lands circa 3000 BC

Then Manishtushu became regent and ruled for 15 years, and was mostly preoccupied with trying to recover the distant colonies which had became mutinous. He too appeared to have died in a palace revolt and was replaced by Naram-Sin. It is not clear if Naram-Sin killed his father in order to assume the mantle of kingship, but in view of his subsequent activities it seems highly likely.

Ruling from 2254 BC to 2213 BC, Naram-Sin subdued the rebellious cities of Mesopotamia and recovered the lost colonies. Unfortunately, his overriding ambition and ruthlessness did not bode well and although he recovered the empire of his grandfather Sargon, he did so at a terrible price. He not only destroyed the space facilities at Baalbek but devastated the lands of Lebanon as well, and poisoned the land so that it was uninhabitable for a thousand years. He boasted of how he destroyed the cities of the west like Ebla.

Naram-Sin proclaimed himself a god and assumed all the trappings of godship, having himself represented wearing a horned headdress, the symbol of a god. He also placed the "dingir" or star symbol before his name, a usage that was restricted to the gods. His policies brought down the Akkad Dynasty and destroyed the lands of Mesopotamia which lay chaotic for a hundred years.

Naram-Sin, the King Who Would be a God

As forceful a figure as his grandfather, Naram-Sin became the subject of many traditions, some complimentary, but most not very flattering. He is remembered as the king who caused the destruction of the city of Agade and the end of a dynasty. He extended the borders of the empire ruthlessly, describing himself as "king of the four quarters," which evidently meant lord of the whole civilized world as it was then known. He also called himself "Conquerer of Arman and Ebla" and boasted that he was the first to destroy these cities. The claim has a ring of truth to it for when archaeologists unearthed Ebla in 1974 they found evidence of a huge conflagration and the city being destroyed at about this time. The ruins of Arman have yet to be located.

There are three main sources which provide most of the information we know of Naram-Sin and his career:

1. A stele which he erected at Sippar, later found at Susa, which shows him climbing a mountain over the prostrate form of his enemies. He faces a large conical object on top of a mountain with the star of Shamash overhead. He wears the horned headdress of a god (figure 59). The conical object he faces is a symbolic representation of the command capsule, the dwelling of the gods.
2. A Sumerian composition known as the *Legend of Naram-Sin,* which relates his expedition to a mountain land where he destroyed a rebellious city but also lost his whole army in the process.
3. A rather long (280 lines) Sumerian histographic poem called the *Curse of Agade*, which was composed soon after his death, perhaps as an exculpation for his destructive policies and his sacrilegious behavior in the plunder of the Ekur, which led to the gods placing a curse on Naram-Sin and his city of Agade.

All three of these sources are believed to be related to the expedition of Naram-Sin to the land of Lebanon and his destruction of the space city at Baalbek.

Destruction of the Rocket Tower and Assembly at Baalbek

The narrative of the *Curse of Agade* begins with the rise of Sargon to power with the support of Ishtar, who made Agade her tutelary city. With Enlil's help, according to the author, the empire of Sargon flourished until the advent of Naram-Sin to the kingship. Soon after he assumed power the gods deserted the city and Ishtar removed her sponsorship, leaving the city weak and impoverished. At first, Naram-Sin accepted his fate with humility, but after seven years of his contrite behavior he consulted an oracle and apparently was repulsed. His humility turned to defiance and according to the poem, he mobilized his army and attacked the "Ekur," desecrated its holy places, and devastated the land. This brought down the wrath of Enlil who unleashed the barbaric tribes of the surrounding hills that spread devastation throughout the land of Mesopotamia.

Fig. 59 – Victory of Stele of Naram-Sin

Found at Susa, dated to about 2200 BC, this stele shows Naram-Sin, the ego-maniac king of Agade, wearing the horned headdress of a god, facing the conical object or "shum" representing the home of the god Shamash. The stars of Shamash and Ishtar are shown overhead. The stele glorifies his victory over the people of the mountain "rebel lands," and the capture and destruction of the "Ekur" or rocket stand at Baalbek in Lebanon.

The key to understanding this story is the identification of the "Ekur" of Enlil whose violation was so serious as to bring down the wrath of the gods who had been called in council. The Ekur has traditionally been equated to the temple of Enlil atop the ziggurat at Nippur, his sacred city, according to usual translations and interpretations. This identification, however, brings many difficulties and contradictions from the text, for nowhere in the text is the city of Nippur mentioned or even suggested.

The Sumerian term E-KUR is composed of E, meaning "house or home" and KUR, the word for "mountain or hill." Besides being used to denote a natural land formation, it is also applied to an artificial mountain such as a ziggurat or to any large man-made edifice. Today's skyscraper would fit the term Ekur very well.

There is no indication in the text that this Ekur was is in the city of Nippur. The text clearly states that the Ekur was located in a forested land, one of boxwoods, cypress, and cedar. There are no forests in the Mesopotamian alluvial plain, particularly near Nippur, nor does any other area of the plain have a history of being wooded. In addition, the cuneiform text makes certain statements that clearly rule out Mesopotamia and rather point to a wooded mountainous land, that of Lebanon.

The legend reveals that Naram-Sin was completely alienated from the Sumerian pantheon, and in particular its chief Enlil, who had blessed Sargon's conquest of Ebla and Dilmun. The poem describes the assault of Naram-Sin on the Ekur of Enlil:

> He defied the word of Enlil,
> Crushed those who had submitted to him (Enlil),
> Mobilized his troops.
> Like a bandit who plunders a city,
> He erected large ladders against the house,
> To destroy the Ekur like a huge ship. . .
> Against the house that was not a mountain,
> Where cedar was felled.
> He forged great axes,
> Sharpened double-edged axes of destruction.
> Leveled it down to the foundation of the land.

The so-called great "axes of destruction" presumably refer to some sort of large-scale destructive weapon. The destruction of the Ekur was complete and so widespread that the effects were felt over the whole land, even that of Mesopotamia. As the poem continues, the land of the Ekur was devastated as:

> Naram-Sin cast into the fire,
> Cedar, cypress, zabalum-tree, and boxtree.
> Its giguna-trees, he pulverized.

The destruction of the land was complete. The structure on the stone platform at Baalbek, the artificial mountain or rocket assembly building and launch structure, was destroyed:

> The people now saw its *cella*,
> The house that knew no light,
> The Akkadian saw the holy vessels of the gods,
> Its great *lahama* of the *dubla*, which stood at the house.

The terms *lahama* and *dubla* have been a puzzle to scholars since they have no Semitic meaning and have been left untranslated. *Cella* is the usual term used for the inner sanctum of a temple or palace, that is, the holy of holiest.

Although the poem is in Akkadian Semitic, it is very probable that these unknown terms are borrowed words from the Sumerian. Words applying to the gods and their activities are considered sacred and are often not translated but carried over into the Semitic language intact. In this case, the Sumerian DU means "bond or connection," while BLA, a form of BAL, means "crossbeam" as applied to buildings or structures. Thus DUBLA may be the framework or "bonded crossbeams" that refer to the tower for the standing rocket vehicle, which in this case would be the *lahama*.

The term LA-HA-MA also lends itself to Sumerian definition. LA means "bright" or "light" in Sumerian, HA or KA is the word for "mouth" or "to speak," and MA is the common term used for ship or craft. Thus *lahcma* probably means "the ship whose mouth speaks loudly and brightly" or in other words, a rocket vehicle. "The holy vessels of the gods" which Naram-Sin saw and destroyed were the rocket ships standing on the rocket stand on the stone platform at Baalbek.

At the same time the lands of Lebanon were also devastated. The *Curse of Agade* also describes the destruction of a wooded land by the weapons of Naram-Sin:

> Leveled it down to the foundation of the land.
>
> He tore up its mes-trees,
>
> The raining dust rose sky high.
>
> He struck down its doorposts,
>
> Cut off the vitality of the land.

Swift retribution came to Naram-Sin. Enlil convened the gods to discuss this terrible tragedy and what to do about it. The seriousness of the affair is shown by the pantheon that decided his fate: Enki, Ishtar, Sin, Ninurta, Adad, and Shamash, all major gods who made the key decisions of the pantheon.

It was first decided to lay waste all of Mesopotamia but the gods relented and decided to punish only the city of Agade. The destruction of the city was so thorough that even to this day the site of the city has not been found. The destruction spread to the rest of Mesopotamia, however, and it lay in a devastated and chaotic condition for a hundred years. It may have been caused by a cloud of radioactive fallout from Lebanon, seeing that Mesopotamia is in the direction of the prevailing winds. The poem describes conditions of hunger and disease, and it relates how the ones "who slept on the roof died on the roof," apparently as a result of exposure to the fallout from the radioactive clouds.

Naram Sin's Army Destroyed

Just as in the *Curse of Agade* there is a similar situation in the *Legend of Naram-Sin* where he is turned down by an oracle and decides to mobilize his army and invade a distant "mountainous land" and destroy the "rebel city." Naram-Sin did battle with the troops of this land which numbered several hundred thousand.

In three successive years, Naram-Sin sent out a huge army to capture the mountainland: 180,000 were sent the first year, 120,000 in the second, and 60,000 in the third year. But not one of them returned alive. The armies appear to have been destroyed by a "floodwind weapon" which caused massive damage and apparently ended the war.

It is not clear who initiated the doomsday weapon, Naram-Sin or the defenders of the mountainland. In any case, the results were devastating to the land of Lebanon and apparently to the civilization of Mesopotamia as well. The lands of Lebanon were scrupulously avoided by eastern kings for the next thousand years. The land may have been contaminated by either chemical or radioactive poisoning.

Naram-Sin, in his overriding ambition, probably tried to imitate the exploits of the hero Gilgamesh and repeat the successes of his grandfather the great Sargon. In declaring himself a god, there apparently was no limit to the excessive ambition of the egomaniac Naram-Sin.

Naram-Sin was not satisfied with just subjecting the cities of the West, but destroyed them as well. In excavating the royal palace at Ebla, the archaeologist Pettinato found that there was "undoubtedly traces of a huge conflagration and that Naram-Sin of Akkad was considered responsible for its fiery destruction."

Generally called the Early Bronze Age, from 3000 to 2000 BC, this period came to an end by widespread destruction. The city of Ai was completely destroyed in 2200 BC and remained a pile of stones for a thousand years. Likewise, Jericho was burned by a great conflagration at about this time. Just as Jericho protected the lower end of the Jordan Valley, Beth-Shan controlled the approaches in the north, dominating the valley at its widest, and guarding the highway which connected it with the seacoast. At the western end of this route, the citadel of Megiddo stood guard. Both Beth-Shan and Megiddo were destroyed at this time.

The fortress of Beth-Shan is of more than passing interest and it is important for another reason. The name Beth-Shan means the "Temple of the Serpent God," and numerous representations of serpents were found here. It may have been the center of the serpent cult which was widespread at that time in Palestine. It is not clear if Naram-Sin is responsible for all these devastations, but he certainly is the prime suspect.

After the death of Naram-Sin, there were a few minor kings of the dynasty but they ruled over a ruined land and could not stem the onslaught of the Gutian tribes which descended from the surrounding mountains. The lands stayed in the hands of the Gutian hordes for about a hundred years, a time when there was no central authority in Mesopotamia.

This leads us up to the days of Abraham who was deeply involved in another attempt by the eastern kings to subjugate the lands of the west and control the remaining facilities of the space complex.

CHAPTER 22

INVASION OF THE WESTERN LANDS: THE REPHAIM, MOUNT SINAI, SODOM AND GOMORRAH DESTROYED

The Days of Abraham: 100 Years of Turbulence

Of all the patriarchal narratives of the Bible, Genesis 14 is unique in being set in a context of world history. It describes an invasion from the east in the year 2085 BC and the role of Abraham in defending the land of Canaan. It is part of a vast panorama of history from the birth of Abraham in 2167 BC until 2067 BC when Sodom and Gomorrah and the other cities of the Valley of Siddim were destroyed.

This time frame coincides with the end of the Early Bronze Age, surmised as between 2100 and 2000 BC, marked by large scale destruction of the cities of the Levant. During these years, the Third Dynasty of Ur rose to prominence in Mesopotamia.

Abraham was born at Ur in lower Mesopotamia in 2167 BC at the time when the land was still under the control of the Gutian hordes. About the year 2109, the Gutians were overcome by Utu-Hegal of Uruk who drove them out of Mesopotamia. One of his governors usurped the throne and seized control in 2102 BC. This was Ur-Nammu who ruled for 18 years according to the Sumerian *King List*.

Abraham and his father Terah were high priests serving the deities of Adad and Utu at the city of Ur. The change in kingship placed them in a dangerous position and in 2106 BC they wisely migrated to Harran in northern Mesopotamia, a city on the edge of the Hittite lands controlled by Adad.

The first invasion of Palestine by Ur-Nammu was in 2099, when he forced a treaty and an assurance of fealty on the cities of the Valley of Siddim: Sodom, Gomorrah, Admah, Zeboiym, and Zoar. These cites were, at that time, located in the valley now covered by the northern part of the Dead Sea.

For twelve years, as reported in Genesis, the pact held firm; in the thirteenth year the cities rebelled and refused to pay tribute. The next year the eastern kings invaded the lands. The rebellion was apparently fomented by Adad, for a few years before they rebelled Abraham was sent to Palestine and then to Egypt, apparently to set up defenses against what was sure to be an invasion from the east.

The year before the invasion, Abraham returned from Egypt and went to Bethel where he divided his forces — Lot took his troops east to defend the city of Sodom in the Valley of Siddim. Abraham deployed his forces south to the Anakim fortress city of Hebron, where he gained valuable allies of the Anakim.

The following year, the eastern kings under the leadership of Ur-Nammu invaded Palestine. With an army numbering 800,000, they easily penetrated the Transjordan and destroyed the fortifications of the Rephaim.

Abraham belatedly engaged the enemy at Dan, north of the Sea of Galilee and again near Damascus, where he liberated Lot and his men and retrieved most of the booty from the rear train of the hastily departing army. It is puzzling why the invaders did not stop and fight the small forces at Abraham's disposal and preserve their loot and prisoners. Had the invading army stood its ground it would easily have defeated the army of Abraham. For some unstated reason, however, the army was in a headlong flight back to its native land. Ur-Nammu is known to have gotten ill on an expedition to a foreign mountainland and died soon after his return to his capital city of Ur.

2167 BC	Abraham is born at Ur in Mesopotamia.
2109 BC	Utu-Hegel sets up the Third Dynasty of Ur.
2106 BC	Terah and Abraham leave Ur and go to Haran.
2103 BC	Ur-Nammu seizes control of the city-state of Ur.
2099 BC	Ur-Nammu forces a treaty with the cities of the Valley of Siddim
2092 BC	Abraham leaves Haran for Canaan on a mission for Yahweh (Adad).
2091 BC	Abraham goes to Egypt to get military support; marries a princess.
2087 BC	The cities of Siddim, i.e. Sodom and Gomorrah rebel.
2086 BC	Abraham returns to Canaan and sets up defenses.
2085 BC	Invasion of the eastern kings under Ur-Nammu. Destruction of the cities of the Rephaim in Transjordan. Capture of Kadesh, the destruction of Mount Sinai, and looting of Sodom and Gomorrah. Abraham gives chase and rescues Lot. Ur-Nammu dies; Shulgi takes over for the next 48 years.
2082 BC	Ismael born of Hagar, the Egyptian princess.
2068 BC	Abraham makes a covenant with Adad; Isaac is born.
2067 BC	The cities of the Valley of Siddim are destroyed by Adad in his last act of vengeance. The Dead Sea is formed. Abraham settles in the Negeb, repudiates his Egyptian connection, and begins a new dynasty with Isaac.
2001 BC	Jacob is born.
1992 BC	Abraham dies and deeds all to Isaac.

Fig. 60 – A chronology for the days of Abraham.

Shulgi then became king and a quiet period seems to have come over the land of Palestine. During this interim period, Abraham apparently broke relations with Egypt as shown in the treatment of Hagar, his Egyptian wife, and their son and heir Ishmael. The cities returned to the aegis of the eastern kings and reaffirmed their loyalty to the Dynasty of Ur.

Considering Adad's inability to defend them successfully against the might of the Mesopotamian power, it seems to have been a logical move. In the person of Yahweh, Adad is portrayed in the Old Testament as a vindictive and vengeful god. Thus, his revenge on the cities of the Plain should have been no surprise. In 2067 BC, seeing that he could not retain their loyalty, he unleashed mass destructive weapons on the cities of the Plain that also ruptured the valley floor, resulting in the formation of the inland sea.

Who Was Abraham?

For someone who is claimed by three major religions — Judaism, Christianity, and Islam, as their Patriarch and founder, there is little information provided by the scriptures on his background in the city of Ur where he was born and raised. The family background of Abraham is given but brief mention in Genesis, which states laconically:

> Terah took his son Abram, his grandson Lot son of Harran, and his daughter-in-law Sarai, the wife of his son Abram, and they

> all left Ur of the Chaldeans to move to the land of Canaan. But when they reached Harran, they settled there.

Obviously, Genesis is no help in obtaining information on the early life and activities of Abraham. Nonetheless, there are other sources that fill in the omissions of Genesis, namely, Josephus in his *Antiquities of the Jews*, the *Book of Jubilees*, the *Book of the Apocalypse of Abraham*, and the rabinnical tradition of the Jews as recorded in the *Haggadah.*

According to Jubilees, Abraham came from a long line of high-priests which served the local deities of the cities of Mesopotamia. His grandfather Nahor learned the special priestly knowledge from his father for

> Nahor grew up and dwelt in Ur among the Chaldeans, and his father taught him the researches of the Chaldeans in order to practice divination and astrology according to the signs of the heavens.

Nahor's son carried on the family tradition; in turn, he was assisted in his priestly duties by his son Abraham. Thus it is recorded that at least four generations served in the priesthood of the city of Ur.

Abraham's father Terah was just not an ordinary priest, for according to the *Haggadah*, he "was a prince and magnate in the house of the king." Jubilee mentions how Abraham in his 60th year differed with his father and burned down the temple which contained the idols. His brother Harran dashed in to save the idols but perished in the fire. It was for destroying the temple, according to this source, that Terah and his family were forced to leave Ur. The real reason for the migration, however, lies in the political turmoil of the times and it may be the temple that they destroyed was that of Enlil or Sin.

Probably the most detailed and fascinating story of Abraham's early life is found in the *Book of the Apocalypse of Abraham.* It is dated to the First Century AD and probably originated in Hebrew in Palestine. It was completely lost to the Western Christian Church until the Eleventh Century. In this document, Terah is described not only as

an astrologer, but also an idolmaker. With his son's help, Terah ran a workshop that manufactured idols for the temples of the Mesopotamian cities as well as for sale to private citizens for home use. These were made of different materials — stone, wood, iron, copper, silver, and gold, with their value determined by the substance and workmanship. These idols were presumably the *teraphim* of the Old Testament, and the animated idols of the Sumerians. They were the portable communication sets which are discussed below.

Abraham Leaves for Palestine on a Mission for Adad

Abraham and his family moved to Harran in northern Mesopotamia in 2106 BC. He remained there for 14 years. Although the scriptures are silent about these years, events elsewhere were rapidly moving to a conclusion. In Ur, the ambitious Ur-Nammu was consolidating his newly won position by gradually subduing the other cities of Mesopotamia. Only then did he turn his attention west to the land of Palestine. The story is narrated in Genesis:

> For twelve years they had served Chedorlaomer, but in the thirteenth year they rebelled. In the fourteenth year, Chedorlaomer and the kings allied with him came.

The pact between the Canaanite kings and the Sumerian kings, presumably led by Ur-Nammu, was therefore enacted fourteen years earlier, in 2098 BC. According to Josephus, this treaty was the result of an incursion by the kings of

Mesopotamia who were "conquerors and imposed a tribute on kings of the Sodomites who submitted to this slavery twelve years." The earlier invasion had occurred during the years that Abraham was at Harran. He must have witnessed these events that saw the policies of Ur-Nammu take fruition.

Utu-Hegal, who rid Mesopotamia of the Gutians, left a memorial of his exploits on a clay tablet wherein he praises the gods Ishkur (Adad) and Utu (Shamash) for their help in defeating the Gutians and returning the kingship to Uruk. Adad and Utu were gods of the Western Lands, and their appearance in Mesopotamia is unusual, the area normally was assigned to Nannar/Sin. Were these the gods that Terah and Abraham served? If so, they were forced to leave Ur when Ur-Nammu established his capital in their home city of Ur. Ur-Nammu had the support of Nannar (Sin) and the whole priesthood was loyal to him; this is shown in the affinity of the kings of this dynasty to attach his name to theirs, for example, Amar-Sin, Shu-Sin, and Ibbi-Sin. Abraham's priesthood was in a precarious position and this explains their sudden exodus to Harran, presumably with a large retinue.

Even from the abbreviated version of Abraham's activities in Genesis it is quite obvious that he was not just an ordinary nomadic chief. He could mobilize a sizable number of troops on short notice and engage a formidable invading horde. There must have been more to the migration than just a vague impulse to settle and populate a new land. Thus, in the year 2092 BC, the fifteenth year of his stay in Harran, Abraham received his marching orders from Yahweh/Adad.

Genesis states tersely that Yahweh appeared to Abraham and told him to take Sarah and Lot and "all the possessions that they had acquired, and all the persons they had obtained in Harran," and set out for the land of Canaan. The statement leaves open the question of the size of his contingent, and "all the persons they had obtained in Harran," could have been a considerable number of people.

Leaving with his entourage, Abraham proceeded to northern Palestine to the area south of Shechem, a site which plays a significant role in the later activities of the Hebrews. Genesis says "Abraham travelled in the land as far as the site of Shechem, by the terebinth (oak) of Moreh."

Customarily, Moreh is translated as a personal name, but its original meaning is "guiding" or "ocular." In the *Book of Judges*, the "moreh" at Shechem is called the "soothsayer terebinth." It was apparently a place where one could contact the gods by radio.

Abraham Goes to Egypt to Seek Military Assistance

At Bethel, Adad (Yahweh) told Abraham to go to Egypt where, according to Jubilees, he remained for five years. What was the real reason for Abraham's visit to Egypt?

Little is known of these years although Josephus implies he moved in the highest circles since he taught the Egyptians many sciences they did not know. Abraham also took an Egyptian wife, a Princess and daughter of the Pharaoh, the usual practice when a treaty is struck between allies. This is not the action of a common nomad and reveals Abraham's aristocratic status and verifies the statement in the *Haggadah* that his father Terah was "a Prince and magnate" in the house that ruled Ur.

Hagar was apparently Adad's choice to start a dynasty under Abraham in the land of Palestine. This is evident in their first child Ishmael being made the heir apparent at the time. The Hittite god was making a power play to seize control of Palestine. It was not until later that a change of fortune caused Adad to initiate a new line of descent under Isaac.

Abraham must have had advanced knowledge of the coming invasion from the east and sought Egyptian assistance in the form of an armed force. In the year 2086 BC, Abraham returned to Palestine and immediately proceeded to Bethel where he had had previous communication with Adad. This took place about a year before the invasion. The cities of the Plain had abrogated their treaty with Ur at this time, probably at the instigation of Adad, but with the promise to provide them with the necessary protection. Abraham was entrusted with the task of setting up defenses. With a strong Egyptian contingent, Abraham also sought help from the Rephaim forces at Hebron.

Proceeding to Bethel, Abraham was told to divide his forces. Lot took part of the army eastward to the Valley of Siddim and deployed them before the city of Sodom to protect it from a direct assault through the Jordan Valley. Abraham led his own forces and Egyptian troops southward to Hebron, at that time a strong citadel of the Anakim (Rephaim), where he received support from the Anakim generals Mamre, Eshkol, and Aner.

It is noteworthy that at this time Abraham did not deploy his forces north of Jerusalem, which would be the logical place to defend that city. Obviously, he was protecting some place south of Jerusalem and Hebron, and as events developed, it was El-Paran in the northern Sinai. The target of the invading army was Mount Sinai.

Thus, the grand strategy of Adad was to defend the land and particularly the space complex in the northern Sinai. The strategy was threefold:

1. A string of fortresses of the Rephaim in Transjordan defended the approach known as the King's Highway. The citadels were believed to be impregnable.
2. The approach through the Jordan Valley was protected by the armies of the five cities of the Plain, reinforced by the army of Lot. Several major citadels like Beth-Shean and Jericho also blocked this approach.
3. The third possible invasion route was through the lands west of the Valley, through Jerusalem. It was protected by the forces of Abraham, supplemented with an Egyptian contingent and the Anakim allies at the fortress of Hebron.

Hence, as the fateful year 2085 BC approached, Abraham had strategically deployed his forces. With his Egyptian, Anakim, and Rephaim allies, his position seemed impregnable.

The Location of Sodom and Gomorrah

Sodom and Gomorrah and the other infamous cities of the Valley of Siddim which were destroyed in the days of Abraham have never been physically located, although tradition places them under the waters of the shallow or southern part of the Dead Sea, the body of water the Jews call *Yam ha-melach* or the Salt Sea. This is a false assumption, just as the age of the Dead Sea is hundreds of thousands of years old and that it existed in this form since recorded time.

There is no scriptural or other evidence to support both suppositions. To the contrary, all indications are that the cities were located in the northern part of the Dead Sea and that this sea dates no further back than the days of Abraham.

The five cities seem to have been a cohesive group. Sodom, Gomorrah, Admah, Zeboiym, and Zoar or Bela were often linked together geographically as though they were neighbors in the Valley of Siddim. The five cities were also associated commercially, and are listed together in the Ebla tablets as a consortium as early as 2500 BC. They rebelled as a group against the authority of the kings of Mesopotamia and refused to pay tribute.

When Abraham and Lot separated their forces, Genesis makes it clear that Lot took his troops to the east, that is, the northern part of the Valley. As Genesis expressed it:

> So Lot chose for himself the whole Jordan plain, and set out eastward . . . and settled among the cities of the plain, pitching his tent near Sodom.

Eastward could only be in the direction of Jericho, the city which marks the northern edge of the present Dead Sea.

Eighteen years later when the cities were destroyed in a cataclysmic explosion, Abraham observed the results from a mountain top near Hebron, only fifteen miles away. The disaster occurred at dawn. That morning Abraham hurried to the mountaintop and as Genesis says:

> As he looked down toward Sodom and Gomorrah and the whole area of the plain, he could see only smoke over the land rising like the fumes from a kiln.

Hebron is due west from En-Gedi and the central part of the Dead Sea. The area of destruction witnessed by Abraham must have been the area in the northern and central part of the valley.

Abraham looked towards the Plain and no mention is made of a body of water. In fact, nowhere in the account of the invasion of the eastern kings nor in the destruction of the cities is any reference made explicitly or implied to the existence of a body of water that could be interpreted as an inland sea.

The Age and Origin of the Dead Sea

The area covered by the Dead Sea is an extension of the Jordan Valley as it would have continued into the Wadi Arabah were it not contained south of Jericho for an area of some 50 miles. Since the lake is a continuation of the valley, what are the characteristics of this important geographical feature which so dominates the land of Palestine?

Today the valley through which the Jordan River flows extends 65 miles between the Sea of Galilee in the north and the Dead Sea in the south. The valley is between three and 14 miles wide, while its river bends and twists in many loops as to complete an overall run of 200 miles.

The river itself is about 90 to 100 feet wide and three to 10 feet deep except in flood at springtime. It falls a distance of 590 feet between the two bodies of water, providing for the swift current of the river. After a torturous descent of 200 miles it loses itself completely in the Dead Sea from which there is not outlet. Historical evidence indicates that this was not so at the time of Abraham.

The Jordan Valley at that time extended all the way from the Sea of Galilee, through what is now the Dead Sea, then called the Valley of Siddim, and exiting into the Wadi Arabah. It may have continued south, exiting into the Gulf of Aqaba.

This valley was extremely fertile. Its lush vegetation made it a veritable Garden of Eden as suggested in Genesis when

> "Lot looked about and saw how thoroughly watered was the whole Jordan plain, all the way to Zoan . . . like Yahweh's own garden, or like the land of Egypt."

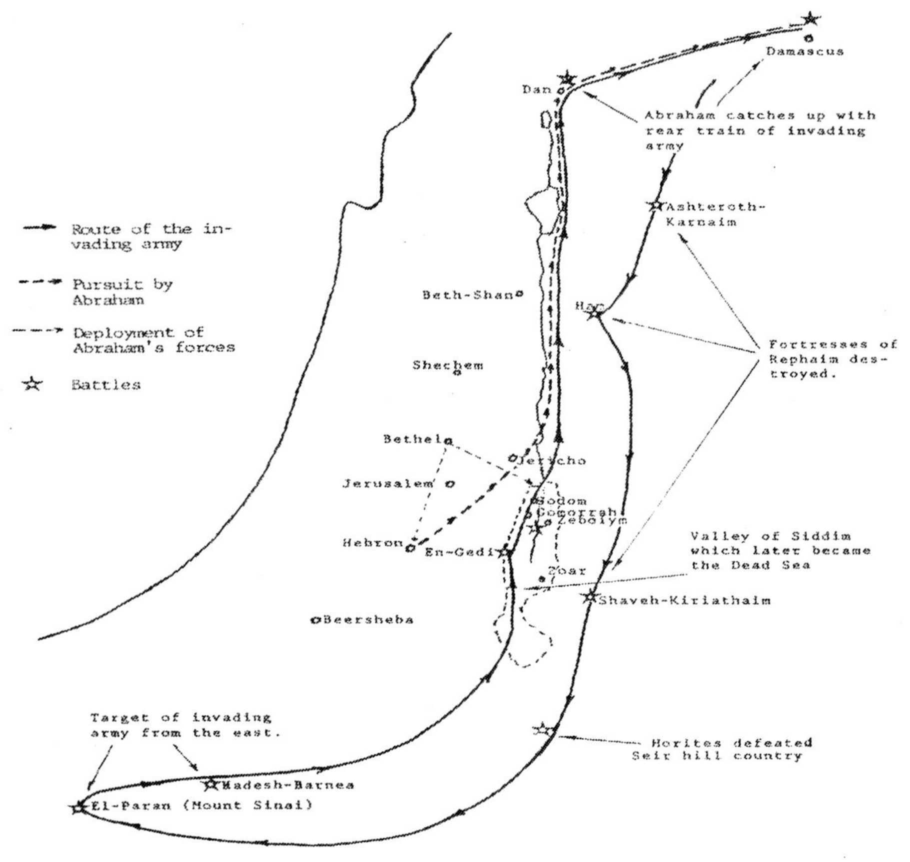

Fig. 61 – Invasion of the Eastern Kings circa 2085 BC.

The Valley of Siddim is thus compared in its green luxuriance to the Garden of Eden and the Nile Valley. In Biblical times, part of the valley of the Jordan was called "The Thicket" or "Jungle of the Jordan," where lions and other animals were so numerous as to be a threat to travellers and sheep herders of the area.

Its many advantages — abundance of water, rich vegetation, and strategic location, made the Valley of Siddim a natural site for many large and prosperous cities. The Jordan-Siddim valley controlled the major trade route from Lebanon and the Mediterranean ports in the north, with the land of Egypt and the Red Sea ports to the south. It was probably for these reasons that the valley was so heavily defended with citadels like Jericho, Beth-Shean, Beth-Nimrah, and En-Gedi, protecting the vital approaches of the north and west. On the eastern side, a natural mountain barrier was supplemented by a number of fortified cities of the Rephaim. In the southern part of the Valley of Siddim, the bitumen pits formed a natural obstacle.

Geological and historical evidence indicates that the lower Jordan Valley in the past was much different from what it is today. The Dead Sea did not exist at the time of Abraham. In fact, studies of the accumulation of the salt content of the Dead Sea place the lake no older that 6000 years. The subject is discussed by Velikovsky in his *Ages in Chaos*. Quoting from research reported in the

British Geographic Journal, Velikovsky contends that if the accumulation of salt (sodium) and other sources of accretion brought in by the Jordan River were taken as a basis of computation for the age of the Dead Sea, its age would be less than 5000 years.

In the Biblical story of the invasion of the four kings from the east, it specifically states that the area now occupied by the Dead Sea used to be called the Valley or Vale of Siddim: "All the latter (that is, the defending kings) joined forces in the Valley of Siddim — now the Dead Sea." The phrase "now the Dead Sea" was apparently added by the chronicler to identify the area of conflict.

The Jordan River evidently flowed through the Valley of Siddim and exited into the Wadi Arabah. It watered the valley and provided for its luxuriant conditions. The *Haggadah* observes that the fertility of the Valley was due to a network of canals which later became the basis for the Dead Sea. It was a well-irrigated land for, according to Genesis, "Lot looked about and saw how thoroughly watered was the whole Jordan plain, all the way to Zoar."

It is generally agreed that Zoar was in the southernmost part of what is now the shallow part of the Dead Sea, somewhere near the Lisan or tongue of land which juts out into the sea. It was to Zoar that Lot retreated in order to escape from the oncoming destruction of Sodom and Gomorrah.

Some catastrophic event must have caused the geological fault (which runs through and underlies the area) to displace, the ground sinking in the process, and forming a seal to allow the accumulation of water from the inflow of the Jordan River.

Josephus in his *Antiquities of the Jews* also asserts that the lake was formed after the destruction of Sodom. When the eastern kings invaded Palestine,

> They pitched camp at the Vale called the Slime Pits for at that time there were pits in that place; but now, upon the destruction of the city of Sodom, that Vale became the lake Asphaltitis, as it is called.

Lake Asphaltitis was the Roman name for the Dead Sea.

Who Was the Actual Leader of the Invading Army?

According to Genesis, the invading kings were Amraphael, King of Shinar; Arioch, King of Ellasar; Chedorlaomer, King of Elam; and Tidal, King of Goiym. Persistent historical research through the years has not been able to associate these monarchs with known Mesopotamian regents either through linguistic affinities or chronological associations.

Shinar of course is Sumer; the land of Ellasar is not identified; Elam is the eastern neighbor of Sumer and traditionally its rival; Goiym is the same as the Hebrew word for "nations" and presumably means he led a polyglot group. According to the Genesis account, Chedorlaomer was the leader of the invading group.

Although it makes Chedorlaomer the leader of the invasion there are many uncertainties arising from the Genesis text. The writings of Josephus, the only other religious source of the invasion, is slightly different. He calls them Assyrian kings and lists them in the following order: Amraphael, Arioch, Chedorlaomer, and Tidal. It would seem he listed them in what he considered their rank of importance. It is also pertinent that the opening sentence of Genesis 14 which provides the account of the invasion also lists them in the same order as Josephus with Amraphael given first and Chedorlaomer third. With that introductory statement, Genesis becomes more specific and states that the cities of the valley had served Chedorlaomer for 12 years, and that Chedorlaomer and the allied kings invaded in the 14th year. Genesis gives their battle order in the Valley of Siddim as Chedorlaomer, Tidal, Amraphael, and Arioch. The next reference in Genesis 14 mentions Abraham's victory over Chedorlaomer and the kings allied with him.

So while the Hebrew chroniclers explicitly state that the invasion was under the leadership of the King of Elam, it is not completely clear that this was actually so, and one is forced to believe that somewhere along the line someone tampered with the text. We are faced with the fact that Amraphael, by virtue of being the King of Shinar (Sumer), would logically be the choice to head the expedition. Apparently something is amiss in the Genesis account and it may be that the Hebrew chroniclers purposely diluted the role of the King of Sumer for reasons of their own, presumably political.

The relations of the Sumerian cities with that of Elam was often tempestuous. Elam was a traditional rival and a persistent threat to the cities of Mesopotamia. By virtue of the assignment of the lands after the Deluge, Elam was assigned to Ninurta, the chief military aide of Enlil. In the Sumerian *King List*, Elam is not listed as one of the cities receiving the kingship and stood out of the pale of legitimate cities. Only the cities of Mesopotamia that were under the aegis of Nannar/Sin were allowed to become capital cities. The only reference to Elam in the *King List* is not a happy one; one of the early kings of Kish is reported to have "smote the weapons of the land of Elam."

It is possible that the king of Shinar (Sumer) had to come to terms with the city of Elam so as not to leave this powerful adversary at his back in Mesopotamia when he took an expedition far away to the Western Lands. Amraphael and Chedorlaomer, the kings of Sumer and Elam, would thus be co-leaders of the expedition as suggested by the Biblical accounts. The next problem is to find which of the dynasties of Mesopotamia that could have produced the invasion king; of these the Third Dynasty of Ur seems the most probable.

It is generally agreed that the Akkad dynasty was much too early to coincide with the days of Abraham. In the interim period after the fall of the Akkad Dynasty, the land of Mesopotamia suffered severe disruptions and depredations at the hands of the Gutian hordes who had descended from the surrounding mountains. These intervening years can be eliminated as producing a candidate for our purpose since the Gutian kings were not strong enough to consolidate the cities of Mesopotamia, much less mount an invasion to the west.

It was one of their puppet kings who ruled Uruk, one Utu-Hegal, who rebelled and finally rid the country of the Gutian occupation. In turn, he appointed a military governor at Ur, who was later to usurp the authority of Utu-Hegal and seize control of the Mesopotamian states, thereby founding what is known as the Third Dynasty of Ur.

This dynasty was followed by the First Babylonian Dynasty and it is generally agreed that it is much too recent to be co-existent with the days of Abraham. In this respect, the Third Dynasty of Ur has been the choice of most scholars.

According to the Sumerian *King List*, the kings which followed the defeat of the Gutians were as follows: Utu-Hegal who ruled at Uruk for 8 years; the kingship was transferred to Ur where Ur-Nammu reigned for 18 years; his son followed and ruled for 48 years; then his son Amar-Sin ruled for 9 years; his son Shu-Sin ruled for 9 years; Ibbi-Sin then reigned for 24 years and ended the dynasty, which had lasted for 108 years according to the *King List*. The reign of Ur-Nammu is believed to have begun in 2103 BC; the dynasty ended in 1995 BC.

Once we have narrowed it down to the Third Dynasty of Ur, one of these kings is sought who fits the requirements based on explicit statements in Genesis 14:

> For twelve years they (the kings of the Valley of Siddim) had served Chedorlaomer, but in the thirteenth year they rebelled. In the fourteenth year, Chedorlaomer and the kings allied with him came . . . and invaded Palestine.

Therefore, our analysis requires a king who reigned at least fourteen years, preferably a little longer. This would allow sufficient time for the monarch to invade the Western Lands, impose his will on the cities of the Valley for thirteen years, and invade again to subdue the rebellious cities.

The second requirement is that there be a period of disintegration before his

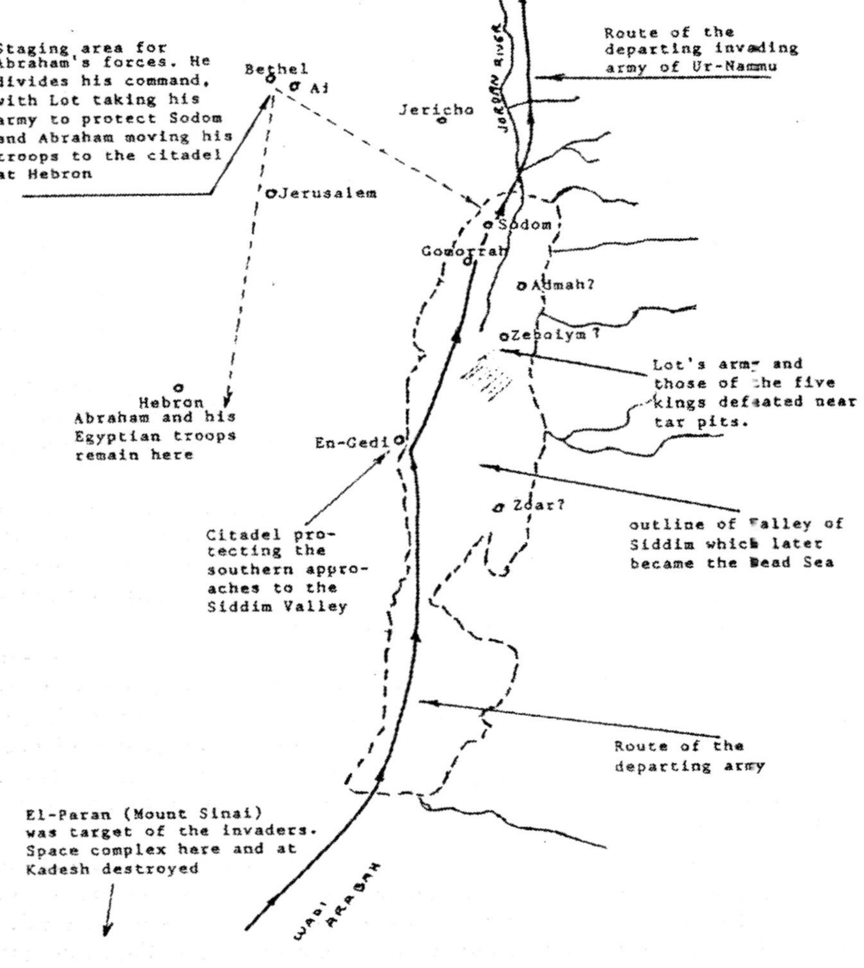

Fig. 62 – Battle of the Valley of Siddim circa 2085 BC.

reign. This king would need several years to pacify and regain control of the city states of Mesopotamia before he could turn his attention to reclaiming the distant cities, the colonies of Sargon the Great, which had become independent during the chaotic period of the Gutian rule.

The third factor concerns a king who would die on a foreign expedition and be brought back hastily by his troops, thereby aborting the invasion to a certain degree.

In summary, these parameters require a king who ruled for at least 14 years, preferably a little longer, whose reign started at the end of a period of chaos and disintegration of the empire, and who died suddenly and unexpectedly while on an expedition to a distant mountain land.

There is only one ruler of the Third Dynasty that meets all these requirements, and that one is Ur-Nammu the founder of the dynasty.

The Rise and Fall of Ur-Nammu of the Third Dynasty of Ur

Ur-Nammu ruled 18 years according to the *King List*. His short reign was due to his dying prematurely on an expedition. It is estimated that he overthrew Utu-Hegal in 2103 BC, at which time he moved the capital city to Ur.

The return of the kingship to the legitimate Sumerian kings after the hundred years of rule by the barbarian Gutians is described in a biographical poem about Utu-Hegal wherein he describes how he went before the shrines of the gods Ishkur (Adad) and Utu (Shamash) and requested their help in dislodging the Gutians and expelling them from the lands of Mesopotamia. The moon god Nannar (Sin) is strangely absent from this poem and his omission is quite significant as we shall see.

It is known from the Sumerian *King List* that the Gutian hordes ruled Mesopotamia for 91 years after the destruction of Agade. Then for eight years the kingship was established at Uruk under the tutelage of Utu-Hegal. The *King List* then cryptically states that "Uruk was smitten with weapons and its kingship carried off to Ur."

Rarely does a kingship change hands in this way in the *King List*. When a city or enemy is "smitten with weapons" it usually refers to unusual widespread destruction such as by non-traditional weapons, the special weapons of the gods.

Utu-Hegal ruled briefly from Uruk for 8 years, apparently with the support of the priesthood of the sun god Utu, a fact which is illustrated by his affixing the name of the deity to his. One of the ambitious governors of the city of Ur seized the kingship, moving the capital to this city. He assumed the name Ur-Nammu, using the city name as a prefix to his.

The details of the palace revolt are not known but it was apparently with the assistance of the priesthood loyal to the moon god Sin. The fact he did not prefix his name with that of Sin is a clue to his character — his overriding ambition and supreme ego which brought on his downfall. Subsequent rulers of the dynasty, such as Amar-Sin, Shu-Sin, and Ibbi-Sin, were careful to attach the deity's name to their own, indicating continuing support of the moon god and his priesthood.

Sumerian cities were ruled by different aristocracies and priesthoods, which owed loyalty to a tutelary deity which supposedly protected the city from harm and supported the king in his many military ventures. Thus the rise of a new king and the transfer to another city also meant a struggle in the ruling aristocracies which also resulted in a major change in the pantheon.

The activities of Abraham are set against this political background, for Terah and Abraham served the ruling king of the city Ur who was at that time Utu-Hegal. In 2106 BC, when Terah and Abraham left Ur for Harran, the struggle for political control was coming to a climax. The support of Terah for Utu and Adad was becoming increasingly dangerous. A few years after they left Ur, Ur-Nammu made his move and seized control of the government and moved his capital to Abraham's native city.

After he had subdued the other cities of Mesopotamia and consolidated his power he turned his attention to trying to recover the lost colonies. In the year 2099 BC, he sent or led an expedition to the cities in the west and reestablished Sumerian control over the former empire that had became independent and rich during the past hundred years. He subdued the cities of the Valley of Siddim and forced a treaty on them, securing their loyalty and tribute for the next twelve years.

During these quiet years, Ur-Nammu turned his attention to internal affairs. Now that the empire was recovered and tribute was pouring in, he was able to rebuild the roads and regain some of the former glory of the empire of Sargon. In a cuneiform tablet he boasted of his outstanding achievements during this period. According to his self-proclaimed deeds, available to us through copies provided by later scribal schools, Ur-Nammu succeeded in codifying the laws which had been suspended during the hundred years domination by the Gutians. These laws antedate the Code of Hammurabi and was the first code of laws known anywhere in the world. Ur-Nammu is also credited with building the great ziggurat at Ur upon which was dedicated the temple to the moon god Sin.

Then for some reason not mentioned, the cities of the west refused to pay tribute and rebelled against the authority of their eastern masters.

The instigator was presumably Adad whose influence over the Western Lands was quite strong. From Anatolia he ruled a Hittite empire that extended as far south as Jerusalem. He certainly must have considered the cities of the Valley of Siddim as his sphere of control, although eastern kings would certainly challenge this claim. According to the division of the lands after the Deluge, the Western Lands had been assigned to Sin.

Invasion and the Battle of the Valley of Siddim

Thus in the year 2085 BC, Ur-Nammu led a mixed army of 800,000 men to the west. He had several purposes — to seize or destroy the space facilities at Mount Sinai and Kadesh which had come under the control of Adad, and to punish the cities of the valley who had rebelled. He must also have wanted to destroy the Rephaim, the semi-divine warrior race, who had also refuted their traditional allegiance to the east and thus presented a serious military threat to the empire.

Genesis is quite unique in that it describes a description of the expedition of Ur-Nammu to the west, the invasion and his battle with the cities of Siddim. It delineates the route taken by the invaders:

> In the fourteenth year, Chedorlaomer and the kings allied with him came and defeated the Rephaim in Ashteroth-Karnaim, the Zuzim in Ham, the Emin in Shaveh-Kiriathaim, and the Horites in the hill country of Seir, near El-Paran, which is on the edge of the wilderness. They then swung back to En-Mishpat — now Kadesh — and subdued all the territory of the Amalekites, and also the Amorites who dwelt in Hazazon-Tamar.

Bypassing the land of Lebanon and the Jordan Valley, the army took the route known as the King's Highway which ran the length of the mountainous land of Transjordan. The passage through this area is also described by Josephus who called the people they encountered the offspring of the Nefilim:

> These kings laid waste all Syria, and overthrew the offspring of the Nefilim.

Destroying this line of fortresses, the army headed for their main target which apparently was El-Paran and Kadesh in the northern Sinai "on the edge of the wilderness." It has been generally accepted that El-Paran was the main goal of the invading army although the strategic or commercial importance of this city has not been fully explained.

Then swinging north through the Arabah, they attacked and reduced the citadel of En-Gedi, formerly called Hazazon-Tamar, which protected the southern approaches to the Valley of Siddim. The kings brought their armies south to face the oncoming threat, or in the words of Genesis:

> Thereupon, the king of Sodom, the king of Gomorrah, the king of Admah, the king of Zeboiym, and the king of Bela — or Zoar — marched forth and engaged them in battle in the Valley of Siddim.

The battle was enjoined near an area of asphalt pits. Here the kings of the cities of the Valley were soundly defeated. Many escaped to the surrounding hills, others were mired in the tar pits and cut down. Lot and his men were taken prisoner.

> Now the Valley of Siddim was one bitumen pit after another. The kings of Sodom and Gomorrah flung themselves into these in their flight; others escaped to the hills. The invaders seized all the possessions of Sodom and Gomorrah and all their food, and departed, taking with them Lot, the son of Abram's brother, together with his possessions.

It is clear that the invaders did not intend to lay waste the rich commercial cities as they had done with the cities of the Rephaim. The cities were much too valuable as subservient commercial cities paying tribute to the city of Ur. On the other hand, the indulgence of the invaders may have been due to the haste in which they left the land of Palestine.

The invading army looted the cities and took many prisoners including Lot. Exiting through the Jordan River Valley, they were attacked by the forces of Abraham at Dan near the Sea of Galilee. Abraham fought them again near Damascus. As a result of these engagements, he liberated Lot and the other prisoners and recaptured the loot taken from the cities of the Plain.

The army of Ur-Nammu at no time stopped and faced the enemy, for reasons unknown, preferring to forfeit their hard-earned gains from Sodom and Gomorrah. In military travel procedure, the supply train, captured booty, and prisoners usually trail the main body of troops. It is clear that Abraham came into contact with the rear guard of the departing army and at not time did he face the main body of troops.

Why Didn't Abraham Confront the Invaders?

It is a mystery why Abraham remained at Hebron with his Egyptian and Anakim allies. Throughout the whole episode — the invasion through Transjordan, the destruction of El-Paran and Kadesh, the battle of the Valley of Siddim — Abraham did not engage the enemy. Military strategy would dictate that he move his army south as the invaders entered the valley and close that exit. He would then have been in a position to execute a classic pincer movement, bottling the Valley at both ends.

Abraham plainly expected the defense line of the Rephaim to hold the invaders, or at least to slow them down. Later, he probably assumed that Lot and the armies of Sodom and Gomorrah could defend the narrow valley It is also possible that Abraham expected a thrust up the Negev towards Jerusalem and waited at Hebron for the attack that never came. Belatedly he may have realized his mistake and chased after the departing armies.

It is more probable that the awesome power demonstrated by the invaders gave Abraham reason for pause and he realized that he did not have the resources to meet the enemy head on.

The invaders moved quickly and resolutely up through the Jordan Valley after looting the cities. They did not tarry and apparently bypassed other fortifications in the area such as Jericho. In fact, the exit through the Jordan Valley and up to Damascus seems more like a headlong flight to return to their homeland as rapidly as possible. Genesis observes that at this time Abraham decided to commit the troops under his command:

> A fugitive brought the news to Abram the Hebrew, who was camping at the terebinths of Mamre the Amorite, kinsman of Eshkol and Aner, these being confederates of Abram. When Abram learned that his kinsman Lot had been captured, he called up his retainers, born into his household, in the number of 318, and gave chase as far as Dan.

The size of Abraham's pursuing army of 318 is unreasonably small, and the number may actually refer to the leaders or chieftains of armed groups or tribes. Hebron was a stronghold of the Anakim and while the assistance of these confederates or allies is not clear, their inclusion in the text would suggest that they supported Abraham in his pursuit of the invaders. These were large and fearsome warriors and presumably equipped with iron chariots. There were probably also Egyptian troops placed under the control of Abraham as a result of his treaty when he married an Egyptian princess.

Abraham and his Anakim cavalry caught up with the rear guard of the army of Ur-Nammu at Dan. A second skirmish was fought near the city of Damascus and they managed to recover most of the booty and prisoners. It is strange that Ur-Nammu did not stand and fight. They would easily have defeated the small force of Abraham; yet they allowed him to seize their war prizes without a strong stand. Evidently, they were in no mood to fight and were in a precipitous haste to leave these lands and return home.

Ur-Nammu as the Victim of his own Devices

It may be that the reason for their rush home was to convey the ill Ur-Nammu back to his capital. The translation of a cuneiform tablet provided by J.V. Kinnier Wilson in his book *The Rebel Lands* provides the story of the expedition of Ur-Nammu and his death in a foreign land. The tablet describes how he fell ill in "the mountain land" and was swiftly taken back to Ur where he was laid on a funeral bier at his palace in Ur.

The people of Mesopotamia were in shock at this disaster for this was not supposed to happen in the cosmic scheme of things. The tablet complains how the king had been "abandoned on the battlefield like a crushed vessel." Although he had served the gods well, so went the complaint, they failed to stand by him in his time of need.

Ur-Nammu may have been the victim of his own ambition. In a tablet commemorating the death of Ur-Nammu it is implied that he used mass destructive-type weapons whose use may have backfired and caused his death. He boasts of using "the mighty *udug* weapon" which is said to have "reduced the enemy land to dust," and to have "overlaid it with poison." There are references to a "fiery gas" which blew into the "house of the rebel lands." These are all symptoms and consequences of nuclear and chemical warfare weapons. They were probably used against the fortresses of the Rephaim in Transjordan and explains the ease with which he captured the land.

Ur-Nammu not only caused his own sickness and death but devastated the lands of Transjordan and the northern Sinai which caused them to remain unoccupied for hundreds of years.

The cities of the Valley of Siddim had a short respite. The death of Ur-Nammu and the change of kingship, with the resultant disorganization, probably allowed them to continue their independent ways. Eighteen years later, the cities were destroyed in a cataclysmic explosion that also ruptured the geological fault that underlies the Jordan Valley, causing the ground to sink and seal off the effluence of the Jordan River. Thus the Dead Sea was formed.

The Quiet Years of 2084 – 2067 BC; Shifting Allegiance and the Coming Storm

With the death of Ur-Nammu, his son Shulgi became king of Ur. He ruled for 48 years bringing in a period of relative peace and prosperity for Sumer. Shulgi relentlessly expanded the limits of the empire over Elam and Anshan to the east and the Zagros mountains to the north. Shulgi assumed divine status and used the dingir or star symbol before his name. Having subdued the land to the east and north, a ruler of Shulgi's ambition would certainly not have left the western provinces unsubordinated.

The scriptures do not reveal any political or military activity for this period and it appears that the cities of the Valley of Siddim had returned to the aegis of the Mesopotamian kings and enjoyed prosperity under the tutelage of Shulgi.

After the events of 2085 BC, Abraham and his retinue settled among the Rephaim at Mamre near Hebron. Here he complained in an exchange with Yahweh/Adad that he had no offspring to continue the family line. Adad promised him a male heir and soon Ishmael was born of his Egyptian wife in the year 2082 BC, three years after the invasion of Ur-Nammu. At this time, Adad had apparently planned to perpetuate the line of Abraham through the Egyptian side, thereby indicating continued cordial relations with Egypt.

Adad Foresakes his Egyptian Connection

Fourteen years later Isaac was born of Sarah, his second wife. Hagar was abruptly banished with the heir apparent Ishmael to the wilderness. In the intervening years since the invasion, Adad must have changed his attitude and relations towards Egypt. The year before the destruction of Sodom, Adad made a new covenant with Abraham — this time choosing Isaac to perpetuate the line of Abraham. There is also a strong indication that Adad himself was the sire of Isaac. What caused the rift with Egypt and the start of a new dynasty under Isaac is not known but the actions presumably were associated with the destruction of the cities of the Valley the following year.

The shift from Ishmael to Isaac is described in Genesis where the change of heart of Adad is described in his announcement to Sarah, that at the age of 90, she is to conceive and bear a son who will be the new heir. It is apparent that Adad wishes to make a new start without the aid of his Egyptian allies. Of this arrangement, Adad informs Abraham, "I will bless her; moreover, I will give you a son by her and when I have blessed her, she shall give rise to nations." Taken literally, it means that Adad will be the sire of the son by Sarah.

It was the policy of the Sumerian deities to mate with human women for the specific purpose of creating an aristocracy of kings, generals, priests, and other important functionaries to run the empire. It was their way of assuring a race of demi-gods they could trust to carry out their wishes and act as a barrier against ordinary humans. Adad was merely following the usual practice of the gods of Sumer. It explains Yahweh's special concern for Isaac and his son Jacob throughout the Old Testament.

As a sign of loyalty and a way to identify his supporters, and to remind them that they are directly descended from a reptilian god, the shedding of the foreskin was introduced at this time in the rite of circumcision. Symbolically, it represented the reptile's sloughing of his skin as the act of renewing his life. It is also perhaps significant, that at the time that Adad was telling Abraham of his new son and heir, he also disclosed his plans to destroy the cities of the Valley.

The Destruction of Sodom, Gomorrah, and Other Cities

In the Genesis account, three angels appeared to Abraham at Mamre to bring the news personally from Adad. The cities, they warned, would be destroyed unless Abraham could provide sufficient reason for not doing so. The angels flew over the cities in reconnaissance, "the men set out from there and looked down upon the face of Sodom." The messengers conducted an aerial survey of the cities presumably to warn any friends and allies of Abraham.

Later, two of them went to Sodom to retrieve Lot and his family. These were "brought out and deposited" outside the city and warned to flee to the hills lest they be caught in the coming destruction. Lot and his family retreated to Zoar in the southern part of the Valley, but warned that they were not safe even there, decided to head for the mountains.

The description of the destruction is provided by Genesis and some added details from Josephus and the *Haggadah*. Genesis says:

> The sun rose upon the Earth as Lot entered Zoar. Then Yahweh rained down upon Sodom and Gomorrah sulphurous fire from Yahweh in heaven. He overthrew the cities and the whole Plain, with all the inhabitants of the cities and the vegetation of the ground.

This account makes it clear that "sulphurous fire" came down from heaven.

Josephus adds more information about the source of destruction with the statement that the Lord "cast a thunderbolt upon the city and set it on fire with its inhabitants." In the *Haggadah*, this thunderbolt comes from the Shekinah, the aerial chariot of the Lord:

> When the angels had brought forth Lot and his family and set them outside the city, he bade them run for their lives, and not look behind, lest they behold the Shekinah, which had descended to work the destruction of the cities.

Lot and his family had been warned not to look behind them lest they be blinded by the flash of the explosion, probably nuclear in nature. According to the *Haggadah* when Lot's wife who had lingered behind turned "and beheld the Shekinah" she apparently was vaporized by the blast. The spaceship of Adad or Yahweh had descended from the sky to fire a mass destructive type weapon to destroy the cities as well as the vegetation of the Plain. The force of the explosion or explosions was so great as to rupture the geological fault underlying the

Valley of Siddim, dropping the valley floor and sealing the fault thereby creating a large inland sea.

At the time of the holocaust, Abraham was at Hebron where he climbed the highest point at dawn to witness the event. Hebron is only 15 miles from the Valley and from his vantage point Abraham must have had an excellent view of the whole event:

> As he looked down toward Sodom and Gomorrah and the whole area of the Plain, he could see only smoke over the land rising like the fumes from a kiln.

Was it a mushroom shaped cloud that Abraham witnessed that destroyed the cities of the plain?

Why Did Adad Destroy Sodom and Gomorrah?

Under the guise of Yahweh, Adad is the prime suspect as the culprit which destroyed the Valley of Siddim. The kings of the Third Dynasty considered these cities too valuable to destroy and preferred to bring them under their control and to collect tribute. They did not destroy the cities when they had the chance. On the other hand, Adad had good reason to destroy them.

He had failed in his attempt to protect the cities from the depredations of the invasion of the eastern kings. He also failed to protect the space complex at Mount Sinai and the support complex at Kadesh, and to prevent their destruction. Seeing that they could not depend on Adad or his resources to protect them from the eastern kings, and being practical commercial entities, the cities apparently decided to revert to the aegis of the eastern monarchs.

Adad and Abraham had broken relations with Egypt, or perhaps it was the reverse — the Egyptians backing down from what they considered to be a bad alliance. Yahweh was known throughout the Old Testament as a vindictive and vengeful god. This appears to have been his last great act of vengeance.

It also appears that Utu deserted Adad at this time. At first occupying Lebanon, Utu presumably shifted his space activities to the Mount Sinai complex after the destructive expedition of Naram-Sin. Now with both space complexes destroyed, he had no base of operations in the west and presumably returned to his home in Mesopotamia. This is indicated in the *Haggadah* where it comments that one of the reasons that the cities of Sodom and Gomorrah were destroyed was because they worshipped the sun and moon gods. Apparently, these cities had transferred their allegiance to Sin, the moon god, and Shamash, the sun god, from that of Adad, known as the thunder god of the Western Lands.

The ruin of the Valley of Siddim was the last of many devastations in the lands of the Levant. Earlier the commercial cities of Ebla and Arman, and the land of Lebanon had been destroyed. Then the fortified cities of the Rephaim in Transjordan, the Mount Sinai/Kadesh complex and the defensive citadels of southern Palestine. Now, as the five cities of the Valley of Siddim disappeared in a fiery cloud and the land eventually flooded to become the Dead Sea, there was little of value left in the Western Lands.

CHAPTER 23

THE AIRSHIPS OF THE ANCIENT SERPENT GODS

Flying Chariots Everywhere!

Many older cultures, particularly non-Western ones, candidly picture their gods flying through the skies in some sort of vehicle. For example, in Hindu mythology, Garuda was prince of birds and is depicted with an eagle's wings and beak, but the body of a man. He served as the personal aircraft of the main Hindu god Vishnu. In the Vedas, which described India before the Deluge, flying cars were quite common. The more recent classic, the Mahabharata, describes a meeting of men and gods, with the gods arriving by aerial cars. Some of these were described as serpent gods, like the Nagas.

Halfway across the world in America, there are also old traditions of flying vehicles. For example, the ancient Anasazi of southwestern United States believed their gods, the Kachinas, flew about from city to city on "flying shields."

Many cultures, particularly those with a Judeo-Christian background, concealed the ability of their gods to fly by using metaphors like dragons and flying serpents. Western religions went through a rigorous process of selection and editing to remove all indications of flying vehicles. This process was not always successful, however, as indicated in the *Book of Ezekiel*, where aerial vehicles are graphically described several times so that it cannot be dismissed as merely an aberration of the text or even a hallucination of the prophet.

Ezekiel is not an exception; these aerial machines appear throughout the scriptures although they are usually interpreted in religious and mystical terms. It is indicative of the mindset of these translators that they refuse to recognize them for what they are.

In Ezekiel's case it is called a "fiery chariot" rather than a flying machine, as if somehow this term is more acceptable. Perhaps because it was the most innocuous way of dismissing a troublesome reference. Nowhere have Biblical scholars translated or referred to the various appearances of these unusual vehicles as aircraft, airships, or even spaceships. Along this vein it is interesting to note that the land-locked Hebrews, who have no naval tradition, refer to the airships as "chariots" while the sea-going Egyptians called them "boats of heaven."

What is also not commonly perceived is that there are numerous references to aircraft in the scriptures but their appearances have been masked through theological interpretation and in many cases just plain false translations.

There are various names used for the vehicles of the ancient astronauts. They had different names for the separate functional sections such as the command capsule or personal housing, the platform or booster rocket on which it rested, and the main rocket itself. We shall try to identify them and separate them by function.

The command capsule or personal housing of the gods is referred to as either a *shekinah* or a *kabod* in the scriptures. The terms seem to be interchangeable since they both rest on a larger vehicle or booster platform called *cherubim.*

This personal capsule housing was considered to be the actual residence of the gods and each civilization revered this cone-shaped object in different ways according to its own traditions. It is was called *beth-el* by the Hebrews, the *betyl* by the Canaanites and Phoenicians, and meaning literally "home of the gods." The Egyptians called the capsule *ben-ben* and revered it at Heliopolis as the home of the sun god. To the Greeks it was the *omphalos*.

To leave the orbiting spaceship or to travel about on Earth, the composite craft of command capsule and booster platform was employed, although the capsule could rise and independently travel by itself for short distances.

In order to leave the Earth's gravity and reach the orbiting spaceship, the command capsule was mounted on a larger booster rocket called a *shem* in the Old Testament, a *shum* by the Sumerians and a *shumu* by the Semitic Akkadians. The rocket vehicle of the ancients was also the source of the legend of the Phoenix bird that rose in fire out of its own ashes.

The "Shum" or Main Rocket of the Sumerians

The most descriptive terms the Sumerian people had for their gods was the composite name U-SHUM-GAL or "great fiery flying serpent," where U stood for fiery, SHUM for flying serpent, and GAL for great or divine. As we have seen, this name was but a euphemism for the rocket ship of the serpent gods.

Like many other words associated with divinity, SHUM was absorbed intact into the later Semitic languages that replaced Sumerian and appears as *shumu*. Since most of the available myths of Mesopotamia are more numerous and complete in Akkadian, Babylonian and other Semitic languages, the term *shumu* is more prevalent. Translators, in despair over translating the term and avoiding its serpent god implications, have rendered the word as "name," a purely arbitrary decision. The *shumu* is mentioned in *Gilgamesh* where it can only be interpreted as a rocket to take him up to the gods in heaven.

As the king of the city of Uruk, Gilgamesh was sad and depressed over the thought of dying. He looked over the city walls and saw dead bodies floating in the river below. Gilgamesh feared that this too would be his fate, being part mortal. He then decided to seek immortality and set his sights on reaching "the land of the living" or the cedar land of Lebanon. Gilgamesh confided in his companion Enkidu that he planned to enter the cedar land in order to set up his *shumu* in the "place where *shumus* have been raised I would raise my *shumu."*

Enkidu informed him that this land was under the sovereignty of Utu and that he must seek his permission, which Gilgamesh proceeded to do. Utu or Shamash was the chief of the cedar land, the land where the space platform was located. It becomes clear that to translate *shumu* as name or reputation makes little sense. Like in Genesis, man would imitate the gods and erect a rocket ship to reach them in heaven since they held all the secrets, especially those of long life.

A similar use of the word *shumu* is seen in the *Tale of Adapa*. After Adapa is summoned to heaven the chief god An wants to know who provided a *shumu* for him so that he could reach the "heavenly abode," or orbiting spaceship. The use of the word *shumu* here clearly means a shuttle craft which took Adapa from the Earth to the heavens.

The "Shem" or Rocket Ship of the Hebrews

The Biblical tale of the Tower of Babel as related in Genesis, deals with events that followed the repopulation of the Earth after the Deluge, when some people "journeyed to the east, and they found a plain in the land of Shinar, and they settled there." The land of Shinar, of course, is the land of Sumer and the plain is the one between the two rivers of Mesopotamia. According to Genesis, the people said:

Let us build a city,
And a tower whose top shall reach the heavens;
And let us make us a name (shem),
Lest we be scattered upon the face of the Earth.
And the Lord came down to see the city and the tower,
Which the children of Adam had erected.
And he said: "Behold, all are as one people and one language,
And this is just the beginning of their undertakings.
Now, anything which they shall scheme to do,
Shall no longer be impossible for them."

The deity then decided to take action and informed some colleagues who are not identified,

Come, let us go down and there confound their language,
So that they may not understand each other's speech.
And the Lord scattered them from there,
Upon the face of the whole Earth.
And they ceased to build the city,
Therefore was its name called Babel,
For there did the Lord mingle the Earth's tongue.

This chapter in Genesis, however, raises more questions than it answers. Why did the ancient residents of Babylon want to "make a name" and why was this "name" to be placed upon a tower or ziggurat whose top would reach the heavens? It is puzzling as to why the making of a name or reputation could counteract the effects of mankind being scattered all over the world. The Lord was so upset over the "making" of this name because such a feat would afterwards make anything possible for man. Obviously, something has been left out of the text. The answers to these questions becomes clear when one reads "rocket ship" instead of "name" for the Hebrew or Semitic word *shem.* The story thus deals with the concern of man to build a tower so as to erect a rocket ship in order to fly over the lands like gods, even to attempt to reach the orbiting spaceship in order to meet the gods. This could not be tolerated by the gods, as only they were permitted to have and to operate rocket and space vehicles.

The *shem* or *shumu* was apparently the main booster that carried the *shekinah* or *kabod*, the command capsule, when it was necessary to leave the Earth and reach the orbiting spaceship. Presumably, the main booster returned to Earth and stood on the launch pad at Baalbek ready for the next mission. Such a large booster was not necessary, however, for the composite craft (shekinah and cherubim) to leave the spaceship and return to Earth, for in such a case only a braking capability was required to slow the reentry of the spacecraft. The personal space capsule or command module apparently also had its own propulsion system, for it could rise from the booster platform or *cherubim* and move freely about for short distances.

The "Kabod" or Spacecraft of Ezekiel

In the Old Testament, the vehicle of the deity is called a *kabod* (occasionally kebod, kavod, or kebod) which is, as we shall see, another name for the "shekinah." In the *Book of Ezekiel*, the famous fiery chariot is a *kabod.*

When Ezekiel stood beside the Chebar Canal near Nippur one summer day, an incandescent cloud bore towards him by a temptuous wind. As the cloud neared, four glowing creatures became visible in the lower part, like humans in their erect posture, with legs and hands, but unlike them in having four faces and four wings. The creatures were arranged in a square and were not connected at their wingtips to each other. They gave the impression of a unity as they moved and, facing in every direction, always went in the direction they faced without needing to turn.

Amidst them was a flashing torch-like apparition, surrounded by a radiance or *hashmal.* The prophet noted that below and alongside each creature was a highly complex wheel, rimmed with eyes, that moved in unison with the creatures. Above their heads was a dazzling icelike expanse.

As they neared, he grew aware of the terrific noise made by the wings in motion. When the wings slackened and the apparition came to a halt, the prophet heard a sound from above the expanse. He saw a sapphire throne standing upon the expanse, upon which a brilliant figure sat, all bright and fiery, and encased in a rainbow-like radiance. Ezekiel realized he had seen the *kabod* of the Lord.

The technical information in the *Book of Ezekiel* was analyzed by the NASA engineer Josef F. Blumrich and published in his book *The Spaceships of Ezekiel.* Using the technical details supplied by Ezekiel, Blumrich has reconstructed what the composite vehicle looks like: a cone-like capsule which sat on a booster platform. He suggested that this platform was composed of four rocket units with each unit having retractable rotor blades and retractable arms.

The appearance of the spacecraft of Ezekiel at the Chebar Canal is also significant since Nippur was the space control center before the Deluge. The second appearance of the chariot to Ezekiel was at Jerusalem and the consistency in the details appears to rule out the possibility of errors in transcription. At Jerusalem, Ezekiel is told to

> "Get up and go out to the plain and there I shall speak to you." So I got up and went out to the plain, and there was the *kabod* of the Lord waiting — like the *kabod* that I saw by the Chebar Canal.

Ezekiel then describes how the *kabod* rose from its platform and flew over the city, then returned to the landing platform of *cherubim:*

> The *kabod* of the Lord went forth off the threshold of the house and halted upon the *cherubim.* The *cherubim* raised their wings and rose off the ground. I watched them depart . . . the *kabod* of the Lord above and upon them.

It seems that while the personal craft or command capsule could fly independently, it needed the larger vehicle or booster platform to travel greater distances and to move freely about the Earth.

The word *kabod* has no Semitic roots and does not appear in the comprehensive study of the Old Testament, *The Encyclopedia Judaica.* The word is apparently an unknown word to the translators and may actually be borrowed from the Sumerian, probably a permutation of KA-BAD, which means "mouth or source of wisdom"

The term *hashmal* has been used in describing the awesome radiance produced by the *kabod.* It is probably also a borrowed word from the Sumerian, which uses the word "ME-LAM" (Akkadian *melammu)* to also mean an awesome radiance attributed to the gods. *Hashmal* may be a form of the Sumerian term HUSH-MELAM, which means "a fiery, awesome radiance."

The "Kabod" of Moses at Mount Sinai

The kabod also appeared numerous times to Moses and the Israelites during the time of the Exodus. For example, when they left the area of the Red Sea and were journeying into the wilderness of the Sinai, the people were grumbling and dissatisfied. According to Exodus 16, Moses and Aaron tried to appease them with the declaration that they would soon see the spaceship of the Lord.

> By evening you shall know that it was the Lord who brought you out from the land of Egypt and in the morning you shall behold the *kabod* of the Lord . . . Then as Aaron spoke the people turned toward the wilderness and there, in a cloud, appeared the *kabod* of the Lord.

The kabod used the flat surface of Mount Sinai (Jebel Halal) as its resting place, where it was usually obscured by a cloud. When the spacecraft stayed among the Israelites it was kept in the Tent of Meeting — a sort of temporary shelter or garage. The Tent of Meeting was set up in the desert when they were traveling and acted as a home for the deity and his vehicle. The inner sanctum or Tabernacle was occupied by the kabod and, as described in Exodus 40:

> "A cloud came down and landed in the Tabernacle. Over it a cloud rested by day; at night a fire would appear from it."

It was also at Mount Sinai that Moses requested the deity to show himself so that Moses could see him and report his appearance back to the Israelites. Moses asked "Oh, let me behold your *kabod.*" The Lord replied that he would pass before Moses but "you cannot see my face, for man may not see me and live." Then he told Moses, "There is a place near me. Station yourself on the rock and as my *kabod* passes by, I will put you in a cleft in the rock and shield you with my hand until I have passed by. Then I will take my hand away, and you will see my back, but my face must not be seen." It appears that Moses was allowed to see the back of the *kabod* or personal housing but not the front, perhaps because the front was transparent and would show the person of Yahweh in all his reptilian splendor.

According to the medieval philosopher Saadiah Gaon of the First Century AD, probably the greatest scholar of Babylonian Jewry, the *shekinah* is identical to the *kavod ha-shem,* a phrase usually translated in religious terms as the majesty of his name. In modern translation, *kavod ha-shem* would mean "the chariot of the rocket" for, as we have seen, the "shem" is none other than the main rocket booster. What is this "shekinah" of the scriptures?

The "Shekinah" and "Cherubim" of the Scriptures

While the term *kabod* seems to have no Semitic antecedents and has not been identified semantically, the word "shekinah," however, means literally "a physical dwelling or resting place." It has been translated as "glory" in the scriptures and given a mystical interpretation to mean a spiritual presence rather than a physical one. In fact, a complete Kabbalistic literature has arisen over this spiritual meaning.

The term "shekinah" is used exclusively for the vehicle of the deity in the Hebrew *Book of Enoch*. Everywhere it is mentioned, it is clearly a physical dwelling or personal vehicle used by the deity. Enoch refers to the "shekinah" as resting on a platform or "cherubim," located in the center of the "heavenly city" or orbiting spaceship. The departure of the shekinah is described in detail as a rocket launch with all the attendant noise of a dangerous rocket blast. It is discussed below.

The term *cherubim* is another interesting one that has received theological interpretations perhaps because its origins or roots are unknown. Customarily, it is translated as a group of winged celestial beings or special kind of angel. The comprehensive study in the *Encyclopedia Judaica* has suggested that the Hebrew word cherub or *keruv* could be a metathesis or inversion of the letters for chariot or *rekhuv.* This makes much sense and this view is supported by the scriptures where the word "cherub" is sometimes equated to an aerial chariot, as it is in the Second Book of Samuel. It is also repeated almost word for word in Psalm 18:

> He bowed the heavens, and came down;
>
> Thick darkness was under his feet.
>
> He rode on a *cherub*, and he flew;
>
> He came swiftly upon the wings of the wind.

In the Rabbinic literature the term *merkabah* is often encountered to mean the chariot of the deity, that is, the craft composed of the kabod and cherub, also known as the shekinah. The term became mystical in the First Century AD and a complete literature developed around it to mean the godly presence. The word actually became taboo in the Middle Ages and was used only by the priesthood.

The "Heavenly Abode" or the Orbiting Mother Ship

There are many indications in the scriptures, particularly in the Hebrew *Book of Enoch*, that the "heavenly abode" was organized very much like a large city or spacecraft. This book describes the trip of the prophet Ishmael to the heavenly abode, where he meets the patriarch Enoch who proceeds to give him a guided tour of the ship. While this book is written in spiritualistic terms, whose purpose is to create an atmosphere of awesome majesty by stripping away the theological verbiage, what emerges is a a large, complex spaceship.

There are seven "heavens" or decks to the spaceship. Each deck has seven "palaces" arranged in concentric circles, with guards at the entrance of each circle of rooms. The obvious comparison would be with that of the Pentagon Building in Washington. The center of the ship was called the *Arabot* and was the residence of the chief deity. It is here that the "shekinah" or dwelling of the deity is located. It sits on a platform called "cherubim."

Various functions are assigned to managers called Princes, who appear to be chiefs of various operational activities associated with the spacecraft.

Of these, Hayliel is the "Prince of the Holy Creatures" or *hayyot.* Since the term is derived from *hayel,* meaning an army, these are presumably the soldiers or guards. Ribbiel is the "Prince of the Cherubim," the platform on which rests the shekinah. Opanniel is the "Prince of the Opannim" and these seem to be the mechanics, for it is their responsibility to maintain the craft: "He polishes their platform, he adorns their compartments, he makes their turnings smooth, and cleans their seats." When the composite craft leaves the heavenly abode or spaceship there is an impressive ceremony called the *Qedussah*, a syllogism for a launch count-down.

The "Qedussah" or Rocket Lift-Off

When the Shekinah leaves, the personnel of the heavenly abode participate in a ceremony called the *Qedussah.* In the words of the Hebrew *Book of Enoch*, there is a "cosmic commotion at the singing of the *Qedussah,*" which sounds very much like the countdown and frantic activity which accompanies the launch of a rocket vehicle. It is said that "all the pillars of the heavens and their bases shake and the gates of the palaces of the heavens of Arabot quiver.

Before this spirited activity begins, "brilliant starry crowns are put on the heads of the angels and princes." These are obviously protective devices or headgear for protection against the deafening noise and brilliant light of the blast-off.

The participants are warned that when the proper procedure is not followed an accident or tragedy can happen, for when they "do not follow the proper order of the *Qedussah*, devouring fire goes out from little fingers of the holy ones and destroys the ministering angels." It warns that the exhaust of the rocket is quite dangerous as "a fire precedes him as he goes devouring all those around him."

Fig. 63 – The Egyptian Ben-Ben

A coin from Byblos of the Emperor Macrimus (217 AD) reproduces a sacred shrine many centuries old. It probably stood at the city of Annu (Heliopolis) in the Nile delta. Byblos was a colony of Egypt until the 15th Century BC.

Like other words relating to rockets and their activity, it is possible that *Qedussah* is also a borrowed word from the Sumerian. *Qedussah* has no Semitic roots and it may be the compound Sumerian word KADUSA, which means "source or thing which creates bright light."

There is an interesting reference in the oral tradition of the Jews which describes where the shekinah went on one of its trips after leaving the spaceship. In the section which describes the destruction of the cities of Sodom and Gomorrah, the shekinah is credited with blasting these cities. It describes how the Shekinah of the Lord had "descended to work the destruction of these cities." Josephus in his *Antiquities of the Jews* seems to support this operation, for on the destruction of these cities he adds that "God cast a thunderbolt upon the city, and set it on fire," suggesting that the spaceship destroyed the cities with some form of missile or beam weapon.

The "Betyl" or the Dwelling of the Gods

In the lands of the Middle East, the command capsule or personal housing of the deity was worshiped as a sacred object. Called *betyl* by the Semitic peoples, a corruption of *beth-el,* meaning the house or dwelling of the god, it appears in various forms. On a coin from Byblos, the Phoenician seaport, the betyl or cone-shaped object is seen set up in a sacred enclosure for veneration, although by that time its real meaning had probably been lost (figure 63).

This "betyl" appears in the literature of the dynasties of Mesopotamia as a "shum." In can be seen visually in the victory stele erected by Naram-Sin of the Akkad Dynasty, which was found at Susa, and is supposed to represent his victory over a local people (figure 59). It depicts Naram-Sin wearing the horned headdress of a god and trodding triumphantly over a prostrate enemy. He faces a large conical object which is dominated by the star symbol of Shamash. Naram-Sin had invaded a "mountainous land," the land of Lebanon, and the conical object signified the betyl or home of the god Shamash who ruled the space facilities at Baalbek.

For the origins of the various words which refer to the home of the gods, we must look into the legend of the Phoenix, the legendary bird that arose in flames from the Sun Stone at the Temple of the Sun at the city of An in the delta in Egypt, called Heliopolis by the Greeks.

CHAPTER 24

THE PHOENIX BIRD AS SYMBOLIZING A ROCKET LAUNCH

The Origin of the Legend of the Phoenix Bird

This fabulous bird, which arose from its own ashes, and thus became a symbol of regeneration, first became known to Western culture through the travels of Herodotus when that famous Greek historian visited Egypt about 455 BC. At the ancient religious center of Annu in the delta, known to the Greeks as Heliopolis, Herodotus was told of a sacred bird which came from the East bearing its father embalmed in a ball of myrrh, and buried him in the Temple of the Sun at the city of Annul. The Egyptians called it the *Benu* bird, but it is better known by its Greek name of Phoenix.

Additional details of the Phoenix were supplied by the Roman writers Tacitus, Pliny, and Ovid, who also visited Egypt and reported further that the Phoenix built its nest on the Sun Stone at the Temple, where it perished in flames. Ovid reported that

> When it has lived 500 years, it builds itself a nest in the branches of an oak. In this it collects cinnamon, spikenard, and myrrh, and of these materials builds a pile on which it deposits itself, and dying, breathes out its last breath. From the body of the parent bird, a young Phoenix issues forth. When this has grown up, it lifts its nest from the tree and carries it to the city of Heliopolis in Egypt and deposits it in the Temple of the Sun.

Herodotus was told that the bird resembled an eagle in size and shape, with gold and red plumage. Early Egyptian depictions, as far back as the 25th Century BC, show the Benu bird as a magpie. In later dynasties it appears as a heron with two long feathers growing from the back of its head.

As we all know, legends are built around a kernel of truth that eventually becomes distorted with time. As each generation adds to the story, it becomes so encrusted that little is left of the former truth. In certain cases, however, like that of the Phoenix bird, sufficient ancient sources are available to enable us to trace its origin back to prehistoric times, and to discover the core of truth which precipitated the legend.

The Phoenix or Benu Bird in the Pyramid Texts

The first available Egyptian reference to the Benu bird is from the times of the Old Kingdom when it is first noted inscribed on the walls of the burial chamber of the pyramid of the Pharaoh Unas, the last king of the Fifth Dynasty, who ruled about 2400 BC.

Called the Pyramid Texts, these carved inscriptions are a collection of spells and directions which gave the dead king all the information he needed for the trip to the afterlife and how to achieve it. Most authorities agree that the Pyramid Texts reflect the belief in a stellar cult that would require the deceased king to journey to the stars. Often he is pictured astride a serpent heading for a star constellation (figure 6). His journey is an imitation of the Sun God himself, who was said to be able to traverse the sky in his “boat of heaven.”

An inscription found on the walls of the burial chamber of this king is of

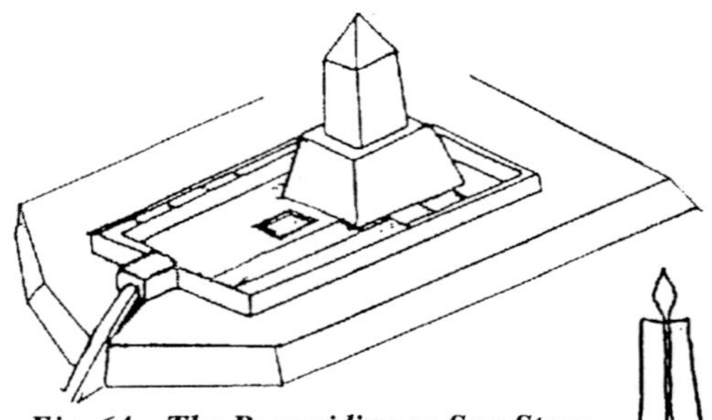

Fig. 64 – The Pyramidion or Sun Stone.

The Sun Stone or Ben-Ben mounted on a stubby stone platform in the sacred precinct of the Temple of the Sun God at Annu or Heliopolis in the Nile delta. The pyramidion, like the betyl, was the residence of the Sun God, in this instance Ra. To the right is the hieroglyphic symbol for the sacred city of Annu. It shows a bolt aimed at the sky.

particular interest because it describes the Sun God as rising from the Sun Stone or Ben-Ben Stone. It states, "O Atum, the Creator, you became high in the sky, you rose up from the Ben-Ben Stone, in the Temple of the Benu in the City of Annu." In the 25th Century BC, Atum had become the dominant sun god and had supplemented Ra, who had dominated the pantheon in the early days of Egypt.

The so-called Pyramid Texts were later adopted by commoners and painted on the wooden coffins. They thus came to be called the Coffin Texts, and eventually they were transcribed to papyrus, becoming known as the *Book of the Dead.* Collectively, the three sets of texts are usually referred to as the *Book of the Dead.* You might say that it was their equivalent of a do-it-yourself manual on how to reach the gods in heaven and thereby achieve immortality

The Sun Temple and the Sacred Ben-Ben Stone

The Benu or Phoenix bird has, since its beginning, been associated with the practice of sun worship in Egypt. This is particularly noted in the coloring of the Phoenix, its miraculous birth, and its connection with fire — all symbolic of the Sun itself. These characteristics, however, lend themselves to a more interesting explanation, as we shall see.

The inner sanctum of the Sun Temple at the City of Annu was the most sacred of all places. It was the home of the Sun Stone, which the Egyptians called the Ben-Ben. Mounted on a truncated pyramid, the Ben-Ben was a square stone platform upon which was set a pyramid-shaped stone or pyramidion, giving the appearance of a stubby obelisk (figure 64). It was on this stone that the Phoenix or Benu bird alighted.

As far back as prehistoric times, the Sun Stone was revered as the dwelling of the Sun God. About 2000 BC, a new version of the Sun Stone appeared in Egypt — the pyramidion. It was placed on a tall square column and it became known as the obelisk. Obelisks were erected by all pharaohs down to the days of Cleopatra.

The capstone on the pyramids themselves were said to be pyramidions, and venerated as the physical dwelling of the Sun God. The dead king buried inside the pyramid was believed thus to be under the direct protection of the god himself. This pyramidion, which represented the Ben-Ben Stone, and used as a capstone on obelisks and pyramids, became the most sacred fetish worshipped by the Egyptians.

The strange feature of the Phoenix legend is that it originated elsewhere and was assimilated into Egyptian sun worship by the priests of Annu or Heliopolis. The legends make it clear that the Phoenix bird came from the direction of the East, some say Arabia, others Assyria, and flies to the Sun Stone in Egypt to repeat its flaming performance. Since the Egyptians were very parochial in their view of the world, the land of Arabia could be any place east of the delta region.

The Middle East as the Home of the Phoenix

In the lands of Palestine, Syria, and Lebanon, the Sun Stone was also revered as the dwelling of the Sun God. It was not only pictured as a stubby obelisk but quite often as an upright conical stone as well.

At Byblos, the oldest of the Phoenician cities which dates to at least 3500 BC, the Egyptian gods were worshipped side by side with those of the Canaanite pantheon. Some of these sanctuaries contained a sacred chapel, an example of which is shown on a coin from Byblos of the Roman Emperor Macronus (AD 217) which evidently represents a shrine many centuries old. It shows a sacred enclosure containing a conical shaped dwelling of the Sun God (figure 64).

The Sun Stone was called a "baetyl" or "betyl" by the Semitic peoples, and its functions are similar to the pyramid shaped stone found in Egypt. Betyl is a Semitic version of the Hebrew term "beth-el" meaning the dwelling or abode of God.

In Palestine, the worship of the Sun Stone or betyl goes as far back as the Eight Millennium. Digging in the ancient ruins of Jericho, archaeologists have found at its lowest level and carbon dated to neolithic times of about 7000 BC, a temple where at its center an oval stone or betyl stood upright on a stone pedestal.

These "betyl" stones were found all over the lands of Palestine and Syria. At Beth-Shean, an altar and betyl were found and dated to the mid-14th Century BC. These betyls are actually the so-called "altars in high places" of the Old Testament. Most of these "pagan" shrines were destroyed by the Hebrews after the division of the Kingdom of Solomon, but many still remain in the more isolated areas, such as in southeast Palestine near Arabia, in the land of the Nabateans. Found on hilltops, these altars appear as stone blocks or stubby obelisks and are believed to be inhabited by their chief deity. At Mada'im Salih, in northwest Arabia, the Nabateans left a necropolis of family tombs, on which many have betyls or sacred stones. In fact, the Black Stone at Mecca called the Kaaba, the most sacred of Islamic shrines, is believed to have fallen from the skies. It is also referred to as a betyl.

The Heliopolis or Launch Site in Lebanon

Besides the one in Egypt, there is another famous Heliopolis nearby, located in Lebanon at a place now called Baalbek. Since antiquity, it has been a city sacred to the Sun God. The Old Testament calls it Beth-Shemesh or the "Abode of the Sun God," Shemesh or Shamash being the Semitic name for the Sumerian Sun God Utu. The land of Lebanon was under the aegis of this Mesopotamian sun god.

At Baalbek, the Greeks erected a splendid temple to their Sun God Apollo or Helios. It is also here that the Romans built a magnificent temple to their supreme god Jupiter. This temple was the largest they erected anywhere in the world, including Rome, indicating the importance they attached to this location. Even today, six of its mighty columns still stand, each 62 feet high and eight feet in diameter.

But what is remarkable about this temple is that it is built on a massive three-tier stone base that must have been here long before the Greeks and Romans. It is raised 30 feet above the ground, and is paved with perfectly hewn and fitted stones ranging from 10 to 30 feet long and 6 to 9 feet wide. The base for this platform was constructed of cyclopean blocks of stone 32 feet long, 13 feet wide, and 12 feet thick. Each slab of stone is estimated to weigh 500 tons

Fig. 65 – The cone-shaped dwelling of the Sun God.

Omphalos found in Egypt in the inner court of the Temple of Amon, the Sun God.

(the largest stone in the Great Pyramid is 200 tons).

But the most spectacular of the three is the middle layer which contains the most massive and gigantic fashioned stone blocks in the world. Referred to as the Trilithon, the three perfectly fitted stone blocks are each 64 feet long, with sides 14 by 14 feet. Each slab is estimated to weigh over 1000 tons! A fourth stone lies in the quarry nearby, readily shaped and cut except for a portion of its base. It is 72 feet long with a cross-section of 16 by 16 feet, estimated to weigh over 1200 tons. The stone was apparently intended to extend the size of the platform but operations seem to have suddenly ceased and the work was never completed.

Such a massive stone platform was obviously designed either to hold an immense weight, or for same operation that must have exerted tremendous pressure on the ground, such as that exerted by a large rocket motor.

The Semitic Sun God Shamash who made his home base at Baalbek was in many ways similar to the Egyptian sun god. Like the Egyptian Ra who appears with the sun disc over his head, Shamash is always shown with a sun disc, containing a four-pointed star and four radiating spokes. And just like Ra, he is often depicted with the head of an eagle. Some scenes also show him holding the symbols of immortality.

When Shamash left Baalbek, one of his destinations was ostensibly the city of Annu in Egypt where his bright arrival and departure in flames became the core of the legend of the gold and red Phoenix bird.

For thousands of years throughout the whole Middle East, the betyl or Sun Stone became a sacred fetish revered as the physical dwelling of the sun god. Its conical or pyramidion shape was their attempt to represent the dwelling of the sun god, that is, the command or personal capsule of the first stage of a composite rocket. In Egypt, the origin of the Sun Stone is partially remembered in the ancient hieroglyphic sign used to represent the City of Annu or Heliopolis. It is shown as a bolt aimed at the sky (figure 64). The origin of the Egyptian name of their sacred city is lost in antiquity but the similarity to the major Sumerian god Anu indicates its Mesopotamian origin.

The Greek Omphalos as the Dwelling of a God

Even the Greeks who came much later adopted the conical shaped stone as a sacred dwelling of their Sun God Apollo. Called an "omphalos" it was the most sacred object at every oracular site (figure 65).

The Sun God Apollo, who later became one of the most important gods of the Greek Pantheon, originally came from Asia Minor, from Ionia. His cult first appeared on the island of Delos from where he leap-frogged to Dodona on mainland Greece. In fact, the island of Delos was considered so sacred that is was inviolate in all the Greek wars. Even the Persians respected its sanctity and bypassed it.

In his *Histories* Herodotus called Dodona the oldest of Greek oracles and archaeologists have traced it back to about 2000 BC. It was the first cult center to Apollo on the mainland. As Dodona declined in importance, Delphi replaced it as a cult center.

Like Dodona, it also had a half-egg stone called an omphalos. Herodotus said that the omphalos here was wrapped with cord, one end of which was held by the Pythia or priestess as she queried the sun god in the stone.

According to the Greek mythologist Robert Graves, the sacred stone at Delphi was also called "baetylos" by the Greeks. He refers to it as a cone-shaped pillar, periodically anointed with oil, and wrapped in raw wool on special occasions. It was the residence of a god, and was said to have fallen from heaven (In Greek mythology, Baetylus was a son of the Sky god Uranus).

While the term "omphalos" means the human navel in Greek, its use here seems to be that of the "navel of the Earth." Besides being the residence of the Sun God, the omphalos was also a geodetic marker.

It is interesting to note that if a line is drawn through the oracular sites of Dodona, Delphi, and Delos, and continued towards the mainland, it runs right through Jerusalem. Like the Greek sites, Jerusalem has often been referred to in ancient documents as "the navel of the Earth." It seems that there was some sort of geodetic grid connecting sacred places in ancient times.

Shamash was also known as the god of justice and measurements. He is shown in one instance with two gods overhead holding cords connected to an altar which bears his sacred symbol (figure 26).

To the Greeks, the conical stone had two meanings, as the "omphalos," it had a geodetic meaning — as a geodetic point of a master grid. On the other hand, it was the residence of a god and used as an oracular device.

In summary, the Phoenix bird rising in flames became symbolic of the lift-off of the rocket craft of the ancient astronauts. Originally shown in conical configuration to represent the command capsule, it later became angular shaped under the Egyptians who used it as a capstone on pyramids and obelisks. Baalbek in Lebanon appears to be the original home of the Phoenix bird, where a gigantic stone platform is all that remains of what was probably the main base for the chariots of the gods.

CHAPTER 25

THE RADIOS OF THE ANCIENTS

Jerusalem as the Main Transmitter

It is implicit that the gods must have had some means to convey their wishes from the heavenly ship to their representatives below — the kings, priests, and generals who carried out their wishes. Conversely, these officials needed to contact the deities and each other on occasion for instruction and guidance, particularly when they were afield on one of their numerous expeditions. How then did they contact each other?

Basic needs would require three basic type of communications equipment: permanent fixed transmitters, field or regional stations, and some sort of portable radio set. All of these forms of communication are found in the ancient literature and art forms.

Before the Deluge, Larak in Mesopotamia had served as the main communication center; however, it was now under the waters of the Persian Gulf. Since it was decided to move the space facilities to the Western Lands, it became necessary to establish a main communication and administrative center.

Ur-Salem, later to be called Jerusalem, is known throughout the scriptures as "the navel of the Earth," attesting to its role both as a main geodetic point as well as the communication center of these lands. It broadcast throughout the Western Lands providing instructions and guidance to the distant colonies of the Mesopotamian empires. Powerful transmitters are suggested in Psalm 29 which is called *Hymn to the God of Storm*, and it states that:

> The voice of the Lord is powerful . . .
>
> The voice of the Lord breaks the cedar,
>
> The Lord breaks the cedars of Lebanon . . .
>
> The voice of the Lord shakes the wilderness.
>
> The Lord shakes the wilderness of Kadesh.

While Jerusalem was the central administrative center for the Western Lands, there were certain places in the land of Canaan and Syria which were considered to be holy or sacred where the patriarchs contact their God. These were the regional or field stations. They also dotted the landscape of Mesopotamia and are mentioned in their literature and seen in their artistic depictions.

The Reed Huts and Other Field Stations

When Abraham and Isaac sojourned into the Western Lands, they would halt occasionally and "set up an altar," a euphemism that meant to communicate with Yahweh and receive further instructions. Certain places like Shechem and Bethel were considered to be sacred by the native population long before the Hebrews arrived. These were apparently the field stations or regional transmitters where radio facilities were available to the privileged few, the aristocracy.

In Mesopotamia, the so-called reed huts were scattered throughout the land and appear quite often in their depictions on cylinder seals and pottery. This is presumably the reed hut that was involved in the case of Utnapishtim when he was informed of the coming Deluge.

In the *Epic of Gilgamesh*, when the gods had decided to bring on the Deluge and destroy mankind for his foibles, only one god remained sympathetic to mankind — his creator and benefactor Enki. Not wishing to see his creation destroyed in the coming catastrophe, Enki decided to forewarn Utnapishtim so that he could make preparations and build a ship. In the epic, Enki addresses the wall of a reed hut:

> Reed-wall, reed-wall. Wall. Wall.
>
> Reed-wall, listen. Wall, pay attention.
>
> Man of Shuruppak, son of Ubaratutu,
>
> Tear down the house. Build an ark.

This verse of the epic has baffled scholars as to why the god would speak to the wall of a reed hut in order to pass information on to the Sumerian Noah. Logically, Enki would at this time be where the gods had just met in council to decide man's fate, probably in the orbiting spaceship. Utnapishtim was presumably listening to the broadcast at a reed hut or radio receiver below, at his home of Shuruppak.

These reed huts which were scattered all over Mesopotamia and the adjacent lands are shown on numerous cylinder seals and paintings with antenna-like projections on the roofs with round eye-like objects attached. These antenna later became stylized as gateposts with streamers, and became a symbol of the goddess Ishtar who seems to have had some association with these reed huts or radio stations. These reed huts were also mobile and could be moved from place to place when required, as shown on a cylinder seal depicting one being transported by boat (figures 66, 67).

Another example of the mobile radio station was the one built by Moses during the Exodus and used specifically to contact Yahweh.

The Ark of the Covenant as a Radio Transmitter

After the Israelites had reached Mount Sinai and when they had been soundly defeated by the Amalekites at Rephidim, it was decided that they would have to enter the land of Canaan by a more indirect route, that is, around the Dead Sea via the Transjordan. During this period of wandering which amounted to 38 years, they would need a means of communicating with Yahweh (Adad). It seems that Adad expected to stay at Mount Sinai and direct Moses from there.

Moses was given specific instructions on how to build the Ark of the Covenant and schematic drawings as well. This is explicit when he was told, "Note well and follow the patterns for them that are being shown you on the mountain."

The box itself was of acacia wood with gold plat-

Seal of the late Uruk period, about 3000 BC, showing cattle gathering around a reed hut with strange antennae-like posts.

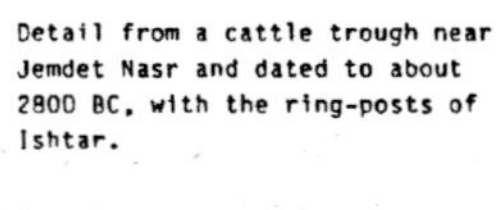

Detail from a cattle trough near Jemdet Nasr and dated to about 2800 BC, with the ring-posts of Ishtar.

Cylinder seal of 3000 BC showing the portability of the reed hut. The original mobile radio?

Fig. 66 – Reed huts with antenna-like posts.

Reed huts with strange eye posts, some with the ring-staff associated with Ishtar, were widespread throughout the countryside of Mesopotamia. Were these the communication stations of the Anunna?

ing. The cover, however, was the key to the device. The cover was to be fashioned of solid gold with a cherub at each end facing one another; solid gold was an excellent choice since it was a good conductor of electricity. It was also specified that the cherubs and the cover must be made in one piece, probably to ensure good electrical contact. The cherubs were to have wings outstretched, facing each other and shielding the cover with their wings, thus forming an antennae. There is no description of what the cherubim looked like, but in view of the Egyptian origin of Moses and his associates, it must have looked something like a winged sphinx.

Fig. 67 – The gatepost symbol of Ishtar.

At right: In early days, the Fourth Millennium BC, Ishtar often appeared with the symbol of the gatepost with streamers, which is also associated with reed huts. Her symbol was replaced with the seven stars of the Pleiades, and eventually the eight-pointed star. At left: From a sculptured vase of the late Uruk period, circa 3000 BC, with Ishtar receiving offerings from humans at her temple.

The cover was to be placed on the box after depositing the tablets provided by Adad. It is significant that it was only after the Ark was constructed that the tablets were provided to Moses. The tablets presumably contained the power source necessary to activate the receiver-transmitter. Moses is then told:

> There I will meet you, and I will impart to you,
> From above the cover, from between the two cherubim
> That are on top of the Ark of the Pact.

This was the form of communication used as they travelled through the wilderness for the next 38 years. According to Numbers 7, Moses "would hear the voice addressing him from above the cover that was on top of the Ark of the Pact between the two cherubim."

The power source and transmission device was presumably incorporated into the two tablets of "stone" upon which was inscribed the Ten Commandments. When Moses broke the first set of tablets upon descending Sinai because he was angry at the sight of the Israelites worshipping a golden calf, it defeated the whole purpose of the Ark. Moses had to go back a second time in order to have another set fashioned. Perhaps this explains the forty days he spent there — it may have taken that long to fabricate a second set or to get the replacement parts.

The Dangers of the Ark: Its Power Source

There is no doubt that there was a power source within the Ark itself and that proved to be dangerous to anyone who ventured near it. At first only Moses, Aaron, and his two sons were allowed to approach the Ark because of its inherent dangers. This was demonstrated when an accident killed the two sons of Aaron. They were hit by a sudden and unexpected discharge of electricity from the Ark for as the *Book of Leviticus* states, "and fire came forth from the Lord and consumed them; thus they died before the Lord."

The Old Testament does not give the full story, however, and we must look to the Hebrew oral tradition for further details on the event. It is recorded in the works of the *Haggadah* how:

> "From the Holy of Holies issued two flames of fire, as thin as threads, then parted into four, and two each pierced the nostrils of Nadab and Abihu, whose souls were burned, although no external injury was visible."

This obvious electrical discharge proved to be a real threat to anyone who dared to enter the tent in order to service the deity. Thus in order to prevent further casualties, Moses is told to warn Aaron:

> "Tell your brother Aaron that he is not to come at will into the shrine behind the curtain, in front of the cover that is upon the Ark, lest he die."

Due to the inherent dangers of the Ark, it was decided to train a group of priests — the tribe of Levi, to care for and to handle all contacts with the Ark. From there on, only a clearly defined group of initiates who wore protective clothing and followed the proper procedures, were allowed access to the Ark. The instructions for fabricating these garments is very detailed and specific, allowing for no margin of error — indicative that its protective nature was woven into the fabric of the material. The Ark was extremely dangerous and even the Levites must have approached it with trepidation and a certain fear of not returning from the Tent alive.

The Tent of Meeting containing the Ark was kept at a safe distance from the Israelite camp. When travelling, the Ark was carried by the Levites and preceded the body of the people. In Joshua 3, the people are instructed to keep a safe distance from it:

> "There shall be a space between you and it, a distance of about two thousand cubits, do not come near it."

Two thousand cubits is roughly one kilometer, what was considered to be a safe distance or buffer zone.

Another fatal discharge is related in the *Book of Numbers*, when a group of 250 members of the tribe of Korah were annihilated by the destructive power of the Ark. When the Israelites were resting near Kadesh after their second and final foray and defeat in Canaan, 250 members of the tribe of Korah were directed to bring copper pans for presenting incense, and to appear at the entrance of the Tent of Meeting.

Suddenly, "a fire went forth from the Lord and consumed the two hundred and fifty men offering incense." The victims appeared to have been completely incinerated for the priests were told to remove, "the charred remains, and scatter the coals." Ironically, their copper pans which had attracted the electrical discharge were hammered into sheets and used as plating for the altar Since the incident happened right after their second defeat at Hormah, it may be as the *Haggadah* insinuates, that the tribe was eliminated for showing cowardice at this battle.

The Ark also appears to have emitted dangerous radioactivity. Numbers 10 relates the incident when Marian, the sister of Moses, was "stricken with scales" at the entrance to the Tent — an affliction that sounds very much like radioactive poisoning. She died not long after.

Subsequent associations with the Ark seems to confirm its radioactive character. After the Exodus, and after the tribes had settled in Canaan, in the days of Eli the Prophet, the Ark was captured by the Philistines and brought to their cities in the hill country of western Palestine.

The *First Book of Samuel* describes how the Philistines suffered from plagues for seven months. Those who came too close to the Ark received sores and tumors and their hair fell out, classic symptoms of radioactive poisoning. The Ark was passed from one Philistine city to another until finally, in fear and disgust, they returned it to the nearest Israelite settlement and abandoned it. Seventy local people were killed who became too curious and approached the Ark.

After that, the Ark acquired a deadly reputation and remained untouched and unmoved until much later when David decided to return it to Jerusalem. In this attempt, one of his men tried to steady the Ark as it began to topple from the wagon carrying it. He was killed outright by a discharge from the Ark. This appeared to be the last activity of the Ark, and this last discharge probably neutralized the power source, for the Ark appears to have remained inactive in the days that followed.

The Portable Radios: The Animated Idols or Teraphim

When the kings of Mesopotamia were away from their home city, particularly when they were afield on one of their numerous military expeditions, they required some sort of mobile or portable communications device to keep in touch with their home base and to receive instructions from the gods. For this purpose they took with them the temple images or statues of the gods. These statuettes were believed to be the active residence of the deity since they spoke to the kings when they were out in the field. They were of different size and composition.

Joan Oates in her monumental work *Babylon* reports that these animated statues which were carried off to war by the kings and priests were fashioned and repaired in special workshops in the city and had to undergo an elaborate and highly secret ritual or consecration which endowed them with "life," and enabled them to speak. This ritual probably consisted of imbedding a radio receiver and transmitter, as well as a power source, inside the statuette.

Abraham and his father Terah are reported to have operated a workshop which fabricated these statuettes. Although Genesis is silent on this activity, it is fully discussed in the works of the Pseudepigrapha. Terah and Abraham were members of the priesthood, the elite class that ruled the city of Ur, and as such would be privy to the secrets of the statuettes.

Their role in producing religious statues is reported in the *Apocalypse of Abraham,* a First Century AD document transmitted in the Slavonic language through Byzantine channels and therefore not available to western scholars until the late Middle Ages. It provides much information on the early days of Abraham.

According to this account, Abraham's father was an idol maker as well as an astrologer. He manufactured idols for the temples and for sale to ordinary citizens and travellers. These idols were of different value and quality, depending on whether they were made of stone, wood, iron, copper, silver, or gold. It was one of Abraham's assigned tasks to take some of these statuettes and sell them to merchants from Egypt at a stall just outside of town. Presumably, these were merely copies of the "animated idols" and had no life of their own. Abraham and Terah seem to have had a lucrative business selling to the "tourists."

When Terah and Abraham left for Harran and thence to the land of Canaan, they presumably had in their possession a number of the animated idols, statuettes with certain devices or power plants implanted. These were probably the *teraphim* or portable communicators of the Old Testament accounts.

The magical nature of the teraphim was well known among the ancient Hebrews. According to Maimonides, the Jewish philosopher of the 12th

Fig. 68 – Teraphim of the Old Testament?

Figure at left is an eye-goddess on altar found in temple at Tell Brak dated to 3000 BC. Other idols are so-called cult objects found at Tepe Gawra near Tell Brak in upper Mesopotamia. Dozens of these "eye" idols were found, dated to 3000 BC. The cone shaped heads of some of these idols may also be the betyl or dwelling of the god. The stones of Kenaz may have been imbedded in the concave eye sockets of the statuettes.

Century AD, the worshipers of the teraphim claimed that, at night as the light of the stars filled the carved statue, it received information or intelligence from distant stars and planets which provided the people with many useful arts and sciences.

Some of these animated statues or teraphim have been unearthed at ancient sites in Mesopotamia. At Tepe Gawra, archaeologists have found dozens of so-called cult statues which have been dated to about 3000 BC. The "cult" objects fit the description of the animated idols of the Sumerians (figure 68).

These large-eyed pagan idols or portable statuettes had concave eye sockets where some fist-sized objects were inserted, probably crystal-like power packs which activated the communicators. These power packs have been described as "stones" — evidently the ancient word for large crystals.

The scriptures describe the teraphim as figurines of different size which were used for divination, that is, they answered specific questions which were posed to them (see Ezekiel 21, Zechariah 10, and Judges 17,18).

The etymology of the word teraphim (it always appears in the plural form) is obscure and its meaning is unknown. The *Encyclopedia Judaica* has suggested that it may come from the Hittite word *tarpis,* which means "animated spirit." In view of the Hittite influence on the Hebrews in the land of Canaan, this derivation is probably true.

The animated idols of Abraham were presumably handed down from generation to generation through Isaac, Jacob, and Joseph, thence to Egypt where they presumably fell into the hands of Moses. References to the teraphim reappear in the days of Joshua and his successor Kenaz, but by this time, about 1400 BC, they had become inactive and were considered to be merely pagan relics or curiosities. From the days of Abraham down to the days of Moses and before the Ark was built, the teraphim was apparently used to communicate with the deity.

They were of various sizes — small enough to hide under a saddle as in the case of Rachel, yet some were large enough to imitate a person sleeping under a blanket as in the case of David, which fooled the assassins sent by Saul. The first explicit reference to the teraphim in Genesis is in the incident of Rachel when she attempted to steal her father's "idols." These may have been part of the cache that Abraham left at Harran with his cousin Laban just before he left for the Western Lands.

The Teraphim of Jacob and Rachel

Jacob and Rachel obviously knew of the value of the teraphim, and considering the lengths that Laban went to retrieve them, he may also have guessed their purpose — although he obviously did not know how to use them. Jacob's sojourn to Harran to live at Laban's house was probably predicated on his obtaining the devices and returning them to the control of Abraham's family. Rachel was obviously in on the plot.

Jacob had been forced by Laban, under one pretext or another, to serve him for twenty years. Finally, Jacob and Rachel, taking advantage of Laban's absence, left secretly, taking with them the idols or teraphim of Laban. Much fuss was made over these idols by Laban when he realized that Jacob had left. He chased after Jacob and finally caught up with the fleeing culprit. Laban was incensed over Jacob's secret departure but seemed more concerned over the theft of the idols: "you had to leave because you were homesick for your father's house, but why did you have to steal my gods?" he complained.

The account mentions only those hidden by Rachel in a camel cushion which she was sitting on. When Laban tried to search it she pleaded that she not be disturbed since it was that time of the month. Laban searched everywhere but could not find the teraphim. While only this teraphim was mentioned in the account, there must have been many more in Jacob's possession which he somehow managed to hide from the prying eyes of Laban.

On the way back to Canaan, Jacob and his household stopped at Shechem, a site sacred to the indigenous people. At Shechem, he ordered all the members of his company to produce their idols or alien gods which they had obtained at Harran (were these the ones of Laban?). These must have been numerous and they were buried at a terebinth (oak) at Shechem. Jacob must assuredly have kept his, yet he was concerned that no one else be allowed to bring one back to his homeland. Shechem was sacred to the people of Canaan and its famous oracle (terebinth) must have been a major link with the deity.

Control and use of the device was a tightly held secret; it would appear that only he and Rachel were privy to the real purpose of the teraphim. In any case, the cache remained buried at Shechem for generations and until the days of Kenaz.

Many years later, these idols and their "stones," or power packs, were unearthed by the followers of Kenaz, the successor to Joshua. When Jacob went to Egypt in the year 1877 BC, he probably took along the communication devices and these were passed down until Moses acquired them several hundred years later and used one to contact Adad on his first visit to Mount Sinai.

The Computer Terminal, the Breastplate of the Ephod

After the disastrous events when the sons of Aaron were killed by the electrical discharge of the Ark, Moses was told by Yahweh to assign a specific group to service and to tend the Ark. The tribe of Levi was selected, hence, the Levite Priesthood came into being. These priests had to wear special protective garments whose design and construction was defined in detail in the *Book of Exodus*. In addition special equipment was provided to them to be able to contact Yahweh for answers to essential questions arising during the Exodus. This was done with the use of the breastplate of the Ephod or garments of the priesthood.

Fig. 69 – The Breastplate of Destiny.

The Hebrew high priest wearing the vestments and the Ephod with the Breastplate of Destiny as described in the Book of Exodus. A "stone" on each shoulder lit up for a yes or no answer.

The Ephod was the upper garment worn by the priests when entering the Tent of Meeting. Later it became the traditional priestly robe to be worn during sacred rites in ancient Israel. The term Ephod usually applies to the ornamental vestment which was worn over the blue robe, but sometimes it is used to mean both the robe and the vest-like Ephod (figures 69, 70).

Golden bells were suspended from the robe and magical power was attributed to these bells since one of their functions was to protect the high priest when he entered the holy place. To the robe, the priest bound the Ephod which contained a breastplate; it in turn had a pouch into which was placed the Urim and Thummim, the sacred dice.

The scriptures contain no clear description of the shape of the Ephod, nor does the Hebrew root of the word furnish any additional clues. The Hebrew word is probably derived from the Semitic Akkadian word *appatu* or plural *appadatu* which means garment, and this may be actually what Ephod meant — garment.

The Ephod is described in Exodus 28 as an embroidered work "of gold, of blue, purple, and crimson yarn, and of fine twisted linen, worked designs." According to other sources it had numerous silver and gold threads interwoven into the design.

To the top there was attached two straps which fastened over the shoulders, and on each of the shoulder straps was set a *shoham* stone. The word shoham has not been identified and does not appear elsewhere. In Exodus 39 the stones were described as lapis lazuli; however, Josephus in his *Antiquities* calls them *sardonyx.*

Josephus also remarks that at times when they were used for divination "there emanated a light" from these stones so that the one worn on the right shoulder emitted a radiance sufficient to be seen by those far away. This was the stone which signified "yes."

The breastplate was bound to the Ephod at the top by rings and chains and at the bottom by a cord of blue, while in the middle it was encircled by a decorative band which was made of gold and other threads.

The breastplate had a pouch inlaid with twelve precious stones, each engraved with the names of the twelve tribes of Israel. This pouch held the Urim and Thummim.

The Stones of the Breastplate

Sitting upon the Ephod, the breastplate was square in shape with four rows of stones; these were given in Exodus as carmelian, crysolite, emerald, turquoise, sapphire, amethyst, jacinth, agate, crystal, beryl, lapis lazuli and jasper. Upon each stone the name of a tribe was inscribed. Rabbinical sources state that Moses had used a special stone called the *shamir,* which means "the stone that splits rocks," to engrave the names of the tribes upon the precious stones of the Ephod.

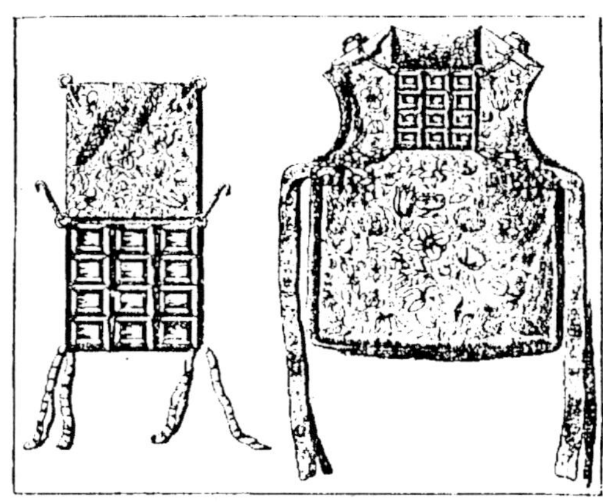

Fig. 70 – The Ephod and Breastplate

On the left, the Breastplate of Destiny unfolded showing its twelve "stones" or gems. To the right, the Breastplate attached to the Ephod worn by the Hebrew priest. Was the Breastplate a computer keyboard?

According to ancient sources the names of the twelve tribes were represented by a letter or initial and that three more were added later to give it the whole Hebrew alphabet. These letters answered queries put to the Ephod by the high priest. Only one question could be asked, however, and if two were asked only the first question was answered.

In his *Antiquities*, Josephus reported that the "shining of the stones" in the breast-plate was used to forecast victory for the Hebrews in battles with the local peoples.

It is problematical what these stone were. It seems more probable that they were all colorless crystals for reasons stated below. When folded it is supposed to have measured a span in each direction, therefore this would mean that its length and breath were from eight to nine inches. In this case the stones themselves would measure about two inches and in view of the number of characters required to express some of the tribal names, this dimension does not seem excessive.

It is also highly improbable that at the time of Moses, precious stones like the ruby, emerald, or sapphire would have been available in these sizes. Another problem inherent in their variety is that they were too diverse in value, with the result that the tribes assigned the less precious stones would certainly be filled with hate and envy at those tribes assigned the more valuable stones.

There is also the problem of identifying the various stones used in the breastplate. The list varies according to the source. Hebrew, Greek, and Latin versions of the Bible differ from one another. Josephus in his *Wars of the Jews,* which was written in Hebrew, carried a different list from the one given by the same author in his *Antiquities of the Jews,* which was written in Greek.

Actually no one really knows what minerals the original Hebrew words referred to. The ancients generally were careless about such terminology, making one word work for several different minerals that might look roughly similar, or else invent words for different colors or types of the same minerals.

For example, the mineral "Yashpeh" is given as Onychion in the *Greek Septuagint*, as Beryl in the *Latin Vulgate* and in Josephus's *Antiquities*, as

Crysolite in his *Jewish Wars*, as Jasper or Onyx in the *King James Bible* and as Amethyst in *Revelations*.

It appears more probable that the twelve stones of the breastplate were all similar, presumably a clear crystal-like quartz. These engraved crystals seemed to function like a keyboard similar to those found on modern typewriters and computers. The priest would type in a question requiring a yes or no answer, which would be provided by the crystals on the shoulder straps of the Ephod, the right stone lighting up for yes, and the left one for no.

The Divine Dice, the Urim and Thummim

In Exodus 28 Moses was told that "inside the breastpiece of decision you should place the Urim and Thummim." This was apparently done after the twelve stones were installed. Little is known about the Urim and Thummim, the material out of which they were made, or the technique of their use. Rabbinical sources state that they were crystals, one smoky dark, and the other light clear crystal. They were supposed to represent opposites, yes and no, or day and night.

Furthermore, the etymology of the words are obscure. From the Greek passage adduced in First Samuel 23 and 30, it seems that the two terms were the names of two separate objects. Hence the conjecture that Urim was derived from "arar," or curse, and Thummim from "tammam," or to be whole, indicating a negation or affirmation.

In use, Urim came to mean accursed or condemned, while thummim meant whole or acquitted. Robert Bolin in his comprehensive study of *Joshua* suggests that they were probably something like dice which were kept in the breastplate and cast as needed. It is clear in Joshua that he consulted the Urim and Thummim before going to battle. Sometimes the reply would be disastrous to the Hebrews such as at the battle of Achan (the Ruin) when 36 of his men were ambushed. It also appears that Joshua used the sacred dice to allot the lands to the individual tribes after the occupation. The two sacred dice were the responsibility of the Levitical priests and only they might query the Lord in order to obtain a divine yes or no to a specific question.

The technical term used by the Israelites for consulting the Ephod and the sacred dice was "to come before the Lord." Aaron was the first high priest to use the devices and according to Leviticus 8, Moses also used the device when he placed a turban or diadem on his head, suggesting that this item may have had something to do with the divination process.

The most recent period for which there is evidence of the use of the Ephod and the Urim and thummim is that of David. The use declined after that time and Josephus says that the oracle ceased to function 200 years before his time, which is about 100 BC. After the days of David, the use of the Ephod for divination is not mentioned, although it continued to be used as a vestment of the high priest.

The origin of the use of the Ephod may have been in Egypt and information on its design and function brought out by Moses at the time of the Exodus. A breast ornament is known to have been worn by the high priest at Memphis which consisted of twelve stones intended to represent hieroglyphics.

Ishtar and Gilgamesh wore similar breastplates and such a device was probably worn in Mesopotamia. Ishtar donned a breastplate and robe before her descent to the netherworld, which she had to surrender to enter certain gates. The breastplate may have been her method of communication with the outside world, just as the PALA robe may have served as protection from radiation.

Gilgamesh also donned a breastplate and robe before facing the monster Humbaba in the cedar forest, suggesting that these accouterments, which we have identified with the Sumerian ME and discussed below, may have been in common use in the Middle East in ancient times.

CHAPTER 26

THE "STONES" OR CRYSTALS OF THE OLD TESTAMENT

There are many strange references to "stones" or "crystals" in the Old Testament and the religious literature which makes up its tradition. For example, there are stones that power instruments and equipment, that shine in the dark, and that seem to have an innate power in themselves. Many of the "stones" of the ancients seem to have some sort of magical power.

Most familiar of all are the stones of the Ephod, the breastplate which the Hebrew priests were told to fashion and to wear during the Exodus when approaching the Tent of Meeting, where the deity made his residence.

Stones as a Source of Power for the Ark of the Covenant

There is little doubt that the Ark of the Covenant which the Israelites built during the days of the Exodus was a radio transmitter and receiver whose source of power killed many people who approached it — the two sons of Aaron, the whole tribe of Korah, and the sister of Moses. It was still active some four hundred years later when it killed thousands of Philistines and Hebrews, and finally a member of the staff of David.

This source of energy was so dangerous that a special priesthood had to be formed, who were trained and specially fitted with strange garments. There are other references to the devices which were contained by the Ark and powered it.

The Ethiopic holy book called the *Kebra Nagast* which is dated to around 850 BC, and which traces the ancestry of the Ethiopian kings back to Solomon and the Queen of Sheba, refers to wondrous crystals which had been placed in the Ark by the deity. This sacred book is not available in English, however, it has been translated into German and parts of it quoted by Erich von Daniken in his book *Signs of the Gods:*

A passage from the *Kebra Nagast* describes these crystal objects:

> Now the heavenly and spiritual (original) within it is of diverse colors, and the work thereof is marvelous, and it resembles jasper and the sparkling stone, and the topaz, and the hyacinthine stone, and the crystal, and the light and it catches the eye by force, and it astonishes the mind and stupefies it with wonder; it was made by the mind of God and not by the hands of the artificer, man, but He himself created it for the habitation of his glory."

This passage describes a number of precious stones and crystals (quartz), all seemingly part of the apparatus which supplied communications. While it does not describe the arrangement of these stones (as for example, the square pattern of the stones in the breastplate) they presumably were all part of some device with each stone playing a different part in its function. Other similar stone arrangements which emitted light are found in the literature.

The Light-Emitting Stones or Crystals of Kenaz and Noah

In the religious literature there is one document that relates what happened after the Hebrews occupied Canaan and after Johsua died. It defines the succession of leaders through Kenaz, Zebul, and finally Deborah. Called the *Biblical Antiquities of Pseudo-Philo* because their attribution to Philo of Aleksandria in the First Century AD is in question, it describes how the tribes were hard-pressed by the Philistines after the death of Joshua when they were seeking a new leader to lead them as they moved into the land of Canaan.

The tribes were hard-pressed by the native peoples and Kenaz was elected with the hope that he not only could lead them, but also find out why they had fallen out of favor with Yahweh. He proceeded to question each tribe of its activities to see if there was any sinful behavior that caused them to stray from the Mosaic Law. Their confessions ranged far afield including sacrifice and cannibalism, but the one which is most interesting for our point of view is that of the tribe of Asher who confessed that:

> We have found the seven golden idols whom the Amorites call the sacred nymphs, and we took them along with the precious stones set upon them and hid them. And behold now they are stored beneath the summit of Mount Shechem. Therefore send, and you will find them.

Kenaz immediately sent a group of men to find them, had them removed and brought to him. He was told by the tribe of Asher that:

> Those precious stones, among which were crystal and prase, were brought from the land of Havilah; and they had a pierced style. And one of them was cut on the top, and another like spotted chrysoprase stone in its cutting as if it revealed the water of the deep lying beneath it. And these are the precious stones that the Amorites had in their sanctuaries, the value of which cannot be estimated; because for those entering by night the light of a lamp was not necessary, so brightly did the natural light of the stones shine forth. But among these that was cut in the pierced style and cleansed with bristles gave off more light.

Some of these clear and light green (prase) crystals had been imbedded in the idols of the Amorites (Canaanites) presumably in the hollow eye sockets. These crystals were alien to the Hebrews, who presumably did not know their purpose except as adornments on the pagan idols. It is a truism that what one does not understand one fears and destroys.

Kenaz found out, however, that these stones or crystals were virtually indestructible. He tried to destroy them several ways first by fire, but then they only quenched the flames. Then he tried to split them with an iron sword but they only dented the blade. Finally in desperation they were offered on an altar to the deity and, according to the account of Philo, they were removed mysteriously during the night by an angel.

These crystals of Kenaz which emitted light and were virtually indestructible were imbedded in the idols taken from the cache found at Shechem under an oak. Presumably they were part of the trove buried by the household of Jacob several hundred years earlier. Long known as a sacred site to the native peoples, Shechem may have been a regional repository for these power packs and other crystal components. These crystals still emitted light after all this time and therefore were active to a certain extent.

The stones by themselves were not very useful for they served to activate various devices such as the teraphim, the Biblical portable radio receiver and transmitter, and perhaps the Ark of the Covenant. It seems that by the time of the days of Kenaz, the late 15th Century BC, and the beginning of the quiet period known as the period of the Judges, the stones had become mere curiosities. Known to be associated with idols of the native Canaanites, they were treated as merely pagan religious artifacts.

The crystals of Kenaz were also described as shining brightly at night so that it was not necessary for those entering to use a lamp. Such a power pack was probably used by Noah for illumination in the Ark during the long period of 150 days that his sealed ship was at sea.

According to the Hebrew oral tradition, the Ark of Noah was illuminated by a precious stone which served to brighten the inside of the ship and made night seem like day.

A similar source of power is mentioned in the *Book of Mormon*, the holy book of the Church of Latter-Day Saints. When the tribe of Lehi left Jerusalem about 600 BC for their trip to the "promised land," they built eight ships for the journey.

These were sealed like the Ark of Noah, and in order to see in the darkened interior, the vessels were given sixteen small "stones," two for each ship, which were "white and clear, transparent as glass." These crystals "shone forth in the darkness" during the 344 days that they were at sea and before they finally reached shore.

The Power Stones of David

Many legends have sprung up around the story of David and his confrontation with the giant Philistine Goliath. The incident as related in the *First Book of Samuel* does not satisfy from a logical point of view — that a giant warrior could be felled by the blow of a small stone from a sling. Something must have been left out of the account and for this reason many stories have sprung up to explain this strange encounter.

According to one legend in the *Haggadah* there was magic power in the stones used by David:

> Scarcely did David begin to move toward Goliath, when the giant became conscious of the magic power of the youth. The evil eye David cast on his opponent sufficed to affect him with leprosy, and in the very same instant he was rooted to the ground, unable to move.

The evil eye may refer to a beam of some sort from one of the "stones" or crystals of David that paralyzed Goliath. These stones of David are also reported to have been special and magical by Pseudo-Philo who said that they were inscribed with the names of his forefathers. The magic possessed by "inscribed" stones is legendary as, for instance, the gemstones of the Ephod which were also supposed to be inscribed with the names of the tribes of Israel.

"Stones" were the general term used by the ancient Semitic people to apply to all kinds of gems and in particular, quartz crystals. Stones are also the term used often in the Sumerian literature to refer to power units and particularly to some of the ME.

CHAPTER 27

THE "STONE" THINGS O
ME'S OF THE SUMERIANS

No civilization can exist without rules to regulate the behavi of its society. Traditionally, Hammurabi of the First Dynasty of Ba 1790 BC, is credited with codifying the laws of the people of Mes largely due to the fact that these rules of behavior have been preserv stone monument.

But long before him, Ur-Nammu of the Third Dynasty of Ur, about 21 BC, boasted of establishing a set of laws to govern his empire. Yet, these man-made rules were preceded by thousands of years by the divine law codes called the ME (pronounced "may"). These rules of behavior applied not only to the gods and mankind, but to the whole universe as well.

The Sumerians believed that since the beginning of time there existed certain fundamental and unalterable authorities and duties, norms and standards, rules and regulations. These prototype laws or MEs related to every facet of civilized life. They controlled the cosmos, the behavior of gods and humans, and affected all cities and countries on Earth.

In order for civilization to run smoothly discipline was required, and this meant that all the activities of god and man ran along predetermined lines which were just as unalterable as the physical forces of the universe. Every aspect of life was clearly defined and its activities strictly regimented. Therefore, there was a standard of ME for both good and evil conduct since these were an integral part of behavior, for both god and human alike.

The Sumerian gods had all the attributes of humans both good and bad, and their rules of conduct included evil, falsehood, violence, oppression, and destruction. Being a reptilian people and lacking human emotions, it was just as essential to define and regulate negative behavior as well as ethical and moral conduct. These had to be defined concisely. From their behavior it is obvious that the Sumerian gods had no moral scruples as we find them in humans, and the "dark side" of nature had to be defined as well. The ME was the only way the alien Sumerian gods knew how to define legitimate behavior which in turn served to define morality as well.

The MEs which controlled Sumerian life must have numbered in the thousands. Over 100 of these MEs have been recovered from Sumerian literature and yet this may account for only a small percentage of the actual number of the MEs since many were specific in nature and seemed to apply to weapons as well.

The Sumerian Stone Things as MEs or Devices

In the story of Ishtar and her trip to the underworld, many of the MEs which she put on were called "stones." It was also found that in combining the various myths related to the story of Zu, that the weapons used by both parties were versions of the MEs and were sometimes called "stones."

In the *Myth of Zu* we have seen where Ninurta complained to the gods that the ME had given Zu absolute control over weapon systems that made it impossible to approach him. He found that Zu could fend off all his weapons which

d. A new weapon or ME was fashioned
in the skies where Ninurta aimed his
craft and managed to disable it. In this
rescued the MEs and who bound up the
uated to the "stone things."

r myth called *Ninurta's Pride and*
ent that Ninurta had knocked the MEs
into the hands of Enki in the Abzu.
to visit the Abzu where he asked Enki
nd Ninurta tried physically to remove
vizier Isimud. An outraged Enki fash-
seized Ninurta and threw him into a
by his mother Ninhursag.

are described both as offensive and
tle" which seized Ninurta may have
other instances the MEs are also equated to
stones." These stones are described in one source as transparent and crystal-like.

We have seen in the *Myth of Zu* that Ninurta is praised as the one "who bound his enemies and tied up the stone things," obviously referring to the MEs of Zu which were used in defense of his stronghold and against Ninurta. In a related myth Ninurta addressed a group of "stones," cursing those which had been his enemy in his battle with the Zu demon, and blessing those which had been his friends.

The Sumerian term NAmeans "stone" and it appears quite often in their literature. The root NA is often combined with other syllables to specifically define the stone. For example, all precious stones are a combination of NA.

Certain MEs are known to use the root NA, as for example NA-U or "bright stone," which was the term used for one of the MEs that Zu used against Ninurta. In the myth *Inanna and Ebih*, a NA-SU weapon is one used against an unidentified land and produces a roaring noise, a thump-thump sound, and a cloud of dust that obscures the Earth. SU usually means "tooth" but here it obviously has a more menacing meaning. The word NA-GAL-GAL is defined as "very big stones" and was used in the same myth to mean an unidentified divine weapon.

Fig. 71 – The mythological dragon of Europe and Asia (author's rendition).

The "Stones" of The Epic of Gilgamesh

"Stones" also play an important part in the adventures of Gilgamesh. In the *Epic of Gilgamesh* the hero is told by the barmaid Siduri, believed to be an epithet for Ishtar, how to reach his grandfather but to do so he must cross the "sea of death," presumably a euphemism for the dangers of space travel. She informs Gilgamesh to see Urshanabi, the boatman or pilot, who is at the edge of the "sea of death." It has been suggested by the author elsewhere that Gilgamesh's trip across the "sea of death" was actually a flight by rocket or spacecraft to see his grandfather Utnapishtim, the Sumerian Noah, who was then in the orbiting spaceship. Siduri tells him:

> The things of stone are with him, In the heart of the forest he picks up the URNU-snakes. If it is possible cross over with him.

Obviously the "stone things" and URNU-snake were needed for the perilous crossing. The URNU-snakes are unidentified but may be a shortened form of U-UR-NU meaning "noble flying snakes." In an old Babylonian version of the story, the boatman explains that the stone things could carry him across the sea so that the waters of death would not touch him. In a Hittite parallel they are called "stone images."

Gilgamesh then enters the forest where Urshanabi lives to fight some unnamed being. The story relates how he attacked its head and pinned back its wings. It is probably the URNU-snakes that were the protective guardians of the things of stone. Gilgamesh has apparently also smashed the "things of stone," for Urshanabi says:

> Your own hands, Gilgamesh, have hindered the crossing, You have destroyed the stone things.

Later, after they have crossed the sea of death and Gilgamesh meets Utnapishtim, his grandfather admonishes Gilgamesh: "Why have the stone things of the boat been smashed?" Because of this they could not cross the sea of death. An alternative method was proposed by the boatman. Gilgamesh was told to go to the forest and produce a number of "punting poles" in order to propel the boat.

As they are crossing the sea of death, there is a strange reference where Gilgamesh makes Urshanabi stand with wings spread. Again we have the possible allusion to winged snakes. The English historian N.K. Sandars in her version of the epic, suggests that the things of stone have something to do with the propulsion of the craft:

> The nature of the things of stone which Gilgamesh rashly smashed remains mysterious and unexplained. All that can be said of them is that the destruction makes necessary the use of punting poles and that they are connected in some way with "wings" or "winged beings or figurines" but beyond this they retain for the present most of their secrets."

It is obvious that the things of stone are some sort of ME connected with the propulsion system of the craft. The destruction of these obliged Gilgamesh to provide a substitute form of propulsion. It was suggested elsewhere that the punting poles were either nuclear reactor control rods or solid propellant rods for a rocket motor.

Sumerian Terms Which Relate to the ME

In the Sumerian language, the term ME meant "power" and it belonged exclusively to the gods. Many Sumerian terms used the element of ME as a combination word to denote aspects of divine appearance, behavior, equipment, and weapons. For example, ME-SIKIL which is translated as "pure power" was often applied to the god's behavior. In the *Myth of Zu* when the MEs of Enlil were stolen, Zu was accused of "taking away the Enlilship, suspended were the MESIKIL to issue decrees," which meant that Enlil had lost his absolute power over the pantheon and mankind.

Of all the various MEs, certain ones were considered to be superior and these were called ME-GAL-GAL or "chief or great ME." It was usually applied to weapons of mass destruction controlled by the gods. For example, the "Floodwind" weapon was a divine weapon often described as a MEGALGAL; it produced blinding light, poisoned the land, and destroyed vast regions in the mountains. While the term GAL had the meaning of "great" it was in the sense of being fearsome and dreadful, and thus came to have the connotation of destroyer.

The transcendent quality of the ME was called ME-LAM and meant something "extraordinary," much like our term "super." It was a quality derived from the gods and used to mean "divine splendor" or "luminous manifestation" and it was an awe-inspiring sheen or radiance inherent to the gods. It presumably originated as a description of the reptilian hide, the smoothness and luminescence which they took great pride in. It was a term also applied to intense forms of life and behavior such as beauty, joy, youth, martial and sexual vigor, and music. Perhaps our closest modern term as used in our mythology or religious texts would be "holy" or "sacred," as applied to the deity.

There were other Sumerian words which seem to be synonyms for the MEs and thus were used interchangeably to mean ME. In the word GISH-HUR, GISH means "essence" and HUR means "great" and was the word applied to the quality of the ME as denoting "great pattern" or "essence." In the story *Ninurta's Pride and Punishment* it is used as a synonym for the ME. When Zu lost the MEs which reverted to the Abzu, he exclaimed: "As I let go the ME out of my hand . . . As I let go the GISHHUR out of my hand."

Two of the best sources for information on the MEs are the myths which concern Ishtar, the great trouble-maker goddess. In one myth she seduces Enki in his Abzu and obtains over 80 of the MEs. In a second story she attempts to seize control of the underworld from her sister; here, seven of the MEs are described in detail. In addition, there are numerous others scattered throughout the Sumerian literature.

CHAPTER 28

THE FOUR BASIS USES OF THE ME'S OR POWER STONES

In cataloging the hundred or so references to the MEs or power stones in the Sumerian literature, it is possible to sort them out by use and function. They seem to fall into four general categories:

1. To set standards of behavior such as laws and regulations.
2. To define and establish various offices and authorities.
3. To provide instructions in the various arts and crafts.
4. And as control devices to operate equipment, if not the equipment itself.

As a Database to Provide Standards of Behavior

The MEs were the prototype system of laws and regulations brought to this planet by alien Sumerian gods. It applied to god and man alike and incorporated all universal laws. Eventually part of this code was adopted by mankind, the gods withholding those sections which they felt applied only to themselves.

Many historians have remarked on the scope and diversity of the MEs. To have rules defining both good and bad conduct seems incongruous to modern minds, but to a reptilian mind these were necessary.

As reptilian forms they did not possess human emotions. The behavior of their mammal children or "lulu," as they called them, must have been puzzling indeed. It reverberates throughout the scriptures as "the weakness of the flesh" and to this innate weakness the Hebrew priesthood who fashioned the books of the Old Testament, added the concept of guilt and sin, which became a guide for moral behavior for Western civilizations.

The Sumerian gods felt no compassion nor did they hate. For this reason, behavior and rules of conduct had to be strictly spelled out for every facet of life and its activities. They knew no evil or immoral conduct, on the one hand, nor moral and ethical behavior on the other, except as it was defined in the ME.

Hence, in their list of MEs we see one devoted to truth and conversely, one on the art of deceit and falsehood. There is one that defines the art of being straightforward and the art of forthright speech or the law, on one hand, and one on slanderous speech or libel. There is even a ME to fill the gray area, one on ornamental speech.

There are MEs on the art of being a hero and how to handle triumph, but on the dark side, there are MEs on the art of treachery, on how to incite strife, and to provoke fear and terror. The plundering and destruction of enemy cities was apparently also well defined and regulated.

There were MEs defining kindness, wisdom and understanding, truth, and how to render judgments. Even sorrow was regulated and defined by a ME which explained how to set up lamentation, and one on the definition of consternation and dismay. These rules and regulations were embedded in data storage devices which could be accessed at will.

As a Database to Define Jurisdiction and Various Offices and Authorities

There are many MEs which dealt with kingly and religious offices, perhaps because the Sumerian hierarchy required a large bureaucracy of retainers to attend to all of the needs of the gods. These included godship, kingship, other royal offices, various offices of high priest, and many types of priestesses which were essential to the operation of the Sumerian empire.

A role of extreme importance in the Sumerian scheme of things were those of palace priestess or votaries since they served a sexual and procreative role. It is difficult to find modern names for these various offices of sexually related functions since western languages like English are riddled with Victorian and Old Testament morality, which treat sexual activities outside marriage in negative terms.

To the Sumerians, these priestesses or hierophants were ordained clergy just as nuns are today in the Christian Church. Their role was not only to serve the gods in mundane matters, but also to act as intermediary in relations with mankind. They served mainly to serve as sexual mates for the various reptilian gods who descended to procreate sons and daughters.

The issue of a god and human was called a "changeling," a hybrid whose function was to rule and to run the empire. Notable examples are Gilgamesh and Sargon the Great who boasted that they were the sons of a god and a mortal. In antediluvian days all the kings, priests, generals, and patriarchs who ran the empire were what you would call homo-saurians, that is, part-reptile and part-human. This arrangement continued for a couple of millennia after the Deluge, and is perceived in the Old Testament where it is clear that Isaac and Ishmael were actually sired by Yahweh.

As a Source of Instructions in the Various Arts and Crafts

No culture would be complete without access and proficiency in the fine arts and the practical crafts. All the arts and crafts were presumably represented by the ME which probably acted like a modern do-it-yourself guide with all the data, plans, and instructions stored in the power stones or quartz crystals.

The design and use of musical instruments, the art of composing songs and singing, are all represented by the MEs. The MEs were strongly preoccupied with sex both as procreation and diversion. Since there was no immoral quality attached to sexual behavior the MEs defined the various techniques of love-making and procreation.

While many of the construction arts are available, many are missing — suggestive of a much more extensive and comprehensive group that covers all facets of civilization. There are many MEs which obliquely refer to complex constructions and equipment, automated devices and robots, and even to advanced weapon systems.

As Control Devices to Operate Equipment or the Equipment Itself

Their use as a power pack to energize communications equipment has been discussed previously. They also served as sources of illumination but in this sense this may have been a secondary function such as seen in the Ephod where the crystals would light up to provide a yes or no answer. The peculiar power sources or stones of the Old Testament are undoubtedly versions of the Sumerian ME.

There are also many curious references to the MEs in connection with their use as a module or control device used to activate certain types of equipment. In this sense they seem to resemble our data storage chips or disks which contain instructions to a computer or mechanical device. In the story of Ishtar's descent to the underworld many of the MEs or stones are clearly communication equipment and protective devices. The constant references to stones and crystals indicate that the ancient astronaut serpent gods had progressed much further beyond magnetic storage devices and used the quartz lattice to store information just as we use magnetic storage memories today.

CHAPTER 29

A CATALOG OF THE ME'S OR POWER STONES

The Mes which Ishtar Stole from Enki

Although individual references to the MEs are found throughout the literature there is one myth which provides a list of over 80 of the divine stones. Called *Inanna and Enki: The Transfer of the Arts of Civilization from Eridu to Uruk*, it circulated throughout Mesopotamia with the main purpose of justifying how the city of Uruk regained its preeminence and leadership in the land, as well as to validate the activities of the priesthood who claimed the blessings of Uruk's tutelary deity Ishtar.

While Uruk had traditionally been one of the great Sumerian cities it could only validate its legitimacy after it had acquired the necessary MEs to provide the authority and thereby obtain the essential instructions and rituals on how to rule a city-state. This myth relates how Ishtar plotted to obtain these MEs by visiting the Abzu of Enki and acquiring them by subterfuge.

As the story begins, Ishtar prepares herself for the trip fully confident of her charms and ability to seduce Enki. There is a festive welcome for the fascinating and attractive Ishtar by Enki in the Abzu featuring a banquet and many alcoholic beverages. Enki and Ishtar settle down to a prolonged drinking bout, competing with each other in draining many a liquor-filled bronze vessel. While in this drunken state, Enki becomes very generous and announces that he will present the enchanting Ishtar with all the precious MEs in his keep.

After Enki's grandiose but somewhat drunken gesture, Ishtar then departs in her "boat of heaven," presumably an aerial craft, loaded with the precious MEs. Later, a sober and repentant Enki, realizing what he had done, attempts to recover the MEs by dispatching his vizier Isimud accompanied by an assortment of "monsters" (probably automatons or robot-like devices), to try to intercept the fleeing Ishtar.

Ishtar is able to repel these many assaults by the minions of Enki presumably because she is armed with many of the defensive MEs. She manages to evade the pursuing craft and arrives at Uruk among the cheers of the populace. According to the myth, Enki eventually capitulated and allowed the ambitious goddess to retain the MEs, which legalized her authority over Uruk.

The 80 MEs which Ishtar extracted from Enki is listed and identified in the Appendix. The MEs are presented in clusters and theoretically each ME within a cluster is interrelated. Dissimilar MEs within the same cluster indicates that the translation of the Sumerian terms must be treated carefully since a distance of some 5000 years separate our cultures. Translators have attempted to apply the best definition possible but this is difficult considering we are locked into the narrow vision of our culture. The meanings of these terms and their relationship within each cluster must have had significance to the ancients. It only emphasizes the fact that we actually know very little of civilizations thousands of years old and how they conceived life and behavior.

For this reason the final definition of the ME is best left to posterity in the hope that more cuneiform tablets will be unearthed in the future and help to cast light on the actual meaning of these MEs.

The Mes that Ishtar Used in Her Descent to the Underworld

A second major source of the Sumerian MEs is the myth *The Descent of Inanna to the Netherworld*, wherein seven MEs are described. Ishtar puts these MEs on her person to protect herself in her descent to the underworld. The Sumerian version of Inanna is inscribed on tablets excavated at Nippur and date to about 2000 BC. It is also found in a later Babylonian version where she is called Ishtar. The death and resurrection of Ishtar was probably one of the better known myths of the ancient Middle East. Presumably the legend was first written down about 2500 BC.

According to the legend, the ambitious Ishtar descends to the netherworld ruled by her older sister Ereshkigal in order to seize control and make herself mistress of this realm. Before she leaves, she collects the appropriate MEs and adorns herself with the MEs before entering "the land of no return." There are seven MEs involved and according to the text they are all physical objects. They appear to have a protective purpose, for when they are removed one by one Ishtar becomes completely vulnerable to attack and the goddess is killed by the underground Anunna using the "eyes of death," presumably a sort of deadly light beam.

Before leaving the surface Ishtar takes sensible precautions. Fearing the worst may happen and that her sister might seize her and try to put her to death, Ishtar instructs her vizier Ninshubur to seek the help of Enlil, Nannar, and Enki, in that order, if she hasn't returned to the surface in three days.

Ishtar then enters one of the entrances to the underworld and descends where she is met by the chief gatekeeper. Upon instructions from Ereshkigal he leads Ishtar through the seven gates of the netherworld. As she passes through each gate one of the MEs is removed from Ishtar in spite of her strong protests.

After passing through the seventh and last gate Ishtar has given up all her MEs and is now vulnerable. She is brought naked and defenseless before her sister Ereshkigal, the Queen of the Underworld, and a group of Anunna gods who are judges in the underworld. They fasten upon her "the eyes of death" and she is turned into a corpse and unceremoniously hung on a stake on a wall.

Meanwhile on the surface, three days and nights have passed, and her vizier Ninshubur is now quite worried. She proceeds to make the rounds of the gods according to the instructions of her mistress. As Ishtar has surmised both Enlil and Nannar (Sin) refuse help. Enki is more sympathetic to the stricken Ishtar, however, and devises a plan to restore Ishtar to life and to rescue her from the underworld.

Enki fashions a KURGARRA (mentioned as a ME in the list, see the Appendix) and a GALATUR, described as sexless creatures. These are automations of some sort. They are given the miraculous "food and water of life" to give to Ishtar to revive her. These creatures are slipped into the underworld "through the cracks in the gates," presumably a secret way to bypass the seven main gates of the underworld. Being non-human they probably are not subject to the laws of god and man and can easily slip into the underworld. These strange creatures which appear to be robots of some sort are discussed below.

Ishtar is rescued by the mechanical men and given the "food and water of life" to revive her. But leaving the underworld is not so simple. There is an unbroken rule of the netherworld that no one who has entered through its gates may return to the world above unless he or she can produce a substitute.

Being a goddess, Ishtar is given special permission to leave the underworld in order to search for an alternate. On this trip she is accompanied by a number of GALLAs, who are described as creatures who "know no food, who know no drink, who eat no offerings, who drink no libations, who accept no gifts," apparently robots or automatons. They are not to let Ishtar out of their sight until she can produce an acceptable substitute. After several attempts to obtain an alternate Ishtar tells them to seize her husband Dumuzi and he is carried off to the netherworld.

Description of the Seven MEs of Ishtar

As the story begins, Ishtar is preparing herself for the journey to the netherworld by adorning herself with a number of MEs:

> She gathered together the seven MEs,
>
> She took them into her hands,
>
> With the MEs in her possession, she prepared herself.

The seven MEs are then described as items of adornment or apparel as she dons them one by one.

First, she placed the SHUGARRA or the "crown of the steppes" on her head. The term is not defined but it seems to be a protective helmet of some kind, for in her visit to the Abzu she also placed the SHUGARRA on her head before leaving for the trip. It may have been some sort of space helmet with breathing apparatus used by the gods when travelling. The term SHU lends itself to this meaning for it means a container or place such as used in SHU-BAT which means "dwelling or place to live." It was suggested elsewhere that the gods, for reason of comfort and perhaps survival, probably travelled about the Middle East in a personal capsule or spacecraft.

Next she placed "stone pendants" on her ears. The generic word "stone" has many meanings and was applied to crystals as well. In view of the fourth item these may well have been a headset of some sort for communications.

The third item Ishtar puts on are "chains of stone around her neck." They may have been a grouping of protective crystals.

The fourth ME she placed on her chest, a breastplate called "Come, come, man." The traditional translation seems nonsensical and may refer to a communication device similar to the Ephod of the Hebrew priest.

The fifth ME is described as a "girdle of stones on her hip which gives life." and again it may refer to a protective device composed of a number of gemstones.

The sixth ME was the "measuring rod and line in her hand." This is similar to the ME on the Abzu list and denotes the symbol of authority, that is, as a dispenser of law and justice. It may have served a defensive or protective purpose as well.

Item seven was the PALA garment which is described as "the royal robe around her body." It is reminiscent of the robe worn by the Hebrew priest under the Ephod and may have protected him from radiation. The Hebrew robe had metallic thread interwoven throughout the material and in this sense would act to protect against microwave and other short wave radiations.

The breastplate as a communication device and the protective robe are also mentioned in the *Epic of Gilgamesh.* When Gilgamesh confronts the mechanical monster Humbaba, he puts on a breastplate called "The Voice of Heroes" and a robe which covers him completely from head to foot, which is highly suggestive of a protective garment.

The seven MEs of Ishtar are apparently the accouterments of the goddess when she travelled, and consisted of protective gear and communication devices. In removing one of these devices at each gate Ishtar became more and more vulnerable until she removed the last ME, a radiation protective garment. The "eyes of death" which the gods of the underworld fastened on her were probably some sort of ray or beam weapon which "turned her into a corpse." A similar weapon is found in the confrontation of Gilgamesh with the monster Humbaba in the cedar forest. The monster fastened "the eye of death" on Gilgamesh but it had no effect on the hero — since it was apparently deflected by the protective gear he was wearing.

Other References to the ME

There are many other single references to the ME which help to describe its vast range of applications as used by the Sumerian Gods. In the self-laudatory poem *Enki and the World Order: The Organization of the Earth and its Cultural Processes*, accolades are heaped on Enki as the great builder and organizer of Sumer. He is called "the USHUMGAL (great, fiery flying serpent) who made the land fertile and productive," and he is:

> The Lord who rides the great ME, the pure ME,
>
> Who stands watch over the great MEs, the pure MEs,
>
> Who is foremost everywhere above and below.

Thus the ME is described as a vehicle of some sort, presumably an airborne craft. A similar reference to a vehicle, except this time it refers to a sea craft, is found in a poem praising Enki's help to mankind, called *Enki and his Word: A Chant to the Rider of the Waves.*

This poem is filled with puzzling and tantalizing references to Enki's power over the ME and the consequences, good and bad, for humankind. It is addressed by the poet to Enki as the "god who rides the waves" — presumably the canal system of Mesopotamia where Enki had his Abzu and where he cruised about in his MAGUR-boat or "runabout."

The poet asserts that after humans had multiplied, Enki brought them to the Abzu to show them the MEs which would be of benefit to mankind.

But from that list he removed the MEs of "life" — presumably referring to either instructions, a restorative, or even a device which conferred long life or immortality. These he fastened to his breast. He warned humankind that they must not covet these MEs, meaning that humans cannot attain immortality. Is this the same breastplate used by Ishtar and Gilgamesh?

Another reference to a ME in the myths refers to one that was used to set the calendar, and may have contained the necessary astronomical data and instructions on how to make adjustments. This is found in a lauditory poem called the *Joy of Sumer* where Ishtar is praised for this ability:

> In order to care for the life of all the lands,
>
> The exact first day of the month is closely examined,
>
> And in the day of the disappearance of the moon,
>
> On the day of the sleeping of the moon,
>
> The MEs are perfectly carried out.
>
> So that the New Year's Day, the day of rites
>
> May be properly determined.

In this respect the MEs used to set the calendar are reminiscent of the "divine names" often mentioned in the scriptures. These divine names conferred extraordinary powers on the owner.

In the the Hebrew *Apocalypse of Enoch*, believed to have originated in Babylonian Jewry and attributed to the Rabbi Ishmael, Ishmael tours the heavenly abode where Enoch, who has been deified, was given "seventy names" which conferred powers and authority over the gods, angels, and humankind. Among the divine names was the power to "control the procession of time and the seasons," which presumably provided the authority and instructions on how to adjust the calendar, when necessary.

CHAPTER 30

THE SUMERIAN ME'S AS ROBOTS OR MECHANICAL DEVICES

There are many creatures mentioned in the Sumerian texts which obviously are not human. It is said that they are "neither male or female," that is, they are sexless creatures. Most translations ignore the ramifications and prefer to skirt the issue by calling them "eunuchs." But this term is not satisfactory, for the text clearly says that they take no food or drink, have no emotions, and have no family life. Obviously these creatures possess no human qualities and have the passivity and traits of artificial machines.

We will try to summarize available references to these creatures which obviously are not human and have all the characteristics of mechanical devices. Five of them are mentioned in the list of MEs that Ishtar obtained from Enki. The robots are called the KURGARRA, GALATUR, SAGURSAG, GIRBADARA, AND GALLA. These are all Sumerian terms for which there is no English counterpart. They are not usually translated for the simple reason that no one knows what they are or how to render the terms into modern language. Other unknown terms also appear to represent artificial creatures — the LILIS, UB, MESI, and ALA have been called "demons." These demons were apparently quite numerous and harassed and oppressed the citizenry of Mesopotamia.

The "Kurgarra" or Bright Mechanical Man

The KURGARRA was one of the creatures created by Enki to enter the underworld and rescue Ishtar. Called "a creature neither male nor female," it was designed to enter the underworld "through cracks in the gates" or, in other words, by surreptitious means. Not being human or godly and not subject to the strict rules imposed by the MEs on entering and leaving the underworld, it could apparently move about at will, unhampered by regulations. This behavior is more characteristic of an artificial creature.

The KURGARRA or as it sometimes appear KURGURRA, is also listed as a ME in the list that Ishtar obtained from Enki (see item 19). A study of the elements which make up the term KUR-GAR-RAor KUR-GUR-RAindicates that it can be translated to mean "bright metallic robot." KUR is often used to mean mighty and it also has a secondary meaning of the underworld; it is often applied to monsters. GUR means to be mobile or to travel about, for example MA-GUR is the runabout that Enki used to tour the canals of Mesopotamia. RA is the term for "bright" in the sense of metallic. It is also possible that GARRA is a form or corruption of GALLA which has been described as a mechanical man. Thus, the KURGARRA or KURGURRA would be a bright metallic-like mechanical creature programmed by Enki to rescue Ishtar from underworld.

The "Galatur" or Small Destroyer

The KURGARRAwas accompanied by another artificial creature fashioned by Enki to rescue Ishtar from the underworld. Called the GALATUR, or GAL-LA-TUR, it too was "a creature neither male nor female." The meaning of GAL is great in the sense of fearsome or destroyer. LA means "glowing" or "bright," and TUR is the term for small (for example, NA-TUR is the Sumerian name for small stone or pebble). It thus appears that GAL-LA-TUR may be a small robot. In this sense the two creatures fashioned by Enki may be large and small robots to make it easier to enter the underworld.

The "Sagursag" or Bright Fearsome Robot

In the list of MEs which Ishtar obtained from Enki there is a creature called a SAGURSAG (see item 21). The SA-GUR-SAG is usually translated as "eunuch" in the sense that it was a sexless creature, but an analysis of the elements which make up the word reveals that it is also a robot. The syllable SA means light or bright; GUR is mobile as previously mentioned. While SAG is usually translated as "head" it is often applied to divine weapons, as something fearsome and menacing. Thus the term SAGURSAG would indicate this creature is a bright, metallic fearsome robot. According to Wilson, ASAG is the name of a major divine weapon.

The "Girbadara" or Clawed Monster

In Ishtar's list of MEs she obtained from Enki there is also a GIRBADARA referred to (item 20). The GIR-BADA-RAis also called a eunuch, that is, a sexless creature. The term GIR-BADA-RA seems to describe a device equipped with pincers or claws. GIR is the Sumerian term for claw or pincer. According to the Sumerian Dictionary, BADA or BAD-A means "outstretched" as in outstretched arms but it also has a secondary meaning "to overturn." Wilson gives BADA the meaning of "to overturn" such as seen in BADA-SHU or "to overturn a chariot." As mentioned above, RA is commonly used to mean bright. Thus the GIRBADARA may be a robot with long arms with claws or pincers attached to the ends.

The "Galla" or Bright Destroyer Robot

When Ishtar was revived by the robots KURGARRA and GALATUR, she was allowed to leave the underworld accompanied by several GALLAcreatures whose purpose was to accompany Ishtar and to keep watch over her to prevent her from escaping. They were also to bring her back or a suitable substitute to the underworld. After many attempts failed to secure a replacement, Ishtar finally named her husband Dumuzi to take her place in the underworld. He was immediately attacked by the GALLA, paralyzed and taken down below.

In another myth Dumuzi manages to escape the GALLA monster. He appealed to the god Utu to change him into a legged snake. Utu acceded and Dumuzi was temporarily saved. The allusion to a reptile may be allegorical, for by appealing to Utu (the Chief Astronaut of the Anunna) for help seems strange unless he would be the one to provide a shuttle or escape craft. The comparison of being turned into a legged serpent or reptile may refer to his becoming a USHUMGAL, or a "fiery, flying serpent," that is, escaping by some sort of air or spaceship.

These GALLAwere obviously mechanical creatures that could move about easily on Earth as well as in the sky, for they are described in the work of Wolkstein and Kramer as those "who flutter over heaven and earth."

In a little known Semitic poem called *Incantation of Eridu,* which was meant to exorcise these demons from among the populace, they are called evil demon gods who live in the heavens but descend to Earth occasionally:

> The evil *utukku* and the evil *alu* — descend to Earth.
>
> The evil *etemmu* and the evil *gallu* — leave the city.
>
> By the great gods you are exorcised.
>
> Into the house they will not enter.

They will not break through the fence.

These are all Semitic names for monsters or demons, of which the GALLA (Semitic *gallu*) are but one type which plagued humankind for millennia. They are described as non-human in the myth concerning the descent of Ishtar to the netherworld:

The GALLA, the demons of the underworld, clung to her side.
The GALLA were the demons who know no food,
who know no drink,
Who eat no offerings, who drink no libations,
Who accept no gifts.
They enjoy no lovemaking.
They have no sweet children to kiss.

Since the root GAL means great and formidable destroyer, as was stated above, and LA means bright, the GALLA can best be described as metallic mechanical devices associated with destruction. The GALLA is among a list of many demons that harassed humans during this period.

In his work on the Anunna, Wilson lists the GALLA as part of a group of seven demons called *lemnu* monsters in Semitic. They are the ALA (*Alu* in Semitic), GALLA (gallu), ILA (Ilu), NAMTAR (Namtaru), UTUKKA (Utukku), Etimna, and *Rabisa*. NAMTAR is the usual Sumerian term for fate or destiny and is often called the "disease demon." There is also a Semitic list of seven called *Kamu* or captive demons and these are *Lamashtu*, *Labasu, Akbazu, Lilu, Lilitu, Ardat, Lili, and Mukil.* It would be a significant study in itself to recover all these terms used to demote monsters and demons and find out their actual meaning in modern terms.

The "Lilis," "Ub," "Mesi," and "Ala," Demons or Robots

These four names are listed as the last four MEs which Ishtar obtained from Enki (items 83-86). They have been tentatively identified by one scholar as musical instruments. However, there is good reason to suspect that all four are actually robots or mechanical machines of some sort, associated with danger and weapons.

The gods had numerous mechanical devices or "demons" that plagued the people of Mesopotamia. These four MEs of Ishtar's list are presumably some sort of manufactured devices in the sense of automatons or humanoids. Let us examine these four words to see if they fit that classification.

The Sumerian word LILI(S) or Semitic *Lilu* has been used to designate a demon that is associated with a whirlwind. In one instance the LILI has been called a great ALA demon of the Anunna.

The word UB (uppu in Akkadian) is applied to a being that was mentioned in a little known myth called *God and Humankind Mixed* where a new creature is fabricated out of clay by Enki to assist mankind and it is called an UB. It is obviously an artificial creature.

The mechanical device MESI is not further identified but may be a combination of SI, meaning strong and righteous and ME, referring to a powerful device of some kind.

ALA is the root word for "image" in Sumerian, such as found in the word ALA-HUL, meaning evil image or demon, and may actually be a foreshortening of the term. As noted above, the LILI demon has been referred to as a great ALA demon of the Anunna.

It was probably their Mesopotamian antecedents that provided the Hebrews with the tradition of the *golem*, or evil robot. According to the Kaballah, there is a statue called *golem* which comes to life under certain conditions, that is, when it is fed paper bearing certain key Kabbalistic formulas. It was a malevolent creature whose escape would start a reign of terror on an unsuspecting world.

Robots or mechanical creatures are also scattered throughout Greek mythology, who seem to have borrowed the idea from the Sumerians. There is also an old Medieval tradition which describes how certain statues in Egyptian temples would come alive at certain times when they were placed in specific places during certain cosmic events. But the most famous of ancient mechanical monsters certainly has to be the one that Gilgamesh fought and destroyed in his historic trip to the land of the gods. Humbaba was the granddaddy of all huge, dangerous mechanical monsters.

"Humbaba," the Guardian Mechanical Monster

Probably the most celebrated of ancient monsters which is clearly a mechanical creature was the one faced by Gilgamesh in the land of Shamash. In their attempt to reach the gods, the hero and his companion Enkidu meet and destroy a monster which was the guardian of the forest land.

There is no specific reference or evidence that Humbaba was a ME itself or that it was activated by a ME, but there is no doubt that it was an artificial creature, a defensive robot or machine. The name HUM-BA-BA itself is merely a descriptive one which means "the great one who metes out the fates," that is, in the sense of a destroyer.

The battle with Humbaba (sometimes called Hubaba or Huwawa) is found in two legends or poems about Gilgamesh. One called *Gilgamesh and the Land of the Living* and the other is the *Epic of Gilgamesh.*

In the Old Babylonian version of the *Epic of Gilgamesh*, Humbaba is called *mimma lemnu* — the Semitic term for supernatural evil or demonic being.

The origins of Humbaba make it clear that it is an artificial creature. The quotes below are from the version of the epic by the historian Sandars. In it Humbaba confides to Gilgamesh that:

> I have never known a mother, nor a father who reared me.
>
> I was born of the mountain, it reared me and Enlil made me keeper of the forest.

In other words, Humbaba is confiding to Gilgamesh that he was not created of human or even divine parents but was created by Enlil. He further says:

> My mother who bore me was a *hurrum* of the mountainland,
>
> My father who engendered me was a *hurrum* of the HURSAG.

The HURSAG is left untranslated by scholars since it fits no known word that would fit the context here. It was probably the launch platform and buildings at Baalbek for HUR-SAG means great artificial mountains. We have seen that SAG means "lion head," thus HUR-SAG would be "that monster that roars." The Semitic *hurrum* is directly borrowed from the Sumerian HUR-RU-UM and presumably was used to mean the rocket preparation building at Baalbek. HUR is an artificial mountain, RU means to rise up, and UM to create or bring forth, an apt description of a launch tower at a rocket facility.

To meet and conquer this monster, Gilgamesh had the technicians at his home base of Uruk manufacture special armor for him and Enkidu.

> They put in their hands the great swords in their golden scabbards, and the bow and the quiver. Gilgamesh took the axe; he slung the quiver from his shoulder, and the bow of Anshar, and buckled the sword to his belt.

These are undoubtedly metaphors for special weapons. Under them he wore a special breastplate and robe reminiscent of those of Ishtar. The Ephod and breastplate of the Hebrew priest was probably similar. Just before meeting with Humbaba he put on this gear.

> He put on his breastplate called "The Voice of Heroes" of thirty shekels weight; he put it on as though it had been a light garment that he carried, and it covered him altogether.

Gilgamesh and Enkidu entered "the mountain of cedars, the dwelling place of the gods, and the throne of Ishtar." Here they apparently witnessed a night launch of a rocket from the stone platform at Baalbek.

> The heavens roared and the Earth roared again, daylight failed, and darkness fell, lightning flashed, fire blazed out, the clouds lowered, they rained down death. Then the brightness departed, the fire went out, and all was turned to ashes fallen about us.

To reach the monster Humbaba, Gilgamesh had to destroy seven defenses. Metamorphically he had to cut down seven "trees" which guarded the approach to Humbaba's inner chamber or home base. As Gilgamesh and Enkidu neared the monster:

> Humbaba came from his strong house of cedar.
>
> He nodded his head and shook it, menacing Gilgamesh;
>
> And on him he fastened his eye, the "eye of death."

It was probably a death ray similar to the one that was used on Ishtar and that the GALLA used on Dumuzi. Humbaba then prepared to arm himself with "seven cloaks" or items of defensive gear.

> When he roars it is like the torrent of the storms, his breath is like fire, and his jaws are death itself. He guards the cedars so well that when the wild heifer stirs in the forest, although she is 60 leagues distant he hears her. The watchman of the forest never sleeps.

According to the *Epic of Gilgamesh*, Humbaba had armed himself with the first of these "splendors" or "terrors" but not yet the other six. Gilgamesh pleaded with Shamash, the ruler of the land of cedars for help. Shamash unleashed eight great "winds" which were weapons of some sort which paralyzed and blinded Humbaba. "The eight winds rose up against Humbaba, they beat against his eyes, he was gripped, unable to go forward or back."

Humbaba was helpless and pleaded for mercy but Enkidu reminded Gilgamesh that they had come this far and could not leave the monster alive or active lest they be sorry later. Then Gilgamesh struck the first blow.

> He took the axe in his hand, he drew the sword from his belt, and he struck Humbaba with a thrust of the sword to the neck, and Enkidu his comrade struck the second blow. At the third blow Humbaba fell. For as far as two leagues the cedars shivered when Enkidu felled the watcher of the forest, he at whose voice (Mt) Hermon and Lebanon used to tremble.

With the destruction of the mechanical defender, Gilgamesh and Enkidu were free to pass through the cedar forest and reach Baalbek, the city of the gods where, "They uncovered the sacred dwellings of the Anunna." Gilgamesh describes the garden of the gods in metaphoric words. It is a city of bright crystals:

> There was the garden of the gods; all around him stood bushes bearing gems. Seeing it, he went down at once, for there was fruit of carnelian, with the vine hanging from it, beautiful to look at; lapis lazuli leaves, hung thick with fruit, sweet to see. For thorns and thistle there were hematite and rare stones, agate and pearls from out of the sea.

What Gilgamesh described was the multicolored apparatus and buildings at the space center. He could only describe the "garden" of the gods in terms he could understand. A similar garden of stones is found in the *Book of Ezekiel* in his diatribe against Hiram of Tyre. Ezekiel describes Hiram as living amidst bright stones:

> You were in Eden, the garden of God:
>
> Every precious stone was your covering,
>
> Carnelian, topaz, and jasper,
>
> Chrysolite, beryl, and onyx,
>
> Sapphire, carbuncle, and emerald,
>
> You were on the holy mountain of God,
>
> And the guardian cherub drove you out,
>
> From the midst of the stones of fire.

Hiram had helped Solomon build his temple and palace when he was King of the Phoenician city-states on the coast of Lebanon, and also the overseer of the internal lands of Lebanon where the cedars came from to build the structures of Solomon. Ezekiel here refers to the "sacred dwellings of the Anunna," or the crystal city of Baalbek, which at one time was the heart of the space facilities of the gods.

EPILOG

The view that aliens or extraterrestrials could have founded ancient civilizations continues to be unfashionable among researchers in general. They believe that these aliens would not be able to get here in the first place because of the vast distances involved. These objections fail to allow for advanced alien technology, one sufficient to enable them to travel between the stars.

It is a most superb irony that a race of intelligent beings may really exist in our neighborhood of space who are reptilian and repulsive by our standards, and yet have founded our human civilization. A race that could traverse space would certainly have achieved genetic engineering and the ability to regenerate themselves and thereby achieve long and extended life.

Is There Really a Missing Link?

Man is a puzzle in the evolutionary chain. The scientific theories of evolution explain the general course of events that cause life forms to develop on Earth, but evolution cannot account for the emergence of Homo sapiens or modern man.

For almost a hundred years, anthropologists and other scientists have been searching for the so-called missing link in order to bridge the enormous evolutionary gap that exists between the ape-man and modern man.

The appearance of Homo sapiens happened virtually overnight in terms of the millions of years that evolution required. There is no evidence of intermediate stages that would indicate a gradual change from Homo erectus the ape-man to Homo sapiens, modern man. While the hominid of the genus Homo is a product of evolution, Homo sapiens is the product of a sudden revolutionary event.

The first being considered to be truly manlike is Australopithecus who existed in Africa some five million years ago. Then it took eons to produce the first primitive ape-man or Homo erectus. About one million years ago he appears on the scene and is called Neanderthal Man.

Then suddenly and inexplicably some 40,000 years ago, a new race appeared from nowhere — Cro-Magnon Man, the creature we call Homo sapiens or thinking man. He looked very much like modern man, so much so in fact, that if he were dressed properly he could pass unnoticed on the street of any city in America.

The arrival of the Sumerians provide the explanation of the sudden appearance of modern man. He seems to have been created and developed in two stages. Man was first conceived as a slave worker; at this time, he was mostly reptilian in appearance and nature, probably only one-third mammal.

The second change increased his mammal nature so that he lost his scaly skin and hide and could reproduce himself. He developed soft skin and hair and now required the use of clothing for comfort and protection. This is metaphorically called "the Fall of Man" in Biblical terms.

The Reptilian Appearance of the Ancient Kings and Patriarchs

The Patriarchs of the Old Testament and the Sumerian antediluvian kings and priests were all part saurian, being the children of the mating of a reptile god and an earthling. This was also true after the Deluge. They would definitely have had a reptilian appearance and, in certain respects, visibly reveal vestiges

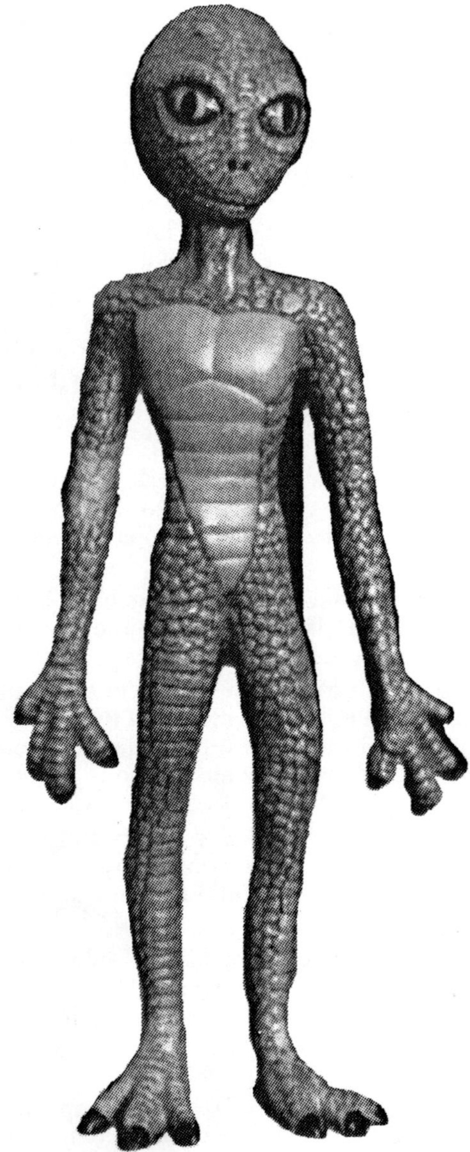

Fig, 72 – Homo-saurus or "Reptile Man"

Is this what the Adam of the Old Testament and the Lulu of the Sumerians may have looked like? Was he created in the image of his gods to do menial tasks such as agriculture, animal husbandry, and the mining of gold and rare metals?

of their origin. In his venture to the land of Shamash, Gilgamesh is challenged by the guards at the gates of the mountain stronghold. Gilgamesh is instantly recognized by the saurian guards "as one of us," since "he has the flesh of the gods." He is allowed to pass unhindered since he is one of the aristocracy.

It is also manifest in the myth *Gilgamesh and Agga.* In this story, the city of Uruk was attacked by Agga, the ruler of Kish. Agga requested Gilgamesh to surrender his city with his army. However, when Gilgamesh presented himself atop the city wall for Agga to see him in person, Agga calls off the seige for no apparent reason, and Agga's army is put to flight. Obviously, there is something in the appearance of Gilgamesh that has satisfied Agga and frightened his army. Like Agga, Gilgamesh was part saurian and apparently the code of chivalry of the day prevented further action against another member of the aristocracy.

What is it about Gilgamesh that is recognizable as saurian and never stated? Ostensibly his appearance is described in the first part of the poem where the details of his birth are provided. The tablet begins with the statement that Gilgamesh is two-thirds divine, being the progeny of a goddess and a priest. The next four lines seem to be devoted to describing his appearance. For some reason, however, they have been mutilated. Were these lines deliberately defaced by later officials and priests in order to hide the true appearance of Gilgamesh?

The patriarchs, god-kings, priests, generals, and other members of the aristocracy were also part saurian, and exhibited certain characteristics which set them apart from ordinary people — probably large patches of scaly skin referred to as "the badge of priesthood." They probably also had horns and chin whiskers.

Perhaps it is these reptilian traits that caused such consternation in Genesis when Noah is seen naked by his sons. The reaction is so completely illogical and baffling that it can only be assumed that Noah was hiding something about his appearance from his sons. Perhaps it was the "badge of priesthood," patches of scaly hide such as was on his brother Nir.

What Did the Ancient Gods Look Like?

The space travelers found our antediluvian Earth much to their liking because it approximated conditions on their home planet. The climate was warm and stable, and more importantly, there was little cyclonic activity. The carbon dioxide and the moisture level of the atmosphere was high within the cloud canopy. These conditions led to luxurious plant growth and giant animal forms. It was the era of the vegetarian dinosaurs. The coming of the Anunna coincided with the end of this period as the Earth began to dry out and the meat-eating dinosaurs and small mammals appeared.

The reptile gods needed moisture and warmth and it was probably the reason why civilizations were founded at the mouth of great river systems — the Nile delta, the Indus river valley, and the Tigris-Euphrates system. The steady drying out of the climate brought discomfort to the Anunna and they were forced more and more to live in an artificial environment — their orbiting spaceship. While on Earth, they lived a great deal of the time in a personal capsule which simulated this artificial environment.

The home planet of our ancestors was probably also covered with a vapor layer of clouds. On such a rather steamy planet it would be necessary to keep cool, and intelligent life there would likely evolve as amphibious and be at home in water as well as on land. It explains the Babylonian legend of Oannes coming from the sea. It also explain's Enki's residence in a water palace which appears to have been submersible as well.

Fig. 73 – What the Serpent Gods may have looked like.

Mythology and literature describe the gods as bearded with horns. Hence, the ibex became sacred to the creator god Enki. The ancient Sumerian gods were usually represented with horned headdresses. The chin whisker was later adopted as a sign of godship by the Egyptian Pharaohs. Male Sumerian gods were always shown with a beard. The sword was the favorite weapon of the gods, especially after the deluge, when it was adopted by the Rephaim which ruled Syria and Palestine for 3,000 years.

Their spaceships would probably contain giant water tanks both for ease of living conditions and for protection from radiation on long space flights. Their form was remarkably adopted to space travel.

Scientists have theorized that the reptile form would be ideal for travel through space on long voyages. Able to hibernate or slow down their metabolism for long periods and immersed in a water or liquid environment, they could thereby survive the perils of space travel which have a deleterious effect on mammal forms.

Radiation has been the major obstacle of space travel for man. Doses of radiation emitted by solar flares would be fatal to space travelers, for one solar flare could emit 800 to 1000 REMs (a measurement of radiation) over a 24 hour period. Man would receive a fatal dose all at once since the lifetime limit for exposure by humans to radiation is 300 REMs. Space scientists have proposed that for protection against these immense doses of radiation, the astronauts would retreat to large tanks of water or liquids during solar storms.

In appearance, the serpent-gods were tall, at least 8 to 10 feet, and walked on two feet. They had a tail like a reptile, and a tough hide somewhat like a lizard but with a large amount of horny or scaly skin. Their hide was generally lustrous and smooth, somewhat like a chameleon, and probably varied in different hues of green and gray. Their natural condition was to go around naked, but they wore clothing such as cloaks as a sign of rank or godship. Because of their need for moisture, they could not stand the direct sun which made their skin dry and uncomfortable.

Their face was somewhat flat with chin whiskers or a goatee, somewhat like a walrus or ibex. They had short horns or their head which they considered to be a sign of divinity. Humans were repulsive to them because they were hairy, had soft skins, and bony limbs. They were particularly upset by man's pungent smells and excretions. The gods did not eat cooked foods at first, but later depended on man to supply these needs. They did not need fires or stoves to keep warm.

Early reptile-man or Adam was not too dissimilar from his creator, except he was smaller, had no facial hair, nor horns. He was more agile and dexterous with his hands. He too ate raw food and ran around naked.

When Did the Serpent Gods Leave, or are They Still Here?

The Period before the Deluge was the heyday of the gods. World mythology refers to this period as the Golden Age when the gods are said to have ruled on Earth.

The Deluge is a watershed in the history of mankind. It ended the Golden Age and started the rule of man. The junior gods seemed to have remained for some time after the Deluge and directed the activities of mankind. Man was used as a tool in their family squabbles. It led to widespread destruction all over the World. The Millennium following the Deluge marked the end of many great civilizations, ostensibly by means of weapons of mass destruction.

After the 24th Century BC, the influence of the gods seemed to have waned. The reign of Sargon the Great, from 2334 to 2278 BC, was marked by restraint and moderation. While he reclaimed all the Western Lands, there was no destruction and cities like Ebla and Sodom thrived under his patronage.

It is with the rise to power of his grandson Naram-Sin in 2254 BC that we see unrestricted use of power and vast destruction. Naram-Sin was also the first Sumerian king to proclaim himself a god and adopt all the trappings of a deity.

Such behavior would certainly not have been tolerated by the senior gods, and his reign seems to mark the end of their control over the activities of mankind.

The unrestrained behavior of Naram-Sin and later Sumerian and Akkadian kings attest to the fact that the orbiting spaceship probably left before the 23rd Century, leaving behind the junior gods and the hybrid forms like the Rephaim or warrior-gods of the Western Lands.

The sightings of strange aerial objects (UFOs) throughout the centuries would indicate either their spaceships have reappeared at intervals or that they may have been here all this time but hidden from human eyes. If they have been here for centuries, where would they find a place that is secure, away from prying eyes, and far from population centers?

The best possibilities for remaining undetected all these years would be underwater or underground. There are numerous caverns and underground tunnel systems throughout the world; some like in Turkey are actually small underground cities. Vast underground tunnel systems have been reported in the Andes, in Tibet, and in many other mountainous places throughout the world. These underground tunnels and cities are reportedly the legendary homes of the serpent-like people such as the Nagas of India.

It is also possible that seas and lakes hide the entrance to these underground bases, which may be more widespread then we realize. For example, the strange activities reported in the Atlantic Ocean known as the Bermuda Triangle may be such an underwater base.

A Great Cultural Shock!

Mankind is probably not yet ready for the truth. The average man and woman needs their fantasies — the myths and religious stories that make life so simple and uncomplicated. Perhaps one of these days we will be shocked into accepting the truth — when our ancestors return to see how their "children" are faring.

Man has been conditioned for millennia to deny the truth of his ancestry and as a palliative we have developed a convenient form of amnesia. We have accepted the interpretation of history propagated by a self-perpetuating priesthood and academia. Nonetheless, the truth can only be delayed for so long.

Eventually mankind will have to learn the truth about his origins and face the fact that his gods and ancestors were reptiles, truly monsters by any of our current definitions.

There will be a great cultural shock as we have never seen before!

A CATALOG OF THE MEs WHICH ISHTAR STOLE FROM ENKI

As Enki presented them to Ishtar in clusters, he described them briefly. A list of the MEs are found with slight variations in both the work by Wolkstein and Kramer, and in the work by Kramer and Maier. There is also a condensed list in Kramer's *The Sumerians*.

Name of the ME	Meaning and Comment
1. EN-ship	The spiritual leader or high priest of the temple.
2. LUGAL-ship	The king or political leader.
3. Godship	This may refer to the power of bestowing divinity on a mortal king.
4. The noble, enduring crown	See item below.
5. The throne of kingship	These two may relate "godship" and probably deals with the accouterments of royalty.
6. The noble scepter	See item above.
7. The staff and nose rope.	This is probably what is called elsewhere as the "holy measuring rod and line" i.e. a stick and rope circle denoting authority and justice.
8. The noble dais or the elevated throne	
9. Shepherdship.	The Sumerian concept on how to lead humankind.
10. Kingship.	
11. EGIZI-ship	The office of princess-priestess.
12. NINDINGIR-ship	The office of the divine queen or priestess.
13. ISHIB-ship	The office of incantation priest.
14. LUMAH-ship	The office of noble priest.
15. GUDU-ship	The office of libations priest.
16. Truth	
(there are two missing here)	
17. Descent to the netherworld	
18. Ascent from the netherworld	
19 The KURGARRA	Referred to in Kramer as a eunuch, that is, a sexless creature, probably a mechanical man or robot.
20. The GIRBADARA	Translated as eunuch by Kramer
21. The SAGURSAG	Also called a eunuch by Kramer
22. The black garment	
23. The colorful garment	Like the above, may be associated with radiation protection. See Ishtar and the PALA garment.
24. The loosening of the nape hair	Significance not known.
25. The binding of the nape hair.	

26. The (battle) standard	See item below
27. The quiver	The standard and quiver may be divine weapons. Wilson calls the "Quiver" a divine weapon or A-MA-URU which produces a raging wind.
28. The working of the penis.	Usually translated without comment.
29. The kissing of the penis	See the above note.
30. The art of prostitution	
31. The art of speeding	Unknown and unexplained by translators.
32. The art of forthright speech or truth.	
33. The art of slanderous speech or libel.	
34. The art of ornamental speech	
(a missing ME here).	
35. The cult-prostitute	
36. The holy tavern	
37. The holy NIGINGAR shrine	A sanctuary devoted to Ishtar.
38. The GUSILIM or resonant musical instrument	
39. The art of song or music	
40. Eldership	
41. The art of being a hero	
42. The art of wielding power	
43. The art of treachery	
44. The art of being straightforward	
45. The plundering and destruction of cities	
46. The setting up of lamentation	
47. The rejoicing of the heart	
48. The art of deceit or falsehood	
49. The rebellious land	The listing of this ME with the above may relate to the Sumerian obsession with subduing the Western Lands of the Levant which continuously rebelled against Mesopotamian kings.
50. The art of being kind	
51. Travel	
52. The secure dwelling place	
53. The craft of the carpenter	
54. The craft of the copper worker	
55. The craft of the scribe	
56. The craft of the smith	
57. The craft of the leather worker	
58. The craft of the fuller	
59. The craft of the builder	
60. The craft of the reed worker	
61. The perceptive ear or wisdom	
62. The art of paying attention	
63. The holy purification rites	

64. The feeding-pen
65. The heaping of the hot coals or maintaining a fire
66. The managing of the sheepfold
67. Fear and terror
68. Consternation
69. Dismay

These last three clusters probably concern the definition and treatment of fear and anxiety

70. The bitter-toothed (word missing)
71. The kindling of fire
72. The putting out of fire
73. The weary arm
74. The (word missing) mouth
75. The assembled family
76. The art of procreation
77. The inciting of strife
78. The handling of triumph
79. The art of counseling
80. The soothing of troubled hearts
81. The giving of judgment
82. The making of decisions

There are an additional four listed in Kramer and which he tentatively called musical instruments. They are the Sumerian words:

83. LILIS
84. UB
85. MESI
86. ALA

BIBLIOGRAPHY

PRINCIPAL SOURCES FOR RELIGIOUS TEXTS

The Torah, The Five Books of Moses. Translation according to the Masoretic text, by the Jewish Publication Society of America, Philadelphia, Second Edition, 1982. It provides recent interpretations of Biblical text in view of significant advances in Biblical Archaeology.

The Holy Bible. Oxford annotated edition published by Oxford University Press, New York, 1962. It is the standard "archaic" version based on the King James translation.

Genesis. Volume 1 of the Anchor Bible Series, with translation and commentary by E.A. Spieser. Doubleday and Co., Garden City, N.Y., Third Edition, 1985. It contains translations and interpretations based on recent Sumerian and Akkadian finds.

Joshua. Volume 6 of the Anchor Bible Series, with translation and commentary by Robert G. Boling, Doubleday, 1984.

Judges. Volume 6a of the Anchor Bible Series, with translation and commentary by Robert G. Boling, Doubleday, 1975.

I Samuel. Volume 8 of the Anchor Bible Series, with translation and commentary by Jacob M. Meyers, Doubleday, 1965.

Ezekial 1-20. Volume 22 of the Anchor Bible Series, with translation and commentary by Moshe Greenburg, Doubleday, 1983.

The following religious sources can be found in *The Old Testament Pseudepigrapha*, which is referenced below.

Apocalypse of Adam
Testament of Solomon
Life of Adam and Eve
Apocalypse of Abraham (Slavonic)
Pseudo-Philo
Pseudo-Eupolemus
Ethiopic *Apocalypse of Enoch (First Book of)*
Slavonic *Apocalypse of Enoch (Second Book of)*
Hebrew *Apocalypse of Enoch (Third Book of)*

The Old Testament Pseudepigrapha. Volume 1, edited by James H. Charlesworth, Doubleday, 1983. Contains apocalyptic literature and testaments, especially valuable for the books of Enoch, Ezra and Baruch.

The Old Testament Pseudepigrapha. Volume 2, edited by James H. Charlesworth, Doubleday, 1985. Contains Old Testament legends, lost Judeo-Hellenistic works and other literary fragments, and more importantly the *Book of Jubilees* and the works of Pseudo-Philo.

Legends of the Bible, by Louis Ginzberg. The Jewish Publication Society of America, 1956. This is an abridged edition of *Legends of the Jews*, originally published in seven volumes in 1909. *The Legends* is a vast store of Jewish stories and lore forming the oral tradition of the Bible known as the *Haggadah.*

Hebrew Myths: The Book of Genesis. Robert Graves and Raphael Patai, Greenwich House, NY, 1983. Good source for the mythical background of the Old Testament.

The Nag Hammadi Library. Editor James K. Robinson. Published by Harper and Row, San Francisco, 1977. It is a veritable gold mine of Gnostic documents.

Antiquities of the Jews, Wars of the Jews, Against Apion from *Josephus: Complete Works*, translated and edited by William Whiston, Kregal Publications, Grand Rapids, MI, 1985. An invaluable companion to the Biblical texts.

Encyclopedia Judaica. Published by the MacMillan Co., Jerusalem, 1971. An indispensible source of collected articles by key researchers. Essential companion to the Old Testament.

The Lore of the Old Testament, by Joseph Geer, published by Little, Brown and Co., Boston, 1951. Contains a treasury of ancient Jewish and Yiddish lore and legend, much of which is not available elsewhere.

The Dead Sea Scriptures, by Theodore H. Gaster, 3rd edition, Anchor Press, NY, 1976.

More Light on the Dead Sea Scrolls, by Millar Burrows, Viking Press, NY, 1958.

The Other Bible. Edited by Willis Barnstone, Harper & Row, San Francisco, 1984. Basic source of non-canonical texts.

Book of Mormon. Published by the Church of Jesus Christ of Latter-Day Saints, Salt Lake City, Utah, 1971 edition. The standard holy test of the Mormon Church.
Articles of Faith, by James E. Talmadge, 49th edition, Church of Jesus Christ of Latter-Day Saints, Salt Lake City, 1968. Standard Mormon religious guide.

PRINCIPALSOURCES FOR MIDDLE EAST TEXTS

The following Sumerian myths were used in this opus and obtained from one or more of the sources cited below.

Atrahasis Epic
Curse of Agade
Descent of Ishtar to the Netherworld
Dispute Between Cattle and Gran
Enki and his Word: A Chant to the Rider of the Waves
Enki and Ninhursag: The Creation of Man
Enki and the World Order: The Organization of the Earth and its Cultural Processes
Enuma Elish
The Epic of Gilgamesh
Gilgamesh and Agga
Gilgamesh and the Land of the Living
God and Humankind Mixed
Inanna and Ebih
Inanna and Enki: Transfer of the Arts of Civilization from Eridu to Uruk
Incantation of Eridu
Joy of Sumer
Legend of Naram-Sin
Legend of Sargon
Myth of Zu
Ninurta's Pride and Punishment
Slaying of the Labbu
Tale of Adapa
Tale of Aghat

Dalley, Stephenie, *Myths from Mesopotamia*, Oxford University Press, NY, 1989,
Gardner, John and Maier, John, *Gilgamesh*, Alfred A. Knopf, NY, 1984.
Heidel, Alexander, *The Babylonian Genesis: The Story of Creation*, Second edition, University of Chicago Press, Chicago, 1951.
Jacobsen, Thorkild, *The Sumerian King List*, Assyriological Studies No. II, University of Chicago Press, 1939.
Kramer, Samuel Noah, *From the Tablets of Sumer*, Falcon's Wing Press, Indian Hills, Colorado, 1956.
Kramer, Samuel Noah, *The Sumerians*, University of Chicago Press, Chicago, 1963.
Kramer, Samuel Noah and Maier, John, *Myths of Enki: The Crafty God*, Oxford University Press, NY, 1989.
Pritchard, James B., editor. *The Ancient Near East: A New Anthology of Texts and Pictures*, Volume 1, Princeton University Press, Princeton, NJ, 1958.
Pritchard, James B., editor. *The Ancient Near East: A New Anthology of Texts and Pictures*, Volume 2, Princeton University Press, Princeton, NJ, 1975.
Sandars, N.K., *The Epic of Gilgamesh*, Revised edition, Penguin Books, London, 1972.
Wilson, J.V. Kinnier, *The Rebel Lands*, Cambridge University Press, London, 1979.
Wolkstein, Diane and Kramer, Samuel Noah, *Inanna, Queen of Heaven and Earth*, Harper & Row, NY, 1983.

INDIVIDUALWORKS CONSULTED

The Author wishes to express his gratitude and sincere acknowledgements to the authors of the literary works enumerated below and to all authorities inadvertently omitted.

Aldred, Cyril, *Egypt to the End of the Old Kingdom*, Thames and Hudson, London, 1982.
Aleksander, Marc, *British Folklore*, Crescent, NY, 1982.
Allaby, Michael and Lovelock, James, *The Great Extinction*, Doubleday, NY, 1983.
Anati, Emanuel, *Palestine Before the Hebrews*, Alfred A. Knopf, NY, 1963.
Anati, Emanuel, *The Mountain of God*, Rizzoli, NY, 1986.

Archaeological Discoveries in the Holy Land, Crowell, NY, 1967.
Bermant, Chaim and Weitzman, Michael, *Ebla: A Revelation in Archaeology*, Times Books, NY, 1979.
Bibby, Geoffrey, *Looking for Dilmun*, Knopf, NY, 1969.
Black, Jeremy and Green, Anthony, *Gods, Demons and Symbols of Ancient Mesopotamia*, University of Texas Press, Austin, TX, 1992.
Blavatsky, H.P., *The Secret Doctrine*, Theosophical University Press, Pasadena, CA, 1963.
Blumrich, Josef F., *The Spaceships of Ezekiel*, Bantam Books, NY, 1974.
Breasted, James Henry, *A History of Egypt*, 2nd edition, Scribner's, NY, 1950.
Budge, E.A. Wallis, *The Egyptian Book of the Dead*, Dover, NY, 1967. Reissue of work originally published in 1895.
Budge, E.A. Wallis, *The Dwellers of the Nile*, Dover, NY, 1977. Reissue of work originally published in 1926.
Campbell, Joseph, *The Masks of God: Oriental Mythology*, Viking Press, NY, 1962.
Campdor, Albert, *Babylon*, Elek Books, London, 1958. Translated from French.
Collon, Dominique, *Near Eastern Seals*, University of California Press, Berkeley, CA, 1990.
Craigie, Peter C., *Ugarit and the Old Testament*, Eerdmans, Grand Rapids, MI 1985.
Curtis, Adrian, *Ugarit (Ras Shamra)*, Eerdmans, Grand Rapids, MI 1985.
Davies, W.V., *Egyptian Hieroglyphs*, University of California Press, Berkeley, CA, 1987.
Desmond, Adrian, *The Hot-Blooded Dinosaurs*, Dial Press, NY, 1976.
Dobin, Joel C., Rabbi, *The Astrological Secrets of the Hebrew Sages*, Inner Traditions, Rochester, VT, 1977.
Dutt, Romesh C., *The Ramayana and the Mahabarata*, Dent & Sons, London, 1910.
The Enchanted World: Dragons, Time-Life Books, Alexandria, VA, 1985.
Faulkner, R.O., *The Ancient Egyptian Pyramid Texts*, Clarendon Press, Oxford, 1969.
Finegan, Jack, *Light from the Ancient Past*, Volume 1, Second Edition, Princeton University Press, Princeton, NJ, 1959.
Finegan, Jack, *Archaeological History of the Ancient Middle East*, Dorset Press, NY, 1979.
Fox, Hugh, *Gods of the Cataclysm*, Harper's, NY, 1976.
Gifford, Douglas, *Warriors, Gods and Spirits from Central and South American Mythology*, Shocken, NY, 1983.
Glubok, Shirley, editor. *Digging in Assyria*, Abridged and adapted from *Nineveh and its Remains*, by Austin Henry Layard, MacMillan, NY, 1970.
Glueck, Nelson, *The River Jordan*, McGraw-Hill, NJ, 1968.
Glueck, Nelson, *Rivers in the Desert*, Farrar, Straus & Cudahy, NY, 1959.
Goetz, Delia and Morley, S.G., *Popol Vuh: The Sacred Book of the Ancient Quiche Maya,* University of Oklahoma Press, Norman, OK, 1950.
Gordon, Cyrus H., *Forgotten Scripts*, Revised edition, Basic Books, NY, 1982.
Gould, Charles, *Mythical Monsters*, Allen & Co., London, 1886. Reissued by Singing Free Press, Detroit, 1969.
Grinsell, Leslie V., *Folklore of Prehistoric Sites in Britain*, David and Charles, London, 1976.
Grey, Sir George, *Polynesian Mythology*, Taplinger Press, NY, 1970.
Gurney, O.R., *The Hittites*, Penguin Books, Middlesex, England, 1952.
Habachi, Labib, *The Obelisks of Egypt*, Scribners, NY, 1977.
Hadington, Evan, *Secrets of the Ice Age: The World of the Cave Artists*, Walker, NY, 1979.
Harding, G. Lankester, *The Antiquities of Jordan*, Revised edition, Frederich A. Praeger, NY, 1967.
Herm, Gerhard, *The Phoenicians*, Wm. Morrow & Co., NY, 1975. Translated from German.
Herodotus, *The Histories*, translation by de Selincourt, Penguin Books, Harmondsworth, England, 1954.
Hitti, Philip D., *A Short History of Lebanon*, St. Martin's Press, NY, 1965.
Hultkrantz, Ake, *The Religion of the American Indians*, University of California Press, 1980. Translated from Swedish.
Jones, Wilbur Devereux, *Venus and Sothis*, Nelson-Hall, Chicago, 1982.
Kenyon, Kathleen M., *Archaeology in Holy Land*, 5th edition, Thomas Nelson, Nashville, TN, 1985.
Kosambi, D.D., *Ancient India: A History of its Culture and Civilization,* Pantheon Books, Random House, NY, 1965.
Kramer, Samuel Noah, *Cradle of Civilization*, Time-Life Books, NY, 1967.
Lloyd, Seton, *The Archaeology of Mesopotamia*, Revised edition, Thames & Hudson, NY,

1984.
Lurker, Manfred, *The Gods and Symbols of Ancient Egypt*, Thames & Hudson, London, 1980.
May, Herbert G., editor, *Oxford Bible Atlas*, 3rd edition, Oxford University Press, London, 1984.
Mertz, Barbara, *Temples, Tombs and Hieroglyphs*, Coward-McCann, NY, 1964.
Moncreiff, A.P. Hope, *Romances and Legends of Chivalry*, Wise & Co., NY, 1934.
Mooney, Richard E., *Gods of Air and Darkness*, Stein & Day, NY, 1975.
Moscati, Sabatino, *The World of the Phoenicians*, Praeger, NY, 1968.
Murray, Margaret A., *The Splendor that was Egypt*, Revised edition, Hawthorne Books, NY, 1963.
Narashimhan, Chakravarthi V., *The Mahabharata*, Columbia University Press, NY, 1965.
Noorbergen, Rene, *Secrets of the Lost Races*, Barnes & noble, NY, 1978.
Oates, Joan, *Babylon*, Thames & Hudson, London, 1979.
Patten, Donald W., *The Biblical Flood and the Ice Epoch*, Pacific Meridian Press, Seattle, 1966.
Pettinato, Giovanni, *The Archives of Ebla*, Doubleday, NY, 1981.
Ragette, Friedrich, *Baalbek*, Noyes Press, Park Ridge, NJ, 1980.
Ruffle, John, *The Egyptians*, Cornell University Press, Ithaca, NY, 1977.
Saggs, H.W.F., *The Greatness that was Babylon*, Hawthorn Books, NY, 1962.
Saggs, H.W.F., *Everyday Life in Babylonia and Assyria*, Dorset, NY, 1965.
Sanders, James A., editor, *Near Eastern Archaeology in the Twentieth Century*, Doubleday, NY, 1970.
Schiller, Ronald, *Distant Secrets*, Birch Lane Press, NY, 1989.
Seeger, Elizabeth, *The Five Brothers: The Story of the Mahabharata*, John Day, NY, 1948.
Sitchin, Zecharia, *The 12th Planet*, Stein & Day, NY, 1976.
Sitchin, Zecharia, The Stairway to Heaven, St. Martin's Press, NY, 1980.
Sitchin, Zecharia, *The Wars of Gods & Men*, Avon Books, NY, 1985.
Sjoberg, Ake W., editor, *The Sumerian Dictionary, Letter B*, The University Museum, Philadelphia, 1984.
Spence, Lewis, *Myths and Legends of Ancient Egypt*, Harrap, London, 1915.
Swaam, Wim, *Lost Cities of Asia: Ceylon, Pagan, Angkor*, Putnam, NY, 1966.
Temple, Robert K.G., *The Sirius Mystery*, Destiny Books, Rochester, VT, 1976.
Thompson, J.A., *The Bible and Archaeology*, 3rd edition, Eerdmans, Grand Rapids, MI, 1982.
Thompson, J. Eric, *Maya Hieroglyphic Writing*, University of Oklahoma Press, Norman, OK, 1960.
Tomas, Andrew, *On the Shores of Endless Worlds*, Putnam's, NY, 1974.
Tompkins, Peter, *Secrets of the Great Pyramid*, Harper & Row, NY, 1978.
Tompkins, Peter, *The Magic of Obelisks*, Harper & Row, NY, 1981.
Unger, Merill T., *Archaeology of the Old Testament*, Zondervan, Grand Rapids, MI, 1954.
Vandenberg, Philipp, *The Mystery of the Oracles*, MacMillan, NY, 1979.
Velikovsky, Immanuel, *Worlds in Collision*, Doubleday, NY, 1950.
Velikovsky, Immanuel, *Ages in Chaos*, Doubleday, NY, 1952.
Velikovsky, Immanuel, *Ramses II and His Times*, Doubleday, NY, 1978.
Velikovsky, Immanuel, *Oedipus and Akhnaton*, Doubleday, NY, 1960.
Velikovsky, Immanuel, *Peoples of the Sea*, Doubleday, NY, 1977.
Velikovsky, Immanuel, *Mankind in Amnesia*, Doubleday, NY, 1982.
Viswanatha, S.V., *Racial Synthesis in Hindu Culture*, Paul, Trench & Trubner, London, 1928.
von Daniken, Erich, *The Gold of the Gods*, Souvenir Press, London, 1972.
von Daniken, Erich, *Signs of the Gods?,* Souvenir Press, London, 1979.
Walker, C.B.F., *Cuneiform*, University of California Press, Berkeley, CA, 1987.
West, John Anthony, *Serpent in the Sky*, Julian Press, NY, 1987.
Woolley, C. Leonard, *The Sumerians*, Norton, NY, 1965.
Wright, Ruth V. and Chadborne, Robert L., *Gems and Minerals of the Bible,* Harper & Row, NY, 1970.

INDEX

Printed in the United States
48598LVS00005B/61-75

9 781885 395382